Bram Stoker's
Dracula

**Sucking Through the Century
1897–1997**

Bram Stoker in 1884 at the age of thirty-seven.
Collection of Ann Stoker.

Bram Stoker's Dracula

Sucking Through the Century 1897–1997

Edited by

CAROL MARGARET DAVISON

with the participation of

PAUL SIMPSON-HOUSLEY

Dundurn Press
Toronto • Oxford

Copy editor: Barry Jowett
Designer: Sebastian Vasile
Printer: Best Book Manufacturers
Front and back cover illustrations: details from *The Triumph of Death* by Pieter
Bruegel the Elder.

Canadian Cataloguing in Publication Data

Main entry under title:
Bram Stoker's Dracula
Includes bibliographical references.
ISBN 1-55002-279-2

1. Stoker, Bram, 1847-1912. Dracula.   2. Stoker, Bram, 1847-1912 – Film and video
adaptations.   3. Dracula films – History and criticism.   4. Horror tales, English –
History and criticism.   5. Dracula, Count (Fictitious character). Vampires in literature.
7. Vampires.   I. Davison, Carol Margaret.   II. Simpson-Housley, Paul.

PR6037. T617D78 1997   823'.8   C97-930620-5

1   2   3   4   5   BJ   01   00   99   98   97

We acknowledge the support of the **Canada Council for the Arts**
for our publishing program. We also acknowledge the support of
the **Ontario Arts Council** and the **Book Publishing Industry
Development Program** of the **Department of Canadian Heritage**.

THE CANADA COUNCIL | LE CONSEIL DES ARTS
FOR THE ARTS | DU CANADA
SINCE 1957 | DEPUIS 1957

 Printed on recycled paper.

Dundurn Press
8 Market Street
Second Floor
Toronto, Ontario, Canada
M5E 1M6

Dundurn Press
73 Lime Walk
Headington, Oxford
England
OX3 7AD

Dundurn Press
250 Sonwil Drive
Buffalo, NY
U.S.A. 14225

CONTENTS

List of

Illustrations

In loving memory of my grandfather
Robert Davison
who was born in Ireland in 1897

and of Colleen McIntyre
(1962–1995)
who died prematurely of AIDS
but left her indelible mark on so many

and to the futures of
Cameron Carl Davison (b. 1994),
Jasmine Natasha Pascual (b. 1995),
and Chelsea-Brooke Pascual (b. 1996),
whose marks have yet to be made.

Notes on
Contributors

RICHARD ANDERSON holds a doctorate in geography from York University, where he teaches part-time. His research has generally followed the theme of engineers and nature, an enquiry into broad themes of modernity. More recently he has developed an interest in applied environmental history, documenting urban pollution and contaminated ground. He runs a small consulting company which specialises in this work.

NINA AUERBACH is the John Welsh Centennial Professor of English at the University of Pennsylvania. She is the prolific author of many articles about nineteenth-century literature, theatre, and culture, whose books include *Communities of Women* (Harvard University Press, 1978), *Woman and the Demon* (Harvard University Press, 1982), *Ellen Terry, Player in Her Time* (Norton, 1987), *Private Theatricals: The Lives of the Victorians* (Harvard University Press, 1990), and *Our Vampires, Ourselves* (University of Chicago Press, 1995). With U.C. Knoepflmacher, she has co-edited *Forbidden Journeys: Fairy Tales and Fantasies by Victorian Women Writers* (University of Chicago Press, 1992).

NATALIE BARTLETT is a graduate from Carleton University, Ottawa, who holds a degree in Film Studies. She has conducted an in-depth research project on horror films by studying the *Nightmare on Elm Street* series in a paper entitled "Slashing the Screen Test of Popularity: Freddy Krueger as Main Protagonist." She has reviewed films for the bi-monthly magazine *Video Verdict*, and produced a radio show on film, television, and photography called "Camera Ready," on CKCU-FM. She is also the author of a murder mystery, and an active member of the National Capital Freenet, a public access electronic network.

BRADLEY BELLOWS is a Mechanical Engineer who currently divides his time between Toronto and Hamilton. He dates his obsession with *anime* back to watching *Battle of the Planets* as a child. As an *anime* resources person, his growing collection of over 300 hours of Japanese animation is always in demand.

JAKE BROWN was born in Ocean Falls, British Columbia. He received a Bachelor's degree from Simon Fraser University and a Master's degree from Queen's University in Kingston. He now teaches English in Westmount, Quebec, and lives quietly and simply with his VCR and his faithful Irish setter Unconditional Amnesty.

MARGARET L. CARTER has specialised, as both fan and writer, in the literature of the supernatural. Her first two books, *Curse of the Undead* (Fawcett, 1970) and *Demon Lovers and Strange Seductions* (Fawcett, 1972), were anthologies of horror stories. Her works on vampire fiction include *Shadow of a Shade: A Survey of Vampirism in Literature* (Gordon Press, 1975) and *The Vampire in Literature: A Critical Bibliography* (UMI Research Press, 1989). She has also edited an anthology of scholarship on Bram Stoker's *Dracula*, entitled *Dracula: The Vampire and the Critics* (UMI Research Press, 1988). Her articles and short fiction have appeared in a variety of publications.

BERNARD DAVIES spent thirty years in theatre, film, and television as an actor and presenter. Over the past twenty years, he has worked in promotion and journalism and, increasingly, as a freelance guide-lecturer and tour consultant on literary interests and allied themes. He has specialised in the worlds of Sherlock Holmes and Dracula, as well as Victorian crime (his grandfather was involved in the hunt for Jack the Ripper!) Mr. Davies is a former Chairman and Honorary Member of the Sherlock Holmes Society of London, an American Baker Street Irregular, and the co-founder and Chairman of the Dracula Society. In 1986 he was made a Freeman of the City of London for services to London tourism.

CAROL MARGARET DAVISON was born in Broxburn, Scotland. A widely published poet and book reviewer, she is a part-time lecturer in Victorian and Gothic literature at Concordia University in Montreal. She is currently completing her doctorate in Gothic literature at McGill University in Montreal. Entitled "Gothic Cabala: The Antisemitic Spectropoetics of Gothic Fiction," her dissertation offers a new theoretical examination of the backdrop of Gothic literature as shaded by anti-Semitism, the longstanding Christian millenarian tradition, and conspiracy fears. She has recently appeared in *Die Blutsauger Victorias*, a documentary on Bram Stoker's *Dracula*, and has also published articles in the areas of African-American, African, and Caribbean literature.

JAN B. GORDON is a professor in the Department of Anglo-American Studies at the Tokyo University of Foreign Studies. A native of Tyler, Texas, he was educated at Rice University (undergraduate) and Princeton University (graduate degrees) under a Woodrow Wilson Fellowship. His work in nineteenth-century British literature is widely anthologised and has also appeared independently in such journals as *The Journal of Aesthetics and Art Criticism, English Literary History, Dickens Studies Annual, Kenyon Review, Salmagundi*, and *The Literary Review*. He is the author of *Gossip and Subversion in Nineteenth Century British Fiction: Echo's Economies* (Macmillan, 1996). He and his wife, Hiromi, who is a Deputy Director of Information at Doshisha Women's University, live in Kyoto.

VERONICA HOLLINGER is an associate professor in the Cultural Studies Program at Trent University in Peterborough, Ontario. She co-edits *Science-Fiction Studies* and has published essays on time travel, feminist and cyberpunk sf, postmodern theatre, and vampires. Her co-edited anthology, *Blood Read: The Vampire as Metaphor in Contemporary Culture*, is forthcoming from the University of Pennsylvania Press.

BENJAMIN H. LEBLANC is a master's student in the Sociology of Religion Department at the University of Montreal. An executive member of the Canadian Chapter of the Transylvanian Society of Dracula, he has lectured on the social integration of new religious movements, and "vampire" night visitations and their relationship to sleep disorders. Mr. Leblanc has undertaken research with Professor Raymond T. McNally on a painting Mr. Leblanc discovered of Vlad Țepeș. He has also appeared in the documentary, *In Search of Dracula*, a one-hour special on vampires by Productions Quai 32 for the Discovery Channel.

JACQUELINE LeBLANC has recently completed her doctorate at the University of Massachusetts, Amherst. In addition to her work in Gothic literature, she studies British Romanticism and literary theory. Her dissertation, entitled "Critique in Aesthetic Ideology: Aesthetic Politics in Romanticism and Critical Theory," examines the radical potential in using art and aesthetic theory as political strategy.

PATRICK McGRATH was born in London and grew up near Broadmoor Hospital, where for many years his father was Medical Superintendent. In 1981, he moved to New York City. He is the author of a collection of stories, *Blood and Water and Other Tales*, and three novels, *The Grotesque* (Ballantine, 1989), *Spider* (Random House, 1990), and *Dr. Haggard's Disease* (Random House, 1993). His latest novel, *Asylum*, was recently published by Random House. He is also co-editor with Bradford Morrow of *The New Gothic* (Random House, 1991). He now lives in New York and London and is married to the actress Maria Aitken.

DENNIS McINTYRE is a teacher at Belgrove Boys School in Clontarf, Dublin. A founding member and former chairman of the Clontarf Historical Society and the author of a three-part history of Clontarf, Mr. McIntyre is the Director of the flourishing Bram Stoker International Summer School which is held annually in Clontarf, Dublin. He is married with two children.

ELIZABETH MILLER is Professor of English at Memorial University of Newfoundland where she specialises in Newfoundland Literature and Nineteenth-Century British Gothic Fiction. In addition to numerous conference appearances she has had articles on *Dracula* published in *Udolpho*, *Locus*, *Transylvanian Journal*, *Lumea* (Romania), *Cinema Monthly Magazine* (Romania), and *Megalon* (Brazil). Her book *Reflections on Dracula* is forthcoming in 1997 from Transylvania Press. Recipient of the honorary title "Baroness of the House of Dracula" in Romania in 1995, she is currently president of the Canadian Chapter of the Transylvanian Society of Dracula.

STEPHANIE MOSS teaches Renaissance Literature at the University of South Florida. Much like a vampire, she is living her second life, having spent her first one in the professional theatre. As an academic, her focus is divided between Shakespeare, Marlowe, other Renaissance dramatists, and Bram Stoker's vampire. She is the author of the forthcoming biographical entry on Bram Stoker in the *Dictionary of Literary Biography*, and of a critical review of Stoker's *The Lair of the White Worm* for Salem Press.

NORMA ROWEN teaches Fantasy and Children's Literature in the Humanities Division of York University, Toronto. Her major interests centre on the Gothic and she has published a number of articles in this area, including two on *Frankenstein*. For the past three years she has taught a course on the vampire, and is currently engaged with a research project about the vampire and the fin de siècle.

CAROL A. SENF is associate professor in the School of Literature, Communication, and Culture at the Georgia Institute of Technology. She has written extensively on vampires and Bram Stoker's *Dracula*. She edited *The Critical Response to Bram Stoker* (Greenwood, 1993), wrote the entry on Stephen King for *The Dictionary of Literary Biography*, and *The Vampire in Nineteenth-Century British Fiction* (The Popular Press, 1988). Current projects include trying to interest publishers in reissuing novels by Bram Stoker that are currently out of print, and exploring changing attitudes to children both in popular culture and public policy. Senf, her husband Jay, and their two sons live in Atlanta, Georgia, with a menagerie of animals.

LESLIE SHEPARD is an author, folklorist, and former documentary film director who has published books on Street Literature (penny balladsheets and chapbooks). He has written widely on the occult as an offshoot of folklore and superstition, and has edited the authoritative *Encyclopedia of Occultism & Parapsychology* through three editions (3rd edition, 2 vols, Detroit, 1991). He is also the author of *How to Protect Yourself Against Black Magic & Witchcraft* (Citadel, 1978). His anthology *The Dracula Book of Great Vampire Stories* (Citadel, 1977) was an alternative choice in the Book-of-the-Month Club in the United States. This and its companion volume, *The Dracula Book of Great Horror Stories* (Citadel, 1981), have been printed in various editions in the United States and Britain.

PAUL SIMPSON-HOUSLEY is full professor in the Department of Geography at York University in Toronto. His books include *Sacred Places and Profane Spaces: Essays in the Geographics of Judaism, Christianity, and Islam* (with Jamie Scott, Greenwood Press, 1991), *Antarctica: Exploration, Perception and Metaphor* (Routledge, 1992), *Writing the City: Eden, Babylon and the New Jerusalem* (with Peter Preston, Routledge, 1994), and *The Arctic: Enigmas and Myths* (Dundurn Press, 1996).

WENDY VAN WYCK GOOD received her M.A. in English Literature from the University of Delaware and her M.S.L.S. from Drexel University. She is the curator of *Bram Stoker's Dracula: A Centennial Exhibition*, which opens in April 1997 at the Rosenbach Museum and Library in Philadelphia.

LIVY VISANO is an associate professor in the department of Sociology at York University in Toronto. The recipient of a number of teaching awards from the province-wide body OCUFA, he has published several books and countless articles on Canadian criminology and the sociology of law. He has lectured world-wide and continues to serve as a member on various public advisory agencies. Among many other current projects, he is researching the nature of crime on the Internet.

GERALD WALKER received his doctorate from the University of California, Berkeley. His academic work has focused on the geography of the countryside in capitalist states, particularly Canada, with an emphasis on the countryside of Toronto. Since 1971, he has been on the faculty of York University in Toronto.

LAWRENCE WATT-EVANS was born at midnight, which seems appropriate. He is the author of some two dozen novels and over a hundred short stories in a variety of genres. His novel *The Nightmare People* and a score or so of horror stories were sufficient to get him into the Horror Writers Association, where he has recently concluded two years as the president of the organisation.

LORRAINE WRIGHT has always had a penchant for vampires and werewolves. She is currently completing her doctorate in geography at the University of Waterloo. While Lorraine's focus is on socio-cultural geography, she also enjoys using computer skills. This includes GIS as well as the challenge of creative computer mapping that allows, for example, for the mood expressions presented in *Dracula*.

JEANNE KEYES YOUNGSON was born in Syracuse, New York, and grew up in Sussex, New Jersey. She attended Maryville College in Tennessee for two years, but left to join the Navy during a national emergency. She later resumed her studies, attending the Sorbonne in Paris, Oxford University (England), and New York University, where she received a doctorate in English Literature. In 1965, she founded the International Count Dracula Fan Club which is still alive and well, with nearly 5,000 members worldwide.

Acknowledgements

LOOD, SWEAT, AND TEARS, QUITE LITERALLY, HAVE gone into the production of this volume. Tremendous thanks are due to many individuals who very generously offered me their time, energy, support, and expertise during its preparation. First thanks go to the contributors who were always patient and receptive to my editorial suggestions. Playing Louis to this variety of noteworthy Lestats was a privilege, a challenge, and an exceptional learning experience. I am very grateful to Patrick McGrath who, despite numerous other commitments, agreed to write the preface after our first, very energetic conversation about my plans for this book in the winter of 1994.

I also flash a fang-filled smile at those individuals who provided me with information for "The Red Pages." These groups and individuals have been the very life's blood of *Dracula* and Stoker-related research for many scholars over the years and have, to my mind, received precious little thanks for their dedicated efforts. I have never met with a group more infectious in their passion for Stoker's creature of the night and feel strongly that, as we take the time to mark *Dracula*'s 100th birthday, we also pay special tribute to them and their incredible efforts. In the face of tremendous indifference from both the "high" academic and "low" pop-culture camps over the years, they have kept Bram Stoker and the spirit of his work alive and biting.

For convincing me not to give up on this book during a severe moment of crisis, I am especially grateful to my longstanding friend and first-time collaborator, Professor Paul Simpson-Housley of York University's Department of Geography. He helped me both to recruit several of the contributors and to secure Dundurn Press, such a wonderful and patient publisher. Without his continued encouragement, this book would never have emerged from my extremely untidy Gothic closet.

Barry Jowett, of Dundurn Press, deserves special thanks for his assiduous editorial work. Romanian designer, Sebastian Vasile, also of Dundurn Press, deserves similar thanks for his impeccable work and signature touches which include the "Transylvania" and "TimesSebastian" fonts. For producing the illustrations accompanying Patrick McGrath's preface I am grateful to the very talented and enthusiastic Lorraine Wright who took crucial time from her dissertation. For producing four of the maps which appear in the chapter by Gerald Walker and Lorraine Wright, I would like to thank the cartography office at York University. I am also thankful to Streamline Pictures for permission to reprint stills from *Vampire Hunter D*. For their impeccable research work and aid, I tip my scholar's cap to the assiduous team at Concordia University's Inter-Library Loans office, Loyola Campus — Nikki Cellucci, Ursula Hakien, Susan Yegendorf, George Franko, Hung-Yeh Tsuei, and Wendy Knechtel. This book hopefully provides proof that I am a vampire scholar and *not* a vampire.

For granting me access to Bram Stoker's working papers for *Dracula*, I thank curator Wendy Van Wyck Good and the staff of the Rosenbach Museum in Philadelphia. Similar thanks go to David Lass, the Honorary Secretary of the Bram Stoker Society and cataloguer for English, Anglo-Irish, and Classical literature at Trinity College, Dublin. His very insightful questions after the presentation of my essay on Dracula and Jack the Ripper in June of 1996 at the Bram Stoker Summer School, Dublin, were helpful to my revising process.

For funding my research work in Romania, Ireland, Philadelphia, and New York over the past few years, I am indebted to a doctoral scholarship from SSHRCC and two substantial grants from the Professional Development Committee of CUPFA (Concordia University Part-Time Faculty Association). For his crucial role in helping me to acquire this funding, his unshakeable faith in my abilities, consistently provocative questions, and relevant reading suggestions, I am extremely grateful to my good friend and unofficial, unpaid advisor, Professor G. David Sheps, Chairman of the English Department, Concordia University.

Thanks are also due to Professors Michael Bristol, Tess O'Toole, and especially Maggie Kilgour, Gothic aficionado and my dissertation advisor, of McGill University's English Department. Their thorough examination of a large section of my dissertation illuminated some of its black holes, thus helping me to decipher the implications of some of my ideas. The theoretical foundation of that dissertation informs my essay here on Jack the Ripper and Dracula.

Others who deserve tremendous thanks are the MLA for allowing me to place a Call for Papers free of charge in the *PMLA*; Sylvie Roy, Robert Murphy, Zeljana Grubisíc, and Rhonda Armstrong who kindly babysat my "kids," Keeper and Katmandu ("Pooks"), while I travelled for research and conferences; Karen Molgaard, Peter Feder, and Erika White who helped me survive the nightmare of moving twice in the space of fifteen months while this volume was being produced; Randall Blackwell who put me up (and put up with me) in Philly; Elizabeth Miller, the greatest Bloofer Lady Internet-networker of them all who retrieved the vampire information I required almost before I requested it (I believe she's plotting to take over the world from her computer terminal!); Veronica Hollinger who repeatedly counselled me to keep my head up and my academic/editorial fangs sharp, and graciously (along with her co-editors) allowed me to reprint a revised version of her essay here which originally appeared in *Science-Fiction Studies*; Nina Auerbach and the University of Chicago Press who courteously allowed the republication of a section of her wonderful book *Our Vampires, Ourselves*; Henry Lai who helped me on the technical computer end of things; Mark Shainblum and Gabriel Morrissette who bent over backwards to locate some rare, but significant, comic books featuring Dracula and Jack the Ripper; Scott MacKenzie who provided this book's subtitle; E. Jean Guérin, who was vital to my initiation into vampire studies; Skon Mouradian for years of invaluable friendship and support; and Ciarán McArdle for always being there when required. I would also like to extend a resounding thank-you to my tried-and-true-blue friends and earnest, supportive, and insightful students who convinced me that this volume had to be produced and never doubted (as I often did) that it would see the light of day.

Finally, I am especially indebted to my greatest backbone of all — my rare, loving, and supportive family with whom I have been truly blessed by the powers that be. As I realised at the age of nineteen when I first undertook professional editing work, editing is a deceptively simple endeavour to the uninitiated. The truth is that writing two, and editing all of these essays on *Dracula* was often complicated and draining. While this might seem fitting given the subject, it does not suit my constitution. It was only thanks to my family's unremitting, Mina-like love transfusions that I only occasionally degenerated into Lucy's damned Bloofer Lady state. Like everything else of interest and value that I have ever and will ever produce, this book is as much my family's as it is mine.

C.M.D.

"The prince of vampires is Bram Stoker's *Dracula*, round whom centres probably the greatest horror tale of modern times."

Devendra P. Varma

Introduction: Bram Stoker's Dracula: Sucking Through the Century, 1897-1997

Carol Margaret Davison

> "Vampires, of course, are supposedly immortal. But Varney wasted away in spite of his 'Feast of Blood' and even J. Sheridan Le Fanu's literary classic, *Carmilla*, is badly in need of a transfusion. Of all the legions of undead in film and fiction, only the Count, born in the same era as Jack the Ripper, lives on."
>
> (Bloch 28)

> "I myself am of an old family ... how few days go to make up a century."
>
> (*Dracula* 23)

A CENTURY AGO IN LONDON, IN MAY OF 1897, A NOVEL was published by Archibald Constable and Company that was to have a profound and unforeseen impact on the popular art and culture of the twentieth century. Sold for six shillings and bound in yellow cloth with its title appropriately embossed in blood red type, Bram Stoker's *Dracula* received uneven reviews from contemporary critics. While some placed Stoker in the ranks of Mary Shelley, Edgar Allan Poe, Ann Radcliffe, and the Brontës, others compared Stoker's novel, rather unfavourably, with such works as Wilkie Collins's 1860 sensation novel *The Woman in White*.[1] Noone reacted more favourably to *Dracula*, however, than Stoker's mother Charlotte. In an enthusiastic letter to her industrious theatre manager son, she wrote, "My dear, it is splendid, a thousand miles beyond anything you have written before, and I feel cer-

Cover of Constable's 1901 paperback edition of *Dracula* featuring the first *Dracula* illustration.

tain will place you very high in the writers of the day — the story and style being deeply sensational, exciting and interesting." A few days later, she added, "I have seen a great review of *Dracula* in a London paper. They have not said one word too much of it. No book since Mrs. Shelley's *Frankenstein* or indeed any other at all has come near yours in originality, or terror — Poe is nowhere. I have read much but I never met a book like it at all. In its terrible excitement it should make a widespread reputation and much money for you" (Ludlam 108–9).

Unfortunately for Stoker, in the domain of his resulting personal and financial success, his mother's prophetic abilities left something to be desired. Although Stoker made some money from *Dracula*, its reputation was only truly established and its lucrative capabilities were only fully realised after Stoker's death when his vampire migrated from the stage to the silver screen, an artistic medium whose conception was concurrent with *Dracula*'s own. Since 1897, "Dracula" has become a household name, Stoker's creature has come to monopolise the word "vampire," and *Dracula* has never been out of print. Indeed, as Wendy Doniger has recently claimed, Stoker's *Dracula* has become vampire literature's "centerpiece, rendering all other vampires B.S. or A.S." (608).

Ironically, while this mesmeric bloodsucker moved into the limelight of popular culture during the twentieth century, his creator remained shrouded in obscurity. Even in academic circles, Stoker remained virtually unknown until recent years when he has been resuscitated from the overpopulated graveyard of forgotten writers. As Margaret L. Carter relates in the invaluable introduction to her book *Dracula: The Vampire and the Critics* (1988), much has happened in this field over the past twenty-five years.[2] Despite claims like that made by James B. Twitchell that "*Dracula*'s claim on our attention is not ... its artistic merit" (135), and thanks to what Ken Gelder describes in *Reading the Vampire* as the "veritable 'academic industry' [that] has built itself around this novel" (65), *Dracula* has become one of the rare popular culture novels to be canonised. Despite his oft-cursed elusiveness and self-effacement, Bram Stoker has also gained long overdue recognition.[3] In the domain of popular culture, nothing served better to put Stoker's name on the literary map than Francis Ford Coppola's 1992 cinematic version of *Dracula*, which was produced under the disputed title of *Bram Stoker's Dracula*.

Interestingly, Stoker's rebirth into literary history may be said to mirror his vampire's foremost activity. As Jan B. Gordon notes in "The 'Transparency' of *Dracula*," an essay included in this volume, every day may be figuratively said to be a (re)birthday for the vampire. Indeed, given what Gordon describes as the vampire's resistance to containment and temporality, it may be argued that a *centenary* celebration is something of a misnomer. Stoker's vampire is certainly characterised by resistance to textual and temporal containment: based on the Count's own statements, his undeath long predated his 1897 literary début and, in the light of his various incarnations since 1897, he clearly managed to survive his death at Stoker's novel's conclusion. In fact, in the light of his myriad appearances, the Count may be said to have become countless. The vampire has not only been "the bogeyman of the decade," as Anne Billson described him in 1992 (Haining 4); thanks largely to the popularity and adaptability of Stoker's *Dracula*, he has truly been *the bogeyman of the century*. Certainly, the scene of his "eternal return" has become almost too familiar — just when we think it's safe to go back into the cinema, yet another of Dracula's innumerable offspring dramatically rises from the crypt with one of Van Helsing's numerous relations invariably in hot and morally-enraged pursuit.

As Philip Martin's 1988 essay, "The Vampire in the Looking-Glass," makes clear, as a result of the tremendous number and varied nature of his celluloid progeny, we have, to some degree, lost sight of Stoker's Dracula: "Few people come to the text having never seen a screen production of some kind, so, while the book remains free from critical molestation, it is still subject to a corresponding process of mediation, as it is commonly read with a number of associations deriving from at least one of the many films" (80). Notably, however, as James B. Twitchell outlines in his popular work, *The Living Dead: A Study of the Vampire in Romantic Literature*, Stoker's Count has yet to be overshadowed by his literary progeny. In Twitchell's words, "There have been many twentieth-century novelists (Ray Bradbury, Robert Bloch, E.F. Benson, Agatha Christie, Virginia Coffman, H.P. Lovecraft, Richard Matheson, Peter Saxon, John Rechy, Fred Saberhagen, Colin Wilson, Desmond Stewart, Anne Rice, to name only a few) who have dealt with the vampire, but none so strikingly as Stoker" (140). Among others, the issue of (re)discovering Dracula in our vampire-obsessed era is considered by Norma Rowen in her essay here entitled "Teaching the Vampire: *Dracula* in the Classroom." Rowen illustrates just how revelatory a reading of Stoker's *Dracula* can actually be in our Dracula-saturated culture.

In *Our Vampires, Ourselves*, her recent examination of twentieth-century cinematic and literary vampires, Nina Auerbach draws connections between the cultural production of vampires and their American presidential counterparts. It is similarly possible to return to the scene of Dracula's 1897 birth and draw some basic links between Dracula and Queen Victoria, that seemingly "undead" monarch who was celebrating her diamond jubilee the year of *Dracula*'s initial publication. Both were of "royal" blood, devoted Anglophiles (Dracula tells Harker that he has "come to know ... [his] great England; and to know her is to love her") and, confronted by the decline of their respective nations, both were nostalgic about the passing of an earlier "Golden Age."[4] Unlike Queen Victoria, however, who was, according to one critic, "in many ways the symbol of the age [who] failed to keep step with the age she symbolized" (Yeazell 10), Dracula proved to be a highly industrious and adaptable aristocrat who recognised the survival potential in relocation, a good blood transfusion, and inter-breeding. In fact, in true versatile vampire fashion, Count Dracula has been consistently able to speak both to his own and other times and cultures. Not only was Stoker's novel, like Jonathan Harker's shorthand, "nineteenth century up-to-date with a vengeance" (36), it has remained equally twentieth century up-to-date as well.

While recognising *Dracula*'s transhistorical adaptability, the essays in this volume are particularly fascinated by two interconnected and socio-historically grounded aspects of the *Dracula* phenomenon: the specific bonds Stoker's novel had with its 1890s point of conception, and the nature of its subsequent transmutations within other socio-cultural contexts. To bring the motif of vampirism to bear here, our focus is on how *Dracula* functioned as both a *vampire text* which derived its lifeblood from a variety of contemporary fin de siècle sources, and a *vampirised text* which was subsequently tapped and retransfused into a variety of cross-cultural artistic productions. If a single citation may be said to capture the spirit of this centenary compilation, it derives from Nina Auerbach's laudable work, *Our Vampires, Ourselves*. Therein, Auerbach articulately and insightfully explains how vampires "promise escape from our dull lives and the pressure of our times, but they matter because when properly understood, they make us see that our lives are implicated in theirs and our times are inescapable" (9).

Bluntly put, vampire-populated Gothic fiction is more than just a diversion. To take things a bite further, and adapt a trademark — *Vampires 'R Us*. Given this seductive spectre's role as a relevant and revelatory sign of our times that encodes our hopes and fears, desires and anxieties, we ignore it at our peril. In order to take a lesson from it, however, we must attain the fine art of *reading between the fictional fangs*, a precarious two-tiered critical process which involves undertaking both a mythic and a socio-cultural reading of this terrifying yet alluring creature. While the former stage involves deciphering the vampire's exact relationship to the narrative's conception of what is human, what s/he holds out to the text's characters, and the price of their seduction, the latter process involves a consideration of the vampire's cultural "make-up" — how s/he speaks both to the text's setting and to its production context. As every experienced cultural-studies-style vampire hunter knows, this bloodsucker's "message" varies greatly from one cultural text and context to another.

With these points of consideration firmly in mind, we may prepare our critical fangs for the prototypical vampire novel — Bram Stoker's *Dracula*. Working from the premise that Stoker "wrote *Dracula* as if he was inspired" (Farson 152), critical analysis to date has focused on uncovering the diverse personal and political influences at work on this giant, grey-eyed, ginger-haired Irishman as he composed this classic novel. Theories on this front have ranged from the enlightening to the ludicrous. Turning first to the latter, we do know that there was an oneiric element involved in *Dracula*'s conception. Stoker, like so many of his predecessors who had penned Gothic fiction, had a vivid and gripping dream that he felt compelled to transcribe. It involved "a vampire king rising from the tomb to go about his ghastly business" (Ludlam 100). The story that Stoker "persistently told" about this dream concerned its apparent biochemical origins, namely that it arose due to the "too generous helping of dressed crab" that he had for supper that evening before bedtime (99). Some critics have seriously considered the significance of this late supper. Joseph Bierman, for example, in his 1972 article, "*Dracula*: Prolonged Childhood Illness and the Oral Triad," proffered a pseudo-Freudian analysis of the dressed crab theory. Adding what Stoker's biographer and great-nephew, Daniel Farson, calls "some remarkable dressing of his own" (154), Bierman deduced, by way of some rather complex and bizarre logic, that the vampire dream that provided the nucleus for *Dracula* was born of Stoker's unconscious desire to kill his youngest brother George who was — prepare yourself — born under the astrological sign of Cancer, the sign of the crab! According to Bierman, the novel's various scenes of infanticide render Stoker's desire evident (156–157).

Ironically, Daniel Farson proved to have a "dressing" talent of his own. In the Postscript to his 1975 biography about the life and literary production of his great-uncle, Farson advanced the theory that Bram Stoker died of syphilis (233). Describing him as "chained to a beautiful but frigid wife" (214), Farson postulated that Stoker sought his sexual pleasure from prostitutes and could have contracted the illness "as early as the year of *Dracula*, 1897." Farson further argued that the effects of this devastating disease became manifest in Stoker's literary works. As he described it, "When his wife's frigidity drove him to other women, probably prostitutes among them, Bram's writing showed signs of guilt and sexual frustration" (234). As with other theories surrounding *Dracula*'s genesis, this one had a veritable snowball effect. It opened the door to Robert Tracy's outrageous claim in 1990 that Stoker, afflicted with syphilis, reenacted in *Dracula*, "with a mixture of moral outrage and prurience, the 1888 murders of Whitechapel prostitutes attributed to Jack the Ripper" (45).[5]

That these speculations have been bandied about as established and indisputable facts in recent years has been the cause of serious concern for at least one scholar. In the Appendix to this volume, Leslie Shepard, the founder and chairman of the Bram Stoker Society in Dublin, Ireland, reconsiders this controversial syphilis theory in his provocative piece, "A Note on the Death Certificate of Bram Stoker." Shepard's companion piece, "The Library of Bram Stoker," considers what might be a more relevant and productive area of examination for the question of influences, namely the books that Stoker owned and might have read while writing his novel. Shepard provides the list of Stoker's books that were sold off by Sotheby, Wilkinson, and Hodge in 1913, the year after his death. It is hoped that this catalogue and other *Dracula*/Stoker resource information provided in "The Red Pages," "The Bloody Bibliography," and the Appendix, will engender and enable further research in the domain of *Dracula* scholarship.

Given current Stoker criticism, it would seem that there is no end in sight for what Farson has dubbed "The Dracula Game," that process of deciphering the influences — especially the "haemosexual" ones (Frayling 79) — underpinning Stoker's classic Gothic horror novel. Longstanding claims about incidents of haemosexual trauma such as Stoker's apparent "childhood experience of blood-letting in a Dublin hospital" (Frayling 79), however, have given way recently to theories regarding incidents of homosexual trauma. Much ink, for example, is sure to be spilled over Talia Schaffer's controversial claim in 1994 that "*Dracula* explores Stoker's fear and anxiety as a closeted homosexual man during Oscar Wilde's trial" (381). While one may suspect, as Nina Auerbach does, "that Dracula's primary progenitor is not Lord Ruthven, Varney, or Carmilla, but Oscar Wilde in the dock" (83),[6] it cannot be overemphasised that Stoker did not require personal experience with such deep-seated contemporary, anxiety-inducing spectres such as homosexuality and syphilis in order to incorporate them into his Gothic morality tale. Contrary to the dictates of some creative writing instructors, it *is* possible to write — and to write well — about something one has never experienced *in the flesh*. My guess is that Stoker had never actually encountered a vampire, and yet he writes about this entirely fantastic phenomenon in a compelling and realistic way.

Putting both the ludicrous and the "in the flesh"-style hypotheses aside, what is indisputable is that *Dracula* was a consummate 1890s creation which responded, albeit sometimes cryptically, to "a distinct constellation of contemporary fears" (Pick 71) including syphilis, homosexuality, feminism, decadence, and imperial decline. The key-word under whose aegis this plethora of fears stood united was "degeneration." As J. Edward Chamberlin and Sander L. Gilman outline in the introduction to their critical anthology *Degeneration: The Dark Side of Progress*, the fin de siècle concept of degeneration was most powerfully associated "with something *unnatural*, even — or perhaps especially — when associated with natural desire or supernatural dread" (ix). *Dracula* functions within these parameters as it inextricably unites supernatural dread with what were regarded by the more reactionary forces within Stoker's society as unnatural desires. Indeed, in the sexually paranoid environment of the fin de siècle which was assaulted by a "rhetoric of medical terrorism" designed to regulate prostitution and demonise certain sexual practices (Showalter, *Sexual* 195), the tendency existed, especially among extremists, to "view ... sexuality [in general] *as* disease" (199). As Elaine Showalter argues, Oscar Wilde's trial for homosexuality in 1895 served a crucial function, for it "created a moral panic that inaugurated a period of censorship" (171). Although it might seem ironic given *Dracula*'s porno-Gothic[7] tenor, Bram Stoker was actually an outspoken advocate of censorship. As Jacqueline LeBlanc outlines in her essay here examining the thematic of censorship in Stoker's original novel and Coppola's 1992 cinematic adaptation, Stoker published two articles on

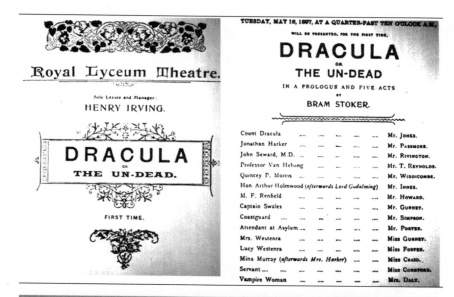

Program for the staged reading of *Dracula* at the Lyceum, 1897.
Courtesy of Jeanne Keyes Youngson.

this subject in the early 1900s for *The Nineteenth Century & After* — "The Censorship of Fiction" (1908) and "The Censorship of Stage Plays" (1909). In the former article, Stoker denounces the "class of works ... meant by both authors and publishers to bring to the winning of commercial success the forces of inherent evil in man" (485). He argues that the people involved in this venture "prostitute their talents" (487), and that women writers are "the worst offenders in this form of breach of moral law" (485). While *Dracula* cannot deny the charge of sexual titillation and graphic violence, Stoker would argue that his novel portrays the truly seductive nature of evil and the terrible price to be paid for succumbing to it. Several literary critics have reiterated this reading, describing *Dracula* as a Christian allegory (Frayling 79) that unapologetically promotes conservative "family values."

Indeed, the reactionary message conveyed by Stoker's morality play is undeniable — in no other British fin de siècle novel is the sex=disease equation so prominent or so uniquely played out as it is in *Dracula*. Vampirism is the ultimate "sexually-transmitted" degenerative disease. Ironically and notably, vampirism is also the ultimate zipless fuck, a thoroughly Victorian displacement of the traditional sex act. For all of its "disguised" sexuality, however, vampirism still delivers more of an erotic bang for the cultural consumer's buck. It elicits more titillation and generates more shock value per word/frame than any graphically detailed sex scene possibly can. Mina's vampire baptism episode perhaps best illustrates this point. It is entirely appropriate, therefore, that in *Dracula*, a novel where sex is figured as an anti-Christian regressive process of succumbing to one's "inner vampire," the only actual acceptable Christian instance of the unmentionable act occurs behind the scenes between a married couple (Mina and Jonathan Harker), and results in a type of immaculate conception (the birth of their son, Quincey).

The alarmist concept of degeneration, however, extended well beyond the realm of sexuality during Stoker's era when it may be said to have spread its tentacles into various discursive domains — cultural, economic, political, and medical. In an article from 1990, Stephen D. Arata argues that degeneration haunted Britain throughout the 1890s, where it effectively threatened the confident Victorian rhetoric of progress. Wittily describing Dracula as a demonic "Occidental tourist" who signifies the erosion of "Victorian confidence in the inevitability of British progress and hegemony" (622), Arata maintains that *Dracula* actually "enacts the period's most important and pervasive narrative of decline, a narrative of reverse colonisation" (623). Arata provides a catalogue of reasons for this erosion which includes the "decay of British global influence, the loss of overseas markets for British goods, the economic and political rise of Germany and the United States, the increasing unrest in British colonies and possessions, [and] the growing domestic uneasiness over the morality of imperialism" (622).

Given this socio-political climate where "fissures ... [were] appearing in bourgeois hegemony, patriarchy and imperial power ... [and] forces [were] gathering ... against and within Victorian society" (Longhurst 65-66), it is not surprising that the literature produced during Stoker's fin de siècle era was "saturated with the sense that the entire nation — as a race of people, as a political and imperial force, as a social and cultural power — was in irretrievable decline" (Arata 622). It is similarly unremarkable that scapegoats were readily found and culturally demonised in order both to account and atone for this decline. Among their number were New Women, homosexuals, Jews, artists (depending on their style and subject matter), and immigrants (especially from Eastern Europe). Bram Stoker's stroke of narrative genius in *Dracula* lay, in part, in the fact that his portrait of a spiritually and physically decadent vampire (he *is* a walking corpse, after all), tapped into and combined the two foremost fears of his day: invasion of the body *and* the body politic by a degenerate "Other." That Stoker's treacherous, alien pollutant finds allies, unwitting and otherwise, *within* Britain, only serves to compound the threat. That Dracula so incredibly resembles an Englishman almost immediately upon his arrival in their country (after a short stint as a wolf), and is literally lovingly embraced by Britain's sacred, domestic angels, converts threat into unspeakable terror.

The fact that Gothic literature was a prominent venue for representing this fin de siècle degeneration crisis is not surprising. As Chris Baldick explains in the introduction to *The Oxford Book of Gothic Tales*, Gothic literature emanated, in part, from "a fear of historical reversion ... of the nagging possibility that the despotisms buried by the modern-age may prove to be undead" (xxi). More than any other single element, the return of the repressed past is at the core of this genre, and it is with a consideration of the role of the past in Stoker's work that this essay collection begins. First, however, Patrick McGrath lends an established Gothic novelist's insights into the relationship between Bram Stoker and his vampire. In this engaging prefatory essay, McGrath illuminates Stoker's achievements in *Dracula* and considers why this work and its eponymous villain have remained decidedly and justifiably undead over the past century. Gerald Walker and Lorraine Wright then escort the reader into the domain of Transylvania, a territory Stoker knew only by way of books and maps which he examined in such places as the British Museum. In "Locating Dracula: Contextualising the Geography of Transylvania," Walker and Wright provide some wonderfully unique maps of their own in their assessment of the actual and imaginary aspects of *Dracula*'s Transylvanian setting. They consider the poetic licence taken by Stoker with both the physical and the human geography of this region in a novel that they maintain enacts "the struggle between antiquity and modernity in a mytho-realistic landscape."

The first section of essays in this centenary collection focuses on *Dracula* as an 1890s "vampire text," and is motivated, in part, by Daniel Pick's agenda of "address[ing] *Dracula* historically ... [in order] to suggest some of its crucial discursive contexts" (71). On this front, the opening section may also be said to respond both to Margaret Carter's claim that "relatively little has been written about Stoker's immediate sources" (8), and to Stephen Arata's allegation that "criticism has consistently undervalued *Dracula*'s extensive and highly visible contacts with a series of [contemporary] cultural issues" (621). Carol Senf begins this section with her essay, "*Dracula, The Jewel of Seven Stars*, and Stoker's 'Burden of the Past,'" which examines Stoker's literary treatment of "the conflict between modernity and the primitive past." Considering Stoker's attitudes towards fin de siècle scientific and cultural developments, and contemporary findings in the area of Egyptian archaeology, Senf argues that *Dracula* enacts a triumph of modernity. Rather intriguingly, Senf illustrates how modernity loses its battle with the past in *The Jewel of Seven Stars*, a novel Stoker published only six years later. Jan Gordon also considers the role of the past in *Dracula* in his provocative essay "The 'Transparency' of *Dracula*." In his examination of the monstrous in Gothic literature, Gordon foregrounds its attendant notion that "the past can never be really past." He argues that *Dracula* is a truly 1890s artistic product that exhibits the fin de siècle preoccupation with double agents and transparencies. The figure of Count Dracula, Gordon claims, acts as a monstrous and "transparent agent of metonymic transfer" that resists transcription. Gordon then outlines the nature and role of this popular "double agent"/transparency motif in a series of fin de siècle intellectual systems, cultural expressions, and artistic interests ranging from Karl Marx's *Grundrisse* and Walter Pater's "Diaphaneitè" to Oscar Wilde's aesthetic theories and Sigmund Freud's *Studies on Hysteria*.

Stephanie Moss's essay "The Psychiatrist's Couch: Hypnosis, Hysteria, and Proto-Freudian Performance in *Dracula*," considers *Dracula*'s Freudian connections in greater detail. She maintains that *Dracula* intervenes in the contemporary debate about hypnosis, and even anticipates Freudian psychology as Stoker manipulates hypnosis and hysteria as metaphors for the effects of repression. As Moss illustrates, the role of hysteria in *Dracula* functions, quite specifically, as a theatrical response to traditional gender roles and rites of passage like marriage. My essay here, "Blood Brothers: Dracula and Jack the Ripper," examines the issue of fin de siècle anti-Semitism and *Dracula*'s relationship to the disturbing and resonant Ripper murders which occurred in London's East End district of Whitechapel in the fall of 1888. Based, in part, on Stoker's introductory comments to the Icelandic edition of *Dracula*, I argue that Stoker consciously fictionalised these serial killings in *Dracula*. Focusing on the issue of "ethnicity" and the Jewish semiotic markers shared by Count Dracula and Jack the Ripper, I illustrate how *Dracula* exhibits signs of fin de siècle anti-Semitism and enacts the contemporary fear of alien invasion.

This volume's second section turns to the issue of *Dracula*'s role as twentieth-century "vampirised text." Many provocative questions arise about Count Dracula's potential to speak to the concerns, anxieties, and desires of the twentieth century. In his essay "Count Dracula and the Martians," R.J. Dingley argues that *Dracula*'s joint alarmist-and-anodyne abilities as "a myth capable simultaneously of exposing and exorcising potential sources of spiritual, political, and moral crisis," explains its continued fascination for our century (22). Although several contributors illustrate how *Dracula* continues to be used as a fable of social control in the twentieth century, in certain cases, as with Werner Herzog's 1979 film *Nosferatu: Phantom der Nacht* (*Phantom of the Night*), the traditional dichotomies of us/them, good/evil are terrifyingly blurred. As Jake Brown and Nina Auerbach independently illustrate, some twentieth-century writers and filmmakers have recognised that "there are social forces more frightening than Dracula" (Auerbach 155). Count Dracula has even suffered greater reduction. As David Boyer has illustrated in his *Might* article examining Satan's recent graduation to popular advertising icon, credibility is a crucial component in the popular response to traditional icons of evil. Turning to another recent publication, Boyer explains, "In his book *The Death of Satan*, Andrew Delbanco argues that, since Americans no longer believe in God or Satan or the battle between good and evil — in a culture that holds nothing sacred — an impotent, cartoonish Satan is the inevitable result" (43). In some instances, as with the conception of a trinity of commercial, cartoonish Counts — General Mills' Count Chocula, Sesame Street's Count, and Disney's Count Duckula — Dracula has experienced a similar emasculation.

Perhaps the most provocative claim about *Dracula*'s relationship to the twentieth century, however, is made by Nina Auerbach in *Our Vampires, Ourselves*. According to her, the fact that Stoker's notorious Count has been "reproduced, fetishized, besequeled, and obsessed over" throughout this century is apt as he perfectly symbolises our evil and impersonal age. As Auerbach unapologetically states, "in his blankness, his impersonality, [and] his emphasis on sweeping new orders rather than insinuating intimacy, Dracula *is* the twentieth century he still haunts" (63). Stoker's alien invader was, in other words, the ideal fin de siècle creation to usher in this century. Although perhaps divested of his original, more obvious anti-Christian vestments, Dracula's ever-shifting face has reflected our culture's ethical debates. Ironically, however, as evil and impersonal as our times might seem to some, the evil vampire is a rare commodity in today's vampire literature market. As several of this collection's contributors suggest, the most fashionable vampire of the twentieth century is a vampire in touch with his/her "inner child," a marginal creature capable of incredible love and intense sexual intimacy. Many recent vampire creators — notably and especially women — have exhibited a strong sympathy for the devil-vampire. In certain instances, they have effected a momentous narrative shift by granting access to the vampire's innermost thoughts, a viewpoint significantly absent in Stoker's Gothic classic.

This volume's second section addresses several of these complex issues while focusing on *Dracula* as a twentieth-century "vampirised text." It begins with an essay by *Dracula* aficionado Margaret Carter, entitled "Share Alike: *Dracula* and the Sympathetic Vampire in Mid-Twentieth Century Pulp Fiction." Commencing with an "against the vein" reading of Stoker's *Dracula*, Carter illustrates how this novel contains the embryo of the twentieth century's most popular bloodsucker — the sympathetic vampire figure. Bringing Harold Bloom's "anxiety of influence" theory to bear on Stoker's novel, Carter maintains that "virtually all twentieth-century vampire fiction labours under an 'anxiety of influence' with regard to *Dracula*." She provides ample evidence in support of this theory from ten vampire stories and novels published between the 1920s and the 1960s. Each of these bloodsucking creations, Carter argues, was crucial in leading the way to the sympathetic vampires who inhabit the novels of Anne Rice and Chelsea Quinn Yarbro.

In her perceptive essay, "Vampires in the 1970s: Feminist Oligarchies and Kingly Democracy," Nina Auerbach continues the chronological assessment of literary vampires in the twentieth century. Focusing on vampire fiction produced in America after the Vietnam War and Richard Nixon's presidency, Auerbach declares the 1970s "a halcyon decade for vampires" during which they, like women, became authorities possessed of an authentic and resonant public voice. Marginalised creatures who advanced desperate social critiques, the vampires in the works of Chelsea Quinn Yarbro and Suzy McKee Charnas resisted patriarchy, a social force Auerbach deems "more frightening than Dracula." While the oppressive nature of patriarchy is retained in the works of Anne Rice and Stephen King — in fact, the vampires in the latter's fiction are described as "so horrible that they may look retrograde" — Auerbach chronicles how the literary vampire became "for the first time, inextricably attached to childhood," a phenomenon which persisted into the 1980s when, she argues, horror became the territory of the young.

Veronica Hollinger's "The Vampire and the Alien: Gothic Horror and Science Fiction," reminds the reader that *Dracula*'s birth was significantly concurrent with the genre of science fiction and, more specifically, with H.G. Wells's *The Time Machine* (1895), "the first great science fiction novel."[8] Although, as Hollinger notes, the vampire is a figure "most typically associated with the horror genre,... it too has, on certain rare occasions, crossed the border from fantasy to science fiction." Her essay focuses on two popular science fiction works featuring vampires — Colin Wilson's *The Space Vampires* (1976), a novel which consciously revises Stoker's *Dracula*, and Jody Scott's *I, Vampire* (1984), a feminist parody of Stoker's *Dracula* — and concludes with a supplement to Auerbach's claim that "every age embraces the vampire it needs" (145). As Hollinger sees it, every *ideology* also "embraces the vampire it needs."

Norma Rowen's illuminating essay "Teaching the Vampire: *Dracula* in the Classroom," completes this section. It explores her experiences and insights after three years of teaching a course on the vampire at York University in Toronto. With *Dracula* as the central course text, Rowen's students explored various twentieth-century cinematic and literary revisions of Stoker's classic work. Perhaps the most interesting insight in Rowen's essay is the fact that for young, marginally-aware, Rice-loving students, Stoker's Transylvanian Count is a disturbingly unsympathetic figure. As Rowen describes the popular student response to *Dracula*, "the journey into the dark and hidden reaches of the self is more difficult when the shadow/guide assumes the form, not of someone youthful and attractive — however murderous — but of a repulsive and unrepentant elder with bad breath."

Section three of this volume, "Mondo *Dracula* — Celluloid Vampires," turns its attention to *Dracula* in the cinema, a medium that Russian author Maxim Gorky intriguingly described in 1896, the year before *Dracula*'s publication, as a type of hypnotic and "technological vampire that promised a kind of living death" (Skal 4).[9] Given the seductive nature of both the vampire and the cinema, it is entirely appropriate that the vampire has had a love affair with the silver screen throughout the twentieth century. An exceptionally popular figure in film since its inception, the vampire was as much drawn to the comfortable hypnotic darkness of the cinema as that medium was magnetically drawn to his superior skills in translating sexual desires — in a manner more acceptable to the censors — to the screen.

Jacqueline LeBlanc's "'It is not good to note this down': *Dracula* and the Erotic Technologies of Censorship," offers a detailed and cogent consideration of the connection between vampirism and technology in the light of Stoker's writings on censorship. Detecting a collusion between eroticism and censorship in *Dracula*, LeBlanc contests the popular perception of a morally "schizophrenic" Stoker who was both Victorian puritan *and* pornographer. *Dracula*, she argues, furnishes a novel and modern treatment of the censorship theme as vampirism is specularly linked to a technology which both produces and polices erotic discourse. LeBlanc concludes her essay with an examination of the "postmodern" technologies of censorship and their ideological significance in Francis Ford Coppola's recent cinematic adaptation of *Dracula*.

In his essay "Draculafilm: 'High' and 'Low' Until the End of the World," Jake Brown argues that adapting Stoker's *Dracula* to the silver screen "has proven to be a daunting task." Maintaining that Stoker's *Dracula* is "all over the ideological map" and straddles the gap between high-brow academic interest and low-brow popular appeal, Brown illustrates how these novelistic features were carried over into the four most famous cinematic adaptations of Bram Stoker's *Dracula* in the twentieth century — F.W. Murnau's *Nosferatu: Eine Symphonie des Grauens* (*A Symphony of Terror*, 1922), Tod Browning's *Dracula* (1931), Werner Herzog's *Nosferatu: Phantom der Nacht* (*Phantom of the Night*, 1979), and Francis Ford Coppola's *Bram Stoker's Dracula* (1992). Brown classifies the Browning and Coppola adaptations as low-brow, box-office successes, and claims that the Murnau and Herzog versions distinguished themselves by appealing to a highbrow academic market. While all four directors managed, to varying degrees, to capture a piece of *Dracula* that appealed to their particular cultural contexts, Brown implies — in agreement with actor/filmmaker Orson Welles — that the definitive, accurate adaptation of Stoker's novel has yet to be produced.

The last essay in this section, "The Supernatural *Ronin*: Vampires in Japanese *Anime*," by Natalie Bartlett and Bradley D. Bellows, turns to the question of *Dracula*'s cultural adaptability. This extensive piece charts the Western vampire's entrance into Japanese culture after World War Two. By way of an in-depth examination of the elements significant to Stoker's narrative, Bartlett and Bellows consider the nature and significance of *Dracula*'s entrance — especially along ethical and aesthetic lines — into Japanese animation (known as *anime*). In addition to offering a detailed historical assessment of the vampire in Japanese film, they focus their critical lenses on two of the most popular vampire animation films produced to date — *Vampire Hunter D* (1985) and *Vampire Princess Miyu* (1988).

This volume's final critical section, "*Dracula* at Large — Vampires and Society," turns to a consideration of *Dracula*'s social impact. That the 1890s are uncannily reflected in our own fin-de-millennium, AIDS-devastated, censorship obsessed, "family values" age accounts, in part, I think for *Dracula*'s current appeal. The Count's influence in the twentieth century, however, has been even more extensive. Not only is he a popular icon in

advertising, his name has been used to designate everything from a hormone purported to increase longevity[10] to an Allied operation in Burma
during World War Two (Ludlam 152). *Dracula* actually played a more significant role in that international crisis, however, for in order to enforce "the
equation of the Hun-like Dracula with the Hun-like Nazi" (Leatherdale
235), free copies of Stoker's novel "were issued to US forces serving overseas" (236).

In more recent years, Dracula has influenced the formation of the
Temple of the Vampire, a splinter group of the Church of Satan which has,
as Benjamin H. Leblanc outlines, its own Vampire Bible, ring, and ritual
medallion. Part of their Vampire Creed reads, "I am a Vampire. I worship
my ego and I worship my life, for I am the only God that is" (Webb).
Perhaps equally sinister is the recently diagnosed borderline psychiatric
disorder known as "cinematic neurosis" where "sufferers believe they have
been bitten by vampires or occupied by a demonic presence."[11] In their terrifying delusions, they "experience feelings of invasion or fear culled from
horror-film imagery, sometimes even experiencing flashbacks to scenes in
the film" (Kingwell 282). This neurosis attests to the vampire's more negative and unsettling social impact, an impact that was intimated — albeit in
a very watered down form — in the 1920s when audience members attending the early stage play based on *Dracula* had to be revived after fainting
spells.[12]

Richard Anderson, an applied urban environmental historian, begins
this essay section with an examination of *Dracula*'s relationship to postwar
suburbia, a place Henry Miller outrageously called an "air-conditioned
nightmare." In "*Dracula*, Monsters, and the Apprehensions of Modernity,"
Anderson delineates how classic horror cinema was not simply an innocuous
form of popular entertainment in that pristine-but-paranoid, Tupperware-
sealed environment. It was also a resonant genre that encoded suburbia's
apprehensions about modernity. More specifically, Anderson focuses on
Dracula's preoccupation with achieving social purification and control
through violence, and its embedded anxiety about the demonic potential of
modernity and science. In his article, "*Dracula* as a Contemporary
Ethnography: A Critique of Mediated Moralities and Mysterious
Mythologies," Livy Visano provides an alternate viewpoint to the popular
claim that *Dracula* reinforced the status quo of fin de siècle Britain. Contrary
to Anderson's interpretation of *Dracula*'s *unconscious* moral apprehensions,
for instance, Visano reads *Dracula* as a *conscious* and provocative fictional
study of the sociology of morality. As Visano sees it, Stoker encouraged his
readers to "interrogate their own credulities and to become estranged from
acts of moral policing." By granting the counter-hegemonic discourse of

superstition a principal role in his novel, for example, Stoker deliberately pointed up the glaring inadequacies of the most important social institutions of his day, among which were science, Christianity, and the law.

Benjamin H. Leblanc's "The Death of *Dracula*: A Darwinian Approach to the Vampire's Evolution," concludes the critical essay component of this volume with the shocking proclamation that Dracula is dead. By way of a Darwinian reading of the history of the vampire in folklore and literature, Leblanc charts the three stages leading to the Count's demise. He chronicles the shift from the supernatural vampire to the romantic vampire then, finally, to the interiorised vampire whose emergence was concurrent with the advent of the New Age movement. Leblanc completes his examination with an assessment of Dracula's "dark legacy" to several of his twentieth-century offspring, which include "psychic vampires" who feed off psychic energy as opposed to blood, and the charismatic, spiritually-enlightened "Vampyre" worshipped by members of the Order of the Vampyre.

This volume would not be complete without statements from those individuals and associations that have been involved with Stoker and *Dracula* studies over the years. Section Five, "The Red Pages," provides seven entertaining and informative pieces from founders of some of the world's most important societies and institutions involved in Stoker/*Dracula* research. Section Six includes an Appendix and "The Bloody Bibliography," which are intended to promote further scholarship. While it may be hard for some to believe, areas of *Dracula* research remain relatively unexplored. Despite much dedicated work to date, so much more remains to be done.

RUMOURS OF DRACULA'S death have been greatly exaggerated. Judging by his countless literary, celluloid, and cyberspace offspring, the Count is certainly alive and sucking.

While James Twitchell has described the vampire as "probably the most enduring and prolific figure we have" (ix), Dracula is inarguably his most memorable incarnation. Indeed, the Count's transmutation skills appear to be far from on the wane. As David J. Skal has described the almost supernatural power of Stoker's novel, "Whatever else it might be, *Dracula* is certainly one of the most obsessional texts of all time, a black hole of the imagination. The story seems to get younger with age, drawing vitality from its longevity, and attracting an ever-widening public" (7).

Short of proffering a primed and exposed jugular, how then is one to say "happy hundredth birthday" to Count Dracula? What, after all, may one possibly offer the demon lover who — endowed with eternal life, an endless supply of swooning virgins, and mounds of glittering gold — essentially has everything? We have chosen to offer this celebratory volume as both a tribute to Stoker's vivid imagination and a gift to ardent fans of his enthralling novel.

Bram Stoker may have died at the age of 64 on the 20th of April, 1912, at 26 St. George's Square, but with the creation of his protean, hypnotic vampire, he enshrined himself forever in literary history. Thanks, in part, to an earnest and ongoing resurrection project undertaken by many scholars and fans, Stoker may rest assured that where his Count goes, he is sure to accompany him. This should prove to be no short journey for, as Harry Ludlam has memorably stated, "The surest thing is that *Dracula* will outlive us all" (196).

Carol Margaret Davison
Montreal, Canada
Hallowe'en, 1996

Illustration by the Rev. William Fitzgerald for Stoker's 1881 collection of stories entitled *Under the Sunset.*

NOTES

1   For contemporary responses to Bram Stoker's novels, see *The Critical Response to Bram Stoker*, an invaluable work by our contributor, Carol A. Senf.

2   For anyone interested in a concise yet comprehensive overview of the developments within *Dracula* criticism since the 1956 publication of Bacil Kirtley's article "*Dracula*, the Monastic Chronicles and Slavic Folklore," Margaret L. Carter's *Dracula: The Vampire and the Critics* is essential reading. On the heels of her captivating and cogent introduction, Carter reprints twenty-one of the most influential critical essays on *Dracula* written between 1956 and 1988. As she notes with regard to *Dracula*'s academic popularity, "Aside from a few articles published from 1956 through the 1960s, serious study of *Dracula* and vampire fiction in general began in the early 1970s" (1).

3   In his biography of Stoker, Daniel Farson outlines Leonard Wolf's opinions about *Dracula*'s creator: "'Bram Stoker eludes me,' says Professor Wolf. But, 'In Stoker's own writing a *person* occasionally shows through, or, better, is exposed. Particularly in his later novels (and of course *Dracula*) there obtrudes the raw, harsh presence of a man endowed with nearly inexhaustible energy who is writing over, around, or under what he knows about loneliness and — predominantly — sexual terror. Referring specifically to *The Lair of the White Worm*, he concludes: 'There is no way to ignore the signs of confusion and loneliness the narrative obtrudes" (224). As to the popular view of Stoker as self-effacing, a perfect managerial type who was always content to take the back seat to Henry Irving, Margot Peters maintains that Stoker's "revenge for life-long self-effacement was *Dracula*" (20).

4   In his innovative novel *Anno Dracula* which unites real and literary figures from the Victorian fin de siècle, Kim Newman forges a ludicrous but intriguing scenario where Dracula actually marries Queen Victoria. The reader only catches a brief glimpse of this couple at novel's end prior to Queen Victoria's suicide. In Newman's disturbing "British Gothic" portrait, marriage literally involves female enslavement. Consider this shocking depiction of Queen Victoria: "The Queen knelt by the throne, a spiked collar round her neck, a massive chain leading from it to a loose bracelet upon Dracula's wrist. She was in her shift and stockings, brown hair loose, blood on her face. It was impossible to see the round old woman she had been in this abused, wretched figure" (447). Despite Newman's sometimes clumsy writing, the Victorian period can never be seen in the same stilted way after a reading of *Anno Dracula*. For further discussion of Newman's novel, see my chapter here "Blood Brothers: Dracula and Jack the Ripper."

5   As Elaine Showalter has outlined in her article "Syphilis, Sexuality, and the Fiction of the Fin de Siècle," a popular rumour circulated during the autumn of 1888 that "the Ripper was a mad doctor avenging himself on prostitutes for a case of syphilis" (94).

6   It is interesting to note, however, that the *Dracula*-Wilde association is not new. It was first advanced in 1966 when critic Grigore Nandris reminded readers that "when *Dracula* was written the minds of Londoners were preoccupied with the trial of Oscar Wilde" (378). Nandris advanced even more specific — although debatable — points of contact between *Dracula* and the trial of Oscar Wilde. He writes, for example, "It may be purely accidental, but it is interesting to recall the resemblance between the scene of the dancing harlots in front of the Old Bailey at Oscar Wilde's condemnation and that of the vampire-women with their sarcastic remarks and debauched gestures in the haunted castle of the Count of Bistritza on the night when the London lawyer became aware of his dreadful master's intentions" (378).

While Talia Schaffer limits her focus to the issue of sexuality and what she calls "the crisis of the closet in 1895" (382), however, Nandris's argument is somewhat more expansive as he postulates that *Dracula* played out the contemporary ideological crisis between "Bohemianism" and conventional Victorian bourgeois mores. Nandris's focus on this clash between lifestyles and worldviews, therefore, comprises issues of established aesthetic principles as well as sexual orientation and ethics. Although I suspect that the differences between Nandris's and Schaffer's critical standpoints are dictated, in part, by the socio-cultural preoccupations of the periods in which *they* wrote, what must be foregrounded is that they both discern in *Dracula*'s intricate narrative web a sense of several fin de siècle preoccupations.

7   In an environment where Gothic classifications continue to proliferate, Robert Druce has recently introduced the category of porno-Gothic. For more details about this genre see his essay "*Pulex Defixus*, Or, The Spellbound Flea: An Excursion into Porno-Gothic."

8   R.J. Dingley's essay, "Count Dracula and the Martians," provides an intriguing comparison between Stoker's Gothic thriller and another of Wells's novels, *The War of the Worlds*, which was serialised in *Pearson's Magazine* in 1897, the same year as *Dracula*'s publication. Dingley classifies both works as invasion stories, a fictional sub-genre popular in fin de siècle Europe. Dingley argues that in both works England is regarded as an inferior territory and the invaders survive by way of sucking blood from humans.

9   David J. Skal provides Maxim Gorky's response to Lumière's Cinématographe in Moscow in 1896, the year before *Dracula*'s publication. "Deeply disturbed by what he beheld," Gorky described the cinema as follows: "Your nerves are strained, imagination carries you to some unnaturally monotonous life, a life without color and without sound, but full of movement, the life of ghosts, or of people, *damned* to the damnation of eternal silence, people who have been deprived of all the colors of life" (4).

10   The drug melatonin, which some researchers have described as a wonder drug that cures insomnia, prevents cancer, extends life, and boosts immunity, has been called the Dracula hormone.

11   Cinematic neurosis seems, in fact, to offer a weird twist on Robert Bierman's 1988 feature film *Vampire's Kiss* where a young literary agent (played by Nicholas Cage) who believes he has been bitten by a vampire, thereafter experiences a mysterious series of transformations.

12   As David J. Skal relates, "a uniformed nurse was ready to administer smelling salts to faint-hearted patrons at all London performances of *Dracula*," produced by the Hamilton Deane Company. Although having this nurse in attendance was initially conceived as a publicity stunt, she turned out to be necessary — "at one performance, thirty-nine audience members took advantage of the offer" (75). In recent years, the vampire has continued to elicit serious physiological reaction. During the screening of Neil Jordan's 1994 adaptation of Anne Rice's *Interview With the Vampire*, for example, some audience members fainted, while others had to be escorted from the cinema.

REFERENCES

Arata, Stephen D. "The Occidental Tourist: *Dracula* and the Anxiety of Reverse Colonization." *Victorian Studies* 33 (1990): 621–645.

Auerbach, Nina. *Our Vampires, Ourselves*. Chicago and London: Chicago UP, 1995.

Baldick, Chris, ed. "Introduction." *The Oxford Book of Gothic Tales*. Oxford: Oxford UP, 1992.

Belford, Barbara. *Bram Stoker: A Biography of the Author of Dracula*. New York: Knopf, 1996.

Bierman, Joseph S. "*Dracula*: Prolonged Childhood Illness, and the Oral Triad." *American Imago* 29 (1972): 186–198.

Bloch, Robert. "Two Victorian Gentlemen." *Blood of the Innocent*. Vol. 1. By Rickey Shanklin and Mark Wheatley. New York: WARP Graphics, January 1986. 27–30.

Boyer, David. "Not Your Father's Prince of Darkness." *Might* 12 (July/August 1996): 42–47.

Bram Stoker's Dracula. Dir. Francis Ford Coppola. Columbia, 1992.

Carter, Margaret L. *The Vampire in Literature: A Critical Bibliography*. Ann Arbor and London: UMI Research Press, 1989.

Chamberlin, J. Edward and Sander L. Gilman, eds. "Introduction." *Degeneration: The Dark Side of Progress*. New York: Columbia UP, 1985. ix–xiv.

Dingley, R.J. "Count Dracula and the Martians." *The Victorian Fantasists*. Ed. Kath Filmer. London: Macmillan, 1991. 13–24.

Doniger, Wendy. "Sympathy for the Vampire." Rev. of *Our Vampires, Ourselves*, by Nina Auerbach. *The Nation* (November 20, 1995): 608–612.

Dracula. Dir. Tod Browning. Universal, 1931.

Druce, Robert. "*Pulex Defixus*, Or, The Spellbound Flea: An Excursion into Porno-Gothic." *Exhibited by Candlelight: Sources and Developments in the Gothic Tradition*. Eds. Valeria Tinkler-Villani and Peter Davidson, with Jane Stevenson. Amsterdam and Atlanta, Georgia: Rodopi, 1995. 221–242.

Farson, Daniel. *The Man Who Wrote Dracula: A Biography of Bram Stoker*. London: Michael Joseph, 1975.

Frayling, Christopher. *Vampyres: Lord Byron to Count Dracula*. London: Faber and Faber, 1991.

Gelder, Ken. *Reading the Vampire*. London and New York: Routledge, 1994.

Haining, Peter, ed. *The Vampire Omnibus*. London: Orion, 1995.

Kingwell, Mark. *Dreams of Millennium: Report From a Culture on the Brink*. Toronto: Viking, 1996.

Kirtley, Bacil F. "*Dracula*, the Monastic Chronicles and Slavic Folklore." *Midwest Folklore* 6 (1956): 133–139.

Leatherdale, Clive. *Dracula: The Novel & The Legend*. East Sussex: Desert Island Books, 1985.

Longhurst, Derek. "Sherlock Holmes: Adventures of an English Gentleman 1887–1894." *Gender, Genre and Narrative Pleasure*. Ed. Derek Longhurst. London: Unwin Hyman, 1989. 51–66.

Ludlam, Harry. *A Biography of Dracula: The Life Story of Bram Stoker*. London: W. Foulsham & Co., 1962.

Martin, Philip. "The Vampire in the Looking-Glass: Reflection and Projection in Bram Stoker's *Dracula*." *Nineteenth-Century Suspense: From Poe to Conan Doyle*. Eds. Clive Bloom et al. London: Macmillan Press, 1988. 80–92.

Nandris, Grigore. *"The Historical Dracula: The Theme of His Legend in the Western and in the Eastern Literatures of Europe."* *Comparative Literature Studies 3 (1966): 367–396.*

Newman, Kim. *Anno Dracula*. 1992. New York: Pocket, 1993.

Nosferatu: Eine Symphonie des Grauens (A Symphony of Terror). Dir. F.W. Murnau. Prana Film, 1922.

Nosferatu: Phantom der Nacht (Phantom of the Night). Dir. Werner Herzog. Twentieth Century Fox, 1979.

Peters, Margot. "The Boss From Hell." Rev. of *Bram Stoker: A Biography of the Author of Dracula*, by Barbara Belford. *New York Times Book Review* (April 7, 1996): 20.

Pick, Daniel. "'Terrors of the Night': *Dracula* and 'Degeneration' in the Late Nineteenth Century." *Critical Inquiry* 30 (1988): 71–87.

Riccardo, Martin. *Vampires Unearthed: The Complete Multimedia Vampire and Dracula Bibliography*. New York: Garland, 1983.

Schaffer, Talia. "'A Wilde Desire Took Me': The Homoerotic History of *Dracula*." *ELH* 61 (1994): 381–425.

Senf, Carol A. *The Critical Response to Bram Stoker*. Westport, Connecticut: Greenwood Press, 1993.

Showalter, Elaine. *Sexual Anarchy: Gender and Culture at the Fin de Siècle*. New York: Penguin, 1990.

—. "Syphilis, Sexuality, and the Fiction of the Fin de Siècle." *Sex, Politics, and Science in the Nineteenth-Century Novel*. Ed. Ruth Bernard Yeazell. Baltimore and London: Johns Hopkins UP, 1986.

Skal, David J. *Hollywood Gothic: The Tangled Web of Dracula from Novel to Stage to Screen*. New York: Norton, 1990.

Stoker, Bram. "The Censorship of Fiction." *The Nineteenth Century & After* 64 (September 1908): 479–87.

—. "The Censorship of Stage Plays." *The Nineteenth Century & After* 66 (December 1909): 974–989.

—. *Dracula*. 1897. Oxford: Oxford UP, 1983.

Tracy, Robert. "Loving You All Ways: Vamps, Vampires, Necrophiles and Necrofilles in Nineteenth-Century Fiction." *Sex and Death in Victorian Literature*. Ed. Regina Barreca. Bloomington and Indianapolis: Indiana UP, 1990. 32–59.

Twitchell, James B. *The Living Dead: A Study of the Vampire in Romantic Literature*. Durham, North Carolina: Duke UP, 1981.

Vampire's Kiss. Dir. Robert Bierman. Hemdale, 1988.

Webb, Don. *The Order of the Vampyre of the Temple of Set*. 1992.

Yeazell, Ruth Bernard. "The World's Worst-Dressed Woman." Rev. of *Queen Victoria's Secrets*, by Adrienne Munich. *London Review of Books* 1 August 1996: 10–11.

Preface:
Bram Stoker and
His Vampire

Patrick McGrath

"I heard recently of one elderly woman who knew Florence [Stoker] and said that she used to be terrified when Bram wrote his horror novels because he '*became*' the personality he was writing about and behaved very strangely at home."

(Farson 231–232)

 RAM STOKER CAME LATE TO THE VAMPIRE. BY THE time *Dracula* was published in 1897, the undead predator had long been a staple of Gothic fiction and, before that, a familiar figure in the folklore of Central Europe. In that incarnation he was not an aristocrat but a plump Slavic peasant in a dirty linen shroud, with long fingernails, a stubbly beard, and a ruddy, swollen face with his mouth and left eye open. Students of the vampire believe that the corpse which not only refuses to stay dead, but returns to bring death to friends and neighbours, is to be found in the folklore of almost every culture in the world, and that the ubiquity of such *revenants* is connected with body-disposal practices and certain peculiarities of the process of decomposition. Human corpses bloat and bleed from the mouth, poke their fingers up through the earth, and can give the impression of still being animate. From such phenomena potent myths arise.

In the late eighteenth century, at about the moment that the Gothic emerged as a distinct literary genre, the vampire graduated from folklore to fiction. Lord Byron's physician, John Polidori, wrote *The Vampyre* in 1819. This was a direct result of the famous storytelling session of the Byron-Shelley circle that also spawned *Frankenstein*. Based on the character of Byron himself, the vampire in Polidori's tale is called Lord Ruthven (pronounced "riven," aptly enough). He shares as many characteristics

Illustration by Lorraine Wright.

with Dorian Gray, the soulless monster created by Stoker's friend Oscar Wilde, as he does with Dracula.

After *The Vampyre* came the hugely successful *Varney the Vampyre*, a lurid and sensational novel by James Malcolm Rymer, and then in 1872, Sheridan Le Fanu invented in *Carmilla* the first great female vampire. Traces of *Carmilla* can be discovered in *Dracula* in the writhing sirens who almost seduce Jonathan Harker when he finds himself at their mercy one desperate night. Tolstoy, de Maupassant, and Hoffmann also wrote vampire stories. In fact, the vampire stalks nineteenth-century literature as persistently as it does twentieth-century cinema, and can be identified as the prototype of George Eliot's Mr. Casaubon in *Middlemarch*. This figure of death lures the heroine, through marriage, into his mausoleum of a mansion where she must dwell with him in dust and shadows and books.

At first glance, Bram Stoker seems a somewhat unlikely figure to have created a vampire of such power and grandeur, such sheer, complex, nuanced evil, as Dracula. Stoker was an outgoing Irishman of apparently boundless vitality who sustained two demanding careers and a large circle of friends. He had a tendency to form strong attachments to vigorous creative men older than himself, Henry Irving and Walt Whitman most notably, the latter once saying of him, "My gracious he knows enough for four or five ordinary men; and what tact!... He's like a breath of good, healthy, breezy sea air" (Roth 12). The friendship with Irving was the more important relationship. It had properly begun after the actor's famous recitation of "The Dream of Eugene Aram" in Dublin in 1876, which so moved Stoker that he had to be carried from the room in a fit of hysterics. When Irving formed his own theatrical company he asked Stoker to be his business and front-of-house manager. Stoker promptly got married and moved to London.

He worked for the charismatic Irving for more than twenty years, running the Lyceum Theatre and organising the company's tours in both Europe and America. He is described by Laurence Irving, Henry's son and biographer, as a "ruddy, bearded gentleman ... of robust appearance and hearty ebullience" (Irving 278), and later as "well-intentioned, vain, impulsive, inclined to blarneying flattery." Irving also remarks with snide asperity that Stoker "worshiped [my father] with all the sentimental idolatry of which an Irishman is capable" (453). He says that Stoker loved to rub shoulders with the great, took himself too seriously, and was susceptible to intense jealousy if Irving showed favour to a rival lieutenant. He does not allude to the blarneying Irishman's literary work.

We can be fairly sure that the Gothic flame was lit in Stoker at an early age. According to Phyllis Roth's biography, Bram's mother "recounted Irish tales of superstition, vividly depicting the banshee, whose wail presaged imminent death, as well as the terrors of the cholera epidemic that killed thousands when she was a child in Ireland" (2). It seems plausible that it was as a result of hearing such stories that Bram nursed his lifelong fascination with death and deathly things, though his was a clever, complicated personality, by no means exclusively preoccupied with morbidity. At Trinity College he threw himself into athletic and intellectual pursuits and was elected president of both the Historical and the Philosophical Society.

After graduation he joined the civil service as a clerk and apparently found the tedium of the work almost unbearable. It is hard to resist the picture of a robust but divided and conflicted man: when he met Henry Irving in 1876 he was writing horror stories, but his best energies were going into a book called *The Duties of Clerks of Petty Sessions*. The passionate and darkly romantic imagination had not been extinguished by clerical work, rather it coexisted, uneasily, with the dutiful, disciplined master of dry legalistic detail. Not until *Dracula*, begun some twelve years later, did Stoker succeed in creatively fusing the mutually antagonistic forces in his own personality: sturdy devotion to all that was good and proper on the one hand, rapt fascination with the idea of evil on the other, specifically its personification in a monstrous figure of unrestrained lust and satanic ambition.

Stoker's triumph in *Dracula* was to depict the stature, origins, and motives of his vampire with such clarity and richness of detail that the book's ability to captivate is as strong today as it was a hundred years ago. There is a lovely touch early in the novel when Jonathan Harker, by now a prisoner in Castle Dracula, returns to his chamber to find the Count *making his bed for him*. It is entirely unexpected, this simple act of domestic intimacy, and the reader remembers that though a monster, Dracula must still move among humans and pass as one of them. The faint tenderness one feels at seeing Dracula behave like a housemaid disappears, however, as soon as Jonathan realises what it means: there are no servants in the castle; he is alone with the ghastly creature. This, in turn, means that the Count must have been the driver of the coach that brought him to the castle — and is therefore able to control a pack of wolves simply by raising his hand — and so it goes.

And it is on that same night that Jonathan is struck by the Count's referring to himself in the plural, as "we." To Jonathan this suggests royal pretensions. We know better, for Dracula is a creature who subverts even the integrity of identity. Not only is he capable of transformation and multiplicity, he is committed to reproducing himself in the human population. He intends to create a world of vampires like himself. So not only is his "we" a precise pronoun, it is a threat, and it is this threat, as soon as it is understood, that drives the novel's great central conflict.

Lesser vampires tend to display selective aspects of Dracula's nature, with the result that many of the Count's characteristics have become clichés of the genre: the aversion to garlic, sunlight, and the crucifix; the ability to change into, among other things, a bat; the attraction to nice girls whom he transforms into creatures of voracious appetite who then require the best efforts of Anglo-American manhood, and Dutch science, to put them back to sleep. But what distinguishes Stoker's vampire from its predecessors, and its later imitators, is the sheer scale of transgression Dracula embodies. No mere thirst for blood drives him. His challenge is to the very idea of mortality itself. What he wants is the breakdown of the distinction between life and death, and the creation of a race of undead beings whose relationship to time, to nourishment, and to daylight, mirrors his own. Like Satan, his real father, Dracula's argument is with God, and with the biological arrangements God made for humanity.

Evil on this diabolical scale demands opposition of more-than-heroic proportions; Stoker manages a masterly fusion of the mediaeval romance tradition with the Victorian cult of manliness. One can almost grow weary of his insistence on the piety, virility, chivalry, and tact of Seward, Morris, Godalming, and Harker; but whatever this may suggest about the author's own homosocial nature, it is structurally necessary, if Dracula's wickedness is to be seen in its true light. The vampire must be a match for not one but four of the finest flowers of Christian manhood that Western civilisation can muster, plus of course the encyclopaedic intellect of Van Helsing.

Connected to this is Stoker's use of documentary evidence as his sole narrative mode. Nowhere is the story left to a mere novelist's construction. It is, rather, a composite of the diaries, memoranda, correspondence, newspaper clippings, and phonographic records produced and/or collected by the characters involved. The illusion of accountability is there to sharpen our sense of the reality of the evil under examination, an evil that comprises not only Dracula's project of raising an army of the undead, but his favoured method of recruitment as well: he exploits the sexual vulnerabilities of his victims, particularly of course the women. Poor Lucy Westenra, for one, is doomed, we suspect, the moment we hear her voice the wish that she might have *all three* of the men vying for her hand. The arousal of uncontrolled female passion is to Dracula's enemies one of the most distressing aspects of the vampire's activity. Lucy, with her sleepwalking and the mild promiscuity of her unconscious desires, is ripe for the plucking.

What does this suggest about the libido of the "red-haired giant," as Laurence Irving called Stoker? In this regard there is a conjecture by

Illustration by Lorraine Wright.

Stoker's grandnephew, the writer Daniel Farson, that after the birth of Stoker's son, Noel, in 1879, Stoker's wife Florence forced on him an unwanted celibacy. Farson guesses that this celibacy broke down twenty years later, and that sometime after the publication of *Dracula*, Stoker contracted from a prostitute the syphilis which Farson claims killed him in 1912 (Roth 20).

The suggestion of chronic sexual repression in a man as hale and vigorous as Stoker sheds a tentative light on the dynamics of that powerful imagination, given the great underground currents of sexuality that surge through the novel, finding sublimated expression in descriptions of vampiric activity. Stoker's Dracula routinely ravishes the throats of his victims, and in one memorable scene with Mina he cuts his own chest and makes her drink from it like an infant. His transaction with his victim is thus more complex than mere rapacity, or parasitism, for it demonstrates the vampire communicating its pathology, that is, *infecting*. It is hard not to hear in this the whisper of syphilis that so haunted the late-Victorian imagination. The point, though, about Dracula's infection is that it is moral as well as organic; it makes the victim evil like himself, and liberates her from the moral world.

What finally sustains *Dracula*'s majestic stature is its ability to make the reader complicit in this activity. In folklore as in Christian doctrine, the idea of the body that lacks a soul is as horrifying as its inverse, the phantom, the disembodied spirit. The vampire kills its victim's soul and introduces her to a condition of moral licence, a pre-Oedipal paradise where all appetites can be unstintingly gratified without thought for consequences. The reader's pleasure is complex, for he, or she, will identify not only with the victim in his/her submission to the sheer passion of the other's need, *but with the vampire as well.*

Bram Stoker's achievement in *Dracula* is thus to give exhaustive expression to the very energies that power Gothic fiction — that is, the drives and terrors of the unconscious mind — and, at the same time, to fully articulate the Gothic's central organising principle, the transgression theme. *Dracula* is a Gothic mandala, a vast design in which multiple reflections of the elements of the genre are configured in elegant sets of symmetries. It is also a sort of lens, bringing focus and compression to diverse Gothic motifs, including not only vampirism but madness, the night, spoiled innocence, disorder in nature, sacrilege, cannibalism, necrophilia, psychic projection, the succubus, the incubus, the ruin, and the tomb. Gathering up and unifying all that came before it, and casting its great shadow over all that came and continues to come after, its influence on twentieth-century Gothic fiction and film is unique and irresistible.

REFERENCES

Farson, Daniel. *The Man Who Wrote Dracula: A Biography of Bram Stoker*. London: Michael Joseph, 1975.

Irving, Laurence. *Henry Irving: The Actor and His World*. London: Columbus Books, 1989.

Roth, Phyllis A. *Bram Stoker*. Boston: Twayne Publishers, 1982.

Stoker, Bram. *Dracula*. 1897. Oxford: Oxford UP, 1983.

Locating Dracula: Contextualising the Geography of Transylvania

Gerald Walker and Lorraine Wright

> "Transylvania is Europe's unconscious."
>
> (Wall 20)

> "Having some time at my disposal when in London, I had visited the British Museum, and made search among the books and maps of the library regarding Transylvania; it had struck me that some foreknowledge of the country could hardly fail to have some importance in dealing with a noble of that country. I find that the district he named is in the extreme east of the country, just on the borders of three states, Transylvania, Moldavia, and Bukovina, in the midst of the Carpathian mountains; one of the wildest and least known portions of Europe. I was not able to light on any map or work giving the exact locality of the Castle Dracula, as there are no maps of this country as yet to compare with our own Ordnance Survey maps; but I found that Bistritz, the post town named by Count Dracula, is a fairly well-known place. I shall enter here some of my notes, as they may refresh my memory when I talk over my travels with Mina."
>
> (Stoker 1–2)

Introduction

HE DRACULA TALE BEGINS AND ENDS SOMEWHERE between 1885 and 1893[1], in the Principality of Transylvania, part of the Hungarian crown of the Austro-Hungarian Empire. The province of Transylvania, the German Seibenburgen, was an ethnically mixed region dominated by Germans and Magyars, but primarily populated by Romanians (Engel 157, Trillmich and Czybulka 130–131). The physical geography is dominated by the Carpathian range, an old uplift geological feature (Moraru 7ff, Giurescu 9ff). The story begins in the stretch of territory in the middle of the Carpathians, starting at the ethnic German town of Bistritz (Romanian Bistriţa), moving through the Borgo Pass from the west and, finally, reaching Castle Dracula in the depths of the mountains. This identifies the core region of the Dracula story.

Subsequently, the action of the story moves to England and is played out in Whitby in the northeast and London in the southeast. The final segments of the story return to the Balkans and ultimately to Castle Dracula as Dracula flees London and is pursued by the six protagonists. They take the Orient Express to Varna in Bulgaria, thence to Galatz (Romanian Galaţi) in Romania and split into three parties, each taking a different route or mode of transport before reassembling at the castle. The final chase returns to the Transylvania region. A different perspective is gained by the final journeys from the south and east into the Dracula core region.

Transylvania, the land beyond the forest, had been a frontier district for centuries. The Turks had advanced into the Romanian lands, to be met by a mix of resistance and collaboration from the princes of Moldavia and Wallachia in the 1400s. German settlers had filtered into the principality from the 1200s onward to meet Magyars who were remnants of the original migration out of the steppes of Asia. The policy of the Habsburg monarchy was to keep the district divided and to function as an outlier of Catholic Christendom. The Turks were overlords in the principality from the early 1500s until Habsburg control was reestablished in the 1690s. By the 1750s, the frontiers were organised as a military district which included that portion of Transylvania in which Castle Dracula is found. After 1851, the district was again reorganised but remained a part of the Hungarian crown lands. It was only after World War One that Romania was granted Transylvania. Simultaneously it received Romanian-speking Bessarabia (the eastern part of Moldavia betweeen the Prut and Nistru rivers which had been conquered by Russia in 1812), and Bukovina, the north-western part of Moldavia which had been conquered by the Habsburgs in 1785. Both areas were contentious and part of continuing

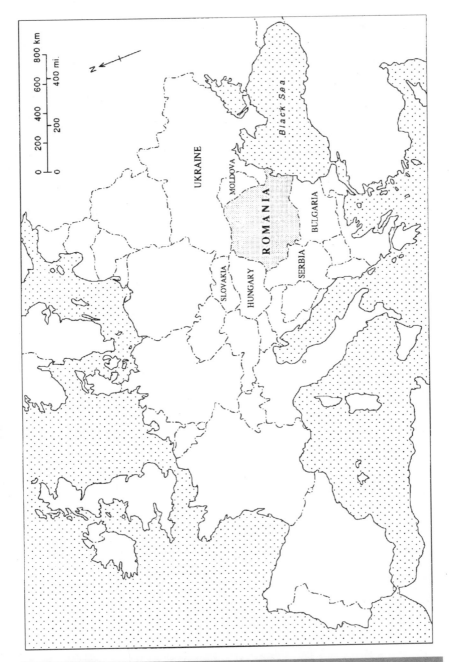

Map of Europe, at present.

struggles in eastern Europe. Bessarabia is now divided between the Republic of Moldova (the Romanian name for Moldavia) and the Ukraine, both of which declared independence in 1991.

Transylvania serves as the mythic centre of the Dracula tale. Its mountains, forests, deep valleys, and extraordinary scenery all play significant roles in the evocation of mystery and horror, especially as the story opens. Transylvania is also the scene for the novel's final resolution. The encounter between ancient superstition and modern science is, rather significantly, set in this frontier between east and west, modernity and the ancient world.

In this essay, we wish to consider the importance of the physical geographic context of this encounter. We will first examine the general characteristics of the northwestern portion of Transylvania in terms of surface geology, land forms, drainage, vegetation, wildlife, ethnic composition, and land uses of the area. This discussion will conclude by considering Castle Dracula's setting within the larger context of the surrounding Magyar and Slavic lands. Finally, we will discuss the paths into Transylvania taken by Jonathan Harker at the novel's beginning and by the chase party at the novel's end.

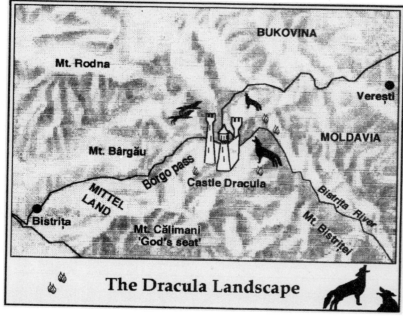

The Dracula Landscape

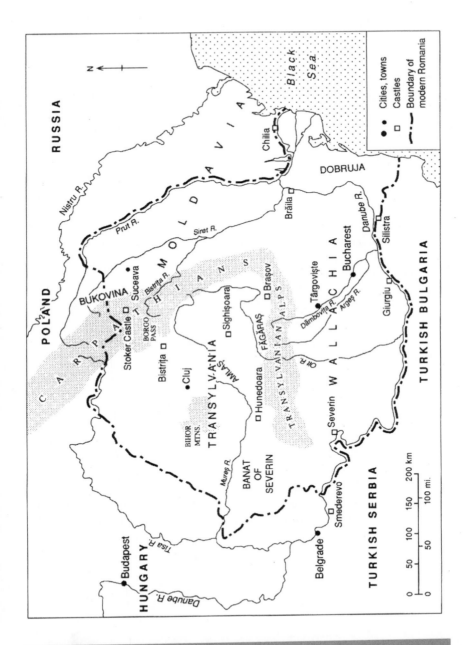

Map of Romania, at present.

The Physical Geography of Dracula Country

TRANSYLVANIA, WHERE *DRACULA* begins, is physically defined by the Carpathian Mountains. There are three segments of the larger mountain system, itself an extension of the Alpine to Himalayas upthrust: the western Carpathians separating Transylvania from the Hungarian Plain to the west, the southern Carpathians separating Transylvania from Wallachia to the south, and the eastern Carpathians separating Transylvania from Moldavia and Bukovina to the east and northeast. It is the eastern Carpathians that contain the core region of the Dracula tale and we shall concentrate on its physical structure. The Carpathians are a mix of crystalline upthrust granites, volcanic extrusions, and pockets of limestone deposits. The mountains are fractured into a number of great blocks, between which there are streams, rivers, and passes. The mountain blocks are morphologically characterised by great steps which create sizeable areas of level land even at high altitudes and lines of formidable peaks.

The centre of the region within which the mythical Castle Dracula lies is bounded roughly by longitude 24°30" East and 25°30" East and latitude 47° North and 48° North. Thus the core region is about a degree in area, or about 34,000 square kilometres. The mountain blocks in this restricted region are between 1500 to 2300 metres in height. There are three great blocks from north to south: Mount Bârgău, Mount Călimani, Mount Bistriţei and, further to the north, the great block of Mount Rodna. Elevations range from 2305 metres on Mount Rodna, to 2102 metres on Mount Călimani, 1864 metres in the Mount Bistriţei block, and 2280 metres on the north slope of Mount Bârgău. Mounts Bârgău and Călimani were created by volcanic action. Mount Rodna and the Bistriţei mountain blocks are crystalline in structure. There are passes around each of these mountain blocks and substantial areas of level, quite farmable land. Hence settlement, though sparse, is found everywhere, even in high elevations.

Immediately adjacent, both west and east of these mountain blocks, outwash and depositional plains are found. On the east, toward the Republic of Moldova, complex areas of outwash from the mountains creates a zone between the mountains and the great plains of Moldova, shading off ultimately to the Ukraine, with depositional features from long periods under inland seas. On the west, in Transylvania proper, the features are predominantly depositional as a result of an inland sea that covered the area up to the Pleistocene. The interior Transylvanian basin is a tableland above 500 metres that is relatively level to undulating up into the edges of the mountains. The Transylvanian tableland has always had relatively dense agricultural settlement.

On both the east and west sides of the eastern Carpathian mountains, streams drain into the Danube River. Much of the southeast of the Transylvanian basin is drained by the Olt, which passes through the southern Carpathian mountains down into the Wallachian plain. Most of the rest of the Transylvanian tableland drains into the Mureș River which flows west to join the Tisa in Hungary and thence south to the Danube. The northern portions of the Transylvanian basin drain into the Someșul, including the Bistrița (Romanian rendering of Bistritz) which flows past the town of that name, and eventually joins the Tisa in the north of Hungary. On the east slopes of the eastern Carpathians, the drainage, including that from the larger Bistrița River, not linked to the Bistrița on the west slope, flows south and tends east to join the Siret (Romanian rendering of Sereth) quite near the 47° parallel, mentioned in *Dracula* (Stoker 357). In its turn, the Siret flows south to join the Danube in Dobrujda near the great delta.

The mountain blocks, with their streams, lead downward through hilly country. One of the important parts of that country is correctly identified by Stoker as the Mittel Land of the valley of the western Bistrița, territory through which Jonathan Harker passes on his way to Castle Dracula at the novel's beginning. This area is relatively high, ranging between 500 and 700 metres in elevation, and slopes upward to the east. Within approximately 20 kilometres, it becomes high mountains. However, the Mittel Land is well tilled, grows fruit trees, and has an upland. The hilly region is separated from the mountains, which quite suddenly rear up as one goes up the pass south of the Bârgău block, or what Stoker refers to as the Borgo Pass. In the mountains, the stepped character of tables of relatively level land and a background of high, oftentimes very sharply-edged peaks transforms the landscape. Stoker uses these sudden transitions very effectively for emotional effect.

Excepting the Mittel Land near Bistrița, the soils draped over the geology of mountain blocks and outwash plains are acidic upland series formed on the slopes since the ice ages. Scattered through the basins in the mountains are bits and pieces of peat bogs, out of which emerge blue flames created from gases formed in the peat that burn spontaneously which Harker notes on his approach to Dracula's castle through the Borgo Pass.

Growing over much of the mountains are substantial forests, populated primarily by beeches and firs. These forests, located mostly on the slopes even up to very high altitudes, are again used by Stoker to develop the dark, sinister character of the landscape and to set the emotional tone of the book. On the lower slopes, particularly in the Mittel Land near Bistrița, cultivation is, and was, general, with cereals and fruit trees dominant. This forms a distinctly humanised landscape. In the mountains, the large blocks of forest are interspersed with smallish stretches of cultivation and considerable upland pasture land. The east sides of the mountain blocks, the zone in which the last chase of the novel takes place, is dominated by forests, scattered cultivation areas, and areas of mountain pasture.

In the basin of inland Transylvania, land uses are more intense and more broad-based, in keeping with the level to undulating character of the topography. In the mountains, forestry and patches of cultivated and pasture land are the norm. In the basin, cereal and sugarbeets are cultivated. Near to the centre of the basin, around Cluj-Napoca, "Klausenburg" in Bram Stoker's novel, is another zone of more intense land uses, in this case market gardens.

The last element about nineteenth-century Transylvania significant to Stoker's novel is its transport web. The Austrians had established a vast system of local militia defense on the edges of the Habsburg domains in the middle of the eighteenth century. That military frontier remained intact until the 1870s, and was supplied by the railways from the middle of the nineteenth century. The railways were pushed forward from the west to the east, with Budapest acting as the hub of the network. Railways crossed Transylvania following the valleys upstream and over the frequent passes toward the old military frontier. In the heart of Dracula country, the railway passed north of the Bârgău through the pass south of Mount Rodna and reached the Siret in Bukovina, to the north and slightly east of the mythic location of Castle Dracula. Another line from the northwest passed to the west and south of Bistriţa (then Bistritz). A spur line ran into Bistriţa, the end of the line.

Thus, the northern portions of Transylvania, with continued links to Budapest and the Hungarian heartland, were relatively well-developed at the time of Stoker's novel, but the mountain interior was linked only by the few roads over the mountain passes and a couple of lines linking Habsburg Bukovina with the rest of the Habsburg dominions.

The Transylvanian principality and the core of the territories which became the focal area in Bram Stoker's novel around Castle Dracula, were part of a larger set of geographic territories. Further, as we shall consider, the Dracula country was part of a very widespread ethno-class mosaic in eastern Europe before the First World War. For our purposes, the lands to the east, the west, and the south are particularly relevant. An important factor in much of the history of Transylvania was the Hungarian Plain, the Alfold, to the west. This extensive plain, mostly under a hundred metres in elevation, was the heartland of the Magyar people and of the Hungarian monarchy. Located inland, it had the great advantage of its topography and soils, and was, like the Transylvanian basin, an agricultural resource of the first importance. The plain could, given some security, become a centre for settlement. In the case of the Alfold, the centre was, very critically, the Danube, with the great cities of Buda and Pesth.

Directly to the south of Transylvania, over the southern Carpathians, is Wallachia. This constituted one of the two core areas of the recently independent Kingdom of Romania, tributary to Turkey for three centuries until independence in 1878. The Wallachian principality, with a long erratic history of good governance and misgovernance, occupied the north portion of the lower Danube valley. This broad valley, with Bucharest near its centre, is the Romanian equivalent of the Alfold in Hungary. It was the metropolitan core of Romania, both at present and in the period in which *Dracula* is set. The combination of plains near the Danube, upward trending to the north with the southern Carpathians at its peak, provided a rich and well-settled base for Romania. Wallachia was also the principality of Vlad Țepeș, Stoker's historical model for Dracula.

Moldavia to the east of Transylvania was the second hearth of Romania. Here, the plains were cut by the great river systems flowing out of the steppe interior of the Ukraine and Russia. Moldavia was always more exposed to the steppes to the east, but was also more removed from the Turkish core at Constantinople in Thrace. Moldavia was mostly a plain, but with inter-riverine hilly sections, usually trending north-south between the large rivers, particularly the Siret and the Nistru (Romanian rendering of Dniester). Many of the inter-riverine uplands were forest-covered in Moldavia, and many remain so to this day. Finally, the duchy of Bukovina represented the furthest eastern portion of the Habsburg domains. Bukovina was the mountainous eastern side of the eastern Carpathians. North of Moldavia, Bukovina was, in its geography and atmosphere, much like the core of Dracula country.

These surrounding regions of Transylvania had the same complex ethno-class arrangements as Transylvania before World War One. Hungarians dominated the Alfold, although there were significant areas of German settlement, from the twelfth century. The Transylvanian basin was primarily populated by Magyars, here separated from the Alfold in some cases for centuries, who were commonly called Szekely. The second resident group, both in Transylvania and elsewhere, were Germans. In Transylvania, these were principally twelfth and thirteenth-century Saxon and Rhenish migrants, planted by the Hungarian monarchy to secure control of the wild regions in the east. German settlements, both urban and rural, were located in islands throughout Transylvania, but particularly in the seven towns of the Siebenburgen. Germans and Magyars were dominant, if separate, populations. Over time, the Germans gained much of the land and became a renting class, losing their earlier mercantile bent. The Magyar Szekely retained the ownership and occupancy of the Transylvanian basin, but were under the lordship of a Magyar aristocracy. In Bukovina in the north, Ukrainian-speaking Slavs inhabited the northern sections of the duchy.

Throughout the region of what was to become Romania after the settlements of World War One, were the Romanic-speaking Vlach populations. The Romanians were found in the large majority in the west of Transylvania, throughout all of Moldavia and Wallachia, and in the southern parts of Bukovina. Romanians almost never appear in *Dracula*. They are part of that invisible indigenous population of areas colonised or dominated by central Europeans.

North of Hungary was the ethnic population of Slovaks. In the novel, and to a considerable degree in reality, the Slovaks are part of the upper working class who function as the teamsters who haul the Count's soil out of Transylvania. The Germans of the Siebenburgen provided, with the Magyar aristocrats, the upper class of the population. Germans provided much of the middle strata of the population, as well as the administrative élite. Magyars also composed the basic peasant population of the basin. In the mountains, the German-Magyar presence thins and even disappears. Bistritz was a German town and the Mittel Country was a German outlier. In the more restricted Dracula territory, the Magyar Szekely were a thin element, and here the invisible Romanians were the large majority. It is interesting that Stoker did not include Romanians as they were the inhabitants of districts his novel identifies as populated only by fierce wolves. Two additional ethnic groups play a part in the novel: Gypsies, called Szgany, and Jews, who inhabited several cities.

Also invisible in Bram Stoker's narrative world, are the changes accompanying the industrialisation of the European world. The railways into Transylvania functioned as military links with the great Habsburg fortresses of Vienna and Budapest, but also led to the reorganisation of the textile industry. At the same time, redefinition of private property in agriculture brought about the dissolution of the peasantry and the creation of an industrial working class. All of this was invisible to Stoker. His was a frozen bit of the antediluvian world surviving in the impenetrable mountain interior. Almost invisible, but on the edge of what Stoker did perceive, were the Jews in the growing cities of Moldavia and Wallachia, who had links to their co-religionists in England. The Jews play a role in the return of the chase party at the end of the novel, and are represented in several passages along racially-stereotyped lines true to the tenets of late nineteenth-century anthropology.

It is into this complex, albeit rather mythicised, mosaic, that Stoker's protagonist Jonathan Harker stumbles, in the spring of 1885/87 or 1893. It is into this world that the party of five men and Mina Harker move in the fall of that year to destroy Dracula in his place of origin. It is to those paths, Harker's and that of the chase party, that we will now turn in order to consider the geographic character of Stoker's *Dracula*.

The Paths to Castle Dracula

ON 1 MAY, JONATHAN Harker leaves Munich by train. He arrives in Vienna early the next morning, and continues on to Budapest. After a brief stop-over, the journey continues to the east. Harker comments that it seems, after crossing the bridges over the Danube, thus leaving the West for the East, that he is entering another world. By the night of 2 May, Harker arrives in Klausenberg, a German town in central Transylvania, where he stays for the night. By 7:30 the following morning, he is aboard a train for the final leg to Bistriţa. This destination is reached in the twilight hours of 3 May. This seems quite a lengthy journey for a distance of only 160 kilometres. Such a trip should have taken no more than about eight hours, even assuming a speed of only 20 kilometres an hour. However, in representing Harker's trip as one of such a duration, Stoker establishes his separation from the world of everyday, modern British life.

During the day of 4 May, Harker takes a coach through the lower Mittel Land. The following night is identified by the innkeeper in Bistriţa as St. George's Day, a time when evil has full sway (4). Up the Borgo Pass, south of Mount Bârgău, Harker and other travelers journey by coach through the upper Mittel Land which trends upward. They then pass under God's seat, Isten szek. This site is identified by one of the travelers and is most likely Mount Călimani. The people along the way are identified as Czechs and Slovaks, peasants suffering from goitre (7). In fact, most of the population here beyond the Mittel Land was probably Romanian. The Mittel Land was hilly but surrounded by increasingly impressive mountains with great slopes covered with birches, beeches, firs, and pines. In the pass are beeches, firs, pines, and oaks. The pass then grows very steep which causes a laboured period, but then levels off as they arrive at the eastern edge of the Borgo Pass. Passengers comment, after crossing themselves, that they have mercifully arrived at the end of the pass one hour before the dreaded St. George's day. After some discussion about the absence of a coach awaiting Harker and the passenger coach's near departure with Harker on board, the Count's coach, pulled by four black horses, draws up beside them.

Harker boards this coach which is driven, unknown to him, by the Count himself. Shortly before midnight, dogs begin to howl, startling the horses. Then, from the distant mountains, wolves begin to howl. Shortly thereafter, the coach turns to the right down a narrow roadway to the southeast. This journey is conducted as if through a tunnel surrounded by trees with great frowning rocks on either side. From time to time, spots of blue flame appear, and the driver-Count dismounts and assembles cairns of stones near the flames. At one point, Harker notices that he can see the flames *through* the driver (13). In the meantime, the howling of the wolves draws closer and black clouds pile up in the mountain sky. The moon emerges and the wolves, now surrounding the coach, renew their howling. The coachman, who had left the coach, returns and waves the wolves away. After the clouds return and blot out the moon, the journey resumes. The roadway now ascends sharply until they reach the courtyard of a vast ruined castle whose broken battlements are outlined against the moonlit sky. Castle Dracula has been reached.

In this drawn-out journey, the world of everyday life is forgotten and Harker enters the heart of a mythic world. Harker arrives at Castle Dracula on 5 May, and remains there as a prisoner until 30 June when he escapes and eventually arrives at Budapest. Gradually, Harker discovers that he is a prisoner. He explores, carefully and with English determination, the world of which he is now part. Between intermittent engagements with the Count, Harker searches the castle, finds himself locked in without a means of escape, locates several sets of apartments and, finally, the Count's crypt.

Perhaps most striking is the antique apartment set over the cliff upon which Dracula's castle is perched. In that apartment, with its loggia, Harker can see the surrounding country. He looks to the west onto a great valley. In the distance are a line of peaks, which are most likely Mount Rodna or, possibly, the Bârgău. He can see mountain ash and thorn on the nearer slopes (35). The Count advises him when abroad in the castle not to sleep anywhere (33), but Harker disobeys this injunction and meets the three young women who almost devour him (37–38). He is saved by the fortuitous appearance of the Count. The women are promised, however, that once Dracula is finished with Harker he will be theirs. They are appeased with a bag containing a baby (39).

Near the end of Harker's ordeal, another child is brought into the castle and its distraught mother is herself devoured in the courtyard by the omnipresent wolves. Harker continues his explorations, now following the Count's lead by climbing lizard-style down the outside walls of the castle, in order to get into the Count's own rooms. Here he finds no evidence of occupancy by the Count, but a great heap of gold covered in dust (47). In one castle episode, Harker finds the Count in a coffin and attempts to kill him, but in vain (51–52). Finally, after the Count receives letters from Harker to be sent to England stating that the business of the purchase of a townhouse in London has been completed and that all is well, it is clear that the Count has done with Harker. The Count uses Szgany (gypsies) and Slovaks to take several boxes of soil to wagons (52–53). Harker's journal ends with the departure of the wagons and the Count asleep in one of the boxes of earth (53). Jonathan is abandoned to the three bloodthirsty beauties. Harker vows he will escape by climbing down the outside of the castle. It would seem that he is successful because later in the novel he arrives in a hospital in Budapest, a ruined man (99).

The novel now turns to Whitby on the northeast coast of England. Here the rest of the characters are introduced. Dracula enters England and the central action of the narrative is developed. Whitby is a seaside town in the northwest of England. It is located north of the Humber River at the outflow of the Esk River into the North Sea. The town is surrounded by the North York Moors, a national park today, which is comprised of Jurassic limestone. This limestone forms caverns, swallow holes, and potholes reminiscent of parts of the Carpathians (Geological Survey, 1957). This is the perfect landscape for the wolf which abandoned the *Demeter* in Whitby and for the bat that in the evenings flutters around Lucy Westenra's window. The landscape fits the mood and requirements of the story because it contains so many secret hiding places. To the east lie the Pennine Hills composed of coal measures, millstone grit, and more massive carbiniferous limestone. For the novel, the important site is the town itself. A number of its central features are particularly important to the arrival of Dracula on the ill-starred *Demeter* from Varna.

The character of the geography of Whitby and its environs shares a certain superficial similarity to Transylvania. The North York Moors are hilly and reach heights of over 1,500 feet or 458 metres. The general character of the area is a dissected upland with exposed portions of harder rock and moor vegetation. The limestone character of the moors provides the perfect setting for Dracula's sinister activities as he stalks, gains access to, and ultimately has his way with Lucy Westenra. It is presumably on the edge of this moorland that the Westenra estate is located. The rest of the regional setting consists of the Cleveland Hills to the north, the Vales of Pickering and York to the south and west, the Pennines still further west, and the Yorkshire Wolds south of Pickering. The basic character of this setting is the dissected and eerie North York Moors and the coastal town with its considerable internal elevation. Stoker thus yokes together tradi-

tional humanised and wild landscapes (or, at least, as wild as English landscapes get).

The action in the novel's Whitby section commences with long
excerpts from the diaries of Mina Murray (soon to be Mina Harker), Lucy

Whitby Abbey, Easter 1923.
These photographs come from snapshots included in an old family photo album, bought
in an antique market in Manchester, U.K. Photographer is unknown.
Collection of Richard Anderson.

Westenra, Drs John Seward and Abraham Van Helsing, and Arthur Holmwood (soon to be Lord Godalming). The principal settings are the Westenra estate, Hillingham, and various locales in Whitby: Tate Hill, the Church of St Mary and its nearby steps, and the cemetery with its seat and grave. Dr. Seward's insane asylum outside London is introduced in this segment of the book, primarily by way of revelations about Renfield, the insane fly eater.

The action in and around Whitby begins well before Jonathan Harker ends his diary after his escape from Castle Dracula. Between 9 May and mid-August, the cast of characters is introduced and Lucy succumbs to the advances of Dracula and gradually, but heroically, fades. In between, Mina Murray is notified on 12 August of the presence and condition of Jonathan Harker in Budapest. Harker had been in hospital in Budapest for the previous six weeks, which means he had come to Budapest in early July, having escaped the castle on 30 June. Mina leaves England, travels to Budapest where she meets Jonathan, helps in his recovery and marries him on 24 August. Meanwhile, Lucy's steady deterioration in Whitby brings Dr. Van Helsing, Seward's old teacher and mentor, from the Netherlands. They, more or less, botch the case. On 20 September, Lucy dies.

At this point the plot shifts to London in the southeast. A variety of settings are introduced which are principally located in and around the Hampstead Heath park area in the northwest of London. Along the way, Mina Harker becomes a victim, but not a fatal victim, of Dracula. The various threads of action centre on Dr. Seward's insane asylum, until the action shifts, again abruptly, when Dracula flees England on the *Czarina Catherine* to return to Transylvania on 5 October. On 7 October, the chase party sets out for Varna in Bulgaria, where they arrive on 15 October. From that point, the chase is on.

Between 15 October and 29 October, the chase party await the arrival of the *Czarina Catherine* at Varna. On the 28th, they are informed that the ship has docked at Galați, in Romania, on the north shore of the Danube near the Delta. They take a train to Galați and arrive there on 30 October. The real chase begins on 30 October from Galați and lasts until 6 November near Castle Dracula where the Count is killed. On 30 October, the larger party of six including Mina, Van Helsing, Godalming, Harker, Seward, and Morris split into three parties, each using a different mode of travel to Castle Dracula. We propose to follow the separate paths of each of these parties and to describe the geographic character of the larger country.

Jonathan Harker and Lord Godalming obtain a steam launch in Galați and proceed on 30 October the few kilometres back up the Danube

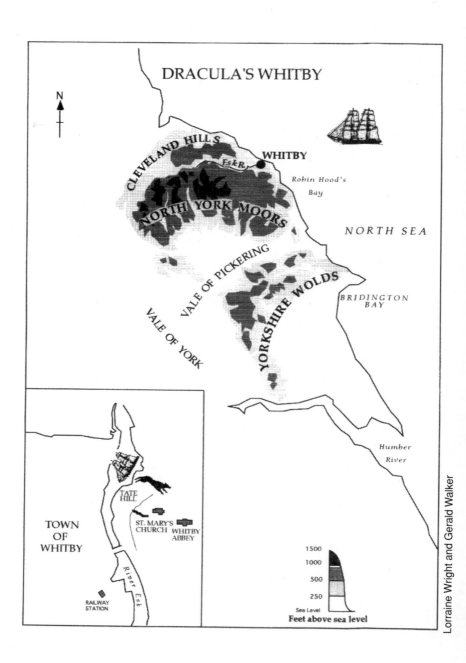

DRACULA'S WHITBY

Lorraine Wright and Gerald Walker

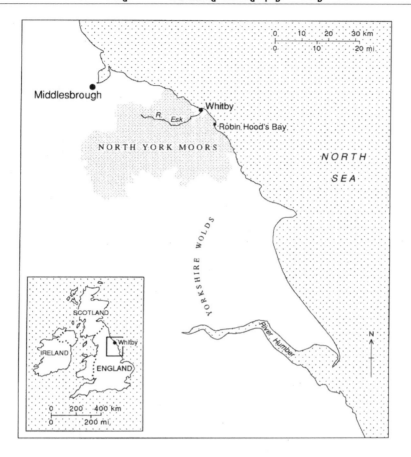

until they reach the confluence of the Siret River. For the next two days, they steam up the Siret through a countryside of low elevation, gradually trending upward and into hilly uplands formed by the down-cutting of a myriad of small streams feeding into the Siret. They then reach a narrows below the confluence of the Siret and the Bistriţa. As they move along upstream, they remain primarily on the western edge of the sown region of Moldavia. During this stretch, they have no difficulty steaming. On 1 November, they steam into the Bistriţa River and obtain a Romanian flag at the confluence town of Fundu, of which we can find no trace. Today, there are several small towns in the general area, but none with a name even faintly like Fundu. Harker comments on the many streams feeding down from the mountains into the Bistriţa. The further upstream they steam, the colder the weather becomes and the more snow appears. On 4 November, the pursuers hear that the Count's launch has experienced an

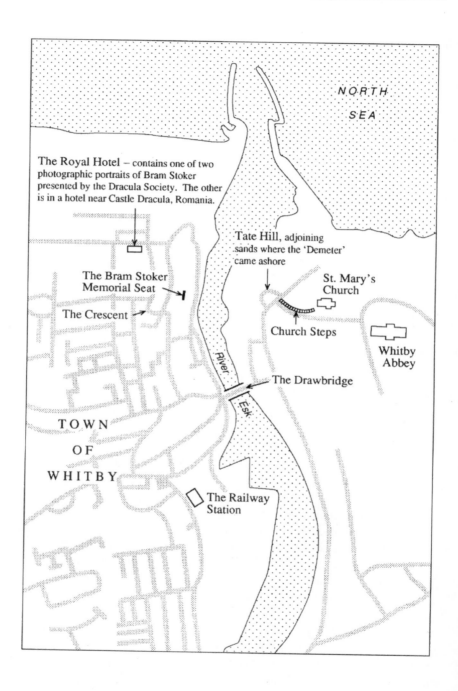

The Royal Hotel – contains one of two photographic portraits of Bram Stoker presented by the Dracula Society. The other is in a hotel near Castle Dracula, Romania.

NORTH SEA

Tate Hill, adjoining sands where the 'Demeter' came ashore

The Bram Stoker Memorial Seat

The Crescent

St. Mary's Church

Church Steps

Whitby Abbey

River Esk

The Drawbridge

TOWN OF WHITBY

The Railway Station

accident but has been able to continue through the rapids. On the 4th, Harker and Godalming suffer an incapacitating accident to their launch and take to horses in order to continue the pursuit into the evening. The horseback stretch continues on for the next day and a half into the mountains away from the river and toward Castle Dracula to the northwest.

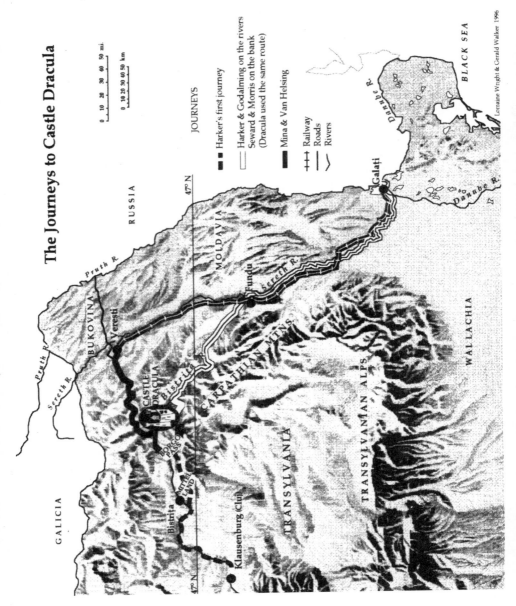

Dr. Seward and Quincey Morris take horses and ride up the same rivers as Harker and Godalming. Quincey Morris, eventually killed in the struggle with the Count's servitors, is an American from Texas whose principal contribution to the expedition is to equip the chase party with Winchester repeating rifles. He himself carries a Bowie knife as well as pistols. For four days, they ride up the river and on the fifth day, 3 November, reach Fundu at the confluence of the Bistrița and the Siret. Hearing that the launch of Godalming and Harker has gone by, they start up that stretch of river. On the 4th, they hear of the accident to the steam launch in the rapids and continue on upstream. On the 5th of November they see a group of Szgany, presumably Gypsies hired by the Count, dashing away from the river with a leiter-waggon, within which is the Count. They continue their pursuit until the 6th of November when they catch up with the Count's party. In the ensuing struggle they are joined by Harker and Godalming, and Quincey Morris is killed, but not before Dracula is killed by the party of men.

The third party chasing Dracula consists of Dr. Van Helsing and Mina Harker. Mina had been attacked by Dracula in London after an elaborate sideshow in which Renfield, the insane fly-eater, allowed Dracula access to the building housing Mina. Not much use to anyone anymore, Renfield is killed. Mina is thereafter contaminated by Dracula and even develops a stigma on her forehead which indicates that she is, at least partially, in the thrall of the Count. After this incident, Mina is excluded from the councils of the men and is effectively placed under the supervision of Dr. Van Helsing.

This party takes the less physically demanding modes of transportation, first the train, and then the carriage. Leaving Galați on 30 October, they journey up a similar route to that taken by the two other parties. The train arrives at Verești in northern Romania near the headwaters of the Siret on 31 October. The principal difference between this party and the others is that instead of taking the Bistrița route they continue on a further stretch of the Siret in order to reach Verești, just inside the Romanian border with Bukovina, a Habsburg possession. A carriage and horses are purchased for the more than 70 miles (113 kilometres) remaining in the journey (360).

The location of Castle Dracula on our map corresponds to that outlined in Jonathan Harker's initial journey. The route from Verești is described by Van Helsing as the quickest way to Bistrița, and links to the Borgo Pass road. On the next two days, 1 and 2 November, they follow this road and reach the Borgo Pass on the morning of the 3rd. Shortly after reaching the Pass, Mina directs them onto the other end of the road taken by Jonathan Harker to the castle. The party takes this side-road for the entire day, making slow progress. They had presumably covered 45 kilometres to the Pass over the two previous days. They travel all of the third day sharply climbing the mountains looming over them. They then, finally, reach the vicinity of Castle Dracula.

Van Helsing camps and creates a fairy ring of protection around Mina by using one of the stolen communion wafers he had earlier acquired. That night they are visited by the vampire women from the castle, but remain safe within their wafer-lined ring. The following morning, Van Helsing leaves the failing Mina in the holy ring and journeys to the castle. The trip is not presented as arduous or lengthy. He carries a blacksmith hammer and other apparatus. The result of his visit to the castle is to incapacitate its defences. He opens the castle to the world by removing its doors, and slays the three lovely women in their crypts. Van Helsing also leaves a wafer in Dracula's tomb, not yet occupied by the Count, so that he may not return to it. On the afternoon of the 6th of November, the party moves east along the side-road in order to join the other parties for the final attack. They trend downward from the castle's heights, near their final campsite, until they find a strategically safe place from the wolves howling in the distance.

From this vantage point, they watch the two parties of men converge on the leiter-waggon in which Dracula lies. The final struggle occurs here. As the party fights with the Szgany, Quincey Morris is wounded, the Szgany are dispersed, and Dracula is slain. At this point, Quincey Morris dies.

Some Interpretations of the Geographical Context of Transylvania

OBVIOUSLY, THE GEOGRAPHY of Transylvania is a creation of Bram Stoker's in the novel *Dracula*. However, Stoker adopts a rigorously realistic style of writing within which the Gothic horror is developed. In order to create a setting for *Dracula*, Stoker researched and presented a vision of Transylvania that was indeed superficially realistic. The places he refers to are usually located approximately where he presents them.

Verești is a good case in point. The town is just to the south of Bukovina, as it was then as a Habsburg province. It is currently located at a junction in the railway. But in the nineteenth century it was located in the northernmost part of Romania and marked the end of the railway which, for military purposes, did not extend from Romania into Habsburg territories. The town is, indeed, about 70 miles or 44 kilometres away from the place where, given other evidence in the book, Castle Dracula ought to be. Nevertheless, the entry into the interior from the last rail stop, which represents the terminal of modernity, is a journey into mythical space. The descriptions of the landscape are realistic, but the emotions evoked by the brooding forests on the great mountains are Gothic.

The sense one gets from reading the passages from the journals of Mina Harker and Abraham Van Helsing is that an enormous world has been traversed. The trip from Vereşti to the edge of the Borgo Pass consumes more than two full days and nights. At the pass, time again slows down as the horses traverse another enormous distance. Here, the story plunges into the heart of the myth and a different time-space continuum is evoked. Stoker uses geography most skillfully by presenting the Transylvanian terrain in the realist mode in order to evoke a mythical state and cultural reality. Even here, the distances presented are plausible: a three-day carriage journey over mountainous terrain into the heart of the Carpathians is believable. Again, it must be underlined that the geography, such as Stoker knew it, is very nicely evoked.

The clever use of regions, barriers, entranceways, and awesome landscapes all create the mythic character of the space of the Dracula story. Bistriţa and Vereşti each act as portals to the inner zone surrounding the castle. At a greater distance, Klausenberg and Galaţi act as portals to that larger zone of Transylvania and Moldavia. The use of an unnamed Moldavia, accurately described but not evoked as a named place, alongside the named agricultural district of Bistriţa, the Mittel Land, betrays a biased Western perspective. The naming of the western side of the approach to Castle Dracula and the non-naming of the eastern approach is also highly significant and betrays a Western outlook. The mountains bound the region as a whole and frame the castle as the novel's core site. The Mittel Land, actually inhabited by Germans, as Stoker was aware, has the symbolic importance of marking the limits of regularly cultivated earth, before entry into the inner zone of the wild castle environs. The sharp separation between the sown and tamed earth and the wild, mountainous world of primeval forces, however thinly disguised to fit into a western conception of the Other's spaces, naturalises a mythic reality. Here, Stoker takes poetic licence in his interpretation of the human geography of the inner region. The block and step structure of the Carpathians allowed cultivation in the midst of the mountains. There were actually farms and villages in the zone Stoker identifies as nearly empty.

Another interesting geographic characteristic of Stoker's representation of Transylvania is the lack of importance ascribed to political divisions. Romania only appears in the ghostly form of a flag the adventurers display to gain respect or fear from the locals. The Habsburg domains are nowhere identified. There is no recognition during the chase, for instance, that the action moves from Romanian to Habsburg territories. This despite several centuries of military organisation of the frontier. Only about a generation before the action of the novel, the Habsburg military frontier had been transformed. One can safely assume that there was a Habsburg military presence in the area, but it is not part of the novel. It is, therefore, a realistic and imperialist gesture that Stoker's English party does not inconvenience themselves with travel documents, visas, and passports. They were not needed at the time of the novel's action, and would not be needed until the time of World War One. In many ways, both Romania and the Habsburgs were scarcely realities. Both states were primarily forces of localised repression. Nevertheless, the progress of several parties of armed foreigners in a country would have been the sort of thing that would have been noticed and, quite plausibly, have affected the story. Most certainly it does not because the party, from Stoker's point of view, are not foreigners. Though their being armed is not something that would have been necessary in England, it is represented as justified given their location and goal.

In addition, the party has the backing of all of the apparatus of modern capitalist technology and power. The aristocrat, Lord Godalming, who funds the project, uses the financial arm of the capitalist establishment, including its local English factors, to equip, inform, and orient the party of adventurers. Most unfortunately, Stoker's characterisation of the Jews bears similarities to the Nazi ideology of a couple of generations later. They are portrayed, economically, as active agents of capitalism and, more narrowly, commercial exploitation. Further, they are represented, physically and culturally, in the most awful stereotyped manner. The manipulation of physical anthropological stereotypes about Jewish merchants as Alpha types is a case in point. Finally, everyone outside of Van Helsing's hunting party are subject to commodification in that they may be bought. Whenever the adventurers need something, including the labour and complicity of a variety of people, it is bought.

Yet, at the same time, during the journey to the castle, the mantle of the West, capitalism, and even Englishness is gradually shed. The Transylvanian interior, the castle, and the mythic core of its surroundings, constitute a land of magic, where autochthonous forces survive, a land where the adventurers are faced with primal powers. However, even here, the Winchesters of Quincey Morris prove to be a match for the earth's forces. During the last struggle, which includes Van Helsing's act of dispatching the undead women, weapons and technology out of the early iron age are used: a hammer, knives, and stakes. What does emerge during this struggle between antiquity and modernity in a mytho-realistic landscape is the display of good English character. The four core characters are English. They are noble (either literally or in spirit), gallant, resourceful, and capable. The other two, Van Helsing and Quincey Morris, are English outliers. The English are the equivalent of a base layer of geological strata and the two others are outliers of that strata. In the case of Morris, the reader is presented with an American who, in the struggle, shows himself to be truly English in his nobility. Van Helsing, though sharing an ideological world with the English, is not English. He represents the wisdom of the continent and of the West put at British disposal.

Equally interesting is what is not represented in the Transylvanian segments of the novel. We have suggested the literal "incorrectness" of Stoker's characterisation of the Borgo Pass as empty. In addition, Romanians, as well as Romania, did not exist in Stoker's perceptual geographic world. Magyars, Germans, Gypsies, Slovaks, and Jews all existed, but Romanians, the vast majority of the population, are invisible. Unless he was going to incorporate the Romanians into the story, and clearly he did not have the need to do so, it seems to have been better just to ignore them. On top of the artistic necessities for this omission, it seems likely that the state of Romania and the Vlach speakers were unknown to Stoker. The myth of the Roman survival through the Vlach-speaking peoples was afoot, but did not yet constitute the central myth of the Romanian state. This represented a potential complication for a story that required the mythic "Otherness" of Germans, Magyars, Gypsies, Jews, and Slovaks in its treatment of locality. These groups were known to the west. The Romanians, however, were not conceptualised because Stoker was probably unaware of them and was not in need of them as a narrative feature.

Thus, Stoker, while rigorously following a realist style, carefully crafted his presentation to both transform the landscape he found in his researches into something mythic while preserving much that was actually there, including the disposition of geographic features. The basic regionalisation Stoker uses — a series of zones around Castle Dracula, each of which gradually becomes more detailed — is a device that helps to enhance the horrifying and fantastic elements of his story. It is not a regionalisation that may be attributed to the on-the-ground realities of Transylvania. Stoker's *Dracula* thus evokes an imaginary world rendered realistically by way of intricate landscape detail.

NOTES

1   The dating of *Dracula* continues to be disputed. As popular Gothic novelist Kim Newman outlines in his concluding Note to *Anno Dracula*, "... Stoker does not specify which year the events of his novel are supposed to take place. Frayling argues persuasively that he intended 1893, while Wolf and Haining pick 1887. The fact is that neither choice will entirely suffice. Published in 1897, the novel ends with a present-day chapter locating the bulk of the story seven years in the past, but numerous small details — like the use of the phrase 'new woman', coined in 1892, or even the comparative sophistication of Dr. Seward's phonograph — jar with this. I have plumped — as did Jimmy Sangster, Terence Fisher and Hammer Films for their 1958 *Dracula* (*Horror of Dracula* to heathen Americans) — for 1885, and opted to shift on to an alternate timetrack half-way through Stoker's Chapter 21.... Stoker's *Dracula* is already an alternate world story, set in a timeline where social and mechanical progress has advanced slightly faster than in our own, where Chicksand Street and Piccadilly are considerably longer thoroughfares than those we make do with, and where London boasts a Kingstead Cemetery in the region of Hampstead Heath presumably corresponding to our own Highgate Cemetery. In reworking history, I have taken as a starting point Stoker's imagined world rather than our own ..." (467).

    Another critic has deduced *Dracula*'s dating by examining (rather appropriately) the phases of the moon. According to Rickey Shanklin, "Based on the phases of the moon as described in Stoker's novel, the story of *Dracula* actually takes place in 1890, two years after Jack the Ripper stalked the streets of Whitechapel" (26).

REFERENCES

Engel, Josef, ed. *Grosser, Historischer Weltatlas, Vol. 3, Neuzeit*. Munich: Bayerischer Schulbuch-Verlag 1957.

Geological Survey, Sheets 1 and 2, 1957. *Geological Map of Great Britain*. Director General of the Ordnance Survey, Chessington, Surrey.

Giurescu, Constantin C. *Transylvania in the History of Romania*. London: Garnstone Press, n.d.

Moraru, Tiberiu, Vasile Cucu, and Ion Velcea. *The Geography of Romania*. Bucharest: Meridiane, 1966.

Newman, Kim. *Anno Dracula*. 1992. New York: Pocket, 1993.

Shanklin, Rickey. "Dracula: Bram Stoker's Bogeyman." *Blood of the Innocent*. Vol. 2. By Rickey Shanklin and Mark Wheatley. New York: WARP Graphics, January 1986. 25–27.

Stoker, Bram. *Dracula*. 1897. Oxford: Oxford UP, 1983.

Trillmich, Werner and Gerhard Czybulka, eds. *Westermanns Atlas zur Weltgeschichte, Vol. III, Neuzeit*. Braunschweig: George Westermann Verlag, 1963.

Wall, Geoffrey. "'Different from Writing': *Dracula* in 1897." *Literature and History* 10 (1984):15–23.

I

Dracula — 1890s Vampire Text

Dracula, The Jewel of Seven Stars, and Stoker's "Burden of the Past"

Carol A. Senf

N THE JUSTIFIABLY FAMOUS FIRST CHAPTER OF *Dracula*, Bram Stoker confronts Jonathan Harker, a representative nineteenth-century Englishman, with a world that differs significantly from the London he ordinarily inhabits. Confident in his own abilities and in the strengths of modern culture, Harker travels to Dracula's castle, located in a region where "every known superstition in the world is gathered" (2). Subsequent chapters pit Harker and a group of other modern Englishmen against a being who is the physical and psychological embodiment of the primitive past, a creature who is both Renaissance warlord and a far more primal destroyer of human beings.[1] In a battle that only one side can win, the representatives of modernity, including scientists, lawyers, and technocrats, use the tools of nineteenth-century science and technology and finally conquer the forces of the primitive past.[2]

Stoker was constantly troubled by the power that the past exerts over the present — so troubled that much of the fiction he wrote after *Dracula* continued to address this issue. *Miss Betty*, published the year after *Dracula*, literally takes place during the first years of the eighteenth century, but addresses issues of gender and nationalism that were relevant to Stoker and his contemporaries. *The Mystery of the Sea* (1902), *Lady Athlyne* (1908), *The Lady of the Shroud* (1909), and *The Lair of the White Worm* (1911) all address the power of the past, although all four are set in Stoker's present. Furthermore, these novels resemble *Dracula* in that all of them suggest that those who understand science and technology are most capable of handling the social and political problems of the day. In fact, most of Stoker's fiction seems to exude confidence that science and technology can correct the problems of the past and provide for a more comfortable future.

The Jewel of Seven Stars, published six years after *Dracula*, is a very different kind of novel. Here, Stoker returns to an issue he had examined in *Dracula*: the conflict between the modern age and the primitive past. However, in this novel, the past is much more powerful, and the result is that the forces of the present are absolutely annihilated by Queen Tera, whose mummy is resurrected by a small group of scientists and Egyptologists. Unlike *Dracula*, which concludes with the representatives of the modern community celebrating their conquest, *Jewel* ends with annihilation, the death of modernity.

Although Stoker's publisher encouraged him to modify the conclusion to make it less bleak and hopeless in editions subsequent to the first [3] (and modern reprints continue to print the sanitised "happy" ending), *The Jewel of Seven Stars* is consistently ambivalent about the power that the past exerts and less optimistic about the power of modern science. In fact, Malcolm Ross, a character who resembles Jonathan Harker in numerous ways, muses throughout the novel about the power of the past. Furthermore, in the first edition, Ross (unlike his fellow characters in the novel who are confident about modern science) is the only character alive and able at the conclusion of the novel to describe Tera's destructive powers.

The remainder of this essay will examine Stoker's attitudes to the past and his visions for the future. In particular, it will explore Stoker's awareness of scientific and cultural developments that were taking place around the turn of the century (including developments in biology, paleontology, and archaeology), his fascination with technology, and his apprehensions about various primitive forces, including certain powers that he associated with women.[4] Most importantly, the essay will examine the way that Stoker incorporates many of the prejudices and predilections of his time. Although Stoker graduated from Trinity College, Dublin, with honours in science, and remained close to his brothers, three of whom were physicians, he was neither a scientist nor an intellectual. Instead, he was a well-educated Irishman who, in his capacity as business manager for the

Lyceum Theatre, hobnobbed with the great and near-great of his time and translated current ideas into popular fiction. Because he rarely had time to revise and polish what he wrote, his concerns often lie near the surface, concerns that a more careful craftsman might have concealed or avoided entirely. Reading these works can therefore provide insights into the world of his day.

Like Conrad's Marlow, Jonathan Harker is plunged into the heart of darkness. He observes early on that he is "not able to light on any map or work giving the exact locality of the Castle Dracula, as there are no maps of this country as yet to compare with our own Ordnance Survey maps" (1). Furthermore, this primitive world is rife with strange customs and inhabited by strange people, the strangest being "the Slovaks, who are more barbarian than the rest" (3). Harker notes the superstitious behaviour and primitive clothing of the inhabitants but is most obviously bothered by the lack of efficiency he encounters: "It seems to me that the further East you go the more unpunctual are the trains. What ought they to be in China?" (2). Thus he suggests that the past and the present are quite different, with the past being inexact, barbarian, superstitious, and inefficient. In stark contrast, the modern age is conceived as exact, civilised, rational, and efficient.

Eventually, Harker leaves behind the vehicles of modern civilisation and is driven first by stagecoach and ultimately by caleche into desolate mountain country where he meets Dracula and becomes a literal prisoner in "a vast *ruined castle*, from whose tall black windows came no ray of light, and whose *broken battlements* showed a jagged line against the moonlit sky" (14, emphasis mine). As its ruined state and broken battlements illustrate, Dracula's castle is a remnant from the distant past.

Stoker spends a great deal of time describing the castle's location and thereby foregrounds the immersion of his modern character in a primitive place, a veritable symbol of the past. More important, however, is the fact that Stoker has Harker confront the human (or inhuman) remnants from that past, for Dracula is both Renaissance warlord and vampire:

> I have had a long talk with the Count. I asked him a few questions on Transylvanian history, and he warmed up to the subject wonderfully. In his speaking of things and people, and especially of battles, he spoke as if he had been present at them all. (28)

Here, Harker identifies Dracula with the past and himself with the present.

In addition to suggesting that Dracula is a figure from the past, Harker also focuses on characteristics that reinforce his bestial nature:

The mouth, so far as I could see it ... was fixed and rather cruel-looking, with peculiarly sharp white teeth; these protruded over the lips.... For the rest, his ears were pale and at the tops extremely pointed.... Hitherto I had noticed the backs of his hands ... and they had seemed rather white and fine; but seeing them now close to me, I could not but notice that they were rather coarse — broad, with squat fingers. Strange to say, there were hairs in the centre of the palm. (17–18)

John L. Greenway notes that this description also identifies Dracula as a criminal, or at least as having physical characteristics usually associated with criminals:[5]

Stoker took some care to describe Dracula and the female vampires as having criminal features.... Seward as a scientist should have done what Mina did unconsciously: recognize Dracula (and vampirism in general) as an atavism, an evolutionary regression to a primordial past. (76)

These characteristics of physiognomy would have been clearer to Stoker's contemporaries than they are to twentieth-century readers.

Although Greenway's reference to atavism and "an evolutionary regression to a primordial past" suggests that vampires are primitive beings — remnants of the past — it is equally important to note that Stoker's description of Dracula (and the women vampires as well) identifies them as more animal than human. This identification links Stoker's concern with the nineteenth-century scientific discussion of humanity's past, a discussion that involved biologists, archaeologists, historians, and laymen. For example, Darwin in *The Descent of Man* (originally published in 1871) discusses at length several of the characteristics that Stoker assigns to Dracula and specifically identifies these traits (among them enlarged canine teeth, pointed ears, and excess hair) as characteristics of more primitive species.[6] Darwin notes that pointed ears are a characteristic of lower animals but not generally of primates (including human beings).[7] Furthermore, Darwin observes that human beings are less hairy than other mammals and that "the hairs thus scattered over the body are the rudiments of the uniform hairy coat of the lower animals" (Appleman 147). Darwin also notes the enlarged canine teeth in the near relatives of human beings and suggests that they were used for aggression. On the other hand, he indicates that social qualities enable humans to compete with physically stronger animals:

> The small strength and speed of man, his want of natural weapons, &c., are more than counterbalanced, firstly, by his intellectual powers, through which he has formed for himself weapons, tools, &c., though still remaining in a barbarous state, and secondly, by his social qualities which lead him to give and receive aid from his fellow-men. (Appleman 175–176)

Darwin, who begins with a discussion of human physical characteristics, concludes by noting human social and moral characteristics — the precise pattern followed by Stoker.[8]

Stoker's contemporaries would likely have associated the physical characteristics of vampires with more primitive human species or with lower animals even if Stoker hadn't emphasised those connections as he does in the following passages. Dracula exits his castle headfirst like a bat, communicates with wolves, and moves with feline grace: "There was something so panther-like ... something so unhuman, that it seemed to sober us all from the shock of his coming" (305). His female companions also behave more like animals than like human beings, a fact that terrifies Jonathan Harker who notes that one of them "licked her lips *like an animal,* till I could see in the moonlight the moisture shining on the scarlet lips and on the red tongue as it lapped the white sharp teeth" (38, emphasis mine).

Most frightening though is the fact that even sophisticated nineteenth-century English women can become animals. Here is Lucy Westenra, virginal bride turned ravenous beast: "When Lucy ... saw us she drew back with an angry snarl, such *as a cat* gives when taken unawares ... she flung to the ground ... the child ... *growling* over it *as a dog growls* over a bone" (211, emphasis mine). As with Dracula, other characters emphasise her teeth which "seemed longer and sharper than they had been in the morning. In particular, by some trick of the light, the canine teeth looked longer and sharper than the rest" (159). The shift underlines Lucy's change from passive bride to aggressive threat. Furthermore, like Darwin and Huxley, Stoker emphasises that human beings in *Dracula* have the moral power of social organisation and the intellectual power of science: "We have on our side power of combination — a power denied to the vampire kind; we have resources of science; we are free to act and think" (238).

Almost every detail in *Dracula* underlines that a sophisticated group of human beings is waging war on a primitive, even animalistic, being. The triumph of the human beings at the conclusion might even be said to reinforce the idea of progress that was so common in the nineteenth century, an idea commonly associated with biological evolutionism. As Peter J. Bowler notes in *Fossils and Progress: Paleontology and the Idea of Progressive Evolution in the Nineteenth Century*:

> [Herbert] Spencer preferred the inheritance of acquired characteristics to natural selection, but his philosophy was easily (if somewhat unfairly) connected with the Darwinian theory.... Indeed it was almost certainly his works that popularized the name "evolution" ... and gave the word a distinctly progressionist flavor. Biological evolutionism became just one manifestation of the universal law of progress.... In Spencer's philosophy man was the head of creation only in the sense that the evolutionary process had succeeded in pushing him further than any of the other lines, into a new phase of development where intellectual and social progress became important.... In the popular mind at least, faith in the universal tendency toward progress could replace the old dependence on direct divine control. (Bowler 128–129)[9]

Whether or not Stoker believed that progress was universal (and *The Jewel of Seven Stars* indicates that he did not always believe it), he concluded *Dracula* by suggesting that the world was evolving toward something better. The old order has been utterly eradicated. The vampires and even Quincey Morris, a representative of a more primitive America, are dead; and the representatives of science, law, and government return to the site of their victory over the vampire. Harker observes:

> Seven years ago we all went through the flames; and the happiness of some of us since then is ... well worth the pain we endured.... In the summer of this year we made a journey to Transylvania, and went over the old ground which was ... so full of vivid and terrible memories. It was almost impossible to believe that the things which we had seen with our own eyes and heard with our own ears were living truths. Every trace of all that had been was

blotted out. *The castle stood as before*, reared high above
a waste of desolation. (378, emphasis mine)

The italicised passage suggests that Harker is on the verge of reexamining
the pervasive power of the past over the present, for the castle and all it
represents continues to loom over the landscape. However, Harker quickly
returns to the happy present and the domestic tranquility of Seward,
Godalming and himself. The conclusion to *Dracula* suggests that the past
has been entirely annihilated. If one were to read *Dracula* in the context of
contemporary social and political ideology, one might say that it exudes
confidence in progressionist notions, in the triumph of the present over the
past. Indeed most of Stoker's fiction seems to suggest that the forces of
modern technology, including motorcars, explosives, and typewriters, will
triumph over everything associated with the past.[10]

The *Jewel of Seven Stars* is far less confident about the triumph of
modernity, as the following discussion indicates, even though it follows
many patterns established by Stoker's other fiction. In fact, like *Dracula*, it
opens with the narrator's acute awareness of the past when Malcolm Ross
is called to the home of a young woman acquaintance, Margaret Trelawny.
Her father, an amateur Egyptologist, is apparently in a cataleptic state, and
Ross, who is asked to watch at his bedside, quickly becomes aware of the
power of the past:

> One might think that four or five thousand years would
> exhaust the olfactory qualities of anything; but experience
> teaches us that these smells remain, and that their secrets
> are unknown to us. To-day they are as much mysteries as
> they were when the embalmers put the body in the bath of
> natron … [Stoker's ellipsis]
>   All at once I sat up. I had become lost in an
> absorbing reverie. The Egyptian smell had seemed to get
> on my nerves — on my memory — *on my very will.* (41,
> emphasis mine)

Ross is acutely aware of the power that past substances exert over his present will, and other characters frequently note that the present age has actually lost the wisdom of the past, including the knowledge exercised by
Egyptian priests to "arrest the natural forces of decay," knowledge which is
"not understood in this later and more prosaic age" (94).

Ross always remains somewhat apprehensive about the power of
the past over the present, but Trelawny is convinced that the present can

learn from the past: "For science, and history, and philosophy may benefit; and we may turn one old page of a wisdom unknown in this prosaic
age" (222). In fact, one reason Trelawny wants to resurrect Queen Tera,
whose mummy he has brought with him back to England, is to share in
her knowledge, knowledge that he sometimes characterises as scientific
knowledge, sometimes as magic: "The experiment which is before us is
to try whether or no there is any force, any reality, in the old Magic"
(224).

Her abilities, whether scientific or magical, occasionally seem to
help her, like Dracula, to overcome natural law:

> She had been an apt pupil; and had gone further than her
> teachers.... She had won secrets from nature in strange
> ways; and had even gone ... down into the tomb herself,
> having been swathed and coffined and left as dead for a
> whole month. (175)

There is even the suggestion that Tera is not really dead but merely in a
state of suspended animation. For example, her wrist bleeds when a
graverobber attempts to steal her hand.

Trelawny mentions specific disciplines that he hopes to learn
about. One of these is astronomy which in old Egypt "developed to an
extraordinary height" and astrology, for which he hopes to find some scientific basis: "And it is possible that in the later developments of science
with regard to light rays, we may yet find that Astrology is on a scientific
basis. Our next wave of scientific thought may deal with this" (227). A
final scientific discipline is acoustics, which was "an exact science with
the builders of the temples of Karnak, of Luxor, of the Pyramids" but "a
mystery to Bell, and Kelvin, and Edison, and Marconi" (228). Thus,
Trelawny suggests that contemporary science can build on scientific
knowledge that had been lost for some time. This belief would seem to
link Trelawny to the progressive beliefs shared by Van Helsing's crusaders
in *Dracula*.

Ross remains sceptical, frequently noting that the mummy had
often been linked to violent activities. The following passage, from a sev-
enteenth-century Dutch text written by Nicholas van Huyn of Hoorn and
later used as a resource by Trelawny and his associates, recounts the first
instance of violence associated with it. Here the victim is a Bedouin who,
after wrenching off the mummy's hand to use for a charm, is found stran-
gled. Stoker leaves no doubt that Tera was responsible because the marks
on his throat match those of her peculiar seven-fingered hand: "There were

seven; and all parallel, except the thumb mark, as though made with one hand. This thrilled me as I thought of the mummy hand with the seven fingers" (159). Ross notes other violence associated with the mummy:

> In the history of the mummy ... the record of deaths that we knew of, presumably effected by her will and agency, was a startling one.... Nine dead men, one of them slain manifestly by the Queen's own hand! And beyond this again the several savage attacks on Mr. Trelawny in his own room, in which ... she had tried to open the safe and to extract the Talisman jewel. (287)

Ross is especially concerned about Tera's power because of his connection with the woman with whom he has fallen in love. Not only was Margaret born on the day that her father discovers Tera's tomb, but she had always resembled Tera more than she resembled her own mother. Furthermore, as the novel progresses, Tera seems to take possession of Margaret. Ross muses about the source of this power, often identifying it with long-forgotten Egyptian religion:

> If the Egyptian belief was true ... then the 'Ka' of the dead Queen and her 'Khu' could animate what she might choose. In such case Margaret would not be an individual at all, but simply a phase of Queen Tera herself; an astral body obedient to her will! (283)

Like the vampires in *Dracula* who seem to exercise profound control over their modern victims, Queen Tera may be controlling Margaret. Furthermore, Ross fears that her control may not be in the direction of progress: "It might be that that other individuality was of the lower not of the better sort! Now that I thought of it I had reason to fear" (287).

While Tera is clearly powerful like the vampires in *Dracula*, she is not identified with the animal world as they are. Instead, as Ross notes, she is a female force that is extremely independent:

> I never knew whether the personality present was my Margaret — the old Margaret whom I had loved at the first glance — or the other new Margaret, whom I hardly understood, and whose *intellectual aloofness* made an impalpable barrier between us. (280, emphasis mine)

In describing the difference in the Margaret that he had grown to love and the changed Margaret, Ross especially notes her growing independence and amoral behaviour, the decrease in her loving care. As a result, she seems to be more intelligent but less feminine, more aloof and less dependent on him or on any other man — characteristics most uncommon for a woman in the nineteenth century:

> In spite of her profession of ignorance Margaret knew a good deal about them [her father's Egyptian artifacts].... She was a remarkably clever and acute-minded girl, and with a prodigious memory; so that her store of knowledge, gathered unthinkingly bit by bit, had grown to proportions that many a scholar might have envied. (121)

Because of the question of possession, it is unclear whether Margaret's knowledge is her own or a manifestation of Tera's control. Certainly, Tera had been known in her own time for her ability to usurp male powers and privilege:

> Prominence was given to the fact that she ... claimed all the privileges of kingship and masculinity. In one place she was pictured in man's dress, and wearing the White and Red Crowns. In the following picture she was in female dress, but still wearing the Crowns of Upper and Lower Egypt, while the discarded male raiment lay at her feet. In every picture where hope, or aim, or resurrection was expressed there was *the added symbol of the North.* (175–176, emphasis mine)

The entire passage focuses on Tera's power, power that manages to subvert nineteenth-century notions of distinctly separate genders and furthermore suggests that Tera had achieved active powers that nineteenth-century thinkers associated with males. Furthermore, the italicised passage also suggests, as with *Dracula*, what Arata characterises as reverse colonisation. In *The Jewel of Seven Stars*, however, ancient Africa comes to conquer England.

In the end, Tera seems to triumph, and Ross, the only survivor of the plan to resurrect her, concludes the novel with horror when he discovers that his companions have managed to resurrect Queen Tera only to be destroyed by her:

> I found them all where they had stood. They had sunk
> down on the floor, and were gazing upward with fixed
> eyes of unspeakable terror.... I did what I could for my
> companions; but there was nothing that could avail.... It
> was merciful that I was spared the pain of hoping.
> (336–37)

Here, the forces of the past triumph in a particularly horrifying way by destroying the very people that Stoker allies with scientific progress.

How are twentieth-century readers to explain the reasons for Stoker's radically different treatments of the past? Because of its emphasis on the vampire's animal traits, *Dracula* seems to be influenced by nineteenth-century discussions in the biological sciences. *Jewel*, on the other hand, seems to be influenced by Egyptian archaeology which, as Wortham notes in *The Genesis of British Egyptology 1549–1906*, "attained an amazing popularity in Great Britain during the nineteenth century" (92–93). Not only did Archibald Henry Sayce, professor of Assyriology at Oxford, spend seventeen years in Egypt (beginning in 1879 and therefore covering the period in which Stoker was collecting the material for his novels), but he sent letters to popular magazines and kept the British public informed of the work that archaeologists were carrying out in Egypt (86). Furthermore, Stoker was personally acquainted with Captain Richard Francis Burton, who is today better remembered for exploring Africa and translating the *Arabian Nights*.[11] Burton also found prehistoric stone implements in Egypt and described them in 1879 along with a defence of John Lubbock's earlier discoveries. Lubbock, a neighbour and friend of Charles Darwin, had founded a new intellectual field, prehistoric archaeology, and had also translated Darwin's theories into the human realm. As Christopher Chippindale observes:

> Despite the inconsistencies of savage virtue and vice,
> Lubbock sees a pattern of progress from savages —
> slaves to their wants, neither noble nor free — to civilized
> persons whose lives are spent, thanks to printing, in com-
> munion with the greatest minds, with the thoughts of
> Shakespeare and Tennyson, and the discoveries of
> Newton and Darwin. Ever the rational optimist, Lubbock
> ends with a peek at the future and sees how mankind
> always progresses towards less pain and more happiness
> as science abolishes the evil that comes from ignorance
> and sin: "Utopia, which we have long looked upon as

synonymous with an evident impossibility ... turns out ...
to be the necessary consequences of natural laws."
(28–29)[12]

In fact, Chippindale foregrounds the progressive ideas found in Lubbock's writing by saying that the central idea of *The Origin of Civilisation and the Primitive Condition of Man* is a social, moral, and cognitive progression of savages that must advance steadily from the beginning of time in just the same manner as technology develops (29).

In general, Stoker seems to share the progressive belief in the power of science and technology over primitive forces. His enthusiasm for science and technology includes engineering and dam building in *The Snake's Pass* (1890), Winchester rifles in *Dracula*, naval armaments in *The Mystery of the Sea* (1902),[13] automobiles in *Lady Athlyne* (1908), airplanes in *The Lady of the Shroud* (1909), and dynamite in *The Lair of the White Worm* (1911). *The Jewel of Seven Stars*, however, introduces a dark and discordant suggestion, sometimes hinted at in *Dracula* as well, that the modern age can neither escape nor supplant the past. The idea that the past was associated with savagery and violence could have been found in many places, including works in evolutionary biology and archaeology. Wortham's book on Egyptology, for example, suggests a possible source for the violence in *Jewel* in the works of one of Stoker's contemporaries, Sir William Matthew Flinders Petrie:

> After comparing his findings at different sites, Petrie arrived at the conclusion that a great social revolution had swept over Egypt sometime during the period of the Old Kingdom. This upheaval had been marked by systematic destruction of tombs, sarcophagi, statues, and other royal relics.... Petrie imaginatively compared this work of destruction to the excesses of the mob during the French Revolution. (117–18)

Stoker, who was personally acquainted with both Sir Richard Burton and Sir William Wilde (noted surgeon, amateur Egyptologist, and father of Oscar), and who often incorporated references to Egyptology in his works, would have probably known Petrie's work. The destruction of Tera's tomb and her conflict with the priests is certainly consistent with Petrie's findings.

While circumstantial evidence suggests that Stoker either knew Petrie's work or knew of it, there is no actual proof of this connection.

Senf • Dracula, The Jewel of Seven Stars, and Stoker's "Burden of the Past"

That Stoker was concerned about the impact of the past on the present, however, is evident in almost everything he wrote. That his fiction usually focuses on modern characters who triumph over characters whose savagery or primitiveness connects them with the past is equally evident. This confidence in science and technology would appear to link him to other nineteenth-century progressionists who believed that human beings were moving toward a better and more civilised future. In *The Jewel of Seven Stars*, however, there is no suggestion that progress is inevitable or even that science and technology can control the forces of the past. In fact, when Trelawny and his allies use the information Tera provides them to resurrect her mummy, she destroys them instead of offering to share her knowledge. Moreover, she presumably goes on to wreak havoc on England as a whole. Unlike *Dracula*, which suggests, in Dracula's defeat, the growth of the bourgeoisie and heralds genuine progress for the future, *The Jewel of Seven Stars* hints only at death and utter annihilation from which no future can spring.

Stoker was persuaded by his publisher to modify this horrifying conclusion to make it less bleak and hopeless (and modern editions continue to print the sanitised "happy" ending which centres on the romance of Malcolm and Margaret rather than the deaths of almost all of the main characters). That Stoker was willing to make this change — essentially changing a tragedy into a comedy — may be evidence of his own uncertainty about the way the world was going or simply of his need for money.[14] Nonetheless, *The Jewel of Seven Stars* is consistently more ambivalent about the power that the past exerts over the future and less hopeful about the powers of modern science than any of Stoker's other novels. It is also the only one of his novels that does not, in its original form, conclude happily.

A comparative examination of *Dracula* and *The Jewel of Seven Stars* suggests that Stoker's attitudes to the past and his visions for the future were complex and ambiguous, expressing the range of possibilities available to people at the turn of the century.[15] In particular, the two novels suggest that Stoker was aware of the scientific and cultural developments that were taking place around the turn of the century, that he was fascinated with technological developments and apprehensive about various primitive forces, including certain forces that both he and the culture that influenced him associated with women and minority groups. The brother of three physicians and a man who experienced poor health at several points in his life,[16] Stoker created physicians and scientists who are complex and interesting, but also ultimately unable to solve the problems put before them, including Renfield's madness and Trelawny's catalepsy. His punishment of independent women (in *Dracula* and *The Man*), people of colour (Africans in *The Mystery of the Sea* and *Lair of the White Worm* and native Americans in *The Shoulder of Shasta*),[17] and other supposedly primitive people (the Turks in *The Lady of the Shroud*) who step outside the boundaries of their gender or class certainly makes him appear both racist and sexist by contemporary standards. It must be underlined, however, that these complex and occasionally ambiguous responses identify Stoker as a man of his time. Faced with the possibilities that science and technology sometimes seemed to hold out, and with the violence and irrationality that he and his contemporaries often associated with the past and with "primitive" people closer to home, Stoker sometimes saw the future as full of infinite possibilities for improvement, sometimes as totally at the mercy of primitive forces, and sometimes offering human beings a range of possible responses much as his own age had done. Although Stoker and most of his works embody the power of the modern age, *The Jewel of Seven Stars* is his tribute to the power of a seemingly unconquerable past.

NOTES

1   Stephen D. Arata notes that *Dracula* "addresses a series of cultural issues, particularly those involving race, specific to the 1890s" (84).

2   John L. Greenway objects to this reading: "The bland, asexual tableau at the end … officially announces the triumph of the Victorian conventions of rationality and progress. At first glance, the Victorian view of history as a conquest of barbarity and superstition seems affirmed in the happy ending. The men, emblems of the establishment as scientist, solicitor, and aristocrat, have become husbands and providers while Mina, who has the best mind of the lot, has become Jonathan's secretary…. The irony in this tableau, however, suggests that these conventions, just as Seward's science, are merely forms of structured ignorance. The novel grows from this irony: not just from the ignorance of the heroes of a world they cannot understand, but the larger irony that the 'other' world is more real than their own" (83–84).

3   Both of Stoker's biographers refer to this alteration though neither provides specific information.

4   Arata notes that the "heroines" of several Stoker novels — Queen Tera, Princess Teuta (in *The Lady of the Shroud*), and Lady Arabella (in *The Lair of the White Worm*), represent "the eruption of archaic and ultimately dangerous forces in modern life". He also notes that "fear of women is never far from the surface of these novels" (86).

5   Greenway's excellent essay examines Stoker's awareness of nineteenth-century science, especially the relatively new science of psychology. He does not look especially at Stoker's use of evolutionary science.

6   Mark Ridley, who edited *The Darwin Reader*, notes that Darwin's contemporaries were intrigued by the material on the pointed ears of human progenitors (145).

7   Darwin comments on pointed ears in *The Descent of Man*: "Why these animals, as well as the progenitors of man, should have lost the power of erecting their ears, we can not say. It may be … that owing to their arboreal habits and great strength they were but little exposed to danger, and so … moved their ears but little, and thus gradually lost the power of moving them…. It has been asserted that the ear of man alone possesses a lobule; but 'a rudiment of it is found in the gorilla;' and … it is not rarely absent in the negro" (143; the quoted passage is from page 396 of St. George Mivart's 1873 publication *Elementary Anatomy*).

8   Thomas Henry Huxley, the great populariser of Darwinian thought, often followed a similar pattern and was eager to suggest that evolution applied to moral evolution as well. See, for example, the following works by Huxley: *Man's Place in Nature* (London, 1863) and "Evolution and Ethics," a lecture originally delivered in 1893. This discussion is not meant to argue that Stoker had necessarily read Darwin and Huxley but that their ideas were commonly known and may have influenced his vampire portraits in *Dracula*.

9   The idea of progressionism was common in other fields as well. As A. Bowdoin Van Riper observes in *Men Among the Mammoths*, "The idea that life on Earth had grown steadily more complex … had become a firmly established part of paleontology during the early nineteenth century. The extensive paleontological work … reinforced the idea of progression in the history of life by providing empirical support from the fossil record…. Progressionists argued that the fossil record showed the advent of increasingly complex classes of animals, and of increasingly complex animals within each class. Thus, the fossil record reflected not only progress toward humanity but also the providential design that suited new species to an increasingly complex environment" (65).

10   Stoker is not only fascinated with the implements of modern technology but apparently proficient in their use. David Skal's *Hollywood Gothic* shows a typewritten page from Stoker's

manuscript of *Dracula* (8). When Stoker wrote about the typewriter, he undoubtedly did so from personal experience.

11   Stoker's *Personal Reminiscences of Henry Irving* suggests that Stoker was fascinated with Burton's ruthlessness and his exotic experiences. Even his vulpine appearance is reminiscent of Dracula: "As he spoke the upper lip rose and his canine tooth showed its full length like the gleam of a dagger. Then he went on to say that such explorations as he had undertaken were not to be entered lightly if one had qualms as to taking life. That the explorer in savage places holds, day and night, his life in his hand; and if he is not prepared for every emergency, he should not attempt such adventures" (I:359).

12   The quotation is from page 492 of John Lubbock's *The Origin of Civilisation and the Primitive Condition of Man* published in 1865. The ellipses are Chippindale's.

13   The material on sea battles may have come from an experience that happened to Stoker and Irving on August 9, 1880, when they hired a boat from a deaf boatman to escape a mob of admirers and found themselves in the middle of a naval drill. Stoker retells the experience in *Personal Reminiscences of Henry Irving*: "I think, however, that we both enjoyed the attack more that night when the actual sham battle was fought. In those days search-lights were new and rare. Both the *Glatton* and Fort Monckton were well equipped with them, and during the attack the whole sea and sky and shore were perpetually swept with the powerful rays. It was in its way a noble fight, and as then most people were ignorant of the practical working of the new scientific appliances of war, it was instructive as well as fascinating. We, who had been out in the middle of it during the day, could perhaps appreciate its possibilities better than ordinary civil folk unused to the forces and horrors of war!" (II:269)

14   Biographical information suggests that the failure of Henry Irving's Lyceum had a devastating impact on Stoker. In fact, Skal suggests that *Dracula* is better written than most of Stoker's other works because Stoker was financially secure during the period when he wrote it, and therefore had more time to work on it. The first edition of *Jewel* was published in 1903, before the death of Henry Irving but not before Irving's company began to have serious financial problems.

15   The collection of essays edited by J. Edward Chamberlin and Sander L. Gilman, *Degeneration: The Dark Side of Progress*, emphasises this multiplicity of views: "The present collection of essays is an attempt to sketch ... this force which complements the idea of progress in the nineteenth and early twentieth centuries. We have selected the term 'degeneration' for it; and like 'progress,' it is a term widely employed in numerous and often contradictory contexts. There is no one area in which the concept of degeneration is dominant. It permeates nineteenth-century thought with a model (or a series of models) for decline, and it permeates nineteenth-century feeling with images of decay. Its roots are ... embedded in biological models and images, but its import soon incorporated, not to say overwhelmed, the purely biological character of the paradigm. It borrows or subverts other terms, such as decadence, but it remains for the nineteenth century the most frightening of prospects, as well as at times the most enthralling" (Preface, vii).

16   It is well known that Stoker was an invalid for the first seven years of his life. Furthermore, if his biographer and grand-nephew, Daniel Farson, is correct in his theory that Stoker died of tertiary syphilis, Stoker may have known of his illness during the period when he was working on *The Jewel of Seven Stars*.

17   Nancy Stepan examines late nineteenth-century racism in her essay "Biological Degeneration: Races and Proper Places." In one excerpt, she writes: "Racial biology ... was a science of boundaries between groups and the degenerations that threatened when those boundaries were transgressed. As slavery was abolished and the role of freed blacks became a political and social issue, as industrialization brought about new social mobility and class tensions, and new anxieties about the 'proper' place of different class, national, and ethnic groups in society, racial biology provided a model for the analysis of the distances that were

'natural' between human groups. Racial 'degeneration' became a code for other social groups whose behavior and appearance seemed sufficiently different from accepted norms as to threaten traditional social relations and the promise of 'progress.' By the late nineteenth century, the urban poor, prostitutes, criminals, and the insane were being construed as 'degenerate' types whose deformed skulls, protruding jaws, and low brain weights marked them as 'races' apart, interacting with and creating degenerate spaces near at home" (98).

Robert Tracy examines Stoker's racial fears in terms that are less geographically remote in his essay "Loving You All Ways: Vamps, Vampires, Necrophiles and Necrofilles in Nineteenth-Century Fiction." As Tracy argues, "For Le Fanu and Stoker, both members of the Protestant Anglo-Irish ruling class of nineteenth-century Ireland, these legends were at once local folklore and metaphors for their class's anxieties about the unhyphenated Irish, who were emerging from centuries of suppression to demand political and economic power. The Anglo-Irish feared intermarriage with the Irish, which would lead to racial degeneration, and the loss of power which would inevitably follow letting the Irish gain ownership of land. These anxieties underlie such works as *Carmilla* and *Dracula*" (38).

REFERENCES

Appleman, Philip, ed. *Darwin: A Norton Critical Edition*. New York: Norton, 1979.

Arata, Stephen D. "The Occidental Tourist: *Dracula* and the Anxiety of Reverse Colonization." *Victorian Studies* 33 (1990): 621–645.

Bowler, Peter J. *Fossils and Progress: Paleontology and the Idea of Progressive Evolution in the Nineteenth Century*. New York: Science History Publications, 1976.

Chamberlin, J. Edward and Sander L. Gilman, eds. *Degeneration: The Dark Side of Progress*. New York: Columbia UP, 1985.

Chippindale, Christopher. "'Social Archaeology' in the Nineteenth Century: Is it Right to Look for Modern Ideas in Old Places?" *Tracing Archaeology's Past: The Historiography of Archaeology*. Ed. Andrew L. Christenson. Carbondale: Southern Illinois UP, 1989. 21–33.

Christenson, Andrew L., ed. *Tracing Archaeology's Past: The Historiography of Archaeology*. Carbondale: Southern Illinois UP, 1989.

Darwin, Charles. *The Descent of Man*. 1871. *Darwin: A Norton Critical Edition*. New York: Norton, 1979.

Farson, Daniel. *The Man Who Wrote Dracula: A Biography of Bram Stoker*. London: Michael Joseph, 1975.

Greenway, John L. "Seward's Folly: *Dracula* as a Critique of 'Normal Science.'" *Stanford Literature Review* 3 (1986): 213–230.

Ludlam, Harry. *A Biography of Dracula: The Life Story of Bram Stoker*. London: W. Foulsham & Co., 1962.

Ridley, Mark, ed. *The Darwin Reader*. New York: Norton, 1987.

Senf, Carol A. *Critical Response to Bram Stoker*. Westport, Connecticut: Greenwood Press, 1993.

Skal, David J. *Hollywood Gothic: The Tangled Web of Dracula from Novel to Stage to Screen*. New York: Norton, 1990.

Stepan, Nancy. "Biological Degeneration: Races and Proper Places." *Degeneration: The Dark Side of Progress*. New York: Columbia UP, 1985. 97–120.

Stoker, Bram. *Dracula*. 1897. Oxford: Oxford UP, 1983.

—. *The Jewel of Seven Stars*. London: Heinemann, 1903.

—. *Personal Reminiscences of Henry Irving*. 2 vols. New York: Macmillan, 1906.

Tracy, Robert. "Loving You All Ways: Vamps, Vampires, Necrophiles and Necrofilles in Nineteenth-Century Fiction." *Sex and Death in Victorian Literature*. Ed. Regina Barreca. Bloomington and Indianapolis: Indiana UP, 1990. 32–59.

Van Riper, A. Bowdoin. *Men Among the Mammoths: Victorian Science and the Discovery of Human Prehistory*. Chicago: University of Chicago Press, 1993.

Worthham, John David. *The Genesis of British Egyptology 1549–1906*. Norman: University of Oklahoma Press, 1971.

The "Transparency"
of
Dracula

Jan B. Gordon

> "I closed my eyes, but could still see through my eyelids."
> Mina Harker's Journal Entry of 1st October.
> (*Dracula* 258)

S WITH SO MANY VICTIMS OF THE GOTHIC NIGHT-mare through the ages, the fitful sleeper, Jonathan Harker, initially encounters Count Dracula as a resistance to any easy transcription:

Midnight. — I have had a long talk with the Count. I asked him a few questions on Transylvanian history, and he warmed up to the subject wonderfully. In his speaking of things and people, and especially of battles, he spoke as if he had been present at them all.... Whenever he spoke of his house he always said "we," and spoke almost in the plural, like a king speaking. I wish I could put down all he said exactly as he said it, for to me it was most fascinating. (28)

The privileged medium of inscription for the "lettred" British commercial patriarchy and its expectant apprentice clerks is a limited tool in reproducing the plurality of the Count's account. In this regard, Harker resembles no one in British fiction more than the urbane Lockwood of *Wuthering Heights* who meets with similar obstacles in his attempt to transcribe an equally alien "misanthrope's Heaven" with which his diary commences: "1801 — I have just returned from a visit to my landlord" (47). It is as a slightly reticent, untraditional host that the Monstrous is often initially encountered in nineteenth-century British fiction, be it the novel of manners or the Gothic.

Perhaps this initial slippage in the traditional representations of inscripted power is suggested in the transmutation of time itself into the spatial plurality of duration: Dracula narrates *as if* he were eternally present as an *idea* or a *fiction* which compels belief. As this "trans-historical" existence is resistant to the enclosure appropriate to Harker's diary, so similarly in *Wuthering Heights*, the Earnshaw family initially presents itself to Lockwood as a *palimpsest*, equally resistant to any univocal recuperation, "a name repeated in all kinds of characters, large and small — *Catherine Earnshaw*; here and there varied to *Catherine Heathcliff*, and then again to *Catherine Linton*" (61). The past can never be really past; one "Catherine" is scratched through, but only incompletely erased as it turns out, leaving in its wake all "Catherines," antecedent as well as successive. There is no longer any distinction between "Catherine" and her genealogical or mnemonic reproductions in history, dream, or fantasy which come thereby to be at least metaphorically elided. This plurality takes possession of the reader as a confusion of names in Brontë's text (much as it has of, first, Heathcliff's affections and later, "our" Lockwood's confused attention) in ways different from those by which a diary would presume to take possession of them. The diary, no matter what the language (*Fr.* "*tenir* un journal"; *Germ.* "ein Tagenbuch *fahren*"; *Jap.* "nikki-o *tsuzukeru*") demands a *singular maintenance*, so as to keep each temporal increment separate, while nonetheless *keeping it going*, as a continuity, a *marked succession*. This may well account for the privileging of the diary as the genre appropriate to the literature of imprisonment: as long as the diary is maintained, its "keeper" is still alive, the *continuous* enclosure that resists society's totalising enclosures.[1]

To be sure, Count Dracula's early resistance to Harker's inscripting enclosure would appear to characterise the very production of Bram Stoker's novel. Dracula is a vampire with no voice of his own, existing derivatively, as he is reproduced in the reading, listening, and writing of others: diaries, letters, newspaper clippings, the notes of medical case histories, Mina Harker's transcriptions from a primitive, scratchy dictaphone. Dracula, Lord Godalming, Quincey Morris, Renfield, and Van Helsing have only recorded or otherwise socially reproduced identities compiled or edited by Jonathan Harker, Dr. Seward, Mina Harker, and Lucy Westenra. Dracula's unconventional procreative strategies are thus mirrored by the equally diverse reproductive techniques of those who would attempt to possess him. Hence, the Monstrous, whatever its other characteristics, operates as a kind of machine-text (with its attendant technological horrors) generating arbitrary subjectivities, but ones which Stoker's novel continually intimates might just as well be differentially determined. This plurality of subjectivity is habitually experienced in one of two ways in *Dracula*: 1) multiple coding wherein a "self" is simultaneously "proper" or self-same and differential in such a way as to occupy two or more ideological or syntagmatic registers simultaneously, or 2) the blurring of differentiating boundaries between a subject and its representations, "reflections," or traces so as to endow it with a largely instrumental existence as an agent of metonymic transfer.

Mina Harker, for example, is enlisted as an ally in the ultimate conquest of Dracula early on in Stoker's novel, but because he can read her mind, her access to the plans and strategies of Harker, Dr. Van Helsing, and the others is censored, inducing yet another symbolic silence. Hence, she is simultaneously part of the Monstrous insofar as she is his "possession," yet, for that very reason, is empowered as a crucial (double) agent in his destruction at the hands of "civilised values." Her operational dynamic is *parasitical* insofar as she colludes with Dracula as an inseparable part of his reproductive potential, while she is nonetheless capable of detaching herself from the sustaining "host" in order to become instrumental to its ultimate demise. In the process, she realises her own independent reproductive potential. Simultaneously Dracula's victim, his compliant extension, and ultimately his betrayer, Mina Harker displays the extra-territoriality which comes to define the proxemics of Bram Stoker's novel.

This extra-territorialisation is shared with Count Dracula and his geographic homeland, *Transylvania*, politically a parasitical (semi-dependent) principality under the Turks until the eighteenth century.[2] In contradistinction to the late Bela Lugosi's interpretation, Stoker's Dracula speaks nearly perfect English, ironic given the exaggerated regional accents exhibited by a Dutchman and a Texan. Told that his noble client is in need of a landed "stake" in England, Jonathan Harker, the emissary of an Exeter estate agent, learns to his surprise that the Count has already acquired a cultural and linguistic interest in his country, from a distance, yet feels this share to be inadequate:

> "But, Count," I said, "you know and speak English thoroughly!" He bowed gravely.
>
> "I thank you, my friend, for your all too-flattering estimate, but yet I fear that I am but a little way on the road I would travel. True, I know the grammar and the words, but yet I know not how to speak them."
>
> "Indeed," I said, "you speak excellently."
>
> "Not so," he answered. "Well, I know that, did I move and speak in your London, none there are who would not know me for a stranger. That is not enough for me. Here I am noble; I am *boyar*; the common people know me, and I am master. But a stranger in a strange land, he is no one; men know him not — and to know not is to care not for. I am content if I am *like the rest....*" (20, emphasis mine)

The Count's expansive library filled with books relating to English life, customs, manners, and law is obviously insufficient to his larger purpose, which is nothing less than a kind of ontological *transparency*. His is not the idea of mastering the local nomenclature à la Sir Stamford Raffles, but a desire to become completely invisible to the British masses so as to share in an imaginary brotherhood. Retrospectively, the Count's dream appears as a mirror-image of certain practices which came to characterise what we might now term "late colonialism." A landed, gentleman patriarch fallen on bad times either economically or as the consequence of some interrupted or otherwise entailed "living," would accept an appointment to serve Her Majesty's civil or commercial interests, often disguised as an extension of parliamentary democracy. In order to more effectively carry out duties which were often blatantly hegemonic, these representatives of (often) established or noble families went "native" in diet, dress, language, or public attitude, so as to be "like the rest." Count Dracula wishes to "lose himself" in Great Britain in much the same way that Conrad's Kurtz of *Heart of Darkness* is lost to his masters, or assumes an altogether different kind of mastery, during the same fin de siècle which witnessed the publication of Stoker's analysis of "cultural demonism."[3] From this perspective, the "life" of Dracula in Stoker's novel might be read as a mock "Pax Draculae" during which hegemonic sexual practices are justified by the need to establish a brotherhood united by a blood bond.

Dracula's *transparency*, that corporeal emptiness which enables him to cleave to a variety of often mutually antagonistic representations — to be somewhat universally "like the rest" — is perhaps initially intimated en route to the castle. Jonathan Harker is astonished to observe that on an occasion when Dracula (as the coachman) stood between his line of sight and the blue flame which signifies Dracula's presence, "he did not obstruct it, for I could see its ghostly flicker all the same" (15). Whatever the Count's other powers, he lacks the opacity which would enable him to univocally *signify*. He instead appears as a floating or "empty" *sign*, a transmitting channel which establishes relationships rather than physically or substantially participating in them. To his carter, he looks so thin "he couldn't throw a shadder" (263).

Dracula's role as a "carrier" of information is again suggested in Harker's encounter with the Count after his first, restless night in the castle. Before the use of mirrors is forbidden altogether by Dracula, he nonetheless manages to evade representation in Harker's shaving glass, in the process drawing the "first blood" from his British guest:

> I only slept a few hours when I went to bed, and feeling that I could not sleep any more, got up. I had hung my shaving-glass by the window, and was just beginning to shave. Suddenly I felt a hand on my shoulder, and heard the Count's voice saying to me, "Good morning." I started, for it amazed me that I had not seen him, since the reflection of the glass covered the whole room behind me.... Having answered the Count's salutation, I turned to the glass again to see how I had been mistaken. This time there could be no error, for the man was close to me, and I could see him over my shoulder. But there was no reflection of him in the mirror! The whole room behind me was displayed; but there was no sign of a man in it, except myself. (25)

Lacking any openness to representation possessed by other objects in the room, Count Dracula functions rather as a mirror "mirrored," his physical presence altogether erased as an object of knowledge. Although the lack of mirrors in the chambers of his castle and the Count's antipathy to them is initially explained by his conviction that the instrument is the "foul bauble of man's vanity" (26), were he in fact to be imagined as a rival instrument of self-reflection, a competing mirror, his distrust in secondary images has a kind of logic which should not be lost on the reader.

By virtue of this antipathy, Dracula has a monopoly on self-reflection that is so totalising, such an inextricable component of his being, that he has no independent knowledge of a "self." He would exemplify the absence or denial of the vaunted Lacanian "Stade du Miroir" which enables a constructed or prosthetic "self" to become the necessary, yet entirely symbolic, foundation of *identity*.[4] His preferred mode of possession is therefore inextricable from complete identification or assimilation, the disappearance of any self, which makes him a stranger in a strange land. This might be imagined as the triumph of the copulative ("A *is* B") over the metaphoric ("A is *like* B") dimension which traditionally grounds judgements of resemblance or comparison. In practice of course, this is experienced by his collusive victims as vampirism, a displacement of traditionally penetrative sexuality (the point of entry leaving barely a trace of a scar), equivalent to reproducing absolute self-sameness among the partners.[5]

If Dracula represents the end of representation, considered as a potentially differential "likeness," his British "victims" seem entirely too dependent upon a reflective representation. Lucy Westenra takes considerable pride in separating a hidden "real" self from its secondary representations consumed by the public. Unlike Dracula, for whom the practice is impossible, the eligible young woman spends hours reading her "self" as a text:

> ... I flatter myself he [a potential admirer] has a tough nut to crack. I know that from my glass. Do you ever try to read your own face? I *do*, and I can tell you it is not a bad study, and gives you more trouble than you can well fancy if you have never tried it. He says that I afford him a curious psychological study, and I humbly think I do. (55)

Doubting her own self-image, Lucy is constantly seeking confirmation by "reading" her own face for clues, just as her friends and acquaintances read diaries in private or listen to a reproduction of a reproduction (as in the dictaphone "copy" of Dr. Seward's "case history" of his patient, Renfield). *Dracula* is structurally a meta-text, the corollary of the palimpsest, in which one "version" is "contained" within or enclosed by another, as characters struggle with reproduction, the attempt to "get everything down" for some record. They live to "pass on" these reproductions.

A corollary to this textual embedding is the production of a space between an act and some secondary "copy." If Mina keeps a diary so as "to do what [she] see[s] lady journalists do" (54), Lucy's diary similarly commences with "I must imitate Mina" (108), and children in the park "play at" reenacted, reconstituted performances of Red Riding Hood and the "bloofer lady" (178) after learning of the seizure of real children in newspapers. British culture appears dedicated to perpetual reenactment, the construction of "texts," which are then "played out," behind which lie some ineffable, foundational "reality." Although Elaine Showalter presumes to find traces of the late Victorian assertive "new woman" in Mina Harker and Lucy Westenra, they are in fact remarkably passive.[6] Lucy imagines herself, along with other women, to be like Desdemona, a rather meek consumer of narratives from a plethora of potential suitors. A culture which so privileges self-dramatisation in everyday life might, for all we know, resemble the world in which Bram Stoker worked, as the stage manager for Henry Irving, one of the era's most popular Shakespearean actors.

But the surplus of signs over signifieds, like the surplus of socially-reproduced texts within the master-text of *Dracula*, forces the characters to make choices. Unlike the Count who has never endured the "mirror-phase" of development and tolerates no instruments of self-reflection, Lucy Westenra has difficulty distinguishing the authentic version from its "copies":

> Here am I, who will be twenty in September, and yet I never had a proposal till to-day, not a real proposal, and to-day I have had three. Just fancy! THREE proposals in one day! (56)

The allusion to a "real proposal" suggests that Lucy has in fact been party to a number of "mimed proposals," dramatisations designed to test her response. She obviously lives comfortably within the highly stylised Victorian courtship rituals prescribing the appropriate forms in which the acceptance or rejection of marital prospects is conducted within the parameters of a social "game." Mina's long engagement to the (relatively) impecunious Jonathan Harker is merely one more of these social conventions. Hence, desire would appear to be largely obedient to a mimetically reproducible order, as Lucy opts for the historically-embedded, en*titled* "text," as represented by Lord Godalming rather than the mixed blood and de-historicised, earned money represented by the figure of Quincey Morris. The mirror in which Lucy Westenra "vamps," symbolically or in fact before becoming a vampire, prompts a reality check against society's expectations.

The Transylvanian Count has no such "prospects," to borrow the eighteenth-century concept which combined economic and visual horizons (given pressures of the distancing sublime), for his castle lies dangerously close to a deep, empty abyss. If Lucy Westenra, to her surprise, has had three marriage proposals in one day, so too has Jonathan Harker early on in his stay at the castle, though his suitors draw attention to their previously rejected object of affection, Count Dracula. When he surprises them in *flagrante delecto* with his foreign guest, the three captive damsels collectively defend any attempt at seduction by accusing the Count of sexual neutrality or impotence: "you yourself never loved; you never love" (39). And yet, the Count seems sufficiently sexually aggressive, albeit homoerotically, in his attempt to protect Harker from their physical advances:

> How dare you touch him, any of you? How dare you cast
> eyes on him when I had forbidden it? Back, I tell you all!
> This man belongs to me! Beware how you meddle with
> him, or you'll have to deal with me. (39)

If this exchange intimates some sexual rivalry over Harker, Count Dracula is quick to correct their assertions regarding his impotency: "Yes, I too can love; you yourselves can tell it from the past" (39). This cryptic comment assumes another dimension altogether when Harker notices that two of his potential seducers have dark complexions and "high aquiline noses, like the Count's" (37). Since they bear a physical resemblance and have, at least from Dracula's corrective comment, experienced his love in the past, Stoker would seem to be raising the possibility of incest among the Count's sexual proclivities. Hence, the Monstrous seems to combine impotency, homoeroticism (in the Count's possessiveness towards Harker), incest, necrophilia (with Lucy), and at least a parodic version of heterosexuality in the practice of bringing infants to his former lovers as a nightly compensation for the diminishment of more traditional physical affection which might also result in infant progeny. So varied and totalising is Dracula's sexual history, as to leave virtually no "inclination" outside his experience!

The polymorphous positioning which enables the polite host to become an aggressive guest of the British in a parasitical economy extends to both blood and money, those vehicles through which vampirism will draw its affective life. Although Dracula takes great pride in the purity of his blood from a noble lineage of Szekelys, martial Huns, he, not unlike the British nobility with whom he shares similar heraldic emblems, is actually of notoriously mixed blood: "We Szekelys have a right to be proud, for in our veins flows the blood of many brave races who have fought as the lion fights, for lordship" (28). Subtly, Dracula's autobiography, as narrated to his guest, seems a mirror image of the British tendency to attribute their cultural domination to an inherent racial homogeneity.

If the trajectory of so many Victorian novels involves the circuitous pilgrimage of an historically discontinuous orphan-figure — the "stain and blot" upon a place, to borrow from the words of an early guardian of Esther Summerson in *Bleak House* — attempting to "clear its name" by recuperating some pure ancestral Origin antecedent to contamination, Dracula appears as some metaphoric counter-orphan. *Always-already* a blended outcast, he first drew fetid breath in that geographic "whirlpool of European races" (28), eastern Europe. There he has sought to preserve his power and lineage, not by recuperating ethnic purity, but by an assimilation which would further mix his blood line! And, as it turns out, one of the (temporarily) effective contraceptives to this dilution is a similar bonding in which a British *blutbrüderschaft* is created by a communal transfusion into poor Lucy's veins.

Dracula's pluralising tendencies, as well as the fostering of it in those committed to his demise, is evident even in his name, for "Dracula" is simultaneously the name of a royal house which "boast[s] a record that mushroom growths like the Hapsburgs and Romanoffs can never reach" (29), the name of a race descendant from Huns with distinctive physiological characteristics, and a *proper* name which designates an individual. In other words "Dracula" is both a *proper* name (in the sense of designating a *propre*, a self-sameness) and an improper name (as a generic indicator of a class of rulers): the Monstrous is both singular and collectively de-nominated. Though Count Dracula insists that his lineage shares nothing with the "mushroom dynasties" that dominated European political life for centuries, he will emulate that parasitical hegemony by seeding himself in dank soil under cover of night. On each occasion when Dracula attempts to establish a racial or historical uniqueness, any differences, upon examination, are revealed as merely arbitrary.

The same totalising amalgam of sexual tastes and blood lines is reflected in the universality of the Count's monetary economy. The Harker who quickly becomes aware of the remoteness of his destination as a consequence of the repeated need to change drivers, language, and currency as he crosses real or imagined frontiers, is surprised to discover a virtual foreign exchange bank inside the walls of Dracula's castle. While looking for a key which might admit him to the castle's secret chambers, he relates the following discovery:

> The only thing I found was a great heap of gold in one corner — gold of all kinds, Roman, and British, and Austrian, and Hungarian, and Greek and Turkish money, covered with a film of dust, as though it had lain long in the ground. None of it that I noticed was less than three hundred years old. (47)

Although Dracula's hoard seems to participate in the more general decay which defines his habitat and lifestyle, with its earthly covering, it is nonetheless gold, the universal general equivalent in which all individual currencies may be *de-nominated*. Later in Stoker's novel, when Dracula is finally apprehended in one of the safe houses he has purchased, Harker deploys his kukri knife against the Monstrous in direct combat. Whereas during his earlier sea passage from the continent to England, the log of the *Demeter* had narrated the futility of a mate's attempt on the life of the "transparency" as "a knife went through It, empty as the air" (84), Harker's attempt, though equally futile, hits a kind of jackpot:

> The blow was a powerful one; only the diabolical quickness of the Count's leap back saved him. A second less and the trenchant blade had shorn through his heart. As it was, the point just cut the cloth of his coat, making a wide gap whence a bundle of bank-notes and a stream of gold fell out. (306)

If blood and money (heart/gold) are more or less convertible, as crucial to circulation for the hook-nosed Dracula as for his compatriot in the history of the Monstrous, Shylock of *The Merchant of Venice*, gold is no less crucial to Dracula's ineffable, even immaterial nature.[7]

In his "The Chapter on Money" in the *Grundrisse*, Karl Marx addresses the question of "value" in such a way as to include observations on the general, physical circulation of money as a commodity. In Marx's prescient analysis, the value of any commodity must be different from the commodity itself, because a specific commodity (say, shoes) is a value (exchange value) only within a *process* of exchange which may be either real or imaginary. Monetary value, and perhaps cultural value, thus becomes a specific exchangeability that has a characteristic metaphoric life, a double-life like that led by Dracula. Value has this dual nature for Marx because it is simultaneously an exponent of the relation in which a particular commodity is exchanged with other commodities, as well as a representation of the relationship in which it has been *historically* exchanged with other commodities. As values, all commodities, though qualitatively equal, do differ quantitatively. Hence, they can be measured against each other in making economic choices.

But considered as an "equivalent," all of the natural properties of a given commodity are repressed. Convertibility creates an economy to the precise extent to which the commodity itself is at least metaphorically dismembered or drained: in the process it no longer assumes a qualitative relationship towards other commodities, but rather becomes a *general measure* (as well as a form of representation, one suspects), the so-called *medium of exchange*. Each time we engage in economic calculations, we are really abstracting commodities from some *natural* (in the sense of *proper*) value. My shoes are equivalent to my watch, for example, insofar as they share the same exchange value (about $120 U. S.) though differing materially. Hence, paper money, for the early Marx, is that *transparency* into which differential commodities are dissolved, and yet it simultaneously dissolves itself into those commodities, insofar as their material essence — that which defines them *essentially* — is negated. The assimilative potential of the Monstrous is inextricably bound to a kind of "double-life." The denomination, usually inscribed upon the upper right-hand corner of a bank note, does not define its "paper" value, but rather an "imaginary" value which is accepted as a matter of public belief (depending upon confidence in the government, rates of inflation, etc.). The purely *nominal value* is defined by Marx as a demon shadow or phantom which pursues, but cannot be separated from, that which it would displace:

> Nominal value runs alongside its body as a mere shadow; whether the two balance can be shown only by an actual convertibility (exchangeability). A fall of real value beneath nominal value is depreciation. Convertibility is when the two run alongside each other and change places with each other. The convertibility of inconvertible notes shows itself not in the bank's stock of bullion, but in the everyday exchange between paper and the metal whose *denomination* the paper *carries*. (132, emphasis mine)

Notions of "authenticity," "false consciousness," "alienation," and "commodity fetishism," all of which permeate the nomenclature of Marxist thought, are surely tied to this rather unique kind of mimesis. Paper money is an "empty transparency," a permeable "carrier" which cannibalises the presumably more "natural" value which defines that real materiality (or labour quotient) which makes the good or service what it inalienably *is*. A bit later in the *Grundrisse*, Marx endows this transparency with more sinister motives:

> Capital posits the permanence of value (to a certain degree) by incarnating itself in fleeting commodities and taking on their form, but at the same time changing them just as constantly…. But capital obtains this ability only by constantly sucking in living labour as its soul, vampire-like. (146)

Even when he is not hoarding or hemorrhaging gold, Dracula's remarkable porosity is much like that which Marx attributes to capital. In a novel where so many of the characters forego thinking in order that "all, big and little, must go down" (289) with the aid of penis, diaries, dictaphones, and "travelling typewriters" to such an extent that the reader is often confused as to the authenticity of whichever recursive "version" he is reading, Count Dracula eschews the inscriptive "trace." He leaves almost no *impressions* upon the surfaces of those he inscribes, but rather unhealed wounds which remain "still open, and, if anything, larger, than before, [with] the edges faintly white" (95), sharing his resistance to closure. So adaptable is the Monstrous that he is able to assume the identity of Jonathan Harker by wearing the latter's clothes (even though the Count and his guest are physically dissimilar), so that any potential local witnesses to Harker's disappearance might testify to having seen the prisoner walking freely in the village. Moreover, when Harker attempts epistolary communication with his English fiancée and employer, Dracula removes the heavy writing paper and substitutes prepostmarked sheets "of the thinnest foreign post" (32), so as to counterfeit a record of Harker's progress in incremental stages during an imaginary return journey. In other words, Count Dracula has sufficient transparency to figuratively displace the letter writer's (or diarist's) subjectivity by giving it a "false cover."

Although they be not nature's laws, Dracula does obey *some* laws; the Monstrous is no more entirely free than is the Imaginary. Not only must he comply with the force of certain material injunctives (garlic, crucifix), but not unlike the British nobility whose tastes and prerogatives he so often doubly mirrors, the Count is trapped between two economies: that which deploys a reserve "currency" as a general equivalent (an empty "carrier" or facilitator of exchange) and another value system, entirely dependent upon ancestral earth (which restricts his mobility in the modern world). In other words, Stoker's Demonic combines the ease of self-effacement with the potential for infinite reproductive multiplication, which differs from most models of biological reproduction insofar as it leaves no visible traces of a previously singular presence: "one vampire meant many" (297). In each instance, the limits on Count Dracula's mobility, from another perspective, are what empowers. As Dr. Van Helsing astutely notes:

> He may not enter anywhere at the first, unless there be someone of the household who bid him to come; though afterwards, he can come as he please. (240)

And, since Dracula has a transhistorical existence, like say Tiresias, he does not exist in time in any measured, chronological sense. His earthly (self-) appointed representative must "summon" the Daimon, either as a longing sexual partner, like Leda does for Zeus disguised as a swan in Yeats's mythology, or, for all we know, like the potential academic celebrants who would hope to bring about an incarnation by granting a (temporary) temporality implicit in the "marking" of centennial birthdays![8] In such a spirit of "summoning" Count Dracula, let us for a moment suggest why the last decades of the nineteenth century, and the fin de siècle in particular, provided such fertile soil for the growth of an interdisciplinary *figure* which often behaves as if it were an intellectual reproduction of Stoker's Imaginary, albeit generally enjoying a better public reputation.

F MARX'S MONSTROUS went into hibernation, usurped perhaps by its creator's evolving interest in "labour capital," William Stanley Jevons was to give it a new life in the figure of *marginal utility*, a self-effacing intruder into economic relationships. In Chapter III of *The Theory of Political Economy*, Jevons, while continuing to define, as the utilitarians had before him, pleasure and pain as the ultimate determinants of a so-called Calculus of Economics, used the curious concept of utility "to denote an abstract quality whereby an object ... becomes entitled to rank as a commodity" (96). Not an inherent quality of commodities, but a vague "circumstance of things" arising out of a relationship to man's requirements and therefore variables, *marginal utility* was a curious "quantity of two dimensions," one consisting in the quantity of a given commodity and another in the intensity of the *effect* produced upon a consumer. In failing to distinguish between the total utility of a commodity and its "final degree of utility," the Welsh professor thought that his discipline had taken a wrong turn prior to 1879.

All human appetites are capable of satisfaction or satiety sooner or later, but, under varying circumstances, great changes take place in the consumption of a commodity which appear not at all to obey the laws of supply and demand. In a time of great scarcity, for example, the utility of barley as food could rise so high as to exceed altogether its utility, even as regards the smallest quantity, say in producing alcoholic liquors. Satisfaction is thus no longer an intrinsic property of a given commodity nor an *a priori* determination of the consumer, but entirely relative to changing circumstances and inversely proportional (time intervals being a negative function) to the quantity consumed. The same articles would vary in utility in inverse proportion to how much of the article we *already* possess:

> The degree of utility varies with the quantity of commodity, and ultimately decreases as that quantity increases. No commodity can be named which we continue to desire with the same force, whatever the quantity in possession. (111)

Jevons's progressively downward-sloping utility curve was paralleled by an upward-sloping disutility function. Applying the concept of marginal disutility to the supply of inputs, the economist was thereby able to predict that "no increment of labour would be expended unless there was sufficient recompense in the produce, but that labour would be expended up to the point at which the increment of utility exactly equals the increment of pain incurred in acquiring it" (221).

Hence, the last unit of a commodity consumed, a kind of "marginal desirability," assumes an added significance in what was, in effect, a theory of incremental pleasure. Although the operation of marginal utility might help to explain the presence of illogical pricing (as say, why raising the price of a 1985 Rothschild Paulliac does not necessarily result in reduced demand, but may in fact increase demand!), Jevons was the first to admit the unverifiability of any interpersonal "cardinal" utility: "no common denominator of feeling is possible" (85). Something demonstrably affected international trade which could not be *contained* by any mathematical notation, save price itself which was determined by its *operation*:

> We cannot really tell the effect of any change in trade or manufacture until we can with some approach to truth express the laws of the variation of utility numerically. To

> do this we would need accurate statistics of the quantities
> of commodities purchased by the whole population at vari-
> ous prices. The price of a commodity is the only test we
> have of the utility of the commodity to the purchaser. (74)[9]

As is the case with those who would hope to pin down Dracula's identity in such a way as to separate it from its effects, neither the substitute of common sense for factual information nor the deployment of induction as a proxy for deduction enables the unquantifiable to be quantified.

The idea of "variable utility," desire taking a different shape depending upon how much of the commodity we already possess — and hence its sufficiency to some "mirror-image" — is precisely what enables it to resist easy quantification, save as an invisible determinant of price. Since everything has a price, there would be no way to "mark" its absence from the calculus. This remarkable tautology bears a resemblance to Van Helsing's explanation for Dracula's power: "... [in] this enlightened age, when men believe not even what they see, the doubting of wise men would be his greatest strength" (321). In a discipline which privileges quantification, Jevons had discovered a "fudge factor" which could be quantified only by an imaginary totalisation of the quantities of commodities purchased by the whole population at various prices, even though its effects could be graphed on a downward-sloping utility curve, or even in the way the last swallow of water drunk by a thirsty consumer assumes (even proportionally) less value than that attached to the first unit consumed.

I F DRACULA'S CONTINUING presence, like marginal utility, is encompassed neither by Life nor Death, but a state (even politically) in between, the "Un-dead," he could find a soul-mate in a peculiar figure of Walter Pater's imagination, the "Diaphaneitè," which, though it appeared early in the critic's career (in the 1857 essay under the same name, later collected in *Miscellaneous Studies*), had a continuing life in the fin de siècle. This figure is neither the "inner light" pursued by Pater's Stoics and children in houses against the world's material demands as a function of aesthetic growth, nor is it the embodiment of the various *Aufklärungen* by which his cultural torchbearers, like the sacrificed Winckelmann of *The Renaissance*, had hoped to illuminate pockets of lingering Gothic darkness. For the "Diaphaneitè," with that peculiar accent as a consequence of a printer's inventiveness

> ... does not take the eye by breadth of colour; rather it is
> that *fine edge of light, where the elements of our moral
> nature refine themselves to the burning point.* It crosses
> rather than follows the main current of the world's life.
> The world has no sense fine enough for those evanescent
> shades, which fill up the blanks between contrasted types
> of character ... (248, emphasis mine)[10]

This de-territorialised figure inhabits the critical margins, "where the veil of an outer life, not simply expressive of an inward becomes thinner and thinner" (249). The Platonic veil separating phenomenal from nominal is subtly removed, along with the metaphysics of infinite regress which grounds the metaphor of the *palimpsest* so crucial to Pater's sensationalist paradigm of aesthetic and historical experience with its emphasis upon "paring down." Though, like Dracula, described as diaphanous, that "colourless, unclassified purity of life," this figure of Pater's critical imagi-nation would nonetheless "fill in the blanks between contrasted types of character" (248). The "Diaphaneitè" is simultaneously an emptiness and an agent of metonymic transfer which works against "one's own confusion and intransparency" (251), having the "double-life" common to vanishing mediators.

From one perspective, in its ability to cleave to contraries, the "Diaphaneitè" might be some principle of universal "in-difference," com-bining, even etymologically, detachment and bonding. But this function involves a radical negation, the cancellation of that rich overlay of "momentary impressions" by means of which historical, cultural, or aes-thetic development is imagined either as the recovery of a moment of instantiation or as the pursuit of some repressed latency. In retrospect, the pattern of rewriting, erasure, and recursivity in Pater appears as a corollary to those archaeological procedures for authentication so prevalent in mid-nineteenth-century thought and among the highly cultured internationalists committed to Dracula's demise in Bram Stoker's novel. If the model of historical or aesthetic experience is the palimpsest whose rich detail we must see through or *behind* and hence is a perfect synecdoche for the reduction of meanings that constitutes the *metaphoric* register, Pater is insistent that his "Diaphaneitè" which "detects without difficulty all sorts of affinities between its own elements and the nobler elements in that order" (251), in fact operates laterally, *metonymically*. The "Diaphaneitè" is simultaneously "a reminiscence of a forgotten culture" and an "edge" which "lets through unconsciously all that is really life-giving in the estab-lished order of things" (251) — antithetical states shared with Dracula.

To ask the question, "what is it?" is in some sense like asking the question, "what is money?" Pater is quite clear that his figural "empty edge" is an aesthetic medium of exchange which "seeks to value everything at its eternal worth, not adding to it or taking away from it, the amount of influence it may have for or against its own special scheme of life" (248). Yet, in some larger sense, again like paper money in a Marxist intellectual regime, the "Diaphaneitè" gives every evidence of some "core negation" which ultimately affects all of Pater's cultural or fictive heroes, including those of the structurally diaphanous "Imaginary Portraits." Winckelmann, Duke Carl of Rosenmold, or the Apollo (borrowed from Heine) in "Pico della Mirandolla" are all revolutionaries who must die or go underground in some political or aesthetic remission in order to bring about change in taste, cultural attitudes, or belief which always chronologically lag behind any historical presence. Only in this way can the revolutionary gain acceptance among those who had been committed to its resistance. Yet, this "core negation" carried by Pater's "Diaphaneitè" and Stoker's Dracula is not the external opposite of *being*, for both writers go to great lengths to distinguish its operational dynamics from some mere contempt of the human or human values.

Rather, we arrive at the peculiar "nothingness" of the "Diaphaneitè" or Dracula simply by trying to specify, to determine the content of its "being." If the palimpsest of a continuously recursive inscription and erasure to which Seward, Harker, Van Helsing and the others are so attached speaks to the impossibility of transcending history regarded as a sequence of historical "successions," Pater's figurative "Diaphaneitè" and Stoker's equally figurative Count enable us to see the "negation of negation." The first negation consists in the slow, underground, nearly invisible change of substantial content which takes place *in the name of form*. Once the antecedent form has lost its substantial right, it falls to pieces by itself: the historical change which had previously been *in itself* becomes *for itself*. This second, self-relating negation, what Hegel had called "otherness reflected into itself" is the vanishing point of "absolute negativity," of the allegedly pure indifference of the palimpsest. This moment is a paradoxical moment, to be sure, for it is sequentially *third*, though in fact the *first* moment which passes over into its own *Other*. In Stoker's novel, this occurs when the pursuers catch an olfactory trace of Dracula's previous presence which, after numerous attempts, Harker finally describes as some odour which "seemed as though corruption had become itself corrupt" (251). What had assumed the characteristics of decadence has become necessity!

In their respective transparencies, the world-historical vanishing mediators vital to the cultural economies of Pater and Stoker doubly reflect the internal contradictions of cultures which seem so antagonistic. The homelessness of a Mina condemned to the sexual extra-territoriality of a long engagement; the Lucy torn between an allegiance to blood (Lord Godalming), and alliance with "folk" (Quincey Morris) and a fascination with scientific research (Dr. Seward); and just perhaps the suggested homoeroticism which binds Mina and Lucy in a kind of "moral sexlessness" like that of Walter Pater's diaphanous, undeveloped "carriers" of cultural meaning — all seem to be reflected in Dracula's ideology. The resistance of both transparencies to conventional, material representation is represented, perhaps not coincidentally, as alternative, more or less permanent flames: the harbinger of Dracula's presence along Harker's route to the castle and the "hard, gem-like flame" of Pater's notorious conclusion to *The Renaissance*. Each flame, like that of Yeats's Byzantium, unable to "singe a sleeve," identifies a space of resistance to conventional demands or experiences for fin de siècle youth.

What is perhaps most intriguing about this increasingly interdisciplinary, migratory transparency is the way in which its affective life seems to embody both epistemological and ideological contradictions. If Count Dracula is in some sense "summoned" as a function of the inscriptive verisimilitude which would presume to "detect" him, so, similarly, Basil Hallward in Wilde's *The Picture of Dorian Gray* paints a precise pictorial "likeness" which is, at the outset, indistinguishable (even in terms of its ownership!) from nature, its sitting subject, Dorian Gray. Dorian Gray even refers to Hallward's portrait as "a diary of my life from day to day which never leaves the room in which it is written" (187). And yet, this myth of quasi-scientific representation or even realism which pervades both Stoker's and Wilde's novels is deflected by its contrary. As the Count is convinced that he transcends historical closure (vampirism being the *modus operandi* in support of the ideology), so Dorian Gray disbelieves any system which would fix the ego as permanent or reliable: "To him, man was a being with myriad lives and myriad sensations, a complex multiform creature ... whose very flesh was tainted with the monstrous maladies of the dead" (175). Later, under the influence of Sir Henry Wotton who is convinced that most people lead other people's lives, Dorian comes to believe in his own plurality; the lives of all "those strange-terrible figures that had passed across the stage of the world ... in some mysterious way ... had been his own" (177). The "imaginary portrait," as it often does in Pater's short stories collected under that name, begins to suck the historical life from its resident subject, but indirectly, as a continuing record of Dorian Gray's transformation by/in gossip and public opinion rather than some "identity" with the natural world.

In the relationship of Dorian Gray to the pictorial image equally "contested" by him, Hallward, and the art-loving public, Oscar Wilde cites the transparency of the figural in ideological convention: "bad art" too readily gives the "lie" to its naturalness by a premature exposure of its artifice. Any effort to foreclose this transparency can never succeed because the consumer — and surely the subject which Stoker, Jevons, Pater, and Wilde share is finally consumption — of an aesthetic or material object could become the narrator (producer) of another, the narrator (producer) of one becoming the consumer of another, *ad nauseam*. It is the unfinished nature of the aesthetic experience in Wilde which lends it a perpetual "likeness" to other transparencies which are the potential subjects of secondary narrations. Art in Wilde or the Monstrous in Stoker can only be *preserved* as appropriations in the progressive evolution of the transparent "fictions" of its attempted closure.

The irreducible achievement of Aubrey Beardsley might offer a similar instance of a difference, fixed entirely arbitrarily, which comes to generate an exchange system. The mirror traditionally "held up to nature" as a model of the operation of mimesis in occidental thought often in Beardsley comes to function simultaneously as a frame, an extension of the picture plane, a material object of consumption like dirty books and pictures, and as a synecdoche for the way Beardsley's work itself was mechanically reproduced in the (often) prurient imagination. In the frontispiece for Wilde's *Salomé* entitled "The Woman in the Moon," Beardsley replaced a worn convention of the Imaginary, the ubiquitous "man in the moon," with a portrait of the play's author, Oscar Wilde, looking either askance or sideways at an exposed pair of homosexual lovers — the page of Herodias and Narraboth. Their love preceded the destructive, vampire-like infatuation of Narraboth with Salomé, which was the ostensible subject of Wilde's drama. The page shields his lover, Narraboth, from the "moon," in which longing is reflected by an Oscar Wilde who must "save him" for a conventionally destructive marriage. Any difference between homosexual and heterosexual love is fixed only arbitrarily. Like the embryoid masker/unmasker which recurrently usurps Beardsley's *oeuvre* — visually indistinguishable from the traditional representations of the balding, equally parasitical "dirty old men" who are in the forefront of its consumption — the "transparency" generates meaning by obliterating the differences which separate, say, the author as creator from the author as subject, birth from death, mimetic repetition from social reproduction, critical or perceptual foregrounding from a work's historical or pictorial "background."[11] A surrogate for the consumer is visually present *within* the picture plane, inseparable from both its embryonic meaning and the attempted repression or censorship of that meaning.

The role of this typical fin de siècle transparency might find an analogue in semiotics in the model that Saussure brought to the concept of the linguistic sign. Although not published until 1912, the *Cours de linguistique générale* was largely reconstructed from lectures delivered in the last decade of the nineteenth century. The arbitrary nature of the linguistic sign endows language itself with a kind of transparency, represented in Saussure's infamous metaphor of the *feuille de papier.*

> Language is, again, comparable to a sheet of paper: thought is the recto and sound the verso; one cannot cut out just the verso; in the same way, in language, one can isolate neither sound from thought nor thought from sound; one would just arrive at an abstraction the result of which would be psychology or pure phonology. (157)

To consider linguistic "value" as the union of a certain sound with a specific meaning would be to isolate one term from its system, implying that one could commence with various terms (phonemic units) and construct the system by locating correspondences. In Saussure's system, however, any word ceases to function as a word when our interest stops at its sensory contour, just as in Stoker's model the Dracula-effect ceases when his "recto," the attempt of scientists to record its operations, either ceases or is revealed to be inauthentic.

According to Saussure, we must "read *through*" the phonetic carrier, since we can never project the semantic level from it alone. In other words, although the linguistic sign continues to be based upon the *assumption* of a solidarity between sound and meaning, the semantic level clings to an exteriority which prevents the generation of one from another. Thus a transparent agent is a metaphoric representation of an obstruction which *continues to function* as a bond. Without this assumption of a (structurally impossible) solidarity, semiotics as a discipline collapses in the same way that the Count meets his end when his maintenance in the recorded traces of his pursuers is called into question.

IN EACH OF these intellectual systems, cultural expressions, or artistic interests, some notion of "excess" threatens to expose the futility of any critique which might have univocity or a self-consistent formalism as a goal. Rather than discovering behind some palimpsest, veil, frame, or obscure aesthetic representation a presumably *authentic* heterogeneity that a dominant ideology or motive suppresses, as in say Jacques Derrida's analysis of western thought, we look behind the representational traces only to discover an apparently *foundational surplus*. Perhaps the most intriguing of these fin de siècle instances of a foundational excess serving as an agent of metonymic transfer is embodied in Freud's *Studies on Hysteria* which shares an approximate contemporaneity with Bram Stoker's novel.

Stoker's Dr. Seward in his treatment of Renfield is surely an "alienist" who has moved a short step beyond the "projection analysis" common to his discipline, though not the giant leap taken by Freud that ultimately resulted in the birth of psychoanalysis. Like Charcot, Freud's early mentor at the Salpêtrière, Seward has begun to focus on the possibilities of hypnotism in the treatment of so-called hysteria. Yet, as Van Helsing reminds the reader of *Dracula* in a passage which makes mention of Charcot's contribution, there are self-imposed limits on Seward's application of hypnotic techniques:

> Then you are satisfied as to it. Yes? And of course then
> you understand how it act, and can follow the mind of the
> great Charcot ... into the very soul of the patient that he
> influence. No? Then, friend, John, am I to take it that you
> simply accept fact, and are satisfied to let from premise to
> conclusion be a blank? No? Then tell me — for I am a
> student of the brain — how you accept the hypnotism and
> reject the thought-reading. (191)

Van Helsing's abstruse research into vampires may be far-fetched, but his knowledge of the evolution of psychoanalysis is very close to the mark. And, here again, we are in the presence of the fin de siècle "transparency" and the curious conversions which occur as part of its operational efficiency.

The "possessed" or hysterical patient suffered from the outset from a complaint that defied logic: as with Dracula's victims, the body is beyond the reach of traditional medicine because it literally speaks a different language. For the hysterical body to be affected, not as the requirements of anatomy dictate, but as popular speech *articulates*, the body would have to belong to the order of language while remaining a repository of symptoms. Freud, pursuing the strategies common to other Victorian disciplines and to its figurative and literal orphans in search of fathers, committed himself to locating an instantiating moment, an Origin in the form of a psychic trauma impacting consciousness. But early on in the *Studies on Hysteria*, he discovered that the mechanism of the psychic trauma is both alien and native to the organic body, like so many fin de siècle double agents with their ease at disguise and dissimulation:

> But the causal relationship between the determining psychical trauma and the hysterical phenomenon is not of a kind implying that the trauma merely acts like an *agent provocateur* in releasing the symptom, which thereafter leads an independent existence. We must presume rather that the psychical trauma — or more precisely the memory of the trauma — acts *like a foreign body* which long after its entry must continue to be regarded as an agent that is still at work.... (6, emphasis mine)

Freud's theoretical departure from Charcot, like Van Helsing's from Seward, involves a subtle rewriting. A psychical mechanism differs from an organic trauma insofar as it only acts "like" a foreign body: the word "like" suggests the possibility of a potential (dis)simulation, since the determining cause is curiously both similar to and different from the organism. In other words, the host organism makes the trauma its own through a mimetic appropriation, while feigning otherwise. As with the highly dramatised relationship of Lucy and Mina in Stoker's novel, Freud's trope of the undercover agent subsidised a large mimetic component in the early literature of psychoanalysis which includes the elements of "family romance," "acting out" before the analyst in the "timelessness" of the unconscious, "screen memories," and the "staging" of conflict. In this departure from the practices of his early mentor, implicitly recapitulated in Dr. Van Helsing's critique of Dr. Seward, Freud opens the door to treating hysteria — and derivatively all mental disorders — not as illnesses of "degeneration," but as errors attendant upon a strategic symbolic eutrophication, one more instance of a fin de siècle foundational *excess*.

In the crucial case of "Fraülein Elisabeth Von R.," who bears an uncanny resemblance to Stoker's Mina, Freud commences his treatment by attempting on a day-to-day basis, Pater-like, to "peel away" the mnemonic residues in order to identify the initiating psychic trauma. To his surprise, however, he notices that the patient throws off entirely new symptoms, not previously present to the analyst. He begins to wonder if in fact there is some heretofore invisible connector:

> The mechanism was that of conversion: i.e., in place of the mental pains which she avoided, physical pains made their appearance. In this way, a transformation was effect-

ed which had the advantage that the patient escaped from the intolerable mental condition; it is true, this was at the cost of a psychical abnormality—the splitting of consciousness that came about.... (166)[12]

Even though the patient is conversationally reticent, her body begins to *speak*: her right leg, for example, becomes painful when the discussion turns on the nursing of a now deceased father. Freud then maps what has become the "hysterogenic" body, just as surely as Dracula's return is so carefully mapped by his adversaries. As his patient speaks of "being unable to stand alone," the analyst notes that the body serves as a paradoxical figure for what is already constituted as a figure of speech. As the body becomes metaphoric, the metaphor becomes a body in a strange osmosis, as startling in its own way as the relationship between Dorian Gray and Basil Hallward's portrait, where one is "written down" as the other is "written up." The hysteric "suffers" from a primordial absence of the metaphoric, made possible only because the symptom behaves with the same arbitrariness as Saussure's sign, allowing it to adhere in entirely unpredictable ways.

Freud's case history makes it clear that what he is really extracting is metaphoric speech, though he uses an anatomical nomenclature which would have pleased the Count:

> The first mention of the young man *opened up a vein of ideas* the content of which I gradually extracted. It was a question here of a secret, for she had initiated no one, apart from the common friend into her relationship with the young man, and the hopes she attached to them. (145, emphasis mine)

The hysterogenic body has become a surface of narrative representations which the analyst "reads" as a text. All of the symbolisations share one unique feature: a verbal displacement has a physiological effect. An intended's unexpected abandonment is never "like a stab in the heart," but *is* a "stab in the heart." Any difference is fixed only arbitrarily. In such a world, anything can be "bonded," made symbolically equivalent, to anything else.

At the end of the *Studies on Hysteria*, the traumatic event has completed its evolution: it is no longer a nineteenth-century metaphysical Origin, nor quite Charcot's *agent provocateur*, but something very close to one of Freud's notorious "boundary ideas" of *The Interpretation of*

Dreams. In the "Psychotherapy of Hysteria," the concluding chapter of *Studies on Hysteria*, Freud suggests that the alien intruder has never been alien at all:

> We have seen that this material behaves like a foreign body, and that the treatment, too, works like the removal of a foreign body from the living tissue. We are now in a position to see where this comparison fails. A foreign body does not enter into any relation with the layers of tissue that surround it, though it modifies them and necessitates a reactive inflammation in them. (290)

In contradistinction, this special pathogenic agent, like the idea of Dracula, will "pass over in every direction into portions of the normal ego" in such a way that any boundary between the two "is fixed purely and conventionally," like that gossamer "feuille" separating sound and meaning in Saussure.

By endowing his agent with a similar transparency, Freud ultimately makes it "far more ... an infiltrate," which, like Wesley Hyatt's invention, extrusive celluloid, bonded itself to a variety of "hosts," thereby initiating the late nineteenth-century development of plastics and plasticity. But, if only arbitrary convention allows us to distinguish a secret, traumatic agent from the resistance to it, then therapy must consist *not* in extirpating the demonic intruder which, given its easy adherence to defence, would be impossible anyway, but rather more modestly, "in causing the resistance to melt" (290). Our demons can only undergo a change in ontic status, or, as Freud sadly told a very skeptical patient who wondered how knowledge could possibly effect a cure, "in transforming your hysterical misery into common unhappiness" (305). One can only wonder if Freud intended the word "common" as in "common cold" or a synonym for "shared." The discipline he founded has not always chosen to recognise those limitations.[13]

Similarly, though the Count may have a bowie knife through the heart when we last see him, the resistance has melted. His blood flows through Mina Harker's veins as a consequence of their voluntary/involuntary tryst. And hence the son, who in Gothic fiction celebrates a birthday on Quincey Morris's death-day (a relationship like that of the two Catherines in *Wuthering Heights*) and will bear his name, must also have Dracula's blood flowing in his veins. Little Quincey perhaps represents the birth of a new, successful "internationalism," like Art Nouveau or psychoanalysis, given his racial and nominative porosity. The disciplines spawned by the fin de siècle "transparency," again like Dracula, eschew the working classes who have other beliefs.

Once Dracula or psychoanalysis takes hold, to borrow from Mina Harker who is equally possessed by both, "sleep has no place it can call its own" (312) because night (largely) becomes a space where eternally wakeful *meaning* rather than rest dwells. *Dracula*, both the novel and the Count, represents some sustained attempt to see *through* the night, to make it, too, *transparent*. If Dracula is the resistance to closure, a resistance which has historically endowed him with the perpetual life of transcendence, he is no more so than Stoker's lovely novel which appears in its penultimate pages, to suffer the indignity of a stake through its representational "heart," the core of verisimilitude which pumps the "life blood" of the nineteenth-century novel:

> I took the papers from the safe where they have been ever since our return so long ago. We were struck with the fact that, in all the mass of material of which the record is composed, there is hardly one authentic document! nothing but a mass of type-writing, except the later notebooks of Mina and Seward and myself, and Van Helsing's memorandum. (378)

The novel must perform the impossible: establish its *own* authenticity in its *own* voice, independent of social reproduction. Its continuous resistance to that demand, as Stoker reminds us in a manoeuvre that seems so, well, "postmodern," is in fact *Dracula*'s life blood, its hold upon generations of readers. Van Helsing's Catholicism may have in fact prepared the way by claiming, along with St. Augustine, that evil has no independent existence, being rather a perversion (a "turning away") from good: "We will not be given over to monsters, whose very existence would defame Him" (320). That same parasitical transparency, a significant inauthenticity which compels belief precisely because its existence, independent of any attempt to quantify it, cannot be verified, is in fact part of a fin de siècle "family" of ideas.

The very transparency of the Monstrous, insofar as it enables evil to resist civilised representation and hence a certain kind of engagement, defines its power over us. Dracula is really too easily absorbed within models of psycho-sexual "degeneration," racial atavism, political marginalisation, or other modes of "deviancing down," subsidised by liberal pluralism(s) which would make his actions comprehensible, if not excusable, on the grounds of historical persecution. It is precisely that absorptive capacity of evil which places civility, then and now, at maximum risk.

NOTES

I wish to acknowledge the help of Ms. Natsue Noda who, during the writing of her senior thesis, continually reminded me of our shared Imaginary.

1   For a delightful commentary on the role of the diary in maintaining the flow of temporality among those spatially or ideologically isolated, see Beatrice Didier's *Le Journal Intime* (Paris: Presses Universitaires de France, 1977).

2   Transylvania consisted of four different "nations" — Magyars, Szeklers, Germans, and Wallachs — against the Muslims. It was hence an "imaginary state," a marginal buffer between Christian and Muslim empires. This "union of convenience" of disparate linguistic partners is remarkably like that of Harker, Van Helsing, Quincey Morris, and Seward. In 1389, the Turks had defeated the Wallachs and Magyars at the now infamous first battle of Kossovo, establishing the Muslim presence which persists in Bosnia-Herzegovnia. It is intriguing that Count Dracula, like his late twentieth-century Serbian descendants, continues to celebrate the occasion as one of collective racial and national humiliation, despite the creation of Transylvania in 1437.

3   The combination of racial or ethnic stereotyping (comic exaggeration of physical characteristics) and the deployment of instruments and techniques designed to limit the "otherness" of the Other (for example, imposing institutions characteristic of parliamentary democracies upon tribes) co-exist. See Chinua Achebe's controversial essay, "An Image of Africa: Racism in Conrad's *Heart of Darkness*." For an intriguing discussion of fin de siècle demonisation, see Patrick Parrinder's "Heart of Darkness: Geography as Apocalypse."

4   Because it is so often the subject of commentary by critics with their own agendas, Lacan's analysis of the "mirror-phase" of development bears a rereading. In Lacan's analysis, development is lived like a temporal dialectic that discursively projects the formation of the individual onto history. Hence, the occasion is metaphorically like the Fall of Adam and Eve. Yet, any illusion of unity which most theories of development might privilege in which the child looks forward to self-mastery, entails a constant danger of sliding back into the chaos from which it, like Dracula, began. The "self" that must be mastered is the product of an anticipatory illusion, the mastery of which would be a realisation of its falsity, and therefore the impossibility of *being self-identical*. The moment of "self-mastery" is thus infinitely deferred, but this same deferred moment would also constitute the revelation of the meaning of the past. Because the comprehension of the past is also deferred, there is a combination of anticipation, anxiety, and jubilation regarding this mirror-phase of development. See page 97 and following in Jacques Lacan's *Écrits*.

5   Dracula's seemingly contradictory combination of impotency and a form of sexual colonialism (the Other becomes him in order to become socio-biologically reproductive in Dracula's world-historical time) is an unstated sub-text of John Stevenson's essay, "A Vampire in the Mirror: The Sexuality of *Dracula*."

6   In *Sexual Anarchy: Gender and Culture at the Fin De Siècle*, Elaine Showalter imagines Lucy and Mina as instances of a new female assertiveness which the "brotherhood" of patrician scientists must struggle to contain (180–1). This is but one of a growing number of essays which treat the female victims of Dracula as "new women" *in situ*. See also, for example, Phyllis Roth's essay, "Suddenly Sexual Women in Bram Stoker's *Dracula*."

7   Judith Halberstam's *Skin Shows: Gothic Horror and the Technology of Monsters* discusses the traits shared by Shylock and Dracula in holding a civilisation (doubly) accountable for its racial prejudices which are then projected as a self-serving, "hoarding" economy (86–107).

8   Since vampires, according to Van Helsing's research, "cannot die by mere passing of time"

(239), successive birthdays are immaterial to its "life." Hence, the vampire's resistance to containment by/in diaries, which would figuratively, make everyday a (re)birthday, stems at least in part from the nature of its *being*.

9 Although Jevons was theoretically opposed to interpersonal comparisons in his assault upon the cost theory of value, Alfred Marshall was intrigued by the possibility of lending it some degree of theoretical respectability. Perhaps for this reason, the debate over marginal utility theory took on an added dimension in the 1890s. See David Reisman's book *Alfred Marshall's Mission*, especially pages 160–173.

10 The figure of the "Diaphaneitè" is less well known than it should be perhaps because the essay was such an early composition in Pater's career, but also because it smacks of an anti-historicism, disguised in *The Renaissance*.

11 Beardsley's *oeuvre*, even without its implicit flattening of the picture plane and the aesthetics of self-reflection, is nonetheless "transparent" in social reproduction. In practice, Beardsley suggests that any difference between advertising, book illustration, marginal (quasi-mediaeval) commentary, pornography, and "high art" was only arbitrary. As a consequence, his potentially large audience encompassed a number of venues: private subscribers, limited edition bibliophiles, the gallery-attending upper classes and, because of the threat or actual practice of censorship, even those in complete ignorance of his work.

12 For a more detailed analysis of this conversion procedure in Freud's *Studies on Hysteria*, see my essay, "Freud's 'Secret Agent' and the *Fin du Corps*."

13 This would be possible of course only if the resistance is precisely what is infiltrating, one manifestation of which might be, in Freud's economy, the "transference" onto the analyst, a problem with which, in some sense, Van Helsing must cope in Stoker's novel.

REFERENCES

Achebe, Chinua. "An Image of Africa: Racism in Conrad's *Heart of Darkness*." *Hopes and Impediments: Selected Essays 1965–1987*. Oxford: Heinemann, 1988. 1–13.

Brontë, Emily. *Wuthering Heights*. 1847. Harmondsworth: Penguin, 1985.

Didier, Béatrice. *Le Journal Intime*. Paris: Presses Universitaires de France, 1977.

Freud, Sigmund and Josef Breuer. *Studies on Hysteria*. 1893–1895. *The Standard Edition of the Works of Sigmund Freud in 24 Volumes*. Gen. Ed. James Strachey. London: Hogarth Press, 1953–66. Vol. 2.

Gordon, Jan B. "Freud's 'Secret Agent' and the *Fin du Corps*." in *Fin de Siècle/Fin du Globe: Fears and Fantasies of the Late Nineteenth Century*. Ed. John Stokes. London: Macmillan, 1992. 117–138.

Judith Halberstam, *Skin Shows: Gothic Horror and the Technology of Monsters*. Durham: Duke UP, 1995.

Jevons, William Stanley. *The Theory of Political Economy*. 1879. Ed. R.D.C. Black. Harmondsworth: Penguin, 1970.

Lacan, Jacques. *Écrits*. Paris: Editions de Seuil, 1966.

Marx, Karl. *Grundrisse: Foundations of the Critique of Political Economy*. 1857–1858. Trans. Martin Nicolaus. Harmondsworth, Penguin, 1973.

Parrinder, Patrick. "*Heart of Darkness*: Geography as Apocalypse." *Fin de Siècle/Fin du Globe: Fears and Fantasies of the Late Nineteenth Century*. Ed. John Stokes. London: Macmillan, 1992. 85–101.

Pater, Walter. "The Diaphaneitè." 1912. *Miscellaneous Studies. New Library Edition of the Works of Walter Pater in 10 Volumes*. London: Macmillan, 1920.

Reisman, David. *Alfred Marshall's Mission*. London: Macmillan, 1990.

Roth, Phyllis. "Suddenly Sexual Women in Bram Stoker's *Dracula*." *Literature and Psychology* 17 (1977): 113–121.

Saussure, Ferdinand de. *Cours de Linguistique Générale*. 1912. Paris: Editions Payot, 1972. Translated for Dundurn Press by Nigel Wood.

Showalter, Elaine. *Sexual Anarchy: Gender and Culture at the Fin de Siècle*. London: Virago, 1992.

Stevenson, John. "A Vampire in the Mirror: The Sexuality of *Dracula*." *PMLA* 103 (1988): 139–149.

Stoker, Bram. *Dracula*. 1897. Oxford: Oxford UP, 1983.

Wilde, Oscar. *The Picture of Dorian Gray*. 1891. Harmondsworth: Penguin, 1985.

The Psychiatrist's Couch: Hypnosis, Hysteria, and Proto-freudian Performance in Dracula

Stephanie Moss

> No one who accepts the view that censorship is the chief reason for dream distortion will be surprised to learn from the results of dream interpretation that most of the dreams of adults are traced back by analysis to *erotic wishes*. A great many [sexual desires] … only find their way to representation in dreams through the assistance of repressed erotic wishes.
>
> (Freud, *On Dreams* 70)

URING THE YEARS 1890–1897 WHEN BRAM STOKER was writing *Dracula*, the late Victorian world was poised at the edge of an epistemological break that would forever alter the view of human psychology. Although the human brain was still generally believed to be responsible as a somatic rather than affective agent of disease, as early as 1877, according to Michel Foucault, the psychiatrisation of sex was occurring. Sexuality was becoming acknowledged as a monolithic impulse categorised by norms and perversions that defined the body as the site of social construction (Faas 7–8, Foucault 154). At the beginning of the last decade of the century, Freud was writing about the sociological etiology of neurasthenia (Strachey 6). In 1893, while Stoker was in the midst of writing *Dracula*, Freud's earliest book on hysteria, *Quelques considérations pour une étude comparative des paralysies motrices organiques et hystériques*, was published.[1] In addition, Stoker's most recent biographer, Barbara Belford, suggests Stoker's acquaintance with Freud's theories:

> Stoker also attended F.W.H. Meyer's [sic] enthusiastic talk on Freud's experiments at a London meeting of the Society of Psychical Research, a group that inquired into thought reading, mesmerism, apparitions, and haunted houses. (212–13)[2]

Another indication of Stoker's interest in psychology and the mind/body connection are the texts listed among *Dracula*'s sources in the Rosenbach collection: the surgeon Thomas Pettigrew's *On Superstitions connected with the History and Practice of Medicine and Surgery* (1844), which examined the power of the mind to effect dramatic changes in the body, and Robert Gray's 1808 publication, *The Theory of Dreams* (Leatherdale 238), an examination of the influence of the human mind on sacred and profane dreams. The interaction of reason and physiology as well as the emerging recognition of the mind as an unconscious agent of self can be seen in the dream-like vampiric state exhibited by Jonathan, Mina, and Lucy during contact with the vampire. This trance, it will be shown, encodes both hysteria and hypnosis, the tool Freud used to examine hysteria as an expression of repressed sexual longing.[3]

Hypnosis emerged from mesmerism in the middle of the nineteenth century when it was used by the surgeon James Braid, whose reputation was ruined by its practice. Franz Anton Mesmer (1734–1815), who developed the technique, worked with hysterical patients and attempted to manipulate cosmic magnetic fluids to provoke a magnetic crisis (Mesmer 5, 13).[4] He filled a *baquet*, or tub, with water and placed iron rods and filings in the water. These protruded from holes in the *baquet* and were applied to the corporeal sites of hysterical symptoms.[5] A disciple of Mesmer's, the Marquis de Puysegur, accidentally discovered that mesmerism also caused a peaceful sleep marked by the expression aloud of thoughts and feelings (Charcot, "Magnetism" 568). It was not until the last two decades of the nineteenth century, however, that mesmerism, now called hypnosis, was legitimised by Charcot, who used hypnosis to provoke both the magnetic crisis and peaceful sleep. Through the consideration of Victorian periodical articles on hypnosis and the application of feminist performance theory, this essay will examine the vampire trance in *Dracula* as analogous to hypnosis. How all three phenomena — the vampire trance, hypnosis, and hysteria — are subversive of Victorian gender norms will also be outlined.

Feminist performance theory reinforces sex and gender as sociological phenomena, demonstrations of established signs of masculinity or femininity that are predetermined by the community. As explicated by Judith Butler, the traditional feminist distinction between sex as biological and gender as socially constructed is problematic: the body does not exist as a social object before it is marked by gender because different genitalia automatically characterise the infant as gendered. Gender and sexual characteristics, therefore, correspond and, if gender is defined as a cultural interpretation of biological sexuality, then gender becomes as essentialist and predetermined as sex (Deats n.p., Butler, *Gender* 8). However, if sex, like gender, is the social identification of the individual as male or female through an established set of "free floating attributes" rather than through fundamentally innate biological characteristics, then both sex and gender become the exhibition of these assigned attributes. Since the individual interiorises society's laws about what is masculine and what is feminine, internalisation becomes the same as outward show and effectively erases the difference between inside and outside. The assigned attributes of gender then conform to the social functions assigned by the biological characteristics of sex. Therefore, "[g]ender is the repeated stylisation of the body, a set of repeated acts within a highly rigid regulatory frame that congeal over time to produce the appearance of substance, of a natural sort of being." Identity is achieved through the incorporation of gender attributes which are then enacted (Butler, *Gender* 24, 33, 134–35). This performance may focus either upon the phallocentric notion of gender or subvert that notion through parody (Deats n.p.). Both types of performance occur in *Dracula*: phallocentric performance in the expression of Victorian values, and parody, or indirect criticism, through hysteria.

The metaphor of performance was also used to articulate both hypnotic and hysterical behaviour. The same year that saw Freud's paper on hysteria translated into French also marked the death of his teacher, Jean Martin-Charcot, the leading specialist in hypnosis as a cure for hysterical symptoms. However, Charcot believed that hypnosis could be an etiology of hysteria as well as a cure. He therefore blurred the boundary between the two:

> For several years the principal towns of Europe have been
> overrun by persons from no one knows where, who, bear-

ing high-sounding titles, invite the people to hypnotizing performances given in the local theaters.... We can track a showman magnetizer of this sort by his victims everywhere. When he has gone, it is noticed that subjects with whom he succeeded best become nervous and irritable. Some of them fall of their own accord into a deep sleep, out of which it is not easy to awake them; thereafter they are unfitted for the performance of the duties of every-day life. Others, and they the majority, are seized with convulsions exactly resembling the crises of confirmed hysteria. (Charcot, "Crime" 166)

Therefore, hypnosis and hysteria are contingent and both are contiguous with the idea of performance. This is reinforced by Charcot's statement that his hysterical patients were "good actors who, consciously or unconsciously enjoyed the attention they received" (Medical 12–13). In addition, his medical demonstrations were presented to students and visitors with a theatrical flair:

[H]e would arrange to bring in and examine a number of patients with successively advanced symptoms of a particular neurological disorder. It was here that Charcot's great visual talents came into play. He would use floodlights and spotlights at particular points in his demonstrations; he would mimic the walk or movements of a particular disorder almost exactly. In one instance, he had the patients wear hats and feathers. (Medical 8)

The European performances of hypnosis noted by Charcot were also found on English stages. Periodicals and newspapers announced hypnotic demonstrations presented to the populace as theatrical performances in public auditoriums in London's St. James Hall and the Royal Aquarium, where theatrical replications of Charcot's demonstrations put hysterical illness on display. According to Ernest Hart, a medical reformer and reporter chronicling these performances, actors were recruited and trained for the demonstrations in the classic regions of Drury Lane where Stoker and Henry Irving worked (Hart, "Eternal" 834, Houghton 941). Pins were stuck into waxen dolls which produced in the actor a predictable response. Vials of metallurgical compounds, magnets, and other objects cued reactions. For example, a tube of alcohol, when placed near the hypnotised subject, produced all the signs of drunkenness. Hart elaborates:

> [S]he fell from the chair onto the floor in a state of com-
> plete inebriety, and with a simulation of the various stages
> of drunkenness so effectively dramatic that I doubt if any
> woman so uneducated could go through such a perfor-
> mance, except an hysteric of this class when 'sleep-wak-
> ing' and freed from the restraint of the fully conscious
> action of the upper brain.[6] It is this mixture of hysteria,
> partially numbed consciousness, trained automatism, and
> imposture, which so often takes in either the wholly cred-
> ulous or ignorantly sceptical spectator. ("Witchcraft" 358)

The medical community was drawn to the performances in order
to establish their credibility. Its consensus was that the demonstrations
were rigged to evince Mesmer's theories of animal magnetism and that the
subjects responded to cues established by the hypnotist. However, along
with Charcot, the medical community believed that the transformations
they witnessed illuminated the true hysterical natures of the performers
(Hart, "Witchcraft" 358). George C. Kingsbury, a medical doctor and prac-
titioner of hypnotism (Houghton 971), reported on the British Medical
Association's official investigation into hypnotic practices:

> Hypnotism is virtually on its trial in this country, a jury of
> twelve medical men having been nominated by the psy-
> chological section of the British Medical Association to
> investigate the argument against, and the pleadings for, its
> recognised introduction into the equipment of the physi-
> cian. (Kingsbury 145)

The Victorian preoccupation with the practice is indicated by the sheer
volume of extant periodical material. *Poole's Index* lists 64 entries under
the subject heading of "hypnosis" between the years 1887 and 1896 (3:
206, 4: 271).

Charcot entered the periodical debates on hypnosis through the
publication of two important articles in which he examined the questions
of morality that arose in connection with hypnosis and hysteria. He agreed
with others that hypnosis could be a cause of hysteria as well as a cure. He
further identified it as "a genuine neurosis" rather than "a physiological
state," and agreed that individuals could be made to perform criminal or
obscene acts against their will (Charcot, "Crime" 160, 166, Kingsbury 151,
Veith 226). Other observers went even further, incorporating ideas about

pathology and morality; it was believed that the mesmerised subject could be led to immoral or criminal behaviour that might result in "infect[ion] with syphilis," and that the personality types susceptible to hypnosis were "those whose morality required strengthening, or whose self-control needed bracing" (Hart, "Witchcraft" 347, 365). Charcot, nonetheless, continued to use hypnosis to cure his hysterical patients while tremendous controversy about its juridical, medical, moral, and scientific employment continued. A variety of articles were generated about Charcot's medical experiments at Salpêtrière (Ewart 253–59), the work done by Bernheim at Nancy (Kempin 278–91), the impact of Darwinian knowledge upon an understanding of hypnotic susceptibility (Jarvis 1–15), the ethical application of the trance state, the question of whether criminal or immoral behaviour could be implanted through suggestion in otherwise non-felonious and upstanding personalities (Ewart 253–59), and the debate over the somatic versus the psychological origin of hypnotic suggestion. As Hart has cogently argued, hypnosis was perceived as medical discourse, but it was also perceived as a "true witches' Sabbath" which rendered victims helpless against the will of the hypnotist ("Witchcraft" 362).

The medico-legal conflict surrounding hypnosis erupted into various courtroom dramas. In 1891, one year after Bram Stoker began to write the tale of his mesmeric vampire, two Parisians, Gouffe and Bompard, were tried for murder using hypnosis as a defence (Kingsbury ff. 145). This case marked neither the first nor the last juridical appearance of hypnosis. Twenty-one years earlier, in 1865, a Castellan was convicted of rape because "the moral force of resistance in the subject" had been broken down by hypnosis (Charcot, "Crime" 162). *Dracula* alludes to the latent moral danger inherent in the unscrupulous use of hypnosis through the Count's transformation of Lucy into an infant-devouring sexual temptress, and through the three female vampires' acts of tempting Jonathan and Van Helsing. In an era profoundly tormented by the impact of science upon cultural values, the issue of free will was examined from a distinctly skeptical perspective. Spinoza, a contemporary of Newton whose mechanical and atheistic philosophy had disastrous implications for organised religion, was quoted in articles about hypnosis. Emily Kempin in *Arena*, a popular nineteenth-century periodical, raised the issue of human autonomy, hypnosis, and the law in connection with Spinoza's philosophy:

> [F]ree will is, as the great philosopher Spinoza says, an illusion and that free will is nothing more than ignorance of the motives of our resolutions. This acknowledgement leads us naturally from the medical to the juridical ques-

tion, What effect has Hypnotism on our system of Law? (Kempin 289)

Stoker was a reader of and contributor to Victorian periodicals, particularly to *The Nineteenth Century* where he published four articles, the first of which appeared in 1890. Its editor, John Knowles, was a close friend, and Stoker's professional and personal association with Knowles and his periodical would have exposed him to the debates on hypnosis (Stoker *Personal* 44–47).[7] Therefore, C. Theodore Ewart's "The Power of Suggestion," Ernest Hart's "Hypnotism and Humbug" and "The Revival of Witchcraft," and George E. Kingsbury's "Hypnotism, Crime and the Doctors," all of which appeared in *The Nineteenth Century* while *Dracula* was being written, would have been familiar to Stoker and may have influenced his portrayal of the vampire trance and the cultural issues it raises. Furthermore, articles on hypnosis also appeared in *Arena* and *Overland*, and Charcot's two articles appeared in *Forum*. In *Popular Science Monthly*, Dr. William Hirsch links hypnotism to hysteria and neurasthenia,[8] and writes of the debilitation of "educated society which is threatened with total overthrow by utter derangement of nerves." Citing mediaeval epidemics of hysteria which resulted in "sexual excitement" and the strangling, boiling, and eating of children, Hirsch attributes this behaviour to *"suggestibility,"* the predominant characteristic of the hypnotisable subject (544, 547, 549). Since Stoker also published articles in *Cosmopolitan*, *World's Work*, *Fortnightly Review*, *North American*, and *Bookman*, he would have kept abreast of periodical data on subjects of interest to him.

That the hypnosis debate was of interest to Stoker is evinced by the pivotal citation of Charcot in Seward's journal as he recalls a conversation with Van Helsing. Charcot's inclusion suggests Stoker's awareness of the psychological use of hypnosis:

"I suppose now you do not believe in corporal transference. No? Nor in materialization. No? Nor in astral bodies. No? Nor in the reading of thought. No? Nor in hypnotism— "

"Yes," I said. "Charcot has proved that pretty well." He smiled as he went on: "Then you are satisfied as to it. Yes? And of course then you understand how it act, and can follow the mind of the great Charcot — alas that he is no more! — into the very soul of the patient that he influence." (191)

This passage suggests a variety of repercussions from Stoker's awareness of Charcot's psychological work. Van Helsing legitimises supernatural phenomena through hypnosis by citing Charcot, a leading empiricist who employed hypnotism. By extension, he proposes to the Victorian reader that the territory previously delineated as "uncanny" can now be justified through scientific investigation. The mention of Charcot implicates his work on the moral ambiguities of the hypnotic trance which, in turn, implies that the characters who succumb to the vampire's will are caught in the double bind of the hypnotic subject: Lucy is not responsible for her vampiric actions because her will is directed by another, but her sexual forwardness defines her as ripe for manipulation. Her trance state, therefore, both condemns and exonerates her expression of desire. As a mediaeval-like hysteric, Lucy is both sexually and cannibalistically voracious. However, these symptoms are now the mark of disease and may be viewed medically rather than as an inscription of the supernatural. Charcot's name further evokes equivocation in relation to the vampire trance because it recalls his citation of the 1865 rape case. Like the Castellan who used hypnosis to perpetrate a rape, the vampire does not seduce, it overpowers. Jonathan is therefore exculpated for his near entrapment by the three female vampires. On the other hand, Charcot's name suggests his therapeutic work with hysterics, paralleled by Van Helsing's use of hypnosis on Mina to gain access to her subconscious in order to "learn that which even [she her]self do[es] not know" (327).

Contemporary periodical descriptions of the behaviour of hypnotised subjects provide a further link between vampirism, hysteria, and hypnosis, this time through connections to Darwin. As Ewart outlined in an article, hypnosis reveals the progression of the human species towards a telepathic future. This is seen in Mina's telepathic link to Dracula. Hypnosis also, however, indicates regression to an animalistic past that Victorian morality repressed (Flower, "Psychical" 318–19, Flower, "Ascent").[9] Entranced subjects often reverted to animal instincts. As Hart outlines:

> I had a patient who in the somnambulistic stage was transformed into a cock and entered into the cock nature. I tried to make him remember when he awoke what he had been thinking of when he was thus transformed, by ordering him to do so when still somnambulistic. I asked him what he had been doing. He said he had been crowing. I asked him why he crowed; he said he did not know; he crowed because he could not help it. I asked him what

he had been thinking of, and his answer was, "Je pensais à mes poules" ("I was thinking of my hens"). (Hart, "Witchcraft" 362)

Hart offers another glimpse into the brute mind exposed by hypnosis:

> She scratched, she mewed to perfection, she washed imaginary whiskers, she spat, she licked her hands, she lapped milk from a saucer; and when you "pressed the button" at her back she sat up rigid as on hind quarters and caressed her face with her paws with a truly feline grace. (Hart, "Witchcraft" 361)

In *Dracula*, Lucy Westenra appears outside her tomb, transformed into a vampire. Her demonstrated animal behaviour suggests that of Hart's hypnotised patients who became cock and cat. After suffering for two months from a lingering malaise, Lucy is buried in the family vault where Van Helsing and the others encounter her in her full-blown vampire state:

> When Lucy ... saw us she drew back with an angry snarl, such as a cat gives when taken unawares; then her eyes ranged over us.... With a careless motion, she flung to the ground, callous as a devil, the child that up to now she had clutched strenuously to her breast, growling over it as a dog growls over a bone. (211)

Feline animal imagery again connects the vampire state to the hypnotic trance as Dracula forces Mina to drink his blood like a "child forcing a kitten's nose into a saucer of milk" (282). Stoker's citation of Cesare Lombroso further substantiates the idea of the vampire as a primitive ancestor that may be awakened under hypnosis.[10]

Hysteria "defies any definition and any attempt to portray it concretely" (Veith 1). A description of the disease is difficult because it "is not clearly defined, because its limits, unfortunately, are very vague" (Janet 18). However, Charcot characterised it as a disease of sexual morbidity, an unhealthy or overly sensitive and gloomy response to sex and sexuality. The association between hysteria and sex dates back to Roman times when Galen noted that the use of manual sexual stimulation without orgasmic release often cured his hysterical patients. Because Galen's patients were often either widows or virgins, sexual abstinence became a cause of the disease (Veith 43, 42, 46). Charcot's experiments with hypnosis allowed the documentation of hysteria as it emerged during trance. Some of these symptoms do not occur during vampire entrancement: the assumption by the patient of a fixed posture due to contractions of the muscle, a catalepsy distinguished by wide, staring eyes, and the retention of whatever attitude may be given to the arms or legs (Charcot, "Magnetism" 572–73). There are, however, other classic signs of the illness that are documented as far back as Egyptian times and that coincide with the symptoms of the vampire spell: fainting, the paralysis that occurs during the nightmares which accompany both hysteria and the vampire trance, sleepwalking, mood swings between hope and despair, suffocation and gasping for breath, anemia (which increases the tendency to hysteria), wounds whose meanings slip between satanic marks of Cain and the religious fanatic's divine stigmata, and loss of voice that marks episodes of both. Garlic both repels the vampire and drives the wandering womb back to its proper place (Veith 23, 205).

These hysterical signs of both hypnosis and the vampire trance suggest a repressed self, not biologically determined by ancestral genes, but shaped by outside forces.[11] Charcot was convinced of the psychosomatic aspects of hysteria and the enormous impact of environment on the development of the disorder. Both Charcot and Pierre Janet, a psychologist who practiced at the fin de siècle, located the origin of hysteria in the social necessity for repression. Hysteria was caused by the subject's efforts to purge "sensibili[ties] that are in opposition to his moral feeling." By refusing to acknowledge those feelings, the patient removed the exciting incident from consciousness only to have it resurface in the hysterical attack (Janet XV).

Like her father before her, Lucy was a sleepwalker since childhood. Her somnambulism, reawakened by Dracula, is marked by the same abundant and copious hallucinations that Janet saw in textbook cases of hysteria:

> [S]he grows more and more gloomy, her health fails, and we may notice the beginning of the singular symptoms we are going to speak of. Nearly every day, at night and during the day, she enters into a strange state; she looks as if she were in a dream, she speaks softly with an absent person.... She rises, goes to the windows and opens them, then shuts them again.... She must be stopped, looked after incessantly till she shakes herself, rubs her eyes, and resumes her ordinary business as if nothing had happened. (27)

The correspondence of the vampire victim to the hysteric suggests a conflict between internal, instinctual needs and external, social dictates. The hypnotised, hysterical, and vampiric subject is a product of the classic Freudian struggle between social and individual desires. The superego, as constructed by social inhibitions, battles against animal instincts which must be suppressed when the child enters society. As Freud remarks in *Civilization and its Discontents*:

> The replacement of the individual by the power of a community constitutes the decisive step of civilization. The essence of it lies in the fact that the members of the community restrict themselves in their possibilities of satisfaction, whereas the individual knew no such restrictions.... The final outcome should be a rule of law to which all — except those who are not capable of entering a community — have contributed by a sacrifice of their instincts.... (47)

A close textual reading of Stoker's novel indicates that this symmetry between hysteric and vampire victim, and the struggle between instinct and conscience, is wedded to gender performance. As outlined above, the feminist distinction between gender and sex has been questioned by Judith Butler, who sees both the social codes that inform gender and the biological markers of sex as socially constructed. The individual's identity as either man or woman, masculine or feminine, is therefore merely a display of socially determined attributes which are labeled either male or female. The concept of performance is a metaphor for that display of gendered characteristics. The performance motif is particularly appropriate for Stoker as he lived and worked nearly every day for twenty-eight years in the world of the theatre. Although most modern readers have assumed Stoker's acceptance of Victorian moral dictates, the theatrical realm remained — and still remains — liminal, operating, with society's permission, outside of society's constraints.[12] The Lyceum, where Stoker worked, was attended by a glamorous circle of famous and respectable people, but its female star, Ellen Terry, had two illegitimate children, was married three times, and her last husband was young enough to be her son (Farson 54–5). Not only, therefore, is Stoker's orthodox Victorianism questionable, but the illumination of *Dracula* by Butler's phenomenological theory of gender as "acts, gestures, the visual body, the clothed body" is particularly descriptive of Stoker's day to day existence in the world of performance and of the ubiquitous presence of staged performances of hysteria and hypnosis ("Performative" 281).

The idea of gender difference enacted within performance disrupts the neatly recuperated Victorian morality that marks the end of the novel. Although the vampires die and Mina's stainless purity is restored, the novel's extensive internal subversion of traditional gender expectations interrupts this ideologically correct ending.[13] Butler describes the process through which Stoker's ending can be mistaken for doctrinal recovery, how gender performance can be mistaken for voluntary enactment:

> Gender is what is put on, invariably, under constraint, daily and incessantly, with anxiety and pleasure, but if this continuous act is mistaken for a natural or linguistic given, power is relinquished to expand the cultural field bodily through subversive performance of various kinds. ("Performance" 282)

Luce Irigaray takes performance theory one step further and, like Charcot, views hysteria as subversive performance, the safety valve that allows for the rejection of socially-sanctioned roles:

> [T]he drama of hysteria is that it is inserted schizotically between that gestural system, that desire paralyzed and enclosed within its body, and a language that it has learned in the family, in school, in society, which is in no way continuous with — nor, certainly, a metaphor for — the "movements" of its desire. Both mutism and mimicry are then left to hysteria ... the hysteric exhibits a potential for ... [a] movement of revolt and refusal. (138, 135)

I suggest that forced performance of gender, the coerced "putting on" of certain attributes, is subverted in *Dracula* by the hysterical displays of Lucy, Mina, and Jonathan. These hysterical episodes signify their discomfort with traditional gender and marital roles in Victorian society: domestic nun wedded to predatory business-man, idle wife espoused to landed gentleman, excluded female protected from the dangerously debilitating rigours of everyday living, enforced idleness, and pristine purity.[14] These were the major causes of the epidemic of hysteria in the nineteenth century (Dijkstra 7).[15] Victorian women, therefore, lay prone upon their sofas in record numbers and men suffered brain fever at the precise moment when that sofa was being reupholstered for use in a psychiatrist's office.

Although a recognition of the psychogenic etiology of hysteria dates back to Edward Jorden's 1603 treatise, *A Briefe Discourse of a Disease Called the Suffocation of the Mother*, Freud was the first to structure a complex psychobiological theory regarding its occurrence.

The presence of Seward, an alienist, introduces the notion of late Victorian psychology into the text. He is an expert forensic doctor who, according to the description given by a momentarily lucid Renfield, is a "humanitarian and medico-jurist," someone who testifies as a witness in criminal cases such as those involving hypnosis (Stoker 244, Wolf 295). For Seward, like Charcot and his patients, Lucy is a scientific text to be interpreted. Stoker's awareness of hidden psychological stimuli, suggested by his description in *Personal Reminiscences* of Henry Irving's psychological rather than supernatural interpretation of *Macbeth* (1. 107–13), is substantiated by Seward's suspicion as to the subconscious, hysterical nature of Lucy's illness:

> [A]s there must be a cause somewhere, I have come to the conclusion that it must be something mental. She complains of difficulty in breathing satisfactorily at times, and of heavy, lethargic sleep, with dreams that frighten her, but regarding which she can remember nothing. (111)

Seward, however, draws no connection between the vampire and the hysteric. Indeed, the existence of the vampire is contrary to what John L. Greenway describes as the "normal science" of the period, a science which supported gender norms by way of such claims as that citing lesser female body weight as the determinant of lesser brain capacity (221). Greenway suggests that "Seward's folly," his embrace of Victorian normal science and his rejection of the vampire, colours a reading of *Dracula*'s overt paternalism, particularly as exhibited towards women. Although "[n]ormal science agreed with William Acton, the leading physician in sexuality of the 1870's, that 'the majority of women (happily for society) are not very much troubled with sexual feeling of any kind,'" Stoker, Greenway continues, is skeptical towards rather than credulous of Victorian sexual conventions:[16]

> These sentimental assumptions lead Seward and all the characters to assume that Lucy falls victim to something alien, but the vampires catalyze a sexuality latent in all the characters. (221)

According to Greenway, Seward's acceptance of Victorian gender distinctions, further evidenced by his decision to exclude Mina from the vampire hunt, is purposefully ironic on Stoker's part (Stoker 242, Greenway 230). Although it is Van Helsing who excludes Mina, Seward later concurs, stating that the vampire hunt "is no place for a woman, and if she had remained in touch with the affair, it would in time infallibly have wrecked her" (256). Seward, therefore, condones the precepts of "normal science," specifically the marginalisation of women and disbelief in the vampire. However, he is unaware that his own display of scientific scrutiny is similar to the vampire's hypnotic intrusion. This is evidenced in Lucy's description of Seward:

> He seems absolutely imperturbable. I can fancy what a wonderful power he must have over his patients. He has a curious habit of looking one straight in the face, as if trying to read one's thoughts. He tries this on very much with me, but I flatter myself he has got a tough nut to crack. (55)

Seward's demeanour as scientist, therefore, connects the scientific to the vampiric, a connection established earlier by the resemblance of vampire behaviour to that of hypnotised subjects. Therefore, metaphorically, the novel calls attention to similarities between scientific procedure and vampiric behaviour and establishes a logical chain which links the validation of vampirism to a repudiation of Victorian gender norms. If the vampire is placed outside "normal science" which views women as biologically inferior, but the amassed data in *Dracula* validates the vampire, then other precepts of "normal science" must be interrogated. This implied disruption of the theories which substantiated Victorian gender ideology is corroborated by the manner in which Mina, Jonathan, and Lucy's hysteria is encoded in the text.

The character of Mina has been critically recognised as a New Woman, an epithet warranted both by Mina's emotional makeup and her active participation in male affairs. Prior to her marriage to Jonathan, she led the "trying" life of an assistant schoolmistress and worked "to keep up with Jonathan's studies" (53). As she explains in an early letter to Lucy:

> ... I have been practising shorthand very assiduously. When we are married I shall be able to be useful to Jonathan, and if I can stenograph well enough I can take

> down what he wants to say in this way and write it out for
> him on the typewriter, at which I am also practising very
> hard ... I shall keep a diary.... I don't mean one of those
> two-pages-to-the-week-with-Sunday-squeezed-in-a-cor-
> ner diaries, but a sort of journal.... I shall try to do what I
> see lady journalists do.... (53–54)

Although Mina's studies are ostensibly for her husband's benefit, it is important to note that in 1891 only 5.1% of clerical employees in England were women (Holcombe 210). Moreover, Mina's subversive proclivity to develop marketable skills considered outside proper feminine behaviour is underscored by the following statement in an 1890 edition of *The Nineteenth Century*, penned by Katie Cowper, a society friend of John Ruskin (Pearsall 515):

> I think it cannot be denied that the change which has
> taken place in the social life of women during the last few
> years has come with giant strides, and is one which
> maybe is justly viewed by some with feelings of alarm....
> Thus, how many women till lately, however talented and
> well-educated they were, ever dreamt of openly writing in
> reviews and newspapers?... These and other like innova-
> tions, which in so short a time have assumed such
> immense proportions, 'give one to think;' and we must be
> excused who do not appreciate and care not to give way
> to this clamour for absolute equality with men. In this
> respect the good old times were better, far better than the
> new. (Cowper 65, 71)

Mina's developing clerical skills and her desire to write journalistically are, therefore, aspects of an emerging feminism that many found disturb-ing. Her stolid emotional character, which is "not of a fainting disposi-tion," is an inversion of gender norms. It is exhibited when she responds to Lucy's death calmly (223). However, these liberated tendencies are threat-ened when Mina becomes a wife and, in place of the New Woman, the Victorian hysteric begins to emerge.

On August 24th, less than a month before Lucy dies, Mina marries Jonathan hurriedly in the hospital in Buda-Pesth (104–5). Lucy is staked on September 28th (103). By October 1st, Mina is exhibiting nascent symptoms of hysteria:

> If I hadn't gone to Whitby, perhaps poor dear Lucy would
> be with us now. She hadn't taken to visiting the church-
> yard till I came, and if she hadn't come there in the day-
> time with me she wouldn't have walked there in her
> sleep; and if she hadn't gone there at night and asleep,
> that monster couldn't have destroyed her as he did. Oh,
> why did I ever go to Whitby! There now, crying again!
> (257)

The unemotional Mina Murray becomes the weeping Mina Harker; this
shift in disposition, symptomatic of hysteria, indicates the tension between
Mina's true self and her performed self. Among the possibilities for this
change is repressed guilt over Lucy's death (Medical 14). However,
October 1st is also the night Mina is thrust from the circle of men, where
she was previously included, and goes "to bed when the men had gone,
simply because they told [her] to" although she "did not feel sleepy" (257).
Her sudden expulsion from male society where decisions occur and power
resides is a consequence of her married state and the performed self she
enacts. There are other symptoms of Mina's hysterical breakdown. She
displays an obsessive nature: "[Jonathan's] awful journal gets hold of my
imagination and tinges everything with something of its own colour"
(180). Van Helsing notes Mina's emulation of Lucy's hysterical characteristics: "[T]here is to her the silence now often; as so it was with Miss
Lucy" (323). Both vampirism and hysteria are contagious, sometimes epidemic in nature: "The principal causes of the spread of ... so-called hysteria are, then, *suggestibility*, emotionalism, [and] the impulse to mimicry"
(Hirsch 549). The combined pressures of her best friend's death and her
own marriage force the Mina Murray who opens the novel to be submerged beneath the Mina Harker whom society mandates. Imitating
Lucy's mode of rebellion, Mina expresses her unconscious animosity
toward her marital role through hysterical symptomology. It should come
as no surprise, therefore, that Dracula visits Mina on the night of October
1st, thirty-seven days after her marriage to Jonathan and the very evening
when she is forcibly removed from the masculine circle of knowledge.

Mina's being is now submerged beneath a performance dictated
by Victorian discourse. The internal struggle provoked by gender constraints can be seen when Van Helsing places her under hypnosis: Mina
exhibits the classic symptoms of the Freudian conflict between id and
superego, her repressed self is at war with her feminine identity performance. As Van Helsing describes her:

At first there is a sort of negative condition, as if some tie were loosened, and then the absolute freedom quickly follows; when, however, the freedom ceases the change-back or relapse comes quickly, preceded only by a spell of warning silence.... [She] bore all the signs of an internal struggle. (329)

Lucy's hysteria may also be traced to her forthcoming marriage. After Mrs. Westenra's death, her entire estate is left to the aristocratic Arthur Holmwood. On the heels of a struggle which brings mother and solicitor almost "into collision" over the matter, Lucy is left, as Seward reports, "either penniless or not so free as she should be to act regarding a matrimonial alliance" (167).

Gender norms are again disrupted by the inscription of male hysteria which, in contradiction to general belief, was recognised by Charcot as common (Medical 12). Jonathan's "violent brain fever," diagnosed by the doctors at the Hospital in Buda-Pesth after he escapes from Dracula's castle, marks the effect of gender roles as he exhibits the hysterical cycle of obsession and amnesia (99). He raves about "wolves and poison and blood; of ghosts and demons" and then returns to a conscious self who "does not remember anything that has happened to him for a long time past" (99, 103). In Dracula's castle his hysteria is expressed in obsessive thoughts of his own demise. His daytime moods are mirrored by his dreams and he is haunted by terrifying forebodings: "I know now the span of my life. God help me!" (41) He later writes, "These may be the last words I write in this diary" (50). Although the episode which precipitates Jonathan's hysteria is his harrowing entrapment in Dracula's castle, there are subtle suggestions that the specific event which haunts him may be his desire for the vampire women. Mina's intuitive perception of Jonathan's desire, expressed by her relief in learning another woman is not responsible for Jonathan's breakdown, is camouflaged by denial:

I believe the dear soul [Sister Agatha] thought I might be jealous lest my poor dear should have fallen in love with any other girl. The idea of *my* being jealous about Jonathan! And yet, my dear, let me whisper, I felt a thrill of joy through me when I *knew* that no other woman was a cause of trouble. (104)

This passage is complex because it displays a classic case of psychoanalytical displacement wherein the unconscious gains partial representation

139

through the transfer of "its intensity or meaning to an indifferent term, allowing the latter to act as its delegate, thus disguising it" (Grosz 87–88). Mina's ardent negation of jealousy suggests both her fear and hope that something may intercede before marriage.

Indeed, something almost does intercede, for the apogee of Jonathan's hysteria occurs during the famous encounter with Dracula's vampire women who are, in fact, the "other women" that Sister Agatha convinces Mina do not exist. Jonathan's harem desires, however, are immediately disrupted by the memory of social sanctions:

> I felt in my heart a wicked, burning desire that they would kiss me with those red lips. It is not good to note this down, lest some day it should meet Mina's eyes and cause her pain; but it is the truth. (37)

One month after their wedding, Jonathan recovers from his "brain fever." However, on the streets of London, Mina sees a beautiful woman at precisely the same moment that Jonathan spies Dracula and falls into a hysterical relapse (172). The juxtaposition of their recent wedding, the Count's reappearance, and the presence of an alluring woman functions as a reminder of the novel's preoccupation with socially-sanctioned and unsanctioned desires. Jonathan awakens, once again, in a state of total amnesia (173).

There are other incidents of hysteria that may be documented, including Van Helsing's hysterical laughter as he prepares to explain to Seward the nature of Lucy's "death." These offer no concrete proof that Stoker consciously employs Freudian theory in *Dracula*. My own belief, based on the subversive nature of the author's life in the theatre, the emerging evidence of his exposure to Freud, and a close reading of the text, is that not only was he aware of Freudian hypotheses, but he consciously manipulated hysteria and hypnosis as metaphors for the effects of repression. What is clear is that the tale of *Dracula* anticipates Freudian psychology. The novel's generally recognised sexuality and the accurate portrayal of hysteria and hypnosis in the vampire trance coincide exactly with the work being done by Freud at precisely the same time. Freud's studies between 1893 and 1895, the period which produced *Dracula*, investigate trauma, not causally in terms of the symptoms of hysteria, but as a catalyst which acts as an irritant, a "foreign body," an "invading alien," terminology descriptive of Dracula's intrusion into the lives of the novel's protagonists (Grosz 52, quoting Freud's 1895 "The Project for a Scientific Psychology" 6).

Ultimately, *Dracula* may be explored in the light of Freud's theories on instinct: the vampire, representing our sexuality, is the death instinct. Considering him to be worth dying for, we willingly sacrifice ourselves to our fundamental human needs. The vampire is, therefore, a proto-Freudian apprehension of post-Freudian sexual fetishism, an incubus who sucks our sexual desires out of our unconscious. As Foucault eloquently theorised about Freud's effect upon our culture: we have exchanged the stigmatised body for one of plenitude, our identity for a once nameless urge, and what we have gained is knowledge that was once thought of only in terms of madness (156). Like Dracula, the tenth scholar in the Scholomance who sacrificed his mortal soul to the devil in exchange for knowledge, we have forged a pact, and it is Faustian.[17]

Notes

1   The inclusion of French titles in the Rosenbach Museum's list of sources for *Dracula* indicates Stoker's reading knowledge of the language. The actual French titles are not given. However L.F. Alfred Maury, whose works include *Essai sur les Légendes Pieuses du Moyen-Age* and *La Magie et L'Astrologie dans L'Antiquité et au Moyen Age: ou, Étude sur les Superstitions Païennes qui sont Perpétuées jusqu'à jours*, a text on the supernatural that was only available in French, is listed as a source (Leatherdale 238).

2   Frederic William Henry Myers (1843–1901) was one of a group of Cambridge dons who, under the leadership of Henry Sidgwick, dominated the Psychical Research Society at the end of the nineteenth century. Their project was to discover scientific evidence for Spiritualism. He went on to author several works on occult phenomena including: *Human Personality and its Survival of Bodily Death* and *The Subliminal Consciousness* (Webb n.p.). Nina Auerbach also suggests that Stoker may have been familiar with Freud's teachings. She sees Seward's attempts to cure Renfield as "a weird forecast of the later Freud rationalizing the obsession of his Wolf Man and Rat Man" (23).

3   Christopher Craft mentions the use of hypnosis in connection with anesthesia in an interesting footnote to his article on gender inversion. He cites Havelock Ellis's theory that the influence of the "upper regions" (reason) may be suppressed by the use of drugs; hypnosis or anesthesia thereby relinquished control of the individual to the lower centres (pelvis) which then displaced the brain as the area of the body directing human actions. This medical theory offered one explanation for the prevailing idea that hypnosis could cause criminal or libidinous behaviour (Craft 193). Ellis's equation of hypnosis and drugs is played out in *Dracula* through the similarity between Seward's and Van Helsing's use of opiates and Dracula's use of entrancement. Both suppress mental influence and release repressed instincts.

4   The magnetic crisis is distinguished by convulsions, defined as "involuntary, jerky movements of all the members and of the whole body, contractions of the throat, subsultus of the hypochondrium and epigastrium [the dropping down of the area of the upper mid-abdomen], disordered vision, shrill cries, weeping, hiccoughing, and immoderate laughter" (Charcot, "Magnetism" 567). Of these symptoms, weeping is symptomatic of Mina's hysteria and immoderate laughter of Van Helsing's.

5   Franz Anton Mesmer, the founder of mesmerism or animal magnetism, fled France in 1792 when Robespierre rose to power. He had been persecuted by the French medical establishment and humiliated by the Academy of Sciences and the Royal Society of Medicine. Mesmer believed that the universe was a mediaeval microcosm/macrocosm where equinoxes coincidental with planetary conjunctions, eclipses, and full moons were named as causations of earthly upheavals such as typhoons, earthquakes, floods, and plagues. Charcot delineates the basic tenets of mesmerism: "Mesmer believed in a fluid diffused everywhere, by the aid of which the heavenly bodies, the earth, and animate bodies exert among themself *(sic)* a reciprocal influence.... [He] believed that [this fluid] is reflected and refracted like light, is communicated from one body to another, is propagated, is augmented by sound, and is capable of being accumulated, concentrated, and transported" ("Magnetism" 568).

6   See note 3 for an explanation of the effects of hypnosis on the upper and lower body.

7   Much of the material in *Dracula* on Transylvanian superstitions was taken from Emily Gerard's article, "Transylvanian Superstitions," published in Knowles's periodical.

8   These diseases are characterised by nervous exhaustion and vague complaints ungoverned by discernible physical causes, symptoms that this article demonstrates are identical with symptoms resulting from a vampire attack.

9   Ewart speaks of the Darwinian aspects of hypnosis and telepathy when he responds to the suggestion of Dr. Voisin, whose private practice was in the Salpêtrière near Charcot's institu-

Moss • The Psychiatrist's Couch: Hypnosis, Hysteria, and Proto-Freudian Performance in *Dracula*

tion, that the "soul, individuality and consciousness, can be annihilated or exchanged for those of another person by the mechanical process of exciting their corresponding brain-notions.... What are love and hate if a magnet applied to a hypnotized patient can transform one into another?" (259) Ewart replies: "The subject put like this is somewhat appalling, and gives rise to an alarming thought that our normal mental life is very closely allied to insanity and graduates away into it by extremely fine transitions. If in the course of human history our nervous system has been gradually developed into its present complex form, it follows that these structures, which have to do with the highest intellectual processes, have been evolved the most recently; consequently they would be the least deeply organized, and therefore the least stable" (259).

10 "Cesare Lombroso (1836–1909) is sometimes called the father of modern criminology. He is still remembered for his belief that there existed among the human species the type of born criminal who was a throwback to his primordial ancestors" (Wolf 403).

11 The thin line between imagined and corporeal symptomology is indicated by the term *"malades imaginaires"* which Dr. A.T. Schofield applies to hysteria, commenting that "it is quite true that if a man is so ill as to imagine he is ill when he is not ill, he must be very ill indeed" (415).

12 There are a few exceptions to the critical tendency to see gender in *Dracula* as an unquestioning inscription of Victorian mores. Carol Senf in her article, *"Dracula*: Stoker's Response to the New Woman," mentions the influence of Stoker's mother, Charlotte, upon the character of Mina. Charlotte Stoker was a feminist who returned to social welfare work after her children were grown. Stephanie Demetrakopoulos also recognises that Stoker evinces feminist leanings. Certainly the character of Mina suggests a woman other than the overly stereotyped "angel in the house" that has now become a part of Victorian mythology.

13 The internal subversion of gender expectations is visible through the gaps in the narratives of Lucy, Mina, and Jonathan. Although on the surface these three seem to enact the traditional gender roles, subtle disruptions in the portrayal of their yearnings indicate that those desires are culturally scripted rather than genuine. Of course, the occurrence of hysterical breakdown, according to feminist theory, suggests unconscious psychological rebellion against cultural gender scripts.

14 For Arthur, the performance of gender norms is not a burden since, according to Foucault, his aristocratic status constructs him as the author and enforcer of gender norms. As Foucault posits, awareness of the relationship of population to resources only resulted in greater stress upon the health of the ruling class. "The primary concern was not repression of the sex of the classes to be exploited, but rather the body, vigor, longevity, progeniture, and descent of the classes that 'ruled'" (Foucault 123).

15 Periodical articles attest to the increase in cases of hysteria during the nineteenth century: "It is a pretty widespread opinion that nervous diseases, and especially hysteria, have alarmingly increased during the last decades, and that they are about to increase much more" (544). The proposed causes for this increase are multiple and beyond the scope of this article, but for various reasons, including increased reporting and documentation, the incidence of hysteria was greater than it had been since the mediaeval epidemics.

16 Greenway cites William Acton's *The Functions and Disorders of the Reproductive Organs in Childhood, Youth, Adult Age and Advanced Life Considered in Their Physiological, Social and Moral Relations*, 3rd edition, published by Blakeston in 1871.

17 For a brief discussion of the theory that Dracula's vampirism owes its origins to his position as the tenth initiate in the Scholomance, see Carol Margaret Davison's chapter on Dracula and Jack the Ripper in this volume. I am indebted to her for bringing it to my attention and suggesting that Dracula's Faustian pact has connections with that which Foucault claims is common to the twentieth century.

REFERENCES

Auerbach, Nina. *Woman and the Demon: The Life of a Victorian Myth.* Cambridge: Harvard UP, 1982.

Belford, Barbara. *Bram Stoker: A Biography of the Author of Dracula.* New York: Knopf, 1996.

Butler, Judith. *Gender Trouble: Feminism and the Subversion of Identity.* New York: Routledge, 1990.

—. "Performative Acts and Gender Constitution: An Essay in Phenomenology and Feminist Theory." *Performing Feminism: Feminist Critical Theory and Theatre.* Ed. Sue-Ellen Case. Baltimore: Johns Hopkins UP, 1990. 270–82.

Charcot, [Jean-Martin]. "Hypnotism and Crime." *Forum* 9 (1890): 159–68.

—. "Magnetism and Hypnotism." *Forum* 8 (1890): 566–77.

Cowper, Katie. "The Decline of Reserve Among Women." *The Nineteenth Century* 27 (1890): 65–71.

Craft, Christopher. "'Kiss Me with Those Red Lips': Gender and Inversion in Bram Stoker's *Dracula*." *Dracula: The Vampire and the Critics.* Ed. Margaret L. Carter. Ann Arbor and London: UMI Research Press, 1988. 167–94.

Deats, Sara. *Sex, Gender, and Desire in the Plays of Christopher Marlowe.* Newark: University of Delaware Press. Forthcoming in 1997.

Demetrakopoulos, Stephanie. "Feminism, Sex Role Exchanges, and Other Subliminal Fantasies in Bram Stoker's *Dracula*." *Frontiers: a Journal of Women Studies* 2 (1977): 105–13.

Dijkstra, Bram. *Idols of Perversity: Fantasies of Feminine Evil in Fin de Siècle Culture.* New York: Oxford UP, 1986.

Ewart, C. Theodore. "The Power of Suggestion." *The Nineteenth Century* 28 (1890): 253–59.

Faas, Ekbert. *Retreat into the Mind: Victorian Poetry and the Rise of Psychiatry.* Princeton: Princeton UP, 1988.

Farson, Daniel. *The Man Who Wrote Dracula: A Biography of Bram Stoker.* New York: St. Martin's, 1975.

Flower, B[enjamin] O. "The Ascent of Life; or Psychic Laws and Forces of Nature." *Arena* 9 (1893): 1–25.

—. "Hypnotism and Its Relation to Psychical Research." *Arena* 5 (1892): 316–34.

—. "Hypnotism and Mental Suggestion." *Arena* 6 (1892): 208–18.

Foucault, Michel. *The History of Sexuality: An Introduction.* Trans. Robert Hurley. New York: Vintage, 1980.

Freud, Sigmund. *Civilization and its Discontents.* 1927. Trans. James Strachey. New York: Norton, 1961.

—. *On Dreams.* 1900. Trans. James Strachey. New York: Norton, 1952.

—. *Quelques considérations pour une étude comparative de paralysies motrices organiques et hystériques.* n.p.: C. Herissey, 1893.

Gaullieur, Henry. "The Wonder of Hypnotism and the Transfer of Sensitiveness From Men to Inert Substances." *Arena* 15 (1896): 33–41.

Gerard, Emily. "Transylvanian Superstitions." *The Nineteenth Century* 18 (1895): 130–50.

Greenway, John L. "Seward's Folly: *Dracula* as a Critique of 'Normal Science.'" *Stanford Literature Review* 3 (1986): 213–230.

Grosz, Elizabeth. *Jacques Lacan: A Feminist Introduction*. London: Routledge, 1990.

Hart, Ernest. "The Eternal Gullible." *Century Illustrated Month Magazine* 48 (1894): 833–39.

—. "The Revival of Witchcraft." *The Nineteenth Century* 33 (1883): 347–68.

Hirsch, William Dr. "Epidemics of Hysteria." *Popular Science Monthly* 49 (1896): 544–49.

Holcombe, Lee. *Victorian Ladies at Work: Middle-Class Working Women in England and Wales 1850–1914*. Hamden: Archon Books, 1973.

Houghton, Walter E. *Wellesley Index to Victorian Periodicals: 1824–1900*. Vol. 2. Toronto: U of Toronto P, 1972.

"Hypnotism in Criminal Investigation." *Littell's Living Age* 19 (1893): 704.

Irigaray, Luce. "The Power of Discourse and the Subordination of the Feminine: Questions." 1985. Trans. Catherine Porter and Carolyn Burke. *The Irigaray Reader*. Ed. Margaret Whitford. Oxford: Blackwell, 1994. 118–39.

Janet, Pierre. *The Major Symptoms of Hysteria: Fifteen Lectures Given in the Medical School of Harvard University*. New York and London: Hafner, 1965.

Jarvis, Stinson. "The Ascent of Life: or Psychic Laws and Forces in Nature." *Arena* 9 (1893): 1–15.

Jorden, Edward. *A Briefe Discourse of a Disease Called the Suffocation of the Mother*. London: John Windet, 1603.

Kempin, Emily. "Hypnotism and Its Relation to Jurisprudence." *Arena* 2 (1890): 278–91.

Kingsbury, George C. "Hypnotism, Crime, and the Doctors." *The Nineteenth Century* 29 (1891): 145–53.

Leatherdale, Clive. *The Origins of Dracula*. 1987. Westcliff-on-Sea: Desert Island Books, 1995.

Mason, R. Osgood. "Concerning a Psychic Medium in Hypnotism." *Arena* 3 (1891): 541–54.

Medical Heritage Society. *Pathfinders in Psychiatry*. Chicago: Medical Heritage Society, 1973.

Mesmer, F. A. *Mesmerism: A Translation of the Original Scientific and Medical Writings of F.A. Mesmer*. Trans. George Bloch. Los Altos: William Kaufmann, 1980.

Myers, Frederic William Henry. *Human Personality and its Survival of Bodily Death*. New York: Longman, 1903.

—. *The Subliminal Consciousness*. New York: Arno, 1976.

Moore, J. Preston. "Hypnotism." *Overland* 16 (1890): 32–44.

Pearsall, Ronald. *The Worm in the Bud: the World of Victorian Sexuality*. Toronto: Macmillan, 1969.

Poole, William Frederick. *Poole's Index to Periodical Literature*. 6 vols. 1892–96. Gloucester, Massachusetts: Peter Smith, 1958.

Schofield, A.T. "Nervousness and Hysteria." *Leisure Hour* 38 (1889): 412–15.

Senf, Carol A. "*Dracula*: Stoker's Response to the New Woman." *Victorian Studies* 26 (1982): 33–49.

Stoker, Bram. "Actor-Managers." *The Nineteenth Century* 27 (June 1890): 1040–51.

—. "The Censorship of Fiction." *The Nineteenth Century* 64 (1908): 479–87.

—. *Dracula*. 1897. Oxford: Oxford UP, 1983.

—. "Irving and Stage Lighting." *The Nineteenth Century* 69 (1911): 903–12.

—. *Personal Reminiscences of Henry Irving*. Vol. 1. New York: Macmillan, 1906. 2 vols.

—. "Question of a National Theatre." *The Nineteenth Century* 63 (1908): 734–42.

Strachey, James. "Introduction." *Civilization and its Discontents*. Sigmund Freud. 1927. Trans. James Strachey. New York: Norton, 1961. 5-10.

Veith, Ilza. *Hysteria: The History of a Disease*. Chicago and London: The University of Chicago Press, 1965.

Webb, James. *The Society for Psychical Research Report on the Theosophical Society*. New York: Arno, 1976.

Wolf, Leonard. *The Essential Dracula: The Definitive Annotated Edition of Bram Stoker's Classic Novel*. 1975. New York: Plume, 1993.

Blood Brothers: Dracula and Jack the Ripper

Carol Margaret Davison

> "... a suggestion also floated in America that *Dracula* is actually a cryptic novelisation of the Jack the Ripper mystery based on certain secret information that was only known to Bram Stoker and a close circle of his friends!"
>
> (Haining 3)

THE YEAR AFTER THE INITIAL PUBLICATION OF HIS compelling thriller, *Dracula*, Bram Stoker was asked to write an introduction to the novel's first foreign-language translation.[1] Entitled *Makt Myrkranna* (*Powers of Darkness*), *Dracula* became available to Icelandic readers in 1901. The curious nature of this linguistic choice aside, two things are particularly noteworthy about Stoker's introduction to *Makt Myrkranna*: his attempt to lend his novel credibility as a historic chronicle, and the significant comparison he draws between it and certain actual macabre events in fin de siècle London. Despite Jonathan Harker's closing note to the novel which foregrounds the unbelievable nature of the *Dracula* "manuscript" — he writes, "We could hardly ask anyone even did we wish to, to accept these as proofs of so wild

a story" (378) — Stoker effectively assumes his Count's role as a bound-
ary-blurrer by extending his novel's crucial fiction-reality theme beyond
its textual parameters in the introduction to the Icelandic edition. There,
Stoker explains that "for obvious reasons,... [he] changed the names of the
people and places concerned." He makes the further claim that "Both
Jonathan Harker and his wife (who is a woman of character) and Dr.
Seward are ... [his] friends and have been for so many years, and ... [he]
never doubted that they were telling the truth" (8). Finally, Stoker attempts
to place his narrative within an actual historical context. Referring to
Dracula's demonic London transactions, he writes:

> I state again that this mysterious tragedy which is here
> described is completely true in all its external respects,
> though naturally I have reached a different conclusion on
> certain points than those involved in the story. But the
> events are incontrovertible, and so many people know of
> them that they cannot be denied. This series of crimes has
> not yet passed from the memory — a series of crimes
> which appear to have originated from the same source,
> and which at the time created as much repugnance in peo-
> ple everywhere as the notorious murders of Jack the
> Ripper.... (7–8)

That the Jack the Ripper serial prostitute slayings should be mentioned in
connection with *Dracula* is not surprising. This reference directly contra-
dicts Stoker's great-nephew's claim that "there is no hint in the novel
[*Dracula*] or any of his writings of either the Ripper's violence or the subsequent panic" (Farson 152).[2] It serves, in fact, to support various critical
claims by such writers as Grigore Nandris, Phyllis Roth, Clive
Leatherdale, and Bernard Davies, that the Ripper slayings were one of several contemporary phenomena that were incorporated into *Dracula's* dense
narrative whirlpool.[3] Curiously, fiction and reality did actually overlap to
some degree for, as Belford relates, 1888 was not only "the year Jack the
Ripper terrorized Whitechapel, bringing evil into the drawing rooms of
Mayfair and Kensington." it was also the year in which Stoker first conceptualised *Dracula*, "a story that would intermingle Shakespeare's dark
psychology with contemporary evils" (202).

Moreover, it could be argued that Dracula's looming spectre was
discernible in the shadows of the popular media representations of the
bloodthirsty and deviant Whitechapel predator. As Judith Walkowitz outlines in her study *City of Dreadful Delight: Narratives of Sexual Danger in*

Late-Victorian London, Gothic literature was, in fact, indispensable to popular media portraits of the Ripper:

> A final element signified by the "mystery" of the [Jack the Ripper] murders was sexual. Faced with a "senseless crime," press commentary invoked the figure of the Gothic sex beast, a "man monster" motivated by "bloodthirsty lust" who "goes forth stealthily and takes his victims when and where he already pleases," akin to the "were wolf" of "Gothic fiction." Declared the *Daily Telegraph*, "we are left ... to form unpleasant visions of roving lunatics distraught by homicidal mania or bloodthirsty lust ... or finally we may dream of monsters, or ogres." (197)

These images of werewolves and Gothic "man monster" sex beasts driven by "bloodthirsty lust" had obvious Draculaesque reverberations, as did the unsettling contemporary rumours of vampirism. As Walter Dews relates in his book *I Caught Crippen*, "People allowed their imagination to run riot. There was talk of black magic and vampires" (125). Perhaps the most direct reference to vampires during the Ripper Terror was provided by the *East London Advertiser* which remarked:

> It is so impossible to account, on any ordinary hypothesis, for these revolting acts of blood that the mind turns as it were instinctively to some theory of occult force, and myths of the Dark Ages arise before the imagination. Ghouls, vampires, blood-suckers ... take form and seize control of the excited fancy. (McNally and Florescu 146)

The poverty-stricken district of Whitechapel also served as the perfect Gothic backdrop for the Ripper's gruesome crimes. Arthur Morrison's description of Whitechapel for the readership of the *People's Palace Journal* in April of 1889 captures this area's haunting atmosphere of physical and moral decay:

> A horrible black labyrinth ... reeking from end to end with the vilest exhalations; its streets, mere kennels of horrid putrefaction; its every wall, its every object, slimy with the indigenous ooze of the place; swarming with human vermin, whose trade is robbery, and whose recre-

ation is murder; the catacombs of London — darker, more tortuous, and more dangerous than those of Rome, and supersaturated with foul life. (Frayling 203)

The image of Whitechapel as a zone of iniquity, the moral underbelly of London, is exquisitely captured in this journalistic passage. An animated, predatorial corpse who deprives others of their vitality, Dracula would be well-suited to this repulsive environment.

The blurring of the fiction-reality boundary between Jack and "Drac" is, at the very least, intriguing. Either figure could have been the subject of the aforementioned "man monster" portrait. Indeed, the predominant depiction of the Ripper provided by contemporary commentators illustrates just how interchangeable London's degenerate serial killer and Dracula could be. The nature of Jack and his crimes, for example, was described as follows:

> ... [the Ripper's] "lust murders" and sexual mutilations of prostitutes were ... unnatural alternatives to heterosexual copulation.... Often imagined as a seasoned urban traveler, the Ripper could move effortlessly and invisibly through the spaces of London, transgressing all boundaries, committing "his" murderous acts in public, under the cover of darkness, exposing the private parts of "public women" to open view. (Walkowitz 3)

The applicability of this description to *Dracula* where Stoker's protean Count, another seasoned traveler, exports vampirism, an unnatural alternative to heterosexual copulation, to England and exposes women's private desires to public view, would be nothing short of uncanny had Stoker not consciously forged the parallel. Thus, while Stoker's *Dracula* was rife with echoes of popular Ripper-obsessed penny "bloods," early Ripper coverage, especially that evoking lusty Gothic bloodsuckers and vampires, foreshadowed *Dracula*. In what was perhaps the apex of the Jack-"Drac" connection, "a suggestion ... floated in America that *Dracula* ... [was] actually a cryptic novelisation of the Jack the Ripper mystery based on certain secret information that was only known to Bram Stoker and a close circle of his friends!" (Haining 3). Given his tantalising introduction to the Icelandic edition, Stoker would no doubt have been delighted by this rumour.

The outrageous claim that Stoker had "secret information" of the Ripper murders aside, this rumour may be said to contain a kernel of truth. The present essay intends to illustrate how, albeit in a very loose way,

Dracula does, in fact, function as "a cryptic novelisation of the Jack the Ripper mystery." Although cursory comparisons have been made to date between Dracula and Jack the Ripper, an in-depth, socio-culturally aware examination of their relationship has yet to be undertaken. While remaining sensitive to the existence of significant distinctions between the historic and the fictional monster, I will focus on the semiotics underpinning the respective portraits of these two figures in an attempt to uncover certain deep-seated social preoccupations in fin de siècle England. In this assessment of the politics and poetics of representation, the issue of the Ripper's true identity actually pales into insignificance. Instead, the primary interest resides with who people *thought* the Ripper was, and the ideological significance of how s/he was represented in the popular worldview.

Indeed, it may be argued that the Ripper, like Stoker's vampire in later cinematic adaptations, actually assumed a life of his own, becoming a type of literary character in his own right in a unique genre that came to be known as Ripperature. As Clive Bloom insightfully notes, "Jack the Ripper [was] given his *nom de guerre* by Fleet Street, [and] was the first major figure to offer himself to, and to become, a creation of journalism." Although Jack's letters "may have been the work of an entrepreneurial journalist providing 'copy' for himself" (123), they are also "a form of *true life confession* heightened to the level of fiction which embraces a 'cockney' persona, a sense of black humour, a melodramatic villain ('them curses of coppers') and a ghoul (sending 'innerds'), and mixes it with a sense of the dramatic and a feeling for a rhetorical climax" (124). In the light of this alternate legendary existence, it must be underlined that fictional monsters not only function, as Michel Foucault and Fred Botting argue, as monitory figures borne of social crises who warn society about potential evils and impending disorder (Foucault 69–70, Botting 140), they also reveal much about the desires and anxieties of the societies within which they are, like Mary Shelley's Frankenstein monster, "created."[4]

What is particularly interesting about the Ripper murders in relation to Stoker's *Dracula* is that both tapped into what Daniel Pick describes as "a distinct constellation of contemporary fears" (71). While *Dracula* is the subject of Pick's statement, Walkowitz makes what amounts to the same claim with regard to the Ripper murders when she explains how his story had a "capacity to play out an elaborate repertoire of contemporary anxieties — from heterosexual violence, to the 'lavender menace,' to the specters of imperial and domestic industrial decline" (4). As the Jack the Ripper and *Dracula* narratives essentially played out a constellation of similar fears ranging from syphilis to alien invasion, I take a certain poetic licence in describing these two predators as blood brothers. However, unlike the "blood brother" crusaders in Stoker's novel (Spear 185) who oppose Dracula and seal a fraternal pact through a series of Christ-like blood transfusions intended to save Lucy Westenra's life, Jack the Ripper and Dracula are bloodthirsty siblings whose kinship is sealed with degenerate, anti-Christian, "black mass"-style acts involving sexual perversion, infection, and death.

Of special importance to this examination is the fact that Dracula and Jack the Ripper may also be said to be blood brothers along ethnic lines. As will be illustrated, both were figured as Jewish, an especially loaded and negative designation which constituted a crucial component in the aforementioned constellation of fin de siècle fears. In fact, during Stoker's era, Jewishness functioned as a signifier under whose aegis the fear of syphilis, alien invasion, sexual perversion, and political subversion, stood united. Judith Walkowitz and Sander Gilman have outlined how "the Ripper ... [was] virtually made to order as an icon for Anglo-America's imagination of the Jew, and itself, at the fin de siècle." Of significance to the Anglo-American Christian brotherhood in *Dracula* is the fact that in "the case of the Ripper narratives, the Jew ... [was] made to embody more pointed threats to the continuity of a newly urgent Anglo-Saxon 'brotherhood,' forged between Britons and Americans in 'a larger patriotism of race'" (Blair 490).

As my forthcoming dissertation[5] outlines, this Gothicisation of the Jew as demonic Other who violated sacred Christian blood-related rituals and taboos long predated the 1890s. While certain of these anti-Semitic seeds were sown in the Middle Ages when the image of the Jew as devil was extremely popular, the reentry of the Jews into England in the seventeenth century precipitated many explosive debates relating to the nature of British economic activity and national identity which were, by the close of the eighteenth century, cryptically channelled into Gothic literature. What I call the cabalistic backdrop of early Gothic fiction — a backdrop that featured the Spanish Inquisition, anti-Christian secret societies (or cabals[6]), secret sciences, the violation of familial bonds (e.g. patricide and incest), and popular millenarian ideas — was grounded in the fear of a social apocalypse like the French Revolution occurring in Britain. Many believed that such a cataclysm would be the result of politically subversive secret societies operated by avaricious Jews advancing their own socio-economic interests to the detriment of British "progress." Compounding this was the threat, as represented by the Great Sanhedrin in France, of Jews gaining national citizenship, thus annihilating the protective distinction between native Briton and foreign Jew. Indeed, the question may be asked, what better figure to press into Gothic literature's service than the anti-Christian figure *par excellence*, the stereotypical vampiric and diseased Jew who was regularly depicted as hyper-sexual and effeminate?[7] Add to these grotesque abnormalities the putative portrait of the male Jew as one who menstruated four times annually (Osborne 129)[8], and engaged in such deviant acts as cannibalism, ritual circumcision, ritual slaughter involving Christian children, and host desecration, and one would be hard pressed to find a more established, pathological bogey in the closet of Christian Britain.

As Dracula's Jewish figuration and the "Jacob the Ripper" theory (Walkowitz 203) illustrate, this sinister Jewish bogey was alive and kicking in the late nineteenth century when, rather notably, his existence was not limited to Gothic literature. Within that fictional domain, however, he rears his head in Oscar Wilde's *The Picture of Dorian Gray* (1891) as the Calibanesque "hideous Jew" theatre manager (80, 48) to whom the "sacred" Sibyl Vane (51) is effectively enslaved by debt. More significantly, he appears as the mesmerising Svengali in George du Maurier's *Trilby* (1894), another deceptive, theatre-associated figure "of Jewish aspect, well-featured but sinister" (11) who threatens to reduce the upstanding British "angel in the house" to the status of seductress. Described by Stoker's longstanding friend du Maurier as "a sticky, haunting, long, lean, uncanny, black spider-cat, if there is such an animal outside a bad dream" (84), Svengali is clearly a relative of Stoker's animalistic Count. In fact, with his "big yellow teeth baring themselves in a mongrel canine snarl" and his ability to "oppress ... and weigh ... on ... [Trilby] like an incubus" (104), Svengali's resemblance to Stoker's own nightmarish incubus is remarkable.[9]

Beyond the realm of Gothic literature, Sir Richard Burton, another of Stoker's close and admired friends, was vital to the dissemination of anti-Semitic ideas in the 1890s. Although anti-Semitism was, as Walkowitz argues, "one articulation of a rising tide of nationalism and racism orchestrated by the popular media" (203), Burton's *The Jew, the Gypsy and El Islam*, published posthumously in 1898, was outrageous in its anti-Semitic statements. In addition to upholding the longstanding blood libel[10] and shamelessly describing the Jews as a "parasitic race" (17), Burton's work sought an "ample motive" for the "tumultuous and wholesale massacres" of Jews throughout history (116). He found such justification in what he implied was the eternal, nefarious Jewish character. It is noteworthy that Dracula could have been the model for Burton's scathing, anti-Semitic portrait:

> His fierce passions and fiendish cunning, combined with
> abnormal powers of intellect, with intense vitality, and

> with a persistency of purpose which the world has rarely seen, and whetted moreover by a keen thirst for blood engendered by defeat and subjection, combined to make him the deadly enemy of all mankind, whilst his unsocial and iniquitous Oral Law contributed to inflame his wild lust of pelf, and to justify the crimes suggested by spite and superstition. (117)

Lusting after blood and pelf and figured as "the deadly enemy of all mankind," Stoker's Count is clearly a product of longstanding anti-Semitic stereotypes. Fleshing out Burton's cameo portrait, Stoker adds the more precise details of Dracula's role as an Eastern European "occidental tourist" (Arata 621) with a stereotypical Jewish physiognomy: once in England he is described as having a hooked nose and "pointed beard" (*Dracula* 137). Dracula also hoards "gold of all kinds, Roman, and British, and Austrian, and Hungarian, and Greek and Turkish money, [which Harker discovers] covered with a film of dust" (47). Compounding this portrait of avarice, the Count is an obsessive treasure-seeker (12–13). He has a distinct odour, or *foetor judaicus* (47) — one of the men who moves the fifty cases of common earth into Carfax comments that one "might 'ave smelled ole Jerusalem in it" (228). Dracula is also a traditional social polluter who is often accompanied by rats, a longstanding symbol of the plague. It was believed that Jews spread this and other infections while, thanks to demonic pacts with the devil, remaining immune themselves.[11] Finally, Stoker incorporates a secret society connection into his vampire portrait by way of Dracula's participation in the Scholomance, an involvement, it is suggested, that probably resulted in his vampire state.[12]

Turning to the case of Jack the Ripper — who, in true Dracula fashion, occasionally consumed his victims — one discovers that many of these anti-Semitic stereotypes were also at play. Not only was the Ripper suspected of being of a "marked Hebrew type" (Walkowitz 204), he was specifically thought by many to be a Jewish *shochet* or ritual slaughterer. This figure was bastardised and demonised in the popular media as a "kosher butcher," one who was perhaps engaged in a type of ritual slaughter of harlots as decreed in the Talmud (Sharkey 115). As Sander Gilman states, "The reality, at least that reality which terrified the London of 1888, was that the victims were butchered" (*Jew's* 112). A result, in part, of the repeated assertion "that no Englishman could have perpetrated such a horrible crime," the popular "Jacob the Ripper" theory led, Walkowitz argues, to "two local developments: denunciation of Jews at the inquests as ritual murderers and widespread intimidation of Jews throughout the East End"

(203). As Christopher Frayling relates, "Official visits were made to kosher abbatoirs, [and] two ritual slaughtermen were arrested" as Ripper suspects (200). This Ripper-as-*shochet* idea is actually incorporated into *Dracula* in the heart-racing scene where the Count is cornered by Van Helsing's crew and figuratively bleeds money after being cut by Harker's Kukri knife. Before taunting them, as was the Ripper's wont, that the girls they love are his, Dracula says, "You think to baffle me, you — with your pale faces all in a row, like sheep in a butcher's. You shall be sorry yet, each one of you!" (306).

As to the Jewish political threat represented by Jack, especially after September 30th, the night of the double murders of Lizzie Stride and Catherine Eddowes, Jewish "revolutionaries" and socialists came under increasing suspicion. While Stride's "body had been discovered in front of the Working Men's International Club, a political club mostly frequented by Jewish socialists, whose members had just finished hearing a lecture on 'Judaism and Socialism,'" a portion of Eddowes's bloodstained apron was found in front of a building on Goulston Street which was inhabited by Jews. Although it is still debated, some argue that the Ripper's scrawled chalk message above the location of Eddowes's apron which read "The Juwes are not the men that will be blamed for nothing" (Walkowitz 204), attested, due to its poor English construction and orthography, to Jack's Eastern European, Jewish background (Gilman, *Jew's* 122).

The "Jacob the Ripper" theory was further supported on the third of December when *The Times* reported that the Ripper was a Russian "nihilist" and a member of a "secret society". While Clive Bloom argues that Jack became "the focal point for an attack on foreigners (in particular Russians) and especially foreigners who … [were] bent on undermining society in secret via covertly ritualised murder" (120–1), the fact is that the "Russians" entering England in the 1890s were predominantly Jews. At a time when England was confronting her position as a declining imperial power and was fearful of revolution (Knight 52), she was also experiencing a tremendous influx of Jews fleeing pogroms, expulsions, and anti-Jewish legislation in Russia and Eastern Europe. According to Jules Zanger in his article "A Sympathetic Vibration: *Dracula* and the Jews," the number of foreign Jews in England increased by approximately six hundred percent between 1881 and 1900 (34). In this climate, the poverty-stricken area of Whitechapel where the Ripper conducted his bloody business became so densely populated with Jewish immigrants that it was called "Jew-town" (Feldman 56). In a country in the throes of an "economic and … social malaise" (Hobsbawm 36) that involved massive unemployment and riots (Feldman 58), the influx of foreign workers who would "take less wages than the native worker and owing to ... [their] lower standard of existence ... maintain ... [themselves] on what would mean starvation to an Englishman" (59) was bound to generate incredible anxiety.

Perhaps Stoker's finest sleight of hand in *Dracula* involves the yoking of this "Jewish" economic and political threat with a sexual fear also associated with the Jew. The fin de siècle was a period of intense moral panic when, in the face of shocking numbers of syphilitics, doctors predicted "the unavoidable 'syphilisation' of the Western world" (Showalter, *Sexual* 188). The terror of contracting syphilis reached such epidemic proportions that the word "syphilophobia" was coined to describe this pathological fear. Within this environment, Jews were particularly anathema as they had been closely related to the spread and incidence of syphilis since the fifteenth century when the disease first appeared in Europe where it was "commonly called the Peste of the Marranos." As Sander Gilman further relates, "literature on syphilis in the nineteenth century contains a substantial discussion of the special relationship of Jews to the transmission and meaning of syphilis" (Gilman, *Freud* 61). This false charge was advanced in various forms, as in Joseph Banister's anti-Semitic work *England Under the Jews* (1901), in which there is "a fixation on the spread of blood and skin diseases" (Gilman, *Jew's* 124).

A type of displaced sex act that involves infection, vampirism tapped into contemporary syphilophobia. At the core of both the Jack and "Drac" narratives, is the association between the Jew and the prostitute who were regarded, in the popular worldview of the period, as syphilis carriers.[13] While there are no prostitutes *per se* in *Dracula*, Lucy's New Woman-style, polyandrous longing to marry three men (59) results in her vampiric transformation into the Bloofer Lady, a supreme and terrifying anti-mother who preys on children in and around Hampstead Heath (178). As *The Westminster Gazette* report in Stoker's novel makes clear, these children were akin to the Ripper's victims as they went missing at night and were discovered with their throats slightly torn or wounded (177).[14] It is also noteworthy that Lucy's metamorphosis into the seductive, prostitute-like Bloofer Lady is presaged by the series of blood transfusions undertaken by Dracula's opponents. Van Helsing explains that this blood-mixing act is a form of marital bond which transforms the "sweet maid" Lucy into a "polyandrist" (176). Rather significantly, this term was also used in Ripper journalism as a euphemism for the word prostitute. In one article concerning the Whitechapel murders, for example, a *Star* reporter was said to have "made inquiries among a number of 'polyandrous' women in the East End" (Walkowitz 203).

What has further bearing on a reading of *Dracula* is the fact that images of vampire women were abundant in fin de siècle culture where they generally represented gold-digging, syphilitic prostitutes. As Bram Dijkstra bluntly describes their presence in the iconography of Stoker's day, "Female vampires were ... everywhere." Dijkstra's description of their symbolic significance illuminates the dynamic between Dracula and the sexually-voracious, polyandrous women in Stoker's novel:

> By 1900 the vampire had come to represent woman as the personification of everything negative that linked sex, ownership, and money. She symbolized the sterile hunger for seed of the brainless, instinctually polyandrous — even if still virginal — child-woman. She also came to represent the equally sterile lust for gold of woman as the eternal polyandrous prostitute. She was the absinth drinker, her fever for the gold of man's essence fed by her addiction, who was seen by Félicien Rops as lurking in the alleyways of Paris. She was the woman cloaked in darkness who beckoned man to his death ... (351)

Like Dracula, the ultimate personification of the *Eros-Thanatos* connection, fin de siècle prostitutes seduced by way of the fruits of decadence, offering total submersion in carnal, worldly pleasures. As a member of the undead, however, Stoker's vampire openly exhibits the price to be paid for such decadence — a living corpse, Dracula is an updated version of the persecuted Wandering Jew figure who is bound to the flesh and denied any spiritual peace.[15]

The polyandrous woman's association with the Jew is actually a conventional motif that dates back, at least, to the sixteenth century when "Jewish usury was likened to the practice of female prostitution." As one observer then reported, "the 'beastly trade of courtesans and cruel trade of Jews is suffered for gain' in Italy; both 'suck from the meanest to be squeezed by the greatest'" (Shapiro 99). Sander Gilman's chapter on Jack the Ripper in *The Jew's Body* examines their traditional "deviant" coupling on the margins of polite society. Posing "'dangers' to the economy, both fiscal and sexual, of the state" (120) as they "represent[ed] a realm of exchange divorced from production" (Gallagher 43), the prostitute and the Jew were united as "lovers of filthy lucre" (Shapiro 99). Their perversion lay in their "sexualized relationship to capital"[16] which entailed regarding money "as a substitute for higher values, for love and beauty" (Gilman, *Jew's* 124). This eroticisation of capital is evident in *Dracula* when Mina

Harker contrasts the vampire's perverse gold-hoarding activity which renders capital unproductive, to the healthy monetary circulation practised by the wealthy Christian Englishman, Lord Godalming, and the American adventurer, Quincey Morris, who unreservedly finance the Dracula crusade (356). These divergent attitudes towards money, "the blood of civilization" (Osborne 131), are both reflected and sexualised in the novel's complex blood thematics: while the Christian crusaders generously provide blood transfusions to their beloved domestic angels, Dracula infects them while draining them to the point of undeath.

Like William Godwin's *St. Leon* (1799), one of the earliest Gothic novels, Stoker's *Dracula* conceptualises the primary menace to Britain as one involving its "Judaisation."[17] This demonic process also involves that nation's figurative "feminisation."[18] Translated into sexual terms, virile Christians were threatened with the circumcised genitalia of the male Jew that, in the familiar racist folklore, were regarded as deviant and symbolically castrated. This threat is certainly central to *Dracula*. Imprisoned in a labyrinthine Transylvanian castle, and at the mercy of three sexually voracious vampire women who love raw babies as a midnight snack, Jonathan Harker assumes the female role in Stoker's compelling, gender-bending, Gothic thriller. Nowhere is this made more more obvious than in the desperate final lines of Harker's opening travelogue of terror when he writes, "At least God's mercy is better than that of these monsters, and the precipice is steep and high. At its foot man may sleep — *as a man*" (53). Stoker's lifesize *vagina dentata*-style "creatures of the night," the pimp-like Count, and his growing harem of polyandrous women, then, threaten to drain the nation of its vitality and infect its sacrosanct Christian "family values." In this regard, it is noteworthy that syphilis specifically symbolised domestic dis-ease in the nineteenth century. As Elaine Showalter outlines, "Whereas in the Renaissance syphilis functioned as a religious symbol of the disease in the spirit, and during the Restoration became a political metaphor for the disease in the state, fin-de-siècle English culture treats it as a symbol of the disease in the family" (*Syphilis* 89).

In his recent provocative work, *T.S. Eliot, Anti-Semitism, and Literary Form*, Anthony Julius provides some sense of the socio-historical factors underpinning two of the foremost fin de siècle spectres:

> In late nineteenth-century Europe, misogyny and anti-Semitism were frequent partners. This alliance represented a reaction, in part, to a certain coincidence in demand by women and Jews for emancipation, especially in Germany and Austria. (19)

This dual threat was found, among other places, at the core of the writings of Viennese theorist, Otto Weininger. In his hugely popular work, *Sex and Character* (1903), Weininger connected women, significantly described along traditional anti-Semitic lines as "human parasites" (Dijkstra 219), with various "degenerate races," among them the Jews. According to Weininger, Judaism was "saturated with femininity" (220), and both women and Jews were decadent creatures devoid of moral sensibility. As Weininger expressed it:

> Greatness is absent from the nature of the woman and the Jew, the greatness of morality, or the greatness of evil. In the Aryan man, the good and bad principles of Kant's religious philosophy are ever present, ever in strife. In the Jew and the woman, good and evil are not distinct from one another. (221)

As Bram Dijkstra notes, "Many of his [Weininger's] ideas had already been elevated to the status of commonplaces among the intellectuals of the 1890s" (218). Further, many of these intellectuals were British. As Ford Madox Ford observed, Weininger's book "had spread through the serious male society of England as if it had been an epidemic" (218). Although British Jews had overcome the final hurdle in their fight for legal emancipation in Britain by 1858 when "Baron Lionel Rothschild was allowed to use a modified oath and take his seat in Parliament" (Stone 235), fiery debates continued over the exact nature of the role of the Jews in what was still regarded as a Christian country. Anthony Trollope's offensive depiction of Jews in 1875 in *The Way We Live Now* as vulgar forgers, impostors, and shyster-style speculators inimical to the progress of honest Christian commerce, was not without a large, appreciative readership. Trollope's novel provides ample evidence that anti-Semitic stereotypes died hard in Victorian Britain. The advent of Zionism in the 1880s and 1890s, during a period of burgeoning right-wing nationalism — which was anti-foreigner, anti-socialist, and anti-liberal in nature (Hobsbawm 142) — added fuel to the well-stoked anti-Semitic fires raging throughout Britain and Europe, and confirmed what many long believed, namely that the Jews could never assimilate into any nation.[19]

In the light of the multifaceted Jewish menace and the advent of the proto-feminist New Woman's "movement,"[20] Daniel Pick's discussion of *Dracula* as a type of ritual text whose "task was to represent, externalise and kill off a distinct constellation of contemporary fears" (71) becomes more intelligible. With specific regard to the syphilis menace at the fin de siècle, the idea of ritual revenge was no stranger to the Jack the Ripper or *Dracula* tales. A popular rumour circulated that "the Ripper was a mad doctor avenging himself on prostitutes for a case of syphilis" (Showalter, *Syphilis* 94), and there is even one critic, Robert Tracy, who advances the highly controversial claim that Stoker, afflicted with syphilis,[21] reenacted in *Dracula*, "with a mixture of moral outrage and prurience, the 1888 murders of Whitechapel prostitutes attributed to Jack the Ripper" (45). Although the mirroring of the deviant woman with the deviant Jew was an established semiotic staple — in their earliest configuration they were considered to be both dangerously seductive and easily seduced by fleshly and material pleasures — it would seem that Stoker puts a spin and some closure on the Ripper tale in *Dracula*.

While, as Gilman argues, "the carrier of disease can only be eliminated by one who is equally corrupt and diseased" (*Jew's* 111) — thus only the deviant Jack the Ripper may kill the deviant prostitute — the tables are turned in *Dracula*. Dracula may respond to the call of the wild polyandrous woman lurking at the core of the sacred angel in the house who, as Mina explains, never entirely loses the taste of the original apple of sin (183). It is also the case, however, that woman, because she exists on the threshold of the sacred and the taboo, the angelic and the demonic, may tap into what Stoker describes as "the mother" in her (230) in order to effect the fall of the devil vampire. Just as female spiritualists, like the famous Georgina Weldon, tried their hand at armchair detection during the Ripper affair by attempting to commune with the spirits of the murdered women (Walkowitz 189), Mina Harker functions as an intriguing "double agent" who supplies the crucial spiritual link to Dracula that precipitates his demise. The exorcism of Mina's "inner prostitute," therefore, is inextricably bound up with Dracula's bloody, violent, and ritualistic death. In fact, both episodes are figured as redemptions. Mina's journal description of Dracula's final moments foregrounds the idea of spiritual salvation: "I shall be glad as long as I live that even in that moment of final dissolution there was in the face a look of peace, such as I never could have imagined might have rested there" (377). The "malignant and saturnine" Count (24) is finally released from his damned, undead state which sentenced him to eternal, carnal bondage. Surely it cannot be sheer coincidence that such a liberation occurs on November 6th, only two days prior to the date of both the Ripper's last murder (Farson, *Jack* 50) and Stoker's birthday (Belford 17) — November 8th.[22]

Turning to the twentieth century, however, the damned, anally-retentive period of the eternal sequel (we can't seem to let anything go),

Cover of the first issue of *Blood of the Innocent*, published in 1986 by WARP Graphics.
Courtesy of Rickey Shanklin and Mark Wheatley.

and Jack and "Drac" may be said to be, unequivocally, alive and killing. In at least two recent narratives, this dynamic duo has even been featured together. In the four-part comic book *Blood of the Innocent* by Rickey Shanklin and Mark Wheatley, Dracula and the Ripper cross paths in the autumn of 1888 in Whitechapel. In England as a type of real estate agent seeking out "new blood" for his homeland (he wants Britons to permanently relocate to Transylvania), Dracula repeatedly encounters the Ripper after his grotesque acts of butchery. In several ironic sequences, Dracula criticises the Ripper for being a slovenly killer who has no respect for the lives he takes. The problem is that the Ripper (who is Queen Victoria's grandson and heir to the throne, Prince Albert Victor, the Duke of Clarence) wastes the blood of his victims! Prince Albert Victor kills these prostitutes in an attempt to revenge himself for his syphilis affliction. Although Dracula occasionally sups on prostitutes himself, in true up-to-date twentieth-century fashion, he is also capable of sexual intercourse and — as the trinity of vampire women in Stoker's novel never would have guessed — love. This proto-Coppola-style Count unfortunately becomes smitten by a prostitute named Mary Jane Kelly who ends up being the Ripper's final victim. After her murder and grotesque mutilation, Dracula vows revenge. Realising that Prince Albert Victor's death by syphilis will be more slow and painful than any death the Count could possibly inflict, he abandons the Prince to his fate. The book's final image of a weeping Dracula, the tormented romantic demon lover doomed to an eternity of love and loss, is typical of the popular "sympathy for the vampire"-style representations of our century.

While a brief episode about one of the actual "Jacob the Ripper" suspects — Jack "Leather Apron" Pizer — is interwoven into the narrative, it is significant that Shanklin and Wheatley do not foreground the Jewish issue. In effect, Stoker's Jewish Dracula is totally absent from this 1980s story. The Count has been adapted to suit the changing tenor of the times and, at this moment in history, Jews do not elicit fear in the modern reader. The focus, instead, is on the devastating effects of syphilis, a disease similar to AIDS in both its transmission and social impact. Further, in keeping with 1980s "victim aware" sensibility, *Blood of the Innocent* exhibits incredible sympathy towards its marginalised characters who include in their ranks both the prostitutes *and* Dracula.

Shanklin and Wheatley's vision of the Count as a marginal, misunderstood, and, therefore, misrepresented figure, does not carry over, however, to Kim Newman's highly inventive novel *Anno Dracula*. Published in

1992, *Anno Dracula* also features the demonic dynamic duo of Jack the Ripper and Dracula. In this instance, Dracula is not only in England during the period of the Ripper murders, he has infiltrated the royal family and is married to Queen Victoria! Against a backdrop of secret society intrigue and vampire wars waged between Republican/socialist and decadent, pro-Monarchist vampires, Dr. *Jack* Seward is revealed to be *Jack* the Ripper. Revenging himself for Lucy's vampire conversion and death, Jack "rips" vampire-prostitutes with medical precision.

Featuring an incredible cast of fin de siècle and vampire-related figures of both the fictional and non-fictional varieties, ranging from Sherlock Holmes and Carmilla to Algernon Charles Swinburne and Oscar Wilde — who has, not surprisingly, "embraced his vampire state with enthusiasm" (65) — *Anno Dracula*'s Dracula is, indeed, a unique creation. Still evil, Dracula is a bloated, infectious, decadent, homophobe who has "grave-mould in his bloodline" (62). More grotesque than terrifying, Dracula is only granted a cameo role (albeit intensely graphic and memorable) at novel's end. Although Stoker never actually appears, he is also a character in *Anno Dracula*. The "now-never-mentioned Bram" (101) is an anti-Monarchist who is rumoured to be held alongside Sherlock Holmes in a work camp called Devil's Dyke on the Sussex Downs (18). Florence Stoker is certainly rolling in her grave over her portrait as a dimwit flirt and invalid who holds salon-style cocktail parties known as "After Darks." Entirely politically disinterested, Florence sometimes wishes that she "had never heard of vampires" (365).

A novel rife with ingenious fin de siècle encounters between real and fictional personages, *Anno Dracula* attests to Kim Newman's extensive knowledge of both the period and the details surrounding the Ripper murders. On the "Jacob the Ripper" theme, Newman incorporates many episodes involving actual, historically-documented Jewish suspects. While Whitechapel remains "a notorious nest of foreigners" (164) which is populated by many Jews, the writing on the wall no longer reads "The Juwes are not the men that will be blamed for nothing." Instead, the message is, "the Vampyres are not the men that will be blamed for nothing" (214). Although Stoker's Jewish Dracula is not incorporated by Newman, the creator of *Anno Dracula* cleverly exposes the nature of the drive to demonise "others," and foregrounds the fact that our "monsters" change with our times. He does this by way of the crusading evangelist, John Jago. Concerning the current 1880s vampire demon, Newman offers a telling description: "A few years ago, he [Jago] would have been preaching against the Jews, or Fenians, or the Heathen Chinese. Now, it was vampires" (38). Newman clearly takes poetic licence with the 1880s in *Anno*

Dracula: in actual, historical fact, the *Jews* were being preached against during the 1880s and 1890s.

History aside, however, in combining this exposure of the arbitrary nature of the demonisation process with the representation of the vampire realm as a type of parallel universe, Newman brings his readers face to face with themselves. Through his strategy of presenting vampirism as "primarily a physical rather than a spiritual condition" (115–116), and locating vampires at both ends of the political and moral spectrum — as the "good" socialist vampire Geneviève Dieudonné unequivocally states, "Vlad Țepeș [one of Dracula's ancestors] hardly represents the best of my kind" (216) — Newman incisively deconstructs the phantasmal vampire/human distinction and advances the inescapable and unsettling point that "Vampires 'R Us." There is no essential difference, in other words, between those inhabitants of England who have, in Newman's fictional vocabulary, "turned," and those who have not.

Contrary to popular Victorian pseudo-science, serial killers like Jack the Ripper are not another species with visible, distinguishing marks. Indeed, it is their combined human-ness and lack of distinction from individuals who are not serial killers that makes them absolutely terrifying.[23] Unfortunately for society, therefore, our social monsters — sexual predators and serial killers, for example — do not physically match our conception of "the Monster." Society's nefarious tendency, however, to locate the monstrous in an "Other" who is figured as alien and different from ourselves — like the Eastern European Jew during Stoker's era — illustrates both our denial of the fact that the Monster *is* us and, tragically and ironically, exemplifies our own monstrous abilities.

It may be said, however, that the vampire figuratively assumes flesh in the form of such figures as Jack the Ripper.[24] Jack's "inner vampire" may be said to have "possessed" him during his gruesome acts of murder. As Robert Bloch has further underlined, Dracula has even come to stand in for Jack in our cultural consciousness. As Bloch provocatively queries, "In a world which hardly recalls Henri Landru, Peter Kurten, Albert Fish, or hundreds of other real-life mass-murderers, torturers of women and children, and drinkers of human blood — why do we all remember a fictional character named Count Dracula?" (27). According to Martin Riccardo in *Vampires Unearthed*, Dracula has even assumed real "historical" flesh. After Adolf Hitler, Idi Amin, Richard Nixon, and Mao Tse Tung, Dracula is reputed to be the world's fifth most hated "person" (3).

As "Jack the Ripper" was an alternate identity of one such serial killer (one who might *not* even have forged this identity), and as his/her true identity was never actually discovered, he is perhaps not a very good example of a "forgotten" serial killer. Jack and "Drac" have, in fact, become celebrity blood brothers. Both have proven to be highly adaptable, seemingly eternal, popular culture icons. As Clive Bloom describes their immortal, blood-brotherhood, "Jack, like any legendary figure ... steps out of historical circumstance and into the imagination of the future. As such, like King Arthur or Robin Hood or Count Dracula, he is the *undead*" (136). Christopher Frayling's elucidations on the Ripper's semiotic versatility may also be said to apply to Stoker's illustrious Count:

> ... "Jack the Ripper", remains the elusive figure he always was: a space in the files, an *absence* which has been given a name by "an enterprising journalist", and a character by successive writers, reporters and members of the reading public. In terms of historical evidence, he does not exist, so, for all sorts of reasons, he has been constantly re-invented. Ever since the autumn of 1888, this space has been used to accommodate the "beasts", "monsters" and "maniacs" of the moment. Each generation has added embellishments to a genre picture which was first created out of the West End's fear of the outcast East, out of a glimpse into the abyss. (214)

Stoker's Count Dracula has also functioned as a monstrous, chameleonic sign that has been constantly reinvented in order "to accommodate the 'beasts', 'monsters' and 'maniacs' of the moment."

Although not generally given to predictions, I can make one basic guarantee. Regardless of the nature of the next millennium's fears, we may rest assured that Jack the Ripper and Dracula, individually and perhaps even jointly, will tap them in relevant and recognisable ways. Like monsters in the hold of the Star Trek spaceship we call time, they are certain to go boldly where no monsters have gone before.

NOTES

1   Although this translation did not appear until 1901, Stoker's introductory comments were
    written in August of 1898.

2   It is noteworthy that, within the space of a few years, Stoker's grand-nephew, Daniel Farson,
    wrote a biography about him and a study of the Ripper murders, yet failed to mention any
    connection between the two. In fact, he denied any association whatsoever. Discussing what
    he called "The Dracula Game," which involves attempting to decipher the influences on
    Bram Stoker when he penned *Dracula*, Farson writes, "The late Professor Nandris suggested
    that Bram Stoker was influenced by the murders of Jack the Ripper in 1888, but there is no
    hint in the novel or any of his writings of either the Ripper's violence or the subsequent
    panic" (152).

3   In his significant essay from 1966, "The Historical Dracula: The Theme of His Legend in the
    Western and in the Eastern Literatures of Europe," Grigore Nandris outlined some of what he
    considered to be the significant sources of, and contemporary influences on, Stoker's
    Dracula. According to Nandris, "To his [Stoker's] reading on folklore the current press of his
    time could have added its contribution. The memories of Londoners at the time of *Dracula*'s
    gestation were haunted by the horror of the undetected murder of women by the criminal sex
    maniac, Jack the Ripper of the 1880's" (Nandris 378). Similarly, in her shopping list of the
    "related contemporary events" that made Stoker "more receptive" to conflating the figure of
    the vampire with the historical Dracula, Phyllis Roth mentions "the horror of Jack the Ripper
    in London; the translation by Sir Richard Burton, whom Stoker knew personally, of twenty-
    five tales about a vampire written centuries before by the Indian sage Bhavabhuti; the publi-
    cation of Frazer's *The Golden Bough* which detailed vampire superstitions, and Stoker's
    membership in an occult lodge called 'Golden Dawn in the Outer' to which Montague
    Summers also belonged" (94). In *Dracula: The Novel & The Legend*, Clive Leatherdale also
    examines contemporary influences on Stoker. He mentions Frazer and then quotes from an
    1888 newspaper saying "This extract confirms the ease with which any unexplained blood-
    shedding could be laid at the door of vampires. The source of these 'vampire' attacks in
    Victorian London? — the activities of Jack the Ripper!" (81). Finally, in a personal letter to
    me dated 28th September 1996, Bernard Davies outlines how Dracula and Jack the Ripper
    essentially "shared a backyard." Count Dracula's East End hideout in Chicksand Street was
    located close to Jack the Ripper's territory. As Davies explains it, "Some of Jack's murders
    were committed within the proverbial 'stone's throw' of Chicksand Street: the first at Buck's
    Row, a little way to the east behind Whitechapel Station; (probably) the second at Hanbury
    Street a little way north; (again probably) the last off Dorset Street, halfway in between.... I
    think the blood-soaked atmosphere of this whole little district then — for he began work on
    Dracula only one year after the last murder, when it was all fresh in the public's mind — fas-
    cinated Stoker."

4   More specifically, Michel Foucault focuses on the etymological grounding of the word "mon-
    ster" and the idea of madness as a form of monstrous spectacle when he writes, "Until the
    beginning of the nineteenth century, and to the indignation of Royer-Collard, madmen
    remained monsters — that is, etymologically, beings or things to be shown" (69–70). Fred
    Botting, on the other hand, is interested in the social climate that generates monsters. As he
    explains, "Most evident in periods of social, political and economic crisis, monsters appear
    as the marks of division and difference that cannot be held together and fixed within the hier-
    archical relations of a social order which sustains the illusion of itself as unified" (140).

5   Tentatively titled *Gothic Cabala: The Anti-Semitic Spectropoetics of Gothic Fiction*, this dis-
    sertation examines what I perceive to be an anti-Semitic backdrop in Gothic literature (espe-
    cially that set during the Spanish Inquisition). After charting this anti-Semitism along socio-

historic lines and explaining how it is manifested, both technically and thematically, in Gothic fiction, I focus on what I call the "Wandering Jew's progress" (which is actually a "regress") in the labyrinthine pages of that genre. This character's significant and dramatic metamorphosis into a vampire is traced over the period of a century in Gothic literature. Texts examined range from Matthew G. Lewis's *The Monk* and William Godwin's *St. Leon* to Charles Robert Maturin's *Melmoth the Wanderer* and Stoker's *Dracula*. A final chapter is devoted to representations of the Wandering Jew in pre-World War Two English literature and cinema, culminating with an examination of his role in German Expressionist cinema and Nazi propaganda films.

6   It is crucial to note that the word "cabal" entered the English language, replete with negative connotations, during the latter half of the seventeenth century when Jews were allowed reentry into Britain. Also noteworthy is the fact that the word "Cabala" became interchangeable with the word "Occult" at the end of the eighteenth century.

7   The Jew's circumcision was popularly regarded as a form of symbolic castration, a "condition" with which he threatened other "healthy" males. As Sander Gilman relates in his book on Freud, some even thought that Jewish men were born circumcised (52).

8   If, as he suggests, Osborne culled this information from Sander Gilman's work *Jewish Self-Hatred: Anti-Semitism and the Hidden Language of the Jews*, he has made an error as to the cycle of Jewish male menstruation. According to Gilman, Franco da Piacenza, a Jewish convert to Christianity, "claimed that the males (as well as the females) of the lost tribe of Simeon menstruated four days a year!" (74).

9   As Barbara Belford explains, du Maurier was at Whitby in the summer of 1890 and "had featured the Stokers in a *Punch* cartoon" (227). According to Belford, du Maurier was completing *Trilby* at this time. Describing the mesmerist Svengali as "an enduring mythic character to rival Dracula", Belford wonders, "Was Dracula born from Svengali, as critic Nina Auerbach suggests, with his powers still further extended over time and space? Both deal with the fear of female sexuality and the loss of innocence, and with brave men who rescue the mother figure from a foreigner's embrace" (228). In the recent Everyman edition of *Trilby*, Leonee Ormond perceptively notes the Dracula-Svengali connection in her introductory comments: "There are parallels here with Bram Stoker's *Dracula*, another man of sinister and Central European origins, practising diabolic arts on British womanhood" (xxviii).

10 As James Shapiro has recently explained, in his inflammatory book *The Jew, The Gypsy and El Islam*, Richard Burton "states that Sephardic Jews still practiced ritual murder and cites specific instances that he knew about in Damascus, Rhodes, and Corfu. Suppressed from publication in this volume, as Burton's editor W.H. Wilkins tactfully notes, was an 'Appendix on the Alleged Rite of Human Sacrifice among the Sephardim'" (101). Shapiro also notes how Montague Summers in *The History of Witchcraft and Demonology* also argued that Jews engaged in ritual murder.

11 F.W. Murnau's *Nosferatu* (1922), the first adaptation of *Dracula* to the screen, retains this plague connection. Rats accompany Graf Orlok to England, and Orlok himself resembles a rat with his pointed ears, rat-like fangs, bald cranium, and inordinately long, claw-like fingers.

12 The Scholomance was a type of secret society school which admitted only ten scholars at a time. There, students were taught nature's secrets, the language of the beasts, and magic spells by the devil himself who claimed, at course's end, the tenth scholar as his payment due. Albeit only brief, this Scholomance reference in Stoker's novel suggests how Dracula became a God-forsaken vampire: he was, it is implied, the tenth scholar. This Scholomance reference also retains the secret society connection from the Gothic literature of the 1790s. What is particularly interesting about Dracula's history, however, is his altered nature from life to undeath. He has essentially metamorphosed from an accomplished and good Christian during his life-time who fought against the Turks, to an anti-Christian, and figurative Jew, in

his undead state. This past is made clear during Mina's bloody baptism ceremony when a furious Dracula tells Mina, "Whilst they [Van Helsing and his Christian brotherhood] played wits against me — *against me who commanded nations, and intrigued for them, and fought for them, hundreds of years before they were born* — I was countermining them" (288, emphasis mine). Curiously, it is Van Helsing, Dracula's foremost opponent and modern-day counterpart who outlines and applauds Dracula's talents as a living man: "As I learned from the researches of my friend Arminius of Buda-Pesth, he was in life a most wonderful man. Soldier, statesman, and alchemist — which latter was the highest development of the science-knowledge of his time. He had a mighty brain, a learning beyond compare, and a heart that knew no fear and no remorse. He dared even to attend the Scholomance, and there was no branch of knowledge of his time that he did not essay" (302).

13   This Jew-prostitute-disease connection is retained in the infamous fictional *Protocols of the Elders of Zion* which was published in its earliest form in Russia in 1901. Presented as a series of twenty-four lectures in which a subversive group known as the Elders of Zion expound their plot to achieve world domination, these Protocols outline how "drunkenness and prostitution must be vigorously fostered" in order to undermine Gentile morality. They explain how any surviving remnants of opposition "can always be inoculated with frightful diseases" (Cohn 3). In recent years, Nation of Islam leader Louis Farrakhan, a notorious anti-Semite, has suggested "that Jewish doctors invented the AIDS virus to infect black children". As Goran Larsson has commented, Farrakhan's claim is but "a modern version of the medieval Black Death-accusation and the superstition that Jews poisoned the wells and even killed Christian children!" (Larsson 52–53).

14   In the introduction to *Makt Myrkranna*, Stoker seems to suggest that Lucy's attacks constitute a fictionalisation of the Ripper murders in *Dracula*. He states, somewhat cryptically, that "the notorious murders of Jack the Ripper ... came into the story [*Dracula*] a little later" (8). My argument, however, is that the Jack the Ripper murders are not only more extensively integrated into *Dracula* along both technical and thematic lines, but that both Drac and Jack share, rather significantly, a certain semiotic "costume."

15   For more on this connection, see my article, "Consanguinity: Bram Stoker's Dracula and Gothic Literature's Wandering Jew."

16   Although George Simmel does not mention Jews in his essay on prostitution, he does outline how "... the nature of money resembles the nature of prostitution. The indifference with which it lends itself to any use, the infidelity with which it leaves everyone, its lack of ties to anyone, its complete objectification that excludes any attachment and makes it suitable as a pure means — all this suggests a portentous analogy between it and prostitution" (122).

17   While this Judaisation fear was prevalent throughout Europe in the late nineteenth century, it is highly significant that a quarter century later in Germany, Adolf Hitler articulated the combined sexual-economic threat posed by the Jew. In *My Struggle* (1925), he writes, "Particularly with regard to syphilis, the attitude of the nation and the state can only be designated as total capitulation.... The invention of a remedy of questionable character and its commercial exploitation can no longer help much against this plague.... The cause lies, primarily, in our prostitution of love.... This Jewification of our spiritual life and mammonization of our mating instinct will sooner or later destroy our entire offspring". As Gilman notes, "Hitler also linked Jews with prostitutes and the spread of infection. Jews were the 'archpimps'; Jews ran the brothels; Jews infected their prostitutes and caused the weakening of the German national fiber" (*Freud* 62).

18   As James Shapiro notes in his remarkably insightful study *Shakespeare and the Jews*, "Paradoxically, even as descriptions of Jews focused almost exclusively on men (except for some notable exceptions in plays), the Jews as a people were often thought of collectively as feminine, especially when juxtaposed to the masculine English (hence the ease with which analogies could be drawn between Jews and female prostitutes)" (38–39).

19   Although the Zionist Organisation was formally established by Theodor Herzl in 1897, the year of *Dracula*'s publication (Shimoni 97), its origins lay in the "Hibbat Zion groups of the early 1880s … [that] articulate[d] an ideology pertaining to the idea of a return to Zion and its restoration as a homeland for the Jews" (85). Leo Pinsker's famous work *Autoemancipation* (1881), a perceptive and cogent analysis of anti-Semitism throughout history, was crucial to the Zionist movement. Therein, Pinsker argued that Judeophobia — hatred of the Jews — was a widespread mental illness among Gentiles. As the Jew, as Pinsker described them, "cannot readily be digested by any nation" (33), the solution to the "Jewish Problem" lay in the establishment of a Jewish nation. Although *Dracula* is quite clearly marked by a fear of Jewish *immigration* rather than Jewish *emigration*, the establishment of the Zionist movement confirmed the longstanding anti-Semitic portrait of the Jew as incontrovertibly alien or, as Count Dracula so aptly describes himself, "a stranger in a strange land" (20).

20   It is noteworthy that the demons in fin de siècle England varied depending on the writer. As Elaine Showalter explains, "By the 1890s the syphilitic male had become an arch-villain of feminist protest fiction, a carrier of contamination and madness, and a threat to the spiritual evolution of the human race. In men's writing of the period, however, women are the enemies, whether as the femmes fatales who lure men into sexual temptation only to destroy them, the frigid wives who drive them to the brothels, or the puritanical women novelists, readers, and reviewers who would emasculate their art" ("Syphilis" 88).

21   Leslie Shepard examines this claim in detail in his piece on Bram Stoker's death certificate in the Appendix to this volume.

22   As Rickey Shanklin notes in his mini-essay, "Dracula: Bram Stoker's Bogeyman," "Based on the phases of the moon as described in Stoker's novel, the story of *Dracula* actually takes place in 1890, two years after Jack the Ripper stalked the streets of Whitechapel. Both events occur in the autumn; coincidentally, Dracula is destroyed in his Transylvanian castle on the same date as Jack the Ripper takes his final victim: November 8th" (26). Although Shanklin gets the date of Dracula's destruction wrong, the convergence of the dates of these two sets of serial crimes seems, as Stoker's introduction to *Makt Myrkranna* strongly suggests, to have been consciously forged. As to the convergence of these dates with Stoker's own birthdate, the coincidence must surely have been recognised by him.

23   Bram Stoker advances a similar point when his Transylvanian Count is shown to be indistinguishable from the general British population when Jonathan Harker first spots him on the streets of London. While Stoker annihilates Dracula's ethnic difference, however, he does not extinguish his moral difference. This is, in fact, inscribed on his physiognomy. As Mina notes when she sees Dracula for the first time, his "face was not a good face; it was hard, and cruel, and sensual, and his big white teeth, that looked all the whiter because his lips were so red, were pointed like an animal's" (172).

24   As the case of John Crutchley illustrates, the "vampire" epithet has also been attached to crimes of sexual violence. Dubbed "the Vampire Rapist," Crutchley raped and kidnapped a 19-year-old hitchhiker in 1985. He thereafter proceeded to drain and drink nearly half of his victim's blood over a 22-hour period before she managed, miraculously, to escape ("Vampire Rapist" A15).

REFERENCES

Arata, Stephen D. "The Occidental Tourist: *Dracula* and the Anxiety of Reverse Colonization." *Victorian Studies* 33 (1990): 621–645.

Auerbach, Nina. "Magi and Maidens: The Romance of the Victorian Freud." *Critical Inquiry* 8 (1981): 281–300.

Belford, Barbara. *Bram Stoker: A Biography of the Author of Dracula.* New York: Knopf, 1996.

Blair, Sara. "Henry James, Jack the Ripper, and the Cosmopolitan Jew: Staging Authorship in *The Tragic Muse*." *ELH* 63 (1996): 489–512.

Bloch, Robert. "Two Victorian Gentlemen." *Blood of the Innocent*. Vol. 1. By Rickey Shanklin and Mark Wheatley. New York: WARP Graphics, January 1986. 27–30.

Bloom, Clive. "The House that Jack Built: Jack the Ripper, Legend and the Power of the Unknown." *Nineteenth-Century Suspense From Poe to Conan Doyle*. Eds. Clive Bloom et. al. London: MacMillan, 1988. 120–137.

Botting, Fred. *Making Monstrous: Frankenstein, Criticism, Theory*. Manchester: Manchester UP, 1991.

Bram Stoker's Dracula. Dir. Francis Ford Coppola. Columbia, 1992.

Brooks, Peter. "The Mark of the Beast: Prostitution, Melodrama, and Narrative." *New York Literary Forum* 7 (1980): 125–140.

Burton, Richard F. *The Jew, The Gypsy and El Islam*. 1898. Hollywood, California: Angriff Press, 1970.

Cohn, Norman. *The Protocols of the Elders of Zion*. Montreal, Quebec: Concordia University, 1982.

Cranny-Francis, Anne. "Sexual Politics and Political Repression in Bram Stoker's *Dracula*." *Nineteenth-Century Suspense From Poe to Conan Doyle*. Eds. Clive Bloom, et. al. London: Macmillan, 1988. 64–79.

Davison, Carol Margaret. "Consanguinity: Bram Stoker's Dracula and Gothic Literature's Wandering Jew." *Journey into the Supernatural: Proceedings of the First World Dracula Congress*. Bucharest: Lumea Publishing House, 1996.

Dews, Walter. *I Caught Crippen*. London: Blackie and Son, 1938.

Dijkstra, Bram. *Idols of Perversity: Fantasies of Feminine Evil in Fin-de-Siècle Culture*. New York and Oxford: Oxford UP, 1986.

Du Maurier, George. *Trilby*. 1894. London: J.M. Dent, 1994.

Edgeworth, Maria. *Harrington. 1817*. London: J.M. Dent, 1893.

Farson, Daniel. *The Man Who Wrote Dracula: A Biography of Bram Stoker*. London: Michael Joseph, 1975.

— . *Jack the Ripper*. 1972. London: Michael Joseph, 1975.

Feldman, David. "The Importance of Being English: Jewish Immigration and the Decay of Liberal England." *Metropolis London: Histories and Representations Since 1800*. London and New York: Routledge, 1989. 56–84.

Foucault, Michel. *Madness and Civilization: A History of Insanity in the Age of Reason*. 1965. Trans. Richard Howard. New York: Vintage, 1973.

Frayling, Christopher. "The House that Jack Built: Some Stereotypes of the Rapist in the History of Popular Culture." *Rape: An Historical and Social Enquiry*. Eds. Sylvana Tomaselli and Roy Porter. 1986. Oxford: Basil Blackwell, 1989. 174–215.

Gallagher, Catherine. "George Eliot and *Daniel Deronda*: The Prostitute and the Jewish Question." *Sex, Politics, and Science in the Nineteenth-Century Novel*. Baltimore and London: Johns Hopkins UP, 1986. 39–62.

Gelder, Ken. *Reading the Vampire*. London and New York: Routledge, 1994.

Gilman, Sander. *Freud, Race, and Gender*. Princeton: Princeton UP, 1993.

—. *The Jew's Body*. New York and London: Routledge, 1991.

Haining, Peter, ed. *The Vampire Omnibus*. London: Orion, 1995.

Halberstam, Judith. *Skin Shows: Gothic Horror and the Technology of Monsters*. Durham and London: Duke UP, 1995.

Hobsbawm, E.J. *The Age of Empire 1875–1914*. London: Weidenfeld and Nicolson, 1987.

Julius, Anthony. *T.S. Eliot, Anti-Semitism, and Literary Form*. Cambridge: Cambridge UP, 1995.

Knight, Stephen. *The Brotherhood: The Secret World of the Freemasons. 1983*. London: Grafton Books, 1990.

Larsson, Goran. *Fact or Fraud? The Protocols of the Elders of Zion*. Jerusalem: AMI-Jerusalem Center for Biblical Studies and Research, 1994.

Leatherdale, Clive. *Dracula: The Novel & The Legend*. East Sussex: Desert Island Books, 1985.

Ludlam, Harry. *A Biography of Dracula: The Life Story of Bram Stoker*. London: W. Foulsham & Co., 1962.

McNally, Raymond T. and Radu Florescu. *In Search of Dracula*. Boston: Houghton Mifflin, 1994.

Nandris, Grigore. *"The Historical Dracula: The Theme of His Legend in the Western and in the Eastern Literatures of Europe."* Comparative Literature Studies 3 (1966): 367–396.

Newman, Kim. *Anno Dracula*. 1992. New York: Pocket, 1993.

Nosferatu: Eine Symphonie des Grauens (*A Symphony of Terror*). Dir. F.W. Murnau. Prana Film, 1922.

Ormond, Leonee. "Introduction." Du Maurier, George. *Trilby*. 1894. London: J.M. Dent, 1994. xxiii – xxx.

Osborne, Lawrence. *The Poisoned Embrace: A Brief History of Sexual Pessimism*. New York: Pantheon, 1993.

Pick, Daniel. "'Terrors of the Night': *Dracula* and 'Degeneration' in the Late Nineteenth Century." *Critical Inquiry* 30 (1988): 71–87.

Punter, David. *The Literature of Terror: A History of Gothic Fictions From 1765 to the Present Day*. London and New York: Longman, 1980.

Ragussis, Michael. *Figures of Conversion: 'The Jewish Question' & English National Identity*. Durham and London: Duke UP, 1995.

Riccardo, Martin. *Vampires Unearthed: The Complete Multimedia Vampire and Dracula Bibliography*. New York: Garland, 1983.

Roth, Phyllis A. *Bram Stoker*. Boston: Twayne, 1982.

Schmitt, Cannon. "Mother Dracula: Orientalism, Degeneration, and Anglo-Irish National Subjectivity at the Fin de Siècle." *Irishness and (Post)Modernism*. Ed. John S. Rickard. London and Toronto: Associated University Presses, 1994. 25–43.

Shanklin, Rickey. "Dracula: Bram Stoker's Bogeyman." *Blood of the Innocent*. Vol. 2. By Rickey Shanklin and Mark Wheatley. New York: WARP Graphics, January 1986. 25–27.

Shanklin, Rickey and Mark Wheatley. *Blood of the Innocent*. New York: WARP Graphics, January 1986. 4 vols.

Shapiro, James. *Shakespeare and the Jews*. New York: Columbia UP, 1996.

Sharkey, Terence. *Jack the Ripper: 100 Years of Investigation*. London: Ward Lock Limited, 1987.

Shimoni, Gideon. *The Zionist Ideology*. Hanover, New Hampshire and London: Brandeis UP, 1995.

Showalter, Elaine. *Sexual Anarchy: Gender and Culture at the Fin de Siècle*. Harmondsworth: Penguin, 1990.

—. "Syphilis, Sexuality, and the Fiction of the Fin de Siècle." *Sex, Politics, and Science in the Nineteenth-Century Novel*. Ed. Ruth Bernard Yeazell. Baltimore and London: Johns Hopkins UP, 1986. 88–115

Simmel, Georg. "Prostitution." 1907. *On Individuality and Social Forms: Selected Writings*. Ed. Donald N. Levine. Chicago: The University of Chicago Press, 1971. 121–126.

Spear, Jeffrey L. "Gender and Sexual Dis-Ease in *Dracula*." *Virginal Sexuality and Textuality in Victorian Literature*. Ed. Lloyd Davis. New York: State University of New York Press, 1993. 179–192.

Stoker, Bram. *Dracula*. 1897. Oxford: Oxford UP, 1992.

—. "Introduction." 1898. *Makt Myrkranna*. Trans. Valdimar Asmundsson. *Bram Stoker Society Journal* 5 (1993): 7–8.

Stone, Harry. "Dickens and the Jews." *Victorian Studies* 2 (1959): 223–253.

Tracy, Robert. "Loving You All Ways: Vamps, Vampires, Necrophiles and Necrofilles in Nineteenth-Century Fiction." *Sex and Death in Victorian Literature*. Ed. Regina Barreca. Bloomington and Indianapolis: Indiana UP, 1990. 32–59.

Trollope, Anthony. *The Way We Live Now*. 1875. Oxford: Oxford UP, 1991.

"'Vampire Rapist' Crutchley finds freedom short-lived." *The Gazette* 10 August 1996: A15.

Walkowitz, Judith R. *City of Dreadful Delight: Narratives of Sexual Danger in Late-Victorian London*. Chicago: University of Chicago Press, 1992.

Wilde, Oscar. *The Picture of Dorian Gray*. 1891. Oxford: Oxford UP, 1994.

Wilson, Colin and Robin Odell. *Jack the Ripper: Summing Up and Verdict*. Ed. J.H.H. Gaute. London: Bantam, 1987.

Zanger, Jules. "A Sympathetic Vibration: Dracula and the Jews." *English Literature in Transition 1880–1920* 34 (1991): 33–44.

II

racula —

wentieth-Century

ampirised Text

Share Alike: *Dracula* and the Sympathetic Vampire in Mid-Twentieth Century Pulp Fiction

Margaret L. Carter

ORE QUICKLY AND THOROUGHLY THAN ANY WORK of fiction in any other field, Bram Stoker's *Dracula* became the definitive model for subsequent vampire fiction. Works that have been written since either consciously imitate or deliberately subvert the conventions established by Stoker.[1] The plot structure modeled in *Dracula* outlines the detection of a vampire — whose depredations are first interpreted in medical terms but finally recognised as supernatural, followed by his destruction. The novel ostensibly tells a story of the exorcism of a diabolical evil by way of the eradication of the Devil's earthly agent, the vampire. That Count Dracula plays the role of Antichrist needs no elaboration here; among many such allusions in the novel's dialogue, Van Helsing identifies the band of heroes as "ministers of God's own wish, that the world, and men for whom His Son die, will not be given over to monsters, whose very existence would defame Him" (320). Yet even in *Dracula* there are traces of ambiguity concerning the vampire's nature — suggestions that he is not a creature of unqualified evil. The text entertains the possibilities that Dracula is himself a victim as well as a villain, that some potential for good remains in him, or that his condition arises from natural rather than diabolical causes.

Most of these hints come from Van Helsing himself. He remarks that the Count descended from "a great and noble race." and informs the other vampire-hunters that "There have been from the loins of this very one great men and good women, and their graves make sacred the earth where alone this foulness can dwell. For it is not the least of its terrors that this evil thing is rooted deep in all good" (241). The vampiric condition, it seems, entails an inextricable confusion of good and evil which is dramatised, perhaps, in the "unclean" state that afflicts even Mina Harker, whom the male characters initially view as utterly pure. As for the individual vampire himself, Van Helsing expresses admiration for Dracula's intelligence, cunning, and persistence. He concludes, "Oh, if such an one was to come from God, and not the Devil, what a force for good might he not be in this old world of ours" (321). In each of these instances, Van Helsing quickly reiterates the contrary assertion, that Dracula is in fact an agent of evil; his potential for goodness, if any, remains unrealised.

One suggestion that vampires may retain some human virtues comes from a surprising source, Jonathan Harker. After Dracula's attack on Mina, Jonathan resolves that "if we find out that Mina must be a vampire in the end, then she shall not go into that unknown and terrible land alone. I suppose it is thus that in old times one vampire meant many; ... the holiest love was the recruiting sergeant for their ghastly ranks" (297). It does not seem to occur to Jonathan that the ability to love absolves vampires from being completely evil. Nor does he recall that, during his stay at Castle Dracula, he overheard the Count remind his three vampire brides, "Yes, I too can love; you yourselves can tell it from the past" (39). Since Stoker's vampires often apply the word "kiss" to their bloodthirsty advances, Dracula's claim to "love" is one statement among many whose ambiguity cannot be resolved.

Throughout the novel, with the exception of Mina Harker, no character pauses to reflect on the possibility that Dracula may not be entirely diabolical. Mina produces the only explicit declaration of sympathy for the villain. She protests against the hatred the other heroes, especially her husband Jonathan, express; she insists that the destruction of the vampire must not be "a work of hate. That poor soul who has wrought all this misery is the saddest case of all. Just think what will be his joy when he, too, is destroyed in his worser part that his better part may have spiritual immortality" (308). In Mina's view, Dracula himself is, like Lucy Westenra, ultimately a victim. We might read Mina's sympathy as a reflection of her saintly character rather than any genuine remnant of goodness within the Count. The same ambiguity surrounds her perception of Dracula's death: "I shall be glad as long as I live that even in that moment of final dissolution, there was in the face a look of peace, such as I never could have imagined might have rested there" (377). Since, in the absence of an omniscient narrator, we have only Mina's word for this transformation, it may or may not reflect objective reality.

In an article that focuses on the subjectivity and potential unreliability of the novel's multiple narratives, Carol Senf draws attention to Dracula's status as victim. The crimes of which the heroes accuse Dracula remain unproven, since the Count never faces formal criminal charges or receives an opportunity to defend his actions. Senf points out that the log of the *Demeter*, the ship whose crew the Count is supposed to have murdered, offers only vague and inconclusive testimony. The death of Lucy might be attributed to Van Helsing's experimental blood transfusions rather than the vampire's predation. Senf reminds us that "even if Dracula is responsible for all the Evil of which he is accused, he is tried, convicted, and sentenced by men (including two lawyers) who give him no opportunity to explain his actions and who repeatedly violate the laws which they profess to be defending" (96). For example, Van Helsing and his cohorts desecrate Lucy's tomb and break into Dracula's houses. According to Senf, the heroes' hostility to Dracula does not arise from the rational and righteous motives they claim, but from fear of their own violent and erotic impulses, which they project onto the vampire and attempt to eradicate. Thus the boundaries between vampire and victim become blurred.

Still more ambiguously, at some points Van Helsing's dialogue suggests that vampirism may constitute, contrary to the novel's dominant ideology, a natural rather than supernatural phenomenon. The Professor speculates that Dracula's unique strengths may spring from unique features of his native land: "With this one, all the forces of nature that are occult and deep and strong must have worked together in some wondrous way. The very place, where he have been alive, Un-Dead for all these centuries, is full of strangeness of the geologic and chemical world" (319). He mentions volcanic gases and "waters of strange properties," postulating "something magnetic or electric in some of these combinations of occult forces which work for physical life in strange way" (319–20). If vampirism is a part of the natural world, it cannot be inherently evil, though Van Helsing and his listeners do not draw this conclusion. Leonard Wolf says of this passage, "Stoker wants to rationalise Dracula's powers by ascribing them to 'forces of nature.' Fortunately, this excursion into science is brief, and we are soon back to a diabolic Dracula" (378n). However, an earlier passage foreshadows this "excursion into science." Shortly after Lucy's death, Van Helsing tries to open Seward's mind to the possibility of vampirism, by means of an extended lecture on the mysteries of the natural world.

Among other extraordinary phenomena, the Professor cites the existence of "one great spider" that "lived for centuries in the tower of the old Spanish church and grew and grew," rumours that "there are some few men that live on always if they be permit; that there are men and women who cannot die," and the case of the Indian fakir who "can make himself to die and have been buried, and his grave sealed and corn sowed on it" yet returns to life months later (192). Van Helsing does not present these instances of extended longevity and miraculous resurrection as supernatural, but simply rare, nor does he stigmatise them as evil. Like Dracula's potential for goodness, however, the suggestion that vampirism may be a morally neutral product of the natural realm remains undeveloped.

Virtually all twentieth-century vampire fiction labours under an "anxiety of influence" with regard to *Dracula*. The individual author need not have read Stoker's novel or even seen one of the many films based on it. The figure of Dracula pervades our culture's conception of vampirism. Authors who choose not to imitate the plot structure and characterisation of the model often deal with its influence by self-consciously subverting it. In many cases they eschew the image of vampire as totally diabolical in favour of a more ambiguous or even sympathetic rendering, often elaborating upon the faint suggestions of sympathy scattered through Stoker's work. Such rewritings reject the image of vampire as radically Other, in favour of foregrounding common traits shared by vampire and human, predator and victim. In the pulp fiction of the early- to mid-twentieth century, we find examples of the following strategies, foreshadowed in *Dracula*, for portraying vampires as less than utterly evil: (1) Vampirism as such is evil, but individual vampires may rise above the curse of their fate. (2) Vampirism is evil, but an individual vampire may prove to be more victim than villain. (3) Vampirism is a morally neutral phenomenon, perhaps natural rather than supernatural, so that the vampire is a free moral agent.

One of the earliest works to be discussed here, Henry Kuttner's "I, the Vampire" (1937), follows the *Dracula* pattern, with the difference that Kuttner's vampire, unlike Dracula, abjures the evil of his existence and embraces self-sacrifice. Kuttner's first-person narrator, Mart Prescott, is assistant director on a movie project. The film, *Red Thirst*, clearly inspired by Bela Lugosi's success in *Dracula*, is to feature a mysterious unknown, the Chevalier Futaine, the subject of strange rumours about "his former life in Paris," of whom the narrator's actress fiancée, Jean Hubbard, says, "Nobody can take a picture of him, scarcely anybody can see him" (208). Even without the cue from the story's title, any knowledgeable reader would suspect vampirism as soon as director Jack Hardy appears on the scene, looking "like a corpse" (209). Mart notices the appalling change in Hardy, from "a stocky, ruddy blond" to "a skeleton, with skin hanging loosely on the big frame" (210). When we learn that another actress, Sandra Colter, wife of leading man Hess Deming, has just died of "pernicious anemia" (208), accompanied by "a throat infection" and "a wound on her neck — two little marks, close together" (211), and that she insisted on being cremated, we know she has been victimised by a vampire. Similar wounds appear on Jack Hardy's throat, confirming the cause of his wasting illness. These symptoms, familiar from *Dracula*, make the situation obvious to the reader, while the characters, committed to a rational world-view, remain oblivious to the danger.

Similarly, the Chevalier Futaine's appearance marks him as a vampire. Mart notices that Futaine's cheeks are rouged and observes "under the rouge ... a curious, deathly pallor that would have made him a marked man had he not disguised it." The mysterious actor's lips, however, are "as crimson as blood" (210). Unlike the reader, Mart does not recognise the meaning of these signs; he attributes Futaine's pallor to disease. Apart from the details of anemia, puncture wounds, the vampire's pale skin and red lips, and Futaine's aristocratic background, Kuttner's story imitates *Dracula* in other respects. In place of the non-reflecting mirror that gives Jonathan Harker the first clue to Count Dracula's true nature, Kuttner uses a more technologically advanced device, a movie camera. During a rehearsal, the cameraman films Jean with Futaine. The print shows "a glowing fog — oval, tall as a man" that "moved forward at about the pace a man would walk" (214). This unnatural phenomenon alerts Mart to the danger posed by Futaine. Mart's suspicions are confirmed when he hears that Sandra Colter "came to life while they were cremating her ... screaming and pounding on the glass while she was being burned alive" (215). Her husband's attempt to rescue her fails, so that she perishes rather than rising as a vampire. Sandra fills the role of Lucy, who becomes a vampire and must be destroyed. Kuttner, like Stoker, uses dual heroines, one who succumbs to the vampire and another who survives. Jack Hardy, who brought Futaine back from Paris, serves the function of Stoker's Renfield, the vampire's human slave, who delivers innocent women into the monster's power. Just as Mina temporarily falls under Dracula's spell, Jean Hubbard, entranced by Futaine, is taken as a captive to his lair, a vault in the cellar of his isolated house.

"I, the Vampire" departs from the *Dracula* pattern with the violent confrontation between Mart and Futaine. Unlike Stoker's heroes, Mart fails to defeat the villain. Also, Futaine's motive for preying on Jean differs from Dracula's reason for attacking Mina. Futaine perceives Jean as a reincarnation of Sonya, his first love, who died by way of a stake through the heart after he had transformed her into a vampire. He intends to transform Jean; Mart, paralysed by Futaine's hypnotic power, can only wait helplessly through the night. The vampire's repentance, not the hero's prowess, effects the heroine's salvation. After freeing both Jean and Mart from his spell, the Chevalier tells Mart his story. Futaine speaks of falling "victim to another vampire.... Deathless and not alive, bringing fear and sorrow always, knowing the bitter agony of Tantalus, I have gone down the weary centuries." Thus he frames himself as a victim, transformed against his will, hating his curse, which includes the vampires' compulsion "to prey upon those they love." He repents making Sonya a vampire, since in undeath only her body, not her true self, walks the earth. His statement, "I put love behind me then, knowing there was none for such as I," reinforces his self-presentation as a creature of sorrow. His memory of love leads him to realise that if he transformed Jean he "would only destroy, as [he] did once before." He therefore renounces his claim on her. Because she "bears the stigmata" (221) and will therefore become a vampire unless Futaine dies, he also renounces his life, giving Mart the key to the vault so that Mart can destroy him after sunrise. The vampire's confession allows the reader direct access to his thoughts, presenting him as a complex individual rather than a murderous monster, an advantage denied Dracula, who, as Senf points out, is the only important character in Stoker's novel of multiple narrators barred from telling his own story.

At the other end of our chronological range, "The Traitor" (1950), by James S. Hart, tells its story from the vampire's viewpoint. As with Futaine's confession, the use of the vampire as point-of-view character does not necessarily mitigate the evil of the vampiric condition. Hart's Lorenz, another aristocratic vampire in the Count Dracula mold, shares with Kuttner's Futaine the perception of vampirism as a curse. Although Lorenz is Italian, the text makes several allusions to eastern Europe, the home of Dracula. When Lorenz recalls preying on dying soldiers on the battlefields of past wars, he reminisces about "the long-past days when the Turk hammered at the Central European gates, leaving his dead and dying strewn along the Danube banks" (137), a clear reference to the history upon which Stoker based Count Dracula's past. Musing about the transformation of the notorious Casanova into a vampire, Lorenz mentions the libertine's "last years at the Castle of Count Waldstein ... in Northern Bohemia — a most likely place indeed" (141). Later, scaling a thirty-five story apartment building, he remembers "ancient days when he had scaled lofty crags and the castle walls atop them in wild East Carpathia" (145). The scene in which Lorenz and his rival, Casanova, climb up this building echoes Dracula's head-down descent of the outer wall of his castle; as Dracula climbs "just as a lizard moves along a wall" (Stoker 34), Casanova appears "[f]lattened to the stone like a lizard" (Hart 142). In another allusion to Stoker, Lorenz beheads Casanova with a kukri knife, just as Jonathan Harker beheads Dracula, and Casanova, like Dracula, crumbles to dust.

By using conventions familiar from *Dracula*, Hart makes Lorenz's nature clear to the reader without using the word "vampire." In the opening scene, the protagonist's mind-reading ability immediately marks him as supernatural, while his mental reference to "a throng of exposed flesh dangerously contained in plunging necklines" (133), his inability to eat or drink, the "intolerable burning … at the butt of his tongue" (135) when he carelessly invokes the name of God, and his haste to leave the party before sunrise demonstrate what kind of supernatural being he is. Lorenz, unlike his undead companions, is striving for "some sort of regeneration, some sort of abatement of his foul condition" (137). He wants to regain his humanity, a goal he pursues by limiting his intake of blood. He finds, oddly, that abstinence causes him to gain weight; one of the other vampire lords remarks that Lorenz is "beginning to resemble one of those on the other side" (138). Lorenz undergoes other changes, which threaten the loss of his powers, a sacrifice demanded for the restoration of his humanity; for instance, he begins to fear heights. He finally redeems himself by rescuing the innocent young Viola Whitney from Casanova's bloodlust. He wins his "greatest victory" by bending over the sleeping Viola, "not to pierce the throat and tap the vein, but to touch his lips lightly to the virgin brow" (145). We become aware that Lorenz is no longer a "true Undead" when another vampire reports that he can now freely cross running water (146), another vampiric convention popularised by *Dracula*. Thus Lorenz, like Kuttner's Chevalier Futaine, wins release from his curse by renouncing the blood of a desired victim; Lorenz, however, gains redemption without the necessity of destroying himself.

Lorenz, unlike Futaine, has apparently chosen his fate and does not assume a victim's stance. Two stories that do present the vampire as victim portray their undead characters in unconventional ways, one as a young woman imprisoned on a boat, the other as an invalid child. Morton, the narrator of Everil Worrell's "The Canal" (1927), discovers a nameless woman on a seemingly abandoned canal-boat one night. She refuses to allow him to swim to the boat, nor will she cross the water. She promises to come across to him only when the canal ceases to flow. Morton's research awakens him to the woman's vampiric nature, but by then he cannot escape her spell and carries her across the river to freedom. She uses him to free a horde of fellow vampires, who together prey upon a community of campers. Morton resolves to dynamite the cavern which is the vampires' lair during the day. In the process he kills himself as well.

Although Morton loathes and fears the girl when he learns the truth about her, at first he views her as an object of desire and pity. She claims to be lonely, dwelling on the old boat with only her father, whom Morton never sees (the father turns out to have died some time previously). The woman presents herself as a victim of persecution: "We have been hardly used, down there in your city. And we have taken refuge here. And we are always — always — on guard" (63). In response to this speech, Morton sees her as "so pale, so pitiful in the night" (63). He is bewitched by "the sadness of the lonely scene, the perfection of the solitude itself" (53). Even at this point, though, imagery of corruption pervades the text. Morton frequently mentions the canal's odour, a "dank, moldy smell that might have been the very breath of death and decay" (64). The tumbledown shacks near the canal, as well as the rotted condition of the girl's boat, emphasise the atmosphere of decay, and foreshadow the revulsion Morton feels when he learns that she is supposed to have murdered a child. The reader becomes aware of her vampiric nature along with Morton when he recalls the legend that vampires cannot cross running water. Later he acknowledges that his vampire lore comes from *Dracula* and "other books and stories. I knew they were true books and stories now — I knew those horrors existed for me" (72).

Worrell's nameless vampire woman resembles Lucy Westenra in that both prey on children. Moreover, Morton's revulsion toward the girl is reminiscent of the demonising of Lucy by Dr. Seward who loves her in life but sees her, after her return from death, as "the foul Thing which had taken Lucy's shape without her soul" and "a devilish mockery of Lucy's sweet purity" (Stoker 213–14). Morton identifies his mystery girl with "women ... who slew to satisfy a blood lust" and "ghosts, specters ... who retained even in death this blood lust" (Worrell, 68). After helping her to escape her imprisonment, he "hardly thought of her now as a woman at all — only as a demon of the night" (71). Various critics have commented on the fear of female sexuality objectified in the treatment of Lucy and Mina in *Dracula*. Gail Griffin associates the characterisation of Lucy with "the idea of woman as a subhuman, wholly animalistic creature" (142). Lucy "outrages the Victorian ideal" (143) with her expressed wish to marry all three men who propose to her, her outbursts of violence as a vampire, and her anti-maternal behaviour of feeding on children. Griffin comments, "It has always been easy for a male-dominated culture to project the beast within upon the woman without, violently repressing her sexuality while just as violently encouraging it" (143). In Lucy's case, the repression consists of first trapping her in her tomb, then driving a stake into her body. In "The Canal," the vampire girl is first driven from her home by the townspeople, then confined like a caged animal aboard the boat. Despite Morton's allusions to the murdered child, his rejection of the vampire (even before he witnesses her freeing the undead hordes to attack innocent people) springs more from what she is — in his view, a demon, associated with odours of corruption, instead of a woman — rather than anything she may have done. He becomes one of her persecutors, like the shanty town inhabitants who drove her from her home. Although the text invites the reader to share the narrator's eventual loathing for the vampire, in the early scenes she is framed as a victim.

An outsider also discovers the true nature of a female vampire in Greye La Spina's "The Antimacassar" (1949). La Spina's protagonist, Lucy Butterfield, staying at a house from which her friend Cora vanished, encounters a little girl, twelve-year-old Kathy, ostensibly confined to her room by rheumatic fever. Mrs. Renner, Kathy's mother, denies any knowledge of Cora. Lucy's discovery of Cora's handkerchief and an antimacassar embroidered by her missing friend, with a plea for help worked into the stitches, confirms her suspicions of Mrs. Renner's deceit. The woman removes sprays of honeysuckle, antipathetic to vampires, from Lucy's room, to allow the starving vampire child to feed. The handyman, Aaron, urges Mrs. Renner to destroy Kathy rather than sacrifice another victim to the child. He finally drives a stake into Kathy himself. As in "I, the Vampire," the reader recognises vampirism at work in "The Antimacassar" before the protagonist does. Aaron's overheard request, "Let me get a sharp stake, missus," alerts the reader to the truth on the second page of the story (258). Lucy dreams of a kiss from a "white-clad child," a caress that "stung cruelly" (263); though she remains ignorant at this point, we know the visit is not a dream. Lucy's subsequent weakness and the "two pin pricks" on her neck reinforce this conclusion (263). Even when Mrs. Renner becomes openly hostile, refusing to let her leave, Lucy does not recognise Kathy's true nature. Her fiancé, Stan, to whom she has sent the antimacassar, rescues Lucy after decoding the rest of the message in the embroidery, with references to vampires; he informs her, "Kathy has been dead for many weeks" (266). Thus, although Lucy takes the initiative that leads to the solution of the mystery, she cannot solve it without help, and like Mart in "I, the Vampire," she cannot save herself from the vampire. After Aaron stakes Kathy, Lucy feels "unable to initiate the next scene in the drama" and "obliged to await her cue" (266). The exclusion of vampirism from her rational world-view (until Stan enlightens her, she interprets the behaviour of Aaron and Mrs. Renner in terms of insanity) prevents her from perceiving facts obvious to the reader, familiar with the conventions of vampire fiction.

Though no child vampires appear in *Dracula*, the possibility of their existence is suggested in that infants and children serve as the preferred prey of the female vampires, Lucy Westenra and Count Dracula's three Transylvanian brides. Since the vampire's bite spreads the contagion, if the children attacked by Lucy had not been rescued, they might well have suffered transformation. The post-mortem fate of the infant drained by Dracula's brides is not revealed. Kathy in "The Antimacassar" does not appear to have become undead through a vampire's attack. Apparently her "death" from rheumatic fever resulted in her transformation. She fits into the paradigm of many cultures' vampire superstitions which maintains that almost anyone who dies in a state of unhappiness or thwarted desire cannot rest. Fatally stricken at a liminal moment, on the verge of puberty, denied normal maturation, Kathy rejects her own death. Stan suggests that Mrs. Renner "probably never realized that Kathy was dead" (267). For all her ruthlessness toward Cora and Lucy, Mrs. Renner appears a pitiable figure, a mother determined to feed her starving daughter. As for the vampire herself, she never appears evil. During the midnight visit, Lucy sees the girl as a "small, shy intruder" (263). Overhearing Kathy's cries, Lucy pities her "alone all day with no one to talk to, and crying all night with hunger" (258). She wonders why Mrs. Renner does not "give the poor child something to eat" (260). Lucy's references to Kathy constantly emphasise the girl's smallness and sickness. In contrast to adult vampires such as Kuttner's Chevalier Futaine and Morton's nameless woman, who pose a more dangerous threat, Kathy evokes only sympathy. When Aaron decides to execute her, the child, unlike the adult vampires, cannot fight her destroyer. An undead child epitomises the strategy of portraying the vampire as victim.

Richard Matheson's little girl vampire in "Dress of White Silk" (1951) narrates her own story. Yet like Kuttner's and La Spina's protagonists, Matheson's narrator also fills the role of the naive character who fails to understand what the reader fully comprehends; the girl's youth and inexperience leave her ignorant of the meaning of her own revelations. Though her age is not stated, her speech mannerisms and the text's omission of apostrophes portray her as very young. The opening sentences of the second paragraph foreground both the child's tender age and her incomprehension: "Granma locked me in my room and wont let me out. Because its happened she says. I guess I was bad" (267). The narrator, whose mother has died, enjoys visiting her mother's bedroom and playing with her dress. One day she shows the mother's photograph and the dress to a friend, Mary Jane, who objects to the darkness in the narrator's house. Mary Jane says that the mother's room "smells like sick people" (270), the dress "smells like garbage" and "has a hole in it," and the adored mother has "buck teeth" and "funny hands" (271). The dress then takes possession of the narrator, who remembers only a sense of being "like grown up strong" (271). In conclusion, locked in her bedroom like La Spina's Kathy, she defiantly claims that her grandmother "doesnt have to even give me supper. Im not hungry anyway. Im full" (272).

The reader, more sophisticated in vampire lore than the child narrator, can fill the lacunae in the text. We realise why the house is kept dark. We know the traditional association between vampires and the stench of decay, strongly emphasised in *Dracula*, and we recognise the hole in the white silk dress as the mark of a stake. We decode the mother's "buck teeth" and "funny hands" as fangs and claws. We infer that during the gap in the narrator's memory she drank the blood of her playmate. Her incomprehension arouses our sympathy; she acts from instinct, not malice. Her orphaned status, emphasised by her solitary play in the darkened house, also predisposes the reader to pity her. Like Kuttner's vampire woman and La Spina's Kathy, Matheson's child lives under the protection of a parental figure who transgresses conventional morality to shelter her. Just as the father of the woman in "The Canal" helps her flee the townspeople's vengeance and guards her daytime rest until his death, and the mother in "The Antimacassar" provides victims for her daughter, the grandmother in "Dress of White Silk" knows the lethal inheritance carried by her granddaughter but takes no steps to mitigate the danger, other than forbidding the child to enter her mother's room (a prohibition the narrator, of course, ignores). The grandmother "cries about the dress" and says "I should burn it up but I loved her so," referring to her deceased daughter (269). In denial about her daughter's vampiric nature, the grandmother constantly tells the child that her "momma is in heaven" (267). Like the child's limited comprehension, the grandmother's willful blindness absolves her of intentional malice. Both characters, with their shared love for the dead woman and their status as victims of prejudice, as illustrated by Mary Jane's unsympathetic perception of the beloved mother, invite the reader's pity.

The first-person, stream-of-consciousness narrative of Matheson's story compels the reader to extract clues to the "facts" of the child's transgression from a subjective account delivered in the voice of a naive protagonist. In contrast, a humorous vampire-viewpoint story by Robert Bloch, also involving a garment that transforms the wearer, ironically distances the reader from the events narrated by consciously manipulating the clichés of vampire fiction as derived from _Dracula_. (As the story's title, "The Cloak," implies, the clichés are borrowed more from the cinematic adaptations of _Dracula_ than from the novel.) The opening lines of "The Cloak" (1939) illustrate this parodic strategy: "The sun was dying, and its blood spattered the sky as it crept into its sepulcher behind the hills.... 'Nuts!' said Henderson to himself and stopped thinking" (369). Henderson's mockery of his own reflective moods characterises him as a modern skeptic. He contrasts the present with past centuries when "the coming of this night [Hallowe'en] meant something.... This new skepticism had taken a profound meaning away from life. Men no longer revered their souls," he muses, linking the belief in "demons and ghouls and elementals" with belief in the spiritual world (369–370). He immediately rejects such philosophic speculations, however. Thus Bloch sketches his protagonist as an unbeliever who will reject vampirism with equal insistence.

When Henderson visits a musty old shop in a shabby neighbourhood in search of a Hallowe'en costume, the proprietor's offer of an "authentic cloak" to wear for the role of a vampire "[l]ike Dracula" (Henderson's own words) bears a significance for the reader to which Henderson is oblivious (372). As a materialist, Henderson notices that "the cloak effected a striking transformation in his appearance" (372) but suspects nothing unnatural in the change. He attributes the chills he suffers when he wears the cloak to illness and his difficulty in seeing his own reflection to eye trouble. After adjusting to the garment, he calls a cab and finds that the driver cringes in terror from his vampiric mannerisms. Other people in the elevator react similarly when Henderson stares at their necks. Unlike the protagonist, we know that the cape, a signifier of vampirism familiar from cinematic clichés, is indeed "authentic." The host of the Hallowe'en party mistakenly assumes Henderson is wearing makeup. Yet Henderson still wonders whether he has merely drunk too much or is "unconsciously acting his vampire role" (374). Even his inability to see himself in a mirror does not open his mind to the possibility of the supernatural; he assumes he must be drunk enough to hallucinate. As a materialist, he continues to rationalise his experiences. Despite his worldly cynicism, he, too, plays the role of a naive protagonist blind to facts obvious to the reader.

He meets a girl, Sheila, dressed as an angel with a dark cape over her white costume. They fall in love at first sight, a phenomenon in which Henderson has disbelieved as thoroughly as in superstitious fears. His flirtation with Sheila emphasises the ambiguity of her "angel" persona. When she remarks on the "queer combination" of an angel and a vampire, he says, "I have a suspicion that there's a bit of a devil in you. That dark cloak over your angel costume; dark angel, you know" (375). This playful remark proves to hold ironic truth, since Sheila, too, acquired her cloak from the mysterious shop, and she, too, has been possessed by the garment's curse; however, Henderson does not discover this coincidence until she reveals it to him. She does so only after he confesses the origin of his own costume. A special edition of the local newspaper reports that a fire has destroyed the costume shop, leading to the discovery of a "skeleton … found in a box of earth in the cellar beneath the shop" in a "Hungarian neighborhood" where the neighbours drop "hints of vampirism" (378). The ethnic reference and the skeleton in the coffin awaken Henderson to the meaning of the other clues he has dismissed, his lack of a reflection, his interest in blood, and his ability to frighten people. Playing the role of both vampire and investigator, he uses his knowledge of vampirism in popular culture to expose himself as the monster whose existence he formerly denied. Now that he believes in love as well as vampires, he aspires to break the curse by proving that his love for Sheila is "stronger than this — thing" (380). Instead, he becomes her victim, since she has no qualms about embracing the power of the cloak.

Because Henderson, in effect, blunders into vampirism by accident, he evokes sympathy rather than loathing. He has an innocent motive for buying the garment — he only wants an "authentic" Hallowe'en costume — and knows nothing of its power until the evidence becomes strong enough to undermine his attachment to stubborn rationalism. When he becomes aware of his new thirst for blood, he resists it and turns to Sheila in an attempt to fight the curse. Thus, he demonstrates his ethical standards and prevents himself from harming anyone. Ironically, neither his new-found love nor his enlightenment regarding the existence of vampires saves him. Unlike the protagonists in *Dracula*, who defeat the Undead by sharing knowledge and bonding together in affection, Henderson is doomed despite these traditional advantages. In addition to presenting the protagonist as an unwitting victim, Bloch suppresses the darker aspects of vampirism through his use of humour and strategy of placing all violence, including the death of the vampire costumer and Sheila's presumed attack upon Henderson, offstage, away from the reader's direct observation.

A science-fiction treatment of vampirism in William Tenn's "She Only Goes Out at Night" (1956) also relegates predatory behaviour to secondhand reportage, thus freeing the vampire from the traditional "monster" role. Tenn's strategy consists of framing vampirism as a natural rather than supernatural phenomenon. His vampire is a young woman, Tatiana, whose vampirism turns out to be an inherited disease. The narrator, Tom, works for a country doctor, whose son, Steve, falls in love with Tatiana. Tatiana preys on children, struggles with guilt over her blood-thirst, and is careful not to take too much from any one victim. Tom, half Romanian, infers Tatiana's secret by recalling the lore he learned from his Transylvanian mother. Like Aaron in "The Antimacassar," he represents the wisdom of the folk, able to recognise the signs of vampirism. In contrast to Tom's folk beliefs about the evil of this phenomenon, Steve and the doctor view the condition from a scientific perspective, as "a sickness like any other sickness" (406).

Once vampirism is redefined as an illness instead of a diabolical curse, the doctor can treat it with "tinted glasses," "hormone injections," and a "daily blood toddy" made from dehydrated blood (407). As demonstrated by her attempts to avoid harming her child victims, her initial refusal to marry Steve, and her attempted suicide, Tatiana is not demonic but capable of moral choice. Tenn reinterprets the Lucy Westenra figure, preying on the blood of children, as a victim of illness rather than the creature of Hell portrayed by Stoker and Everil Worrell. Where the protagonists of *Dracula* first perceive the mystery of Lucy's illness in medical terms and gradually shift to a supernatural interpretation, Tenn's narrator begins by assuming the supernatural, demonic nature of vampirism and concludes by embracing a medical explanation. Tom, the reader's surrogate, begins with the assumption, derived from folk belief and reinforced by *Dracula*, that vampires are inherently evil. As he learns otherwise, he leads the reader through the process of enlightenment. He recognises that Tatiana is "enough in love with [Steve] to try to kill herself the *only* way a vampire could be killed" (407). Expecting "one of these siren dames" (the seductive "vamp" of film conventions), Tom meets instead with "a very frightened, very upset young lady" (407). Thus the vampire becomes humanised by way of Tatiana's ethical, self-sacrificing behaviour and the emphasis on her youth and vulnerability. Tenn portrays her as capable of love, a possibility touched upon but not openly acknowledged in *Dracula* when Jonathan speculates about "the holiest love" serving as a "recruiting sergeant" for the vampires' "ghastly ranks" (Stoker 297).

Though neither young nor, in any obvious sense, vulnerable, the vampire in "Share Alike" (1953) by Jerome Bixby and Joe E. Dean also represents a reinterpretation of the traditional monster in science-fiction-based, morally neutral terms. After a shipwreck, Craig, the human protagonist, finds himself alone in a lifeboat with Eric Hofmanstahal, the vampire. Hofmanstahal, a Romanian with a "colorful past" (423), never eats his share of the rations. From these two details, along with Craig's increasing weakness, the reader infers the truth about the vampire before the protagonist. Craig realises what Hofmanstahal is when he awakens one night to find the other man at his throat. This vampire, however, is a member of the natural order, a representative of another species rather than a creature transformed by the Devil. By implication he contrasts himself to the sharks circling the boat, which "rend and kill, and give nothing in return for the food they so brutally take. They can offer only their bodies, which are in turn devoured by larger creatures" (424). The vampire, also a part of the food chain, at least refrains from killing Craig and rewards the younger man by ceding him the unneeded food rations. Craig at first rejects this "symbiotic relationship" (426), as Hofmanstahal classifies it, but finally yields despite his qualms. Under the influence of his late father, a Baptist minister — who, though not physically present, functions in this tale as the Van Helsing figure who urges the exorcism of evil — Craig first interprets the vampire as a spawn of the Devil.

Like Tom in "She Only Goes Out at Night," Craig, once he realises that the "monster" is not supernatural and therefore not inherently evil, learns to see the vampire as an individual rather than a demon. The vampire disillusions Craig, literally, by deconstructing his illusions about vampirism. When, under the influence of popular culture, Craig challenges Hofmanstahal to turn himself into a bat, the vampire disclaims any such power. "Nor do I sleep in a coffin. Nor does daylight kill me," he says, dismissing the literary and cinematic conventions that distort human perceptions of his kind (426). Analogous to Van Helsing's brief speculations about geologic, chemical, magnetic, or electric sources of Count Dracula's powers, a range of natural explanations for his species' existence is offered by Hofmanstahal — perhaps they originated on another planet; perhaps "when *Homo sapiens* and the ape branched from a common ancestor, there was a third strain which was so despised by both that it was driven into obscurity"; perhaps vampires are "a species which was quite different from man but which, because of man's dominance over the earth, imitated him until it developed a physical likeness to him" (427). He scorns the theological hypothesis of the vampire's diabolical origin as a pernicious legend due to which his people "have been persecuted, imprisoned, burned alive … all because our body chemistry is unlike that of man" (427).

Making the familiar strange, forcing us to view ourselves through alien eyes, he points out that vampires "drink from the fountain of life while man feasts at the fleshpots of the dead, yet [vampires] are called monsters" (427). He compares humanity to the sharks that swarm around the boat. Thus he presents himself as a victim of persecution, revealing that his grandfather "died with a white ash stake through his heart" and maintaining, "We variants have more to fear from the ignorant and superstitious than they from us. There are so many of them, and so few of us" (426). Vampires are framed, therefore, as a persecuted minority race. In view of the intimacy between Craig and Hofmanstahal, the "almost lascivious" feeling of "comfortable warmth and lassitude" (427) that the vampire's bite confers upon Craig, and Hofmanstahal's "almost sexual avidity" (429) in feeding, homoerotic overtones cannot be ignored. Vampires are persecuted as "maniacs and perverts" (427), as well as a threatening alien species. Craig's initial reaction of nauseated revulsion, far out of proportion to Hofmanstahal's behaviour, invites a reading of homophobia. This aspect of the relationship becomes clear when a ship finally appears on the horizon, and Hofmanstahal drinks "for the last time" to mark the end of the "little idyll" (429). Craig sees the approaching ship as a symbol of "[n]ormalcy and sanity, cities and machines and half-forgotten values" (429). The imagined phantom of his late father, the minister, arises to damn him for "lying in the arms of" a monster (430). In panic he struggles, throwing the vampire overboard to be killed instantly by the sharks. Although Craig immediately repents killing his friend, the momentary lapse into a theological rather than naturalistic reading of vampirism transforms him into one of the persecutors. With his shift back to affection for the vampire, and the final exorcism of, not the "demon," but his father's image, Craig awakens to a "new awareness ... coming over him in a hot flood" (430): repeated doses of Hofmanstahal's venom have transformed him into a vampire. Although the text does not explain how this transmutation can work in terms of the vampire's status as a member of a separate species, Craig has become the Other he originally feared.

Through the protagonists' gradual enlightenment about the true nature of vampirism in such stories as "The Antimacassar," "She Only Goes Out at Night," and "Share Alike," the vampire's self-disclosure in "I, the Vampire," and "Dress of White Silk," or the sharing of the "monster's" viewpoint as in "The Cloak" and "The Traitor," the reader comes to view the vampire as a victim of persecution, the involuntary object of a disease or curse, or a member of the natural order capable of moral choice. Direct access to the vampire's thoughts and motives invites the reader to share, if only temporarily, the "monstrous" point of view. Stories such as these foreshadow the convention of the monster's self-disclosure that characterises the typical vampire narrative in contemporary fiction.

At the end of our period, two novels, both reinterpreting vampirism in science-fiction terms, admit the reader to the vampire's viewpoint and invite sympathy for the monster. Both authors use references to *Dracula* to highlight, by contrast, their own rational, rather than supernatural, reading of vampirism. Richard Matheson's *I Am Legend* (1954) embodies the most elaborate development of the "vampirism as disease" hypothesis. A bacterial plague leaves the protagonist, Robert Neville, the only living man on earth, everyone else having been either killed or transformed. Neville mounts a solitary crusade against the vampires. For information, he alternately reads *Dracula* and medical texts on blood diseases. Stoker's novel proves an unreliable source of knowledge full of superstitions without foundation, such as the beliefs that vampires have no reflections and cannot cross running water. Yet although Neville considers *Dracula* "a hodgepodge of superstitions and soap-opera clichés," he acknowledges that it holds one central truth: "The strength of the vampire is that no one will believe in him" (13). Guided by trial and error, sifting fact from legend, Neville spends his days staking the undead and his nights barricaded in his house. Finally, however, he meets a young woman who has contracted the disease without either dying or becoming a mindless undead; she and her companions live in symbiosis with a mutated form of the bacteria. At the last, with his death approaching, Neville realises, "I'm the abnormal one now" (121). To the new race, he is "some terrible scourge they had never seen ... an invisible specter who had left for evidence of his existence the bloodless bodies of their loved ones" (122). Through Neville's deathbed enlightenment, the reader comes to share the viewpoint of the alien Other.

The first-person narrative of a natural "vampire," a blood-drinking sociopath, forms a substantial part of Theodore Sturgeon's epistolary novel, *Some of Your Blood* (1961). An Army psychologist, a medical detective like Van Helsing and Seward, unravels the mystery of "George" (a pseudonym), a young private referred for psychiatric treatment after striking an officer. Part of this young man's therapy involves writing his autobiography. He does not mention his blood-drinking habit; Dr. Outerbridge must decode the text to extract George's secret. Thanks to the young man's first-person narrative, which emphasises the loneliness of his childhood with an abusive father and battered mother, and Dr. Outerbridge's gentle, nonjudgemental therapeutic approach, the reader does not perceive George as a monster. Though Dr. Outerbridge gleans clues to his patient's pathology from the works of Richard Krafft-Ebing[2] and confirms his hypothesis through hypnosis and other recognised therapeutic tools, the text links the scientifically rationalised "vampire" to the preternatural world of *Dracula*. George is the son of a Hungarian-American couple, and his real name is Bela. At the novel's conclusion, the frame narrator invites the reader to choose among several alternative dénouements for the story. Should the young man be cured or killed? "Would you like him shot in the chest? Or in the belly? Why *that*; what is he to you?" (142). If the fate of the Other holds emotional importance for us, we cannot presume to pass disinterested judgement. Nor can we maintain the unexamined assumption that the "monster" is wholly Other.

As Ken Gelder notes in his comments on *Dracula*, in the realm of vampire fiction "consumption is never just consumption; it always entails the production of new knowledges, new interpretations, new texts" (85). Vampire stories feed, as it were, upon their predecessors, consciously misreading earlier tales to construct "new interpretations" out of preexisting material. Though all the works discussed here show, to a more or less explicit degree, the influence of *Dracula*, they extrapolate from ambiguities implicit in Stoker's novel to develop the figure of the vampire in new directions. Each story challenges assumptions embodied in *Dracula* and embedded in popular culture about the vampire as a demonic creature of absolute evil. Works such as these prepared the way for the sympathetic vampire-viewpoint fiction that has come to dominate the field since Anne Rice's *Interview with the Vampire* (1976) and Chelsea Quinn Yarbro's *Hotel Transylvania* (1978). This kind of narrative, by inviting us to share the viewpoint of the Other, forces us to examine our assumptions about our absolute difference from the so-called "monsters" among us.

NOTES

1 *Dracula* maintained its definitive status until the publication of Anne Rice's *Interview with the Vampire* in 1976. Among present-day vampire fans and writers, many were first introduced to the literary vampire by Rice, rather than Stoker, and consider her their principal influence.

2 Krafft-Ebing was a German neurologist (1840–1902) who was a pioneer in the field of sexual pathology.

REFERENCES

Bixby, Jerome, and Joe E. Dean. "Share Alike." *Beyond* 1 (1953). *Weird Vampire Tales.* Ed. Robert Weinberg, et al. New York: Gramercy Books, 1992. 421–430.

Bloch, Robert. "The Cloak." *Unknown* 1 (1939). *Weird Vampire Tales.* Ed. Robert Weinberg, et al. New York: Gramercy Books, 1992. 369–380.

Gelder, Ken. *Reading the Vampire.* New York: Routledge, 1994.

Griffin, Gail B. "'Your Girls That You All Love Are Mine': *Dracula* and the Victorian Male Sexual Imagination." *International Journal of Women's Studies* 3 (1980): 454–65. *Dracula: The Vampire and the Critics.* Ed. Margaret L. Carter. Ann Arbor: UMI Research Press, 1988. 137–148.

Hart, James S. "The Traitor." *Magazine of Fantasy and Science Fiction* 1 (1950). *The Supernatural Reader.* Ed. Groff Conklin. New York: Collier, 1962. 133–147.

Kuttner, Henry. "I, the Vampire." *Weird Tales* 29 (1937). *Weird Vampire Tales.* Ed. Robert Weinberg, et al. New York: Gramercy Books, 1992. 207–222.

La Spina, Greye. "The Antimacassar." *Weird Tales* 41 (1949). *Weird Vampire Tales.* Ed. Robert Weinberg, et al. New York: Gramercy Books, 1992. 257–267.

Matheson, Richard. "Dress of White Silk." *Magazine of Fantasy and Science Fiction* 2 (1951). *Vamps.* Ed. Martin H. Greenberg and Charles G. Waugh. New York: DAW, 1987. 267–272.

—. *I Am Legend.* New York: Fawcett, 1954.

Rice, Anne. *Interview with the Vampire.* New York: Alfred A. Knopf, 1976.

Senf, Carol A. "*Dracula*: The Unseen Face in the Mirror." *Journal of Narrative Technique* 9 (1979): 160–70. *Dracula: The Vampire and the Critics.* Ed. Margaret L. Carter. Ann Arbor: UMI Research Press, 1988. 93–103.

Stoker, Bram. *Dracula.* 1897. Oxford: Oxford UP, 1983.

Sturgeon, Theodore. *Some of Your Blood.* New York: Ballantine, 1961.

Tenn, William. "She Only Goes Out at Night." *Fantastic Universe* 6 (1956). *Weird Vampire Tales.* Ed. Robert Weinberg, et al. New York: Gramercy Books, 1992. 403–407.

Wolf, Leonard, ed. *The Essential Dracula.* New York: Penguin, 1993.

Worrell, Everil. "The Canal." *Weird Tales* 10 (1927). *Weird Vampire Tales.* Ed. Robert Weinberg, et al. New York: Gramercy Books, 1992. 59–73.

Yarbro, Chelsea Quinn. *Hotel Transylvania.* New York: St. Martin's, 1978.

Vampires in the 1970s: Feminist Oligarchies and Kingly Democracy

Nina Auerbach

HE 1970s WAS A HALCYON DECADE FOR VAMPIRES, one in which they not only flourished, but reinvented themselves. Hammer vampires, young and swollen with desire, had teased pompous authorities before retreating into solemnity and the old roles. Vampires in the 1970s *become* authorities. Hovering between animal and angel, they are paragons of emotional complexity and discernment, stealing from Van Helsing the role of knower but adding a tenderness and ineffable sorrow human beings have become too monstrous to comprehend.

In 1975, Fred Saberhagen's *The Dracula Tape* allowed a witty and humane Dracula to tell his own story, one that exposed the sadistic idiocy of the vampire-hunting men and the profundity of his love for Mina. Saberhagen's sophisticate is an acute critic of Stoker's ambiguities and contradictions, but his rich sympathy, his keen awareness, could never come from the "child-brain" of the original Dracula. Saberhagen's Dracula — or Vlad, as he prefers to be called — is not a variation on Stoker's but a differ-

---

This essay was taken from *Our Vampires, Ourselves* (1995). Reprinted with the permission of the University of Chicago Press and Nina Auerbach.

ent character altogether. As a new being with an old name, he is the type of the new vampires who, for the first time, belong in the age that bred them.

The sophistication and variety of the 1970s horror cycle is easy to appreciate, but difficult to explain. After a decade of violent social division and political upheaval, monsters sank into American self-perceptions. At the time, the few critics who cared about them explained their insurgence in terms of a national Armageddon of the spirit. With an urgency that now seems endearing, Robin Wood argued that the horror film "is currently the most important of all American genres and perhaps the most progressive, even in its overt nihilism — in a period of extreme cultural crisis and disintegration, which alone offers the possibility of radical change and rebuilding" (28).

More than twenty traumatic years later, the "extreme cultural crisis and disintegration" of the 1970s seems difficult to discern, particularly for a woman. In retrospect, the 1970s seem, to me at least, a decade of reintegration, full of hope for new beginnings. The Vietnam War ended, and so did Nixon's presidency. With an assurance that seemed to me miraculous, women were moving into the public world, not as isolated anomalies, but on our terms. Vampire literature, however, like my own frame of mind, was more reintegrative and less nihilistic than the horror films Wood was seeing: *The Texas Chainsaw Massacre* was doom-ier than the two *Draculas* that appeared in that decade. Like women, vampires were assuming an authority unprecedented in their history. No doubt they were able to do so because, in the 1960s and '70s, so many official authorities had fallen.

The assassinations that peppered and created the 1960s — not only John Kennedy's, but those of Malcolm X, Robert Kennedy, and Martin Luther King Jr. — were eerily replayed in the two American presidencies that followed Kennedy's. In 1968, Lyndon Johnson was forced out of the presidency by broad repudiation of the officially nonexistent Vietnam War, and also (as I remember it) by an orgy of popular hate. In 1974, the more official and sedate Watergate investigation forced Richard Nixon to resign. Leaders fell like extras in movies. As I remember it, the ease with which they crumbled into death or disgrace aroused as much glee as anxiety, but whether Americans feared cultural crisis and disintegration or relished the new beginnings they promised, authority in the 1970s was, before all things, mortal. Vampires rushed in to fill the vacuum.

The 1970s: Feminist Oligarchies and Kingly Democracy

No, amica mia, I am not the ravenous thing you think me.
You could fill the ruby cap I gave to Laurenzo with what
I take from the living. But just the blood is not enough. It

will keep me … alive … but it is not enough. So when it is possible, I have intimacy as well. It is not only the blood that nourishes me. It is nearness, pleasure, all intense emotions. Only those who come to me knowingly are … tainted by me. Only those who accept me as I am will be like me. (Yarbro, *The Palace* 152)

CHELSEA QUINN YARBRO's Count Saint-Germain, who at this writing is still thriving in a seemingly inexhaustible series of historical horror novels, epitomises the highly evolved vampire of the late 1970s, whose refinement is an implicit reproach to humanity. Like that of his nineteenth-century predecessor Carmilla, the vampirism of Yarbro's Count flows from a thirst for intimacy — the romantic intimacy Stoker's Dracula destroyed in his estranged rage for dominance. Unlike Carmilla's, though, Saint-Germain's thirst is the symptom of a despairing social critique.

Tender vampires like Saint-Germain are more plausible when they hunt and love beyond Stoker's boundaries: when they call themselves Dracula as Frank Langella does, they spend an inordinate amount of energy fighting their preordained script. Saint-Germain's life creates its own history, as do his cohorts in vampire fiction by women: Suzy McKee Charnas's Weyland, Anne Rice's Louis and Lestat, and Tanith Lee's Sabella are superior beings whose lives the mortal reader is too ensnared to emulate.[1] Saint-Germain is more socially committed than Weyland and the rest, but the history he experiences always tells the same story: from pre-Christian Egypt through Nazi Germany, Saint Germain watches with helpless anguish as mass brutality snuffs out frail enlightenment.

In virtually every novel, Saint-Germain tries to rescue a grand woman in thrall to a sadistic patriarchal system by transforming her into a vampire. Sometimes the saving transformation succeeds: Madelaine de Montalio in *Hôtel Transylvania*, a brilliant girl trapped in the degenerate intrigues of pre-Revolutionary France, and Olivia Clemens in *Blood Games*, whose sadistic husband Justus epitomises the sick abuse of power in Nero's Rome, are saved from lethal marriages to become wise, tender, erotically knowing vampire companions. More often, though, the woman is disheartened or dismembered before she can turn. No matter when they live, civilisation offers Yarbro's women no recourse but transformation or destruction.

Yarbro claims that she is more interested in history than horror, but since horror fiction is more marketable, she included a vampire.[2] Her vampire, however, is the only character strong enough — because he has learned from the tragic centuries he has lived in, because it is difficult though not impossible for him to die — to provide a humane perspective on the mass carnage that finds its domestic epitome in the degradation of women. Her mortal characters are too corrupt or too weak to appreciate the human tragedy. In Yarbro's long Saint-Germain series, history and horror are inseparable, a dark union that distinguishes her Count from some of the sweet-natured vampires that followed him.[3]

The xenophobic fear that inspired Stoker's *Dracula* was the vision of a racially alien foreigner ruling and transforming England. The fear that inspires Yarbro's historical horror series is the impossibility of such rule. Saint-Germain, who is scathingly nicknamed "Foreigner" in all countries and times, is a perennially wise and learned counselor who is always forced into exile. The reader is allowed to imagine an egalitarian triumvirate governing the world — Saint Germain and the two brilliant women he has saved into vampire life — but the world will never be ready for them. The superior species, which understands not only government, but healing, sexuality, and art, will always be expelled.

A supreme artist and scientist, Saint-Germain excels at everything. Schooled in ancient medical arts, an alchemist who adapts the principles of transmutation from jewels to the human body, he is an artful healer. But the societies he tries to live in never accept his cures: his medical artistry makes for him vulnerable to accusations of witchcraft. The antithesis of the disease-bringing vampire of *Nosferatu*, Saint-Germain has the wisdom and skill to heal the societies that cast him out.

No matter how barbarous his circumstances, his clothes proclaim his artistry. Even in the Dark Ages of Saxony, he is a monument to the luxury of earlier, more advanced civilisations: "He had changed from the bliaut he had been wearing to the dark wool roc he had persuaded Enolda to make for him four months earlier: like the Roman tunica circula he had worn six hundred years before, the shoulders were pleated to take up the fabric, and the sleeves of his heavy woolen chemise were revealed, and his dark braies below the knees" (*Better* 286).

Christopher Lee's flamboyant taste in castles hinted at a stylish, post-Victorian future — lived on Carnabay Street perhaps. Saint-Germain's gorgeous clothes are monuments to the forgotten artistry of the lost past. Christopher Lee looked toward modernity; Saint-Germain looks back. Worshipped by those few who know him as the spirit of civilisation and culture, Saint-Germain is a yardstick by which to measure society's recurrent falls. The horror of Yarbro's history is humanity's rage to persecute chosen spirits.

Though he is an erotic virtuoso, Saint-Germain is scarcely a body. He needs blood to live, a fact that embarrasses him, but animal blood will do for a time: his primary satisfaction lies in giving women pleasure in intimately nonphallic ways that suit his peculiar artistry, for since vampirism has dried up his bodily fluids, he has no penile life. Yarbro's many sex scenes make vampirism a celebration, not only of nonviolence, but of a sexuality richer and more variable than penetration. Feminists in the 1970s were discovering, just as the vampire's lovers do, the multiorgasmic versatility of women's eroticism, which, despite the admonitions of male experts, requires no penis for arousal. Vampire and alchemist, Saint-Germain knows the erotic secrets patriarchs withhold.

Artist though he is, Saint-Germain is scarcely an animal; his body doesn't extend beyond his clothes and his small, deft hands. Moreover, this master of centuries of erotica is doomed by his nature to frustration, for sexual communion between vampires is impossible. Once Saint-Germain's love for a mortal is consummated in her transformation, these chosen spirits can be lovers no longer. The erotic intimacy for which Saint-Germain longs is, by the laws of his being, eternally withheld. This vampire is by nature a denial of animality.

To his own eternal sadness, Yarbro's vampire has evolved beyond his body. The aloof, scholarly Edward Weyland in Suzy McKee Charnas's contemporaneous *The Vampire Tapestry* is Saint-Germain's complementary opposite: wryly ironic and brilliant, Weyland is nevertheless essentially animal. Saint-Germain turned Dracula's foiled sovereignty over mortals into a tragic loss of authentic leadership; Weyland turns Dracula's animalism into a token of a similar loss. By the late twentieth century, animals are no longer the evolutionary menace they had been a hundred years earlier; they are reminders of lost integrity, just as Saint-Germain's clothes are monuments to lost arts. One of Weyland's few acolytes, a lonely teenage boy, knows animals only as endangered species: "The documentary film ... first lovingly detailed the cleverness of the coyote, his beauty and his place as part of nature, and then settled into a barrage of hideous images: poisoned coyotes, trapped coyotes, burned coyotes, and coyotes mangled by ranchers' dogs. Mark didn't think he would ever be cool enough to stand that kind of stuff" (74). An animal is by definition a sacrificial victim.

Weyland has none of Saint-Germain's grace; he shuns eroticism, art, and empathy as dangerous human invasions of his predator's integrity. Saint-Germain is all memory; Weyland preserves himself by forgetting. Renewing himself by periodic hibernations, he retains when he wakes only the survival skills acquired in his many past lives. Intercourse with him is scarcely transfiguring. His sole approach to love — the night he spends with his therapist, Floria, at her own urging — is, for both, more perplexing than enhancing. Floria may or may not be renewed, but her troubling

abandonment of professional ethics erodes her hard-won independent identity.[4] For Weyland, as for the unicorn in the tapestry, nonviolent intercourse
with a trusting mortal is a dangerous loss of autonomy from which he can
recover only by the long sleep of forgetfulness. Charnas refuses to turn her
tapestry into a Yarbro-like romance. No saviour, her predator leaves
behind an untransfigured city: "Same jammed-up traffic down there, same
dusty summer park stretching away uptown — yet not the same city,
because Weyland no longer hunted there. Nothing like him moved now in
those deep, grumbling streets" (180).

Charnas evokes myths of salvation she refuses to believe in. Male
writers of the '70s also dreamed of a superior species among us, even feeding on us, but their New York does not grumble with desolation. Whitley
Strieber, a more visionary, less ironic fantasist than Charnas, finds a consola-
tion she refuses in the image of a beast hunting in New York. The climax of
The Hunger (1981) is Sarah's ravenous prowl around New York's east side,
a neighbourhood vitalised by her metamorphosis. Perhaps because Strieber's
master vampire is a woman. *The Hunger* and Sarah repudiate her at the end,
but *The Wild* celebrates its hero's change as he stalks through New York as
a wolf: "He was a generous man, and at that moment his heart burst with one
wish, that all human beings everywhere could just for one instant experience
the world in this new way. He had not known it was like this, had never
dreamed what a difference really powerful senses could make. Human eyes
were strong, but not so strong as wolf ears, not nearly so discriminating as a
wolf's nose" (250). Strieber's central saving myth of intercourse with a higher species crystallises in *Communion: A True Story* (1987), an account of
his own gradual transformation by extraterrestrial mentors. Moving from
Gothicism to beast fable to scientific revelation, Strieber increasingly celebrates the interspecial communion whose impossibility women fantasists —
tougher, perhaps, and more socially aware — lament.[5]

Despite the differences in their vampires (the disengaged Weyland
sometimes turns into a sardonic commentary on Saint-Germain), Yarbro
and Charnas both use fantasy to survey social loss. It is easy to dismiss
their vampire romances as, by definition, escapist, but both use their vampire as a yardstick by which they measure American society in the late
1970s. Unlike Strieber, whose wolves, vampires, and extraterrestrials are
virtually omnipotent, Yarbro and Charnas carefully limit the saving powers of their vampires. Even Saint-Germain manages to transform only a
remnant of mortals who, like him, can become only horrified spectators of
power abused. Male authors give far more power to their vampires,
although, in their imaginative exuberance, they pay less attention to the
untransfigured majority.

The corporate corruption revealed by the Watergate investigations seems to have been decisive in the transformation of vampires into potential saviours. Not only Nixon's duplicity, but his self-revelations on tape, might well inspire dreams of extrahuman majesty: the witty and literate self-justifications via cassette tape of Fred Saberhagen's Dracula in 1975 and of Anne Rice's Louis in 1976 are more edifying than nasty Nixonian mutterings. Even the vampires of Yarbro and Charnas, Strieber and Talbot, who are too preoccupied to define themselves on tape, are survivors from an aristocratic age. They have dignity, manners, sensuous intensity, in all of which the Watergate conspirators were deficient. The past that threatened late Victorian England with savage reversion became, for late-twentieth-century Americans, the fantasised source of a finer nation, a more authentic civilisation.

THE BEST-KNOWN VAMPIRES of the 1970s are those of Anne Rice and Stephen King. Neither species is paralysed by social awareness. Weyland, Saint-Germain, and their peers are vampires' vampires: they fascinate their admirers, arousing a longing for national as well as personal transformation, but their audience is relatively specialised. These vampires may live in our houses, but they are not household words. Anne Rice's Lestat, the vampire who is, is more beautiful than Saint-Germain, more self-absorbed than Weyland. He has cosmic longings, but these concern the discovery of his own origin, not the salvation of mortals; he yearns after humanity en masse, but individually humans are too dull for him to worry about. Saint-Germain and Weyland were trapped in human history; Lestat inhabits a spectacular universe of his own.

When we first see him refracted through Louis's gloomy eyes in *Interview with the Vampire* (1976), he shatters all the old smelly stereotypes at once: "Of course, you must realise that all this time the vampire Lestat was extraordinary. He was no more human to me than a biblical angel" (16). Neither as wise as Saint-Germain nor as animal as Weyland, Lestat and his company are a species apart. They scarcely participate in history, even as an oppressed race. When Louis and, later in *The Vampire Chronicles*, Lestat seek the origin of vampires, that origin is unrecognisable to the human reader: these vampires live without reference to us, composing a mythic landscape of their own. Nevertheless, the fraught ménage of Louis and Lestat is a return to vampire beginnings. Their irritable mutual obsession recovers literary vampires' lost origin: the homoerotic bond between Byron and Polidori.

Our midcentury Draculas were free to subvert patriarchy, but all were hygienically heterosexual. They released chosen women from sadistic husbands, but oppressed men had to look out for themselves. The early Saint-Germain romances seem startlingly homophobic today: wicked husbands are often degenerate homosexuals who abandon to vampires the intricate responsiveness of a woman's body. Charnas's Weyland finds cruising men an outcast group on whom it is conveniently easy to prey, but the novel never suggests that they, like Floria, might be aroused by Weyland's animal touch. The taboos that Stoker institutionalised in the 1890s held for almost a hundred years of vampire fiction. Saint-Germain tries vainly to drink an earlier, lost intimacy, but only Louis and Lestat can admonish each other with the old assurance of affinity: "Remember your oath."

But this oath has become too momentous for mortals: only vampires can tolerate its intensity.[6] Putatively a new species with its own alternate history and mythology, the vampires of Anne Rice reclaim their literary origin, if not their prehistoric source, by limiting their feverish admiration to each other. The homoeroticism that infuses vampire life — imagined by a woman writer who finds male homosexuality as glamorous as vampirism is to the smitten (and finally bitten) boy who tapes Louis's confession in *Interview* — restores a lost birthright. Rice's infraction of this final Stoker-instigated taboo brings a special electricity to *Interview with the Vampire*, giving its predators a glamour more socially engaged vampires lack.

The insularity of *Interview* was profoundly appealing in the leaderless 1970s.[7] Its vampirism is a select club, a fraternity of beauty and death whose members are expected to be handsome and refined enough not to irritate each other throughout eternity. They do little, but they are superb spectators. When they are not killing, they flex their highly developed vampire sight: "It was as if I had only just been able to see colors and shapes for the first time," Louis reminisces. Though the entire world is the vampire's spectacle, the most satisfying sight is each other: "I was so enthralled with the buttons on Lestat's black coat that I looked at nothing else for a long time. Then Lestat began to laugh, and I heard his laughter as I had never heard anything before" (20).

This self-reflexive gaze is far from Saint-Germain's horrified fixation on human history. Amoral aesthetes, Rice's vampires are beautifully devoid of social consciousness, another major attraction for disaffected readers. Claudia, the little girl Louis and Lestat transform and adopt, is, in her enforced perennial childhood, bristling with feminist significance, but unlike Yarbro's Madelaine and Olivia, she secretly articulates her complaint: like Hawthorne's Pearl, she is a visual icon of arrested development.

This lovely little vampire, worshipped and controlled by two fatherly lovers, reminds us of the Hammer Lucy *before* Dracula bit her into brief adulthood. For the Claudia who will always look like a doll, vampirism is no release from patriarchy, but a perpetuation of it until the end of time. Her only alternative is her futile attempt to kill Lestat; immolation for this treachery is her only respite from undeath. So suggestively angry and still that she is almost an allegorical figure, Claudia, like Stoker's Dracula, tells no story: we see her as a refraction of Louis's self-love and self-hate. "Claudia was mystery," he concludes. "It was not possible to know what she knew or did not know. And to watch her kill was chilling" (101). Rice's vampires are compulsive storytellers, but Claudia, the ultimate spectacle, is unable to break free of paternal narrative. Instead of being released by vampirism, she is trapped in a mock-family as self-enclosed and strangling as was the Holmwood household in *Horror of Dracula* before it admitted Christopher Lee.

Louis and Lestat may be patriarchs, but they are dreadful fathers. Far from subverting paternal tyranny, Louis bemoans paternal ineffectiveness. His story is his futile search for an adequate mentor, but there is no one to initiate him into the permutations of undeath. Lestat, the fetid folklore predators of Varna, even Armand and the Parisian precision of his Théâtre des Vampires, all provide spectacle, but not authority. The final irony of Louis's account of abandonment is his own assumption of paternity at the end: he bites the pleading boy to become that boy's Lestat. Even though his last words to his swooning acolyte are "I don't know" (345), Louis has become the spectacle of authority, and for these vampires, spectacle is the only credible substance.

The ornamental self-enclosure of Rice's select society saves her vampires from the excessive virtue that threatened their species in the 1970s. The visionary novelists who resurrected and remade vampires know that there are social forces more frightening than Dracula: tyranny, dullness, brutality, unbelief, mass self-deception and self-destruction. Deliberately, they drain fear from their vampires, admonishing thrill-seeking readers to look closer to home. These vampires who are more frightened than frightening become, at their worst, edifying, Superman-like rescuers — as, for instance, Saberhagen's Vlad does in the novels that follow his *Dracula Tape*, in which Dracula, under a variety of names, uses his powers to save friends persecuted by villains. The vampire who is a symptom of lost authority becomes, too often, too nice.

But the most famous vampires of the 1970s are not nice: Stephen King's down-home hordes in *'Salem's Lot* (1975). Deader than the finer spirits who followed them — *Interview with the Vampire* was published the year after *'Salem's Lot*, *Hôtel Transylvania* three years later — King's vampires are so horrible that they may look retrograde.[8] They are surely unsympathetic. No one could call them chosen spirits or leaders manqué. For women writers like Anne Rice and Chelsea Quinn Yarbro, new vampires must undergo a selection process as hairsplitting and fastidious as academic tenure; so must the recruits in later feminist novels like Jewelle Gomez's *The Gilda Stories* (1991). Even Stoker's Dracula chose his prey thoughtfully: his predations were power strategies through which he gained primacy over the charmed circle of hunters, the heart of the West. But vampirism in *'Salem's Lot* is open to all.

There are no elect spirits in *'Salem's Lot*. Anyone can become a vampire, and almost everyone does. It scarcely matters whether the citizens of the Lot have turned or not; even at their most human, the embittered Father Callahan smells in his flock "a mindless, moronic evil from which there was no mercy or reprieve" (149). Since evil is stupid, victimisation is random; anyone exposed in the night can become a vampire. Vampires multiply so quickly that it scarcely matters who begins the chain. Metamorphosis is not a discipline, but an epidemic as indiscriminate as fire, as majority-ridden as democracy. Stephen King's vampires may not inspire sophisticated moral probing, but they are as iconoclastic as those of Anne Rice, for they too thrive without authority or rules.

One principle that does direct vampirism in *'Salem's Lot* is an abyss of which we heard much in the 1970s: the generation gap, which takes on sinister new import when vampires invade the mean little town. Though anyone, young and old, can become a vampire, only the young expect them. Mark Petrie, one of those charmed Stephen King children born with apprehension of evil, understands the invasion because he has learned life from the random grue of horror comics. He is polite enough to love the parents who discuss him in temperate clichés, but he is scarcely surprised when Barlow knocks their heads together "with a grinding, sickening crack" (351), for in comic books death is neither logical nor sacramental: "Understand death? Sure. That was when the monsters got you" (139).

Mark is not cute; he is right. King has often claimed that Stoker's *Dracula* is the source of *'Salem's Lot* (*Danse Macabre* 38-39), but his is a *Dracula* without pattern or rationale or rule-giving elders. Not only is there no viable Van Helsing;[9] vampires are so abundant that there is virtually no Dracula. Somehow, though, the young have access to terror their rationalist parents are denied. They are not guides or seers; they are seismographs. The generation gap becomes an almost visible abyss in *'Salem's Lot*, one from which Hiroshima, the violent lives of the

Kennedys, and Vietnam peep out to divide the growing generation from its conventional parents.

Watergate is a silent but essential collaborator. According to Stephen King, its climate of lies shapes *'Salem's Lot*:

> I know that, for instance, in my novel *'Salem's Lot*, the thing that really scared me was not vampires, but the town in the daytime, the town that was empty, knowing that there were things in closets, that there were people tucked under beds, under the concrete pilings of all those trailers. And all the time I was writing that, the Watergate hearings were pouring out of the TV. There were people saying "at that point in time." They were saying, "I can't recall." There was money showing up in bags. Howard Baker kept asking, "What I want to know is, what did you know and when did you know it?" That line haunts me, it stays in my mind. It may be *the* classic line of the twentieth century: what did he know and when did he know it. During that time I was thinking about secrets, things that have been hidden and were being dragged out into the light (*Bare Bones* 5).

Bred on these buried horrors, the young people in *'Salem's Lot* seem always to have known that life was inhuman. If the monster-bred Mark Petrie — who finally knows only enough to get out of town — is the book's closest approximation to Van Helsing, his friend Danny Glick is the Lot's most memorable vampire. Danny's attack on a sick man inspires the novel's most quoted line:

> And in the awful heavy silence of the house, as [Matt] sat impotently on his bed with his face in his hands, he heard the high, sweet, evil laugh of a child — and then the sucking sounds. (165)

Danny is one of the more ravenous demon children who proliferate in popular horror of the 1970s,[10] but unlike Rosemary's baby, *The Omen*'s Damien, and the toothsome babies of *It's Alive* (1974) and *It Lives Again* (1978), Danny, in this scene at least, is neither possessed nor a mutant. "The high, sweet, evil laugh of a child," the ensuing "sucking sounds," might, in any other context, be naturalistic descriptions; the adjective "evil" could simply characterise a cranky observer. The vampire Danny is

Danny the child. Tobe Hooper's TV movie (1979) gives the transformed Glick boys clownish white makeup and rubbery fangs, but in the novel there is little distinction between child and vampire — or vampire knower. Even when Danny first peers out of his coffin, there is nothing unnatural about him: "There was no death pallor in that face; the cheeks seemed rosy, almost juicy with vitality" (135).

Whether they are vampires like Danny or vampire-knowers like Mark — whose toy cross is a more effective vampire repellent than Father Callahan's "real" one — boys are the heart, though not the cause, of the vampire epidemic in 'Salem's Lot. They are not, like other demon-children of the '70s, occult invaders of a benevolent adult society; they are the essence of that society. Danny Glick is a different sort of child from Claudia in *Interview with the Vampire*, for Claudia is an adult male construction, a stunted woman with no identity apart from the obsessions of the fatherly lovers who made her.

For Anne Rice, childhood is a monstrous imposition on an adult consciousness. For Stephen King, childhood is the essence of experience, one so haunted and frightening that adulthood is evasion. The degradation of Claudia's undeath is her enforced existence as a doll. At the end of *'Salem's Lot*, a forgotten doll is a mute truth-teller: "And perched in one corner of the sandbox, a floppy arm trailing on the grass, was some child's forgotten Raggedy Andy doll. Its shoe-button eyes seemed to reflect a black, vapid horror, as if it had seen all the secrets of darkness during its long stay in the sandbox. Perhaps it had" (425).

Significantly, Anne Rice's resistant child/vampire/doll is female, while Stephen King's oracular Raggedy Andy is male. As is so often true, the woman writer wants to free herself from the childhood the male writer exalts. For both King and Rice, however, vampirism becomes for the first time inextricably attached to childhood, not an imposition by oppressive elders, as it was in the 1930s, or a strategy through which sexy young people evaded stuffy old ones, as it was in Hammer films. Children's innate affinity with horror means that vampirism is, for the first time, symptomatic of fear of the future, not the past. The horrors on youth's side of the generational abyss — which King calls by the names of Hiroshima, Vietnam, the Kennedy lives and deaths, Watergate — are not tokens of a savage past that refuses to die, but portents of a dreadful new nation.

In the 1980s, horror will belong to the young. Vampire movies like *Fright Night* and *The Lost Boys*, as well as horror cycles like *Friday the Thirteenth* and *Nightmare on Elm Street*, make monstrosity a teenage phenomenon, not an invasion from antiquity. Stephen King, with his passionate allegiance to pre-adulthood, helped shift the axis of horror, but only *'Salem's Lot* depicts the appropriation of horror by the young as a historical event. *Fright Night, Nightmare on Elm Street,* and the rest are set in timeless American small towns closer to movies than to life. *'Salem's Lot* sees a small town evolve through American history to a point where vampires are known before they arrive. Heavy, slovenly, unrefined, Stephen King could not on the face of it be farther from Chelsea Quinn Yarbro, but like her — and like so many other writers of the 1970s — he writes historical horror. Their urgent political vision generates conventions that will become routine and unexamined in the 1980s, a decade when history seems to disappear.[11]

'Salem's Lot produces no Van Helsings, not even travesties like Laurence Olivier in John Badham's movie; the best knowledge one can have is the assurance that something is wrong. No authentic leaders emerge because there are no clear vampire rules. The townsfolk dredge up memories of Stoker's novel and Hammer movies, they hunt frantically for crucifixes none of them owns, but the rules that were once so reliable splutter and sometimes stop working altogether in 'Salem's Lot.

Mark's toy cross repels Danny Glick because Mark believes; so does the good doctor Jimmy Cody, who makes a functional cross out of two tongue depressors (though it saves neither Jimmy's neck nor his life). Jimmy's tongue depressors are more potent than the candlestick cross Peter Cushing held up to Christopher Lee in *Horror of Dracula,* which needed scalding reinforcement by the sun, but when Father Callahan, the only character whose crucifix is authentic, tries to repel Barlow's invitation of the Petrie kitchen, the cross fails embarrassingly.[12] Barlow's diagnosis seems to make smooth sense: "Without faith, the cross is only wood.... The boy makes ten of you, false priest" (355).

But nothing in 'Salem's Lot is comprehensible except its plausible vampires. Father Callahan's cross may fail to work for the same non-reason that my computer could give out as I write this, or your car could stop dead on the freeway, or the predictable universe itself could (as our bodies will) lose a gear. In a seminar at the University of Pennsylvania, Stephen King described in a burst of eloquence, seeming to scare himself, a potential vampire story in which "the garlic doesn't work, the cross doesn't work, the running water doesn't work, the stake doesn't work, *nothing works*: and basically you're fucked. There's nothing you can do."[13] Father Callahan's humiliation brings us momentarily into this dysfunctional territory.

Nothing works in 'Salem's Lot because its vampires, like its mortals, have no palpable design and no identifiable leaders. Their invasion seems to follow the old xenophobic *Dracula* pattern: two evilly suave Europeans, Barlow and Straker, come to the Lot to open an antique store. Identified with un-American attributes like wit, homosexuality, and "old things, fine things" (99), Barlow and Straker seem as contaminatingly foreign as Bela Lugosi was, but what is the role of the native Marsten House that seems to bring them? Is it, as Ben postulates, "a kind of psychic sounding board. A supernatural beacon, if you like" (112)? And who is Dark Father who, according to Matt (319), is Barlow's Master? — is he Hubert Marsten or some sort of satanic essence (European or American?) hovering over the action?

This overdetermined chain of command is left undefined.[14] As in Rice's *Vampire Chronicles*, there are no rules and no clear vampire origin, demonic or divine. This vacuum of vampire leadership is the diffused authority of American democracy. Father Callahan muses on its Kafkaesque amorphousness:

> It was all out of control, like a kid's soapbox racer going downhill with no brakes: *I was following my orders.* Yes, that was true, patently true. We were all soldiers, simply following what was written on our walking papers. But where were the orders coming from, ultimately? *Take me to your leader.* But where is his office? *I was just following orders. The people elected me.* But who elected the people? (305)

The vampires themselves have no doubt that they are under authority. Danny Glick explains to Mark, "*He* commands it"; Ed Miller awakens his wife into vampirism reassuringly: "Come on, darlin'. Get up. We have to do as he says" (240, 372). These vampires lack even the illusion of autonomy; they could never produce a wise and sophisticated Olivia, or even a Hammer woman welcoming her transformation with a knowing grin. Transformation in the Lot holds no promise of freedom. Yet, though these vampires are willingly led, Barlow could not be their Master, for after he is staked in a pseudo-climax, his creations survive him: in an egregious rejection of hierarchies of dominance, the death of the head has no effect on the creatures he made, who continue to drift around aimlessly, perhaps assuming they are still obeying orders.

These floundering, directionless killers pay occasional lip service to Dracula, but they have no access to his individuality, his efficiency, even his tyranny. Rather, they are cousins of the utterly American vampires in George Romero's possessed Pittsburgh, who in *Night of the Living Dead*

(1968) and *Martin* (1978) devour, for no reason they know, the squabbling citizens of a city that has no authorities beyond woozy television and radio chatterers.

IKE THE OTHER vampires born in the American 1970s — Weyland, Saint-Germain, Louis and Lestat — the citizens of Stephen King's Lot are wholly new creations, leaderless and lethal, uncertain what to do. The rules that control them are so indeterminate that they flow easily into psychic vampires, the quintessence of twentieth-century predation who pervade everything in mortal life except mortality.

Whether they are lovable elitists like Frank Langella or ignorant shamblers like Stephen King's populace, vampires in the twentieth century inhabit a lush but senseless world. In the 1970s, humans and vampires seem to cry together for a leader, a master-vampire who will guide them beyond the corrupt morass of muttering voices that supposedly constitutes authority. When, in 1980, Ronald Reagan assumed that role, the vampires who had longed for him were systematically stripped of their powers.

NOTES

1   Since the gorgeous Sabella is an extraterrestrial from a future planet known as "Novo Mars," she doesn't quite belong in this discussion of a superior species intersecting with contemporary human society. See Tanith Lee, *Sometimes after Sunset* (New York: Doubleday, 1980).

2   Quoted in Joan Gordon, "Rehabilitating Revenants, or Sympathetic Vampires in Recent Fiction." In Gordon's view, Saint-Germain is so nonviolent that these novels are scarcely horror fiction at all. Gordon's exclusive focus on vampires prevents her from investigating the plausible horror of Yarbro's violent mortals.

3   Gordon finds sympathetic vampires largely a phenomenon of the 1980s, as does Margaret Carter in her "What Makes a Vampire 'Good'? Sympathetic Vampires in Contemporary Fiction" (delivered at the International Conference of the Fantastic in the Arts, 1993). But like so many pious fictions of the Reagan-Bush years, sympathetic vampires are dilutions of a once-potent reformist impulse: they originated as social scourges in the bolder 1970s.

4   In February 1991, Suzy McKee Charnas described to my class at the University of Pennsylvania her own dramatisation-in-progress of *The Vampire Tapestry* in which Floria's unprofessional embrace of the vampire is unequivocally destructive, not the hinted-at release through romance it almost becomes in the novel.

5   Michael Talbot's *The Delicate Dependency: A Novel of the Vampire Life* (New York: Avon, 1982) is a more extravagant epic of salvation by vampires who are virtual angels. For Talbot, who sweeps over human history with the assurance (though not the detailed accuracy) of Yarbro's historical horror, vampires are the *illuminati* who by elaborate mind-control have always saved humans — whom they need in order to reproduce — from their own self-destructive tendencies. Like Saint-Germain and Strieber's intense aliens, Talbot's vampires are healers, not diseases.

6   *The Tale of the Body Thief*, the fourth book of *The Vampire Chronicles*, is a definitive statement of the incompatibility between vampires and humans. After an awkward attempt at union through a body exchange between Lestat and the mortal David, Lestat forces a happy ending by turning David into a vampire. Only then is communion between them possible.

7   The later novels in *The Vampire Chronicles* (1985–) strenuously expand the airless world of the self-contained *Interview*, but these later works express a different historical moment than the elitist yearnings of the late 1970s.

8   In the decade of its publication, Robin Wood called *'Salem's Lot* "unambiguously reactionary" because "the novel's monster is unequivocally evil and repulsive, and onto him are projected all the things of which the book is clearly terrified (including gayness, which provides the novel with a whole sub-text of evasions and subterfuges)" (25). Had Wood called "the monster" "the *monsters*," an entire community of stalwart if corrupt citizens, he would have gotten closer to the heart of King's fear.

       Homosexuality is spread more widely in *'Salem's Lot* than Wood suggests: the decadent Barlow and Straker surely suggest a gay couple invading smalltown America from wicked Europe, but despite his peripheral love affair with a town girl who eagerly becomes a vampire, the hero, Ben Mears, is similarly implicated in homoerotic couplings first with the high school teacher, Matt, then with Mark, the monster-ridden child who alone recognises vampires and evades them. Focusing on families, King's novels generally have little interest in homosexuality, but like *Interview*, *'Salem's Lot* steeps vampirism in male homoeroticism. If that homoeroticism makes villains villains, it also makes heroes heroes.

9   On p. 322, a well-meaning doctor claims coyly to Ben that Matt Burke, the local schoolteacher, reminds him of Van Helsing, but since Matt is at that point hospitalised with a terror-induced heart attack, he is scarcely Stoker's monumental knower; he is even further from

those invulnerable paragons, Edward Van Sloan and Peter Cushing. Moreover, Matt has to cram, futilely, to learn the rules that were the stuff of Van Helsing's wisdom. "And now, if you don't mind, I'm very tired. I was reading most of the night," he tells his perturbed friends. This "authority" would do better to abandon his rule books for Mark Petrie's horror comics.

10   Of whom David J. Skal writes superbly in *The Monster Show*, pp. 287–305, though he excludes vampire children like Danny Glick and Rice's Claudia from his infantine company.

11   King's vampires adjust to changing idioms. *Stephen King's Sleepwalkers* (1992), a TV movie, is set in the timeless small town typical of the Reaganesque years. Like most '80s and early '90s horror, it limits its focus to the family: incest replaces politics as the vampire breeding ground. The handsome teenage vampire and his sexy mother are reassuringly un-American: they look like extraterrestrials and, like many '80s vampires, they come from ancient Egypt.

12   One of my students at the University of Pennsylvania was so dismayed by this breakdown of the rules that she wondered whether Father Callahan simply ranked too low in the hierarchy. "It would have worked if he'd been a bishop or something," she claimed, searching for controlling hierarchies in a book that valorised, for a time at least, tongue depressors and toys.

13   Robert Lucid's seminar on popular literature, University of Pennsylvania, April 1, 1991.

14   In one of the best *'Salem's Lot* spin-offs, Robert R. McCammon's *They Thirst*, whose vampires take over Los Angeles, Stoker's imperial rules and hierarchies are restored: there is a definite head vampire, Vulkan, who aims to conquer the world by creating a new dominant race. Does McCammon graft Stephen King's nightmare American epic to the new decade of the '80s that aimed to restore the rules flouted in the '60s and '70s?

REFERENCES

Carter, Margaret. "What Makes a Vampire 'Good'? Sympathetic Vampires in Contemporary Fiction." Essay delivered at the International Conference of the Fantastic in the Arts, 1993.

Charnas, Suzy McKee. *The Vampire Tapestry.* 1980. New York: Pocket, 1981.

Gordon, Joan. "Rehabilitating Revenants, or Sympathetic Vampires in Recent Fiction." *Extrapolation* 29 (1988): 227–234.

King, Stephen. *'Salem's Lot.* 1975. New York: Signet, 1976.

———. *Danse Macabre.* New York: Berkley, 1981.

Lee, Tanith. *Sometimes after Sunset.* New York: Doubleday, 1980.

McCammon, Robert. *They Thirst.* 1981. New York: Pocket, 1988.

Rice, Anne. *Interview with the Vampire.* 1976. New York: Ballantine, 1977.

———. *The Tale of the Body Thief.* New York: Knopf, 1992.

Strieber, Whitley. *The Wild.* New York: Tor, 1991.

Skal, David J. *The Monster Show: A Cultural History of Horror.* New York: Norton, 1993.

Talbot, Michael. *The Delicate Dependency: A Novel of the Vampire Life.* New York: Avon, 1982.

Underwood, Tim, and Chuck Miller, eds. *Bare Bones: Conversations on Terror with Stephen King.* New York: Warner, 1988.

Wood, Robin. "Return of the Repressed." *Film Comment* 14 (July-August 1978): 24–32.

Yarbro, Chelsea Quinn. *The Palace.* New York: St. Martin's Press, 1978.

———. *Better in the Dark.* New York: Tor, 1993.

The Vampire and the Alien: Gothic Horror and Science Fiction[1]

Veronica Hollinger

RAM STOKER'S *DRACULA* (1897) IS, ARGUABLY, THE last of the great Gothic horror novels. In its dramatisation of the battle between the monstrous Count and his human adversaries, we can read the tensions between the ideological worlds of Gothic fantasy and the late nineteenth-century ideologies of human rationality and technological progress. H.G. Wells's *The Time Machine* (1895) is the first great science-fiction novel, an early "scientific romance" which responded to those same tensions within the conventions of a genre which has become the twentieth century's quintessential imaginative response to the technologisation of contemporary life.

It is hardly coincidental that these two fin de siècle novels appeared at almost the same moment, nor that they both demonstrate an obsession with overcoming humanity's powerlessness in the hands of time.[2] Their imaginative solutions are very different, however: Dracula makes an unholy pact with the powers of darkness and sustains an eternal, although inhuman, life by drinking human blood; the Time Traveller, that epitome of the rational man of science, uses his knowledge of the laws of nature to invent a machine which enables him to travel freely into the future.

Generically, these two novels are poles apart and their differences are crucial to an understanding of what happens when Gothic monsters are introduced into the worlds of science fiction (sf). While sf has frequently been associated with fantasy in the popular imagination, it has always tended to situate the marvellous within a context more consonant with material reality. For this reason, science or pseudo-science usually provides the rationale behind the unusual or wonderful events which may appear in the sf narrative.

It has, in fact, become something of a critical cliché that sf is capable of evoking in its readers "a sense of wonder."[3] A closely related side of the sf coin, however, is its role in what we might term "the domestication of the fantastic." Wells, for one, introduced this issue in his "Preface to the *Scientific Romances*" (1933). "Nothing," he writes, "remains interesting where anything may happen." For this reason, the sf writer should provide the reader with orderly ground rules for his or her fictional universes. Wells concludes that "[the writer] must help [the reader] in every possible unobtrusive way to *domesticate* the impossible hypothesis" (241). This is reiterated, in different terms, by Eric S. Rabkin, who argues that

> what is important in the definition of science fiction is ...
> the idea that paradigms do control our view of all phe-
> nomena, that within these paradigms all normal problems
> can be solved, and that abnormal occurrences must either
> be explained or initiate the search for a better (usually
> more inclusive) paradigm. (121)

Consequently, while the sf genre expands the scope and the variety of the physical universe, it often does so — ironically perhaps — at the expense of what cannot be explained in terms of natural law and scientific possibility — that is, at the expense of the supernatural or the unnatural, the ontologically indeterminate area of the fantastic.

From the generic perspective of sf, this territory lies just across the border, and sf has always been effective at expanding its own scope through the scientific rationalisation of elements originally located in the narrative worlds of fantasy. In Colin Manlove's words, "the science fiction writer throws a rope of the conceivable (how remotely so does not matter) from our world to his [or hers]" (7). Manlove points out that "as soon as the 'supernatural' has become possible we are no longer dealing with fantasy but with science fiction" (3).[4]

A classic example of this domestication of the fantastic occurs in Arthur C. Clarke's *Childhood's End* (1953), a novel which draws the conventional figure of the devil — bat-wings, barbed tail, and all — across the border of the supernatural into sf territory. *Childhood's End* not only provides a "plausible" narrative framework for its demystification of the devil-figure; it also aims to explain the powerful ongoing presence of this figure in our collective race-memory. Clarke thus manages to transform mythic fantasy into alien reality while maintaining the "sense of wonder" inscribed in the original figure.

The vampire, a less grandiose but equally horrific archetype, is one satanic figure which is currently enjoying a resurgence of literary and critical popularity.[5] And while the vampire is still most typically associated with the horror genre, it too has, on certain rare occasions, crossed the border from fantasy to sf, undergoing varieties of domestication in works such as Richard Matheson's *I Am Legend* (1954), Tanith Lee's *Sabella: Or the Blood Stone* (1980), and Brian Aldiss's *Dracula Unbound* (1991).

I want to concentrate here on two other texts which introduce the figure of the vampire into the narrative worlds of sf: Colin Wilson's *The Space Vampires* (1976) and Jody Scott's *I, Vampire* (1984). Although each may be said to parody — in the broadest sense of the term — both traditional vampire narratives and traditional sf treatments of the alien-invasion story, it is interesting to examine the extent to which Wilson's compliance with previously established conventions serves to consolidate a conservative ideology, while Scott's skeptical rejection of the absolutes of generic boundaries both derives from and results in a more radical ideological positioning. As Linda Hutcheon notes in her study of the forms and functions of parody, "the presupposition of both a law and its transgression bifurcates the impulse of parody: it can be normative and conservative, or it can be provocative and revolutionary" (76).

The Space Vampires is strongly influenced by A. E. van Vogt's sf novella, "Asylum" (1942), as Wilson acknowledges in an introductory note to his story. The makers of *Lifeforce*, the film version of *The Space Vampires*, took their title from van Vogt's story of evil aliens whose "unnatural lusts" include a passion for human energy (611). Wilson's vampiric aliens share this appetite for the "life force" and are thus not particularly remote displacements of Stoker's quintessential blood-drinker, Count Dracula.

Wilson's text is directly concerned with the expansion of scientific paradigms to include the "abnormal occurrence" of the vampire in ways which will rationally account for its existence. His narrative is based upon the theory that a kind of metaphorical vampirism is natural to human beings and that it may be either malevolent — as when one deliberately drains another's psychic energy — or benevolent — as when one shares one's own energy. This theory is developed after the discovery of "the space vampires," ruthless aliens who suck the life-energy from their victims and leave them either dead or helplessly enslaved.[6]

The story follows the efforts of Wilson's human characters, led by the heroic Commander Carlsen, to find and then expel three of these vampire-like aliens who have inadvertently been brought back to Earth by a team of human explorers who mistakenly assume they are dead. Wilson rather neatly plays by the rules of popular vampire lore here, since, as the text later reminds us, "it is a characteristic of vampires that they *must* be invited. They cannot take the initiative" (95).

While Scott's novel was published by Ace Books under the sf rubric, it is rather more careless of generic boundaries than is Wilson's. It, too, peoples its narrative world with aliens from outer space, but, apart from a casual reference to the defective gene inherited by its vampire protagonist (1), it makes very little effort to explain the "abnormal occurrence" of this figure within its fictional world. Among the ironically surreal events which take place in *I, Vampire*, there are no fewer than two alien invasions. The background conflict of the novel is between the benevolent race of Rysemians, who are determined to drag humanity up the evolutionary ladder in spite of itself, and the sinister Sajorians, for whom humanity provides a booming market in intergalactic slaves. Scott's vampire, however, is neither human nor alien: a kind of link between the two, Sterling O'Blivion remains an inexplicable phenomenon inhabiting a narrative world which accommodates both "semi-mythological creature[s]" like herself (22) and genuine sf aliens.

While *I, Vampire* can be read as a self-contained narrative, it is also the sequel to Scott's earlier novel, *Passing for Human* (1977). The protagonist in the latter novel, Benaroya, is the repulsively fish-like Rysemian "anthropologist" who reappears in *I, Vampire* disguised as Virginia Woolf. It is interesting to note here that, in *Passing for Human*, Scott, like Clarke in *Childhood's End*, makes use of a "domesticated" version of the devil. In her satiric fiction, however, this devil-as-alien is no benevolent saviour but the quintessentially evil leader of the Sajorian invasion. Scaulzo, "the Prince of Darkness," is able to mesmerise his human victims because of their inherent gullibility: "primitives always go for that type of schmaltz" (23).

Passing for Human has been reprinted by The Women's Press in its feminist sf series; *I, Vampire* continues Scott's critique of contemporary social and sexual politics. Specific to the latter novel, however, is her satiric attack on the repressive nature of social and discursive representations of the Other, accomplished through the delineation of Sterling O'Blivion's struggles against "readings" which attempt to appropriate her both as a woman and as a vampire. Benaroya/Woolf addresses this problem directly at the end of the narrative: "What is a vampire? Who projected that image onto you? My guess is, the people of Transylvania *created* you out of boredom and frustration" (210). Even before this, however, Sterling refuses to either rationalise or justify her existence: "if my actual history sounds like outtakes from a tacky B movie, or worse, well, that's not my problem. I am what I am, as God and Popeye both say when you wake them out of a sound sleep" (13).

After centuries of keeping a low profile, Scott's vampire finds herself enlisted by the Rysemians in their battle against the Sajorians. And thanks to a time-travel machine which she has invented in her spare time, she also finds herself jumping five years into the future to market the Famous Men's Sperm Kit as part of the Rysemian effort to hasten the evolution of the human race. Most importantly, perhaps, courtesy of Rysemian lessons in "psychic evolution," Sterling overcomes her craving for blood, repudiating, within the terms of Scott's fictional world, the limitations projected onto her by the representations of others.

What both Wilson and Scott have produced are intertexts. *The Space Vampires* and *I, Vampire* inevitably invoke the entire history of the vampire in literature, film and television at the same time as they make use of previously established narrative codes and conventions for their own purposes. Within the terms of Hutcheon's analysis of parody, this history is "grafted onto the text[s]" (24) and becomes available to readers as a significant contextual element which, as "decoders of encoded intent" (34), it becomes the role of these readers to activate.[7] While Wilson and Scott's texts are also traversed by typical sf conventions in general and, in the case of *The Space Vampires*, by details of previous sf stories in particular,[8] I want to focus here upon the way in which the figure of the vampire is positioned within each narrative structure and the ideological implications of its positioning. In the process, I will, for the most part, confine my own activation of background material to certain aspects of Stoker's classic treatment of the vampire in *Dracula* (1897).

In Stoker's text, the sinister Count is the enemy in one version of the eternal battle between good and evil. This opposition, which is central to romance narratives, is always constructed upon specific ideological foundations. In his discussion of "magical [that is, romance] narratives" in *The Political Unconscious*, Fredric Jameson explains the foundation of this opposition as follows:

> The concept of good and evil is a positional one that coin-
> cides with categories of Otherness.... The essential point
> to be made here [about the Other] is not so much that he
> is feared because he is evil; rather he is evil *because* he is
> Other, alien, different, unclean, and unfamiliar. (115)

And in his consideration of "fantasy antagonists," R.E. Foust reminds us of
Freud's theory of the *doppelgänger* and the latter's postulation of the "phenomenon of the 'double'" (442): the Other is a projection of certain undesirable aspects of the self, a "monstrous adversary" (443) constructed
out of repressed psychological material. As such, it is a source of fear and
loathing whose return threatens to overcome the forces of Consciousness
and Culture — the forces in whose interests it has been repressed in the
first place. "The fantasy conflict," Foust concludes, "is structured upon an
implicit assumption of the binary, rather than the unilateral, relationship
between nature and culture" (445). As I shall presently argue, it is this kind
of binary thinking, endemic to our present historical and geographical
moment, which is sustained — even as it is parodied — in Wilson's text
and deconstructed in Scott's.

   One of the ways in which Stoker's text maintains the position of
the vampire as evil Other is through its epistolary narrative technique. The
entire novel is a compendium of diaries, journals, letters, newspaper articles, and other forms of I/eye-witness reports. The ideological outcome of
this narrative method, of course, is that it keeps the outsider on the outside.
As has been frequently noted, Stoker's narrative voices are exclusively
human. Indeed, Dracula himself appears on only 62 pages of the original
390-page edition of the novel (Wolf 350). As Nina Auerbach describes
this:

> Dracula begins the novel by telling an unresponsive
> Jonathan Harker his history in almost flawless English,
> but thereafter he is silent. In the massive, impeccably col-
> lated testimony that comprises the long English portion of
> the novel, Dracula has no voice: he leaps in and out to
> make occasional florid boasts, but his nature and aspira-
> tions are entirely constructed — and diminished — by
> others, especially Van Helsing. (82)

In *Dracula*, the Other has no voice, no point of view; he merely *is*. While
this, of course, ensures that he is all the more terrifying because almost
completely unknown, it also effectively silences him.[9]

As we might expect from its narrative strategies, *Dracula* is an extremely conservative text, one that valorises human reason and privileges human over "alien" life. The inhabitants of its narrative world are neatly divided into "us" and "them." Recalling Foust's argument that the construction of fantasy antagonists depends upon binary/oppositional assumptions, it is not surprising that we can read *Dracula* as a narrative carefully structured by exactly this kind of thinking. Auerbach argues that

> *Dracula* is less in love with death or sexuality than with hierarchies, erecting barriers hitherto foreign to vampire literature; the gulf between male and female, antiquity and newness, class and class, England and non-England, vampire and mortal, homoerotic and heterosexual love, infuses its genre with a new fear: fear of the hated unknown. (66–67)

The narrative perspective of *The Space Vampires* achieves very much the same kind of result. Although Wilson replaces Stoker's I/eye-witnesses with an omniscient narrator, the point of view is again that of the human characters and, in particular, that of Olaf Carlsen, the commander of the *Hermes*, leader of the expedition which brings the three aliens to Earth and the central character in the subsequent battle to overcome them. There is no real attempt in *The Space Vampires* to explore the point of view of the aliens. Like Stoker's Count, they are more often off-stage than on, objects of human fear and loathing, variously described as "deadly unknown germs" (69) and "galactic criminals" (187–88). During the course of the narrative, their vampirism is equated with sexual perversion (39), criminality (136), and outright evil (137).

Unlike Stoker, however, Wilson does provide his alien vampires with one opportunity to speak for themselves: when the human heroes trap one of the three "Nioth-Korghai" in the body of a human victim, they wrest a confession from him of his people's fall into vampirism and their subsequent history. He admits to these crimes but makes it clear that the alternative to their vampirism is death: "After all, this seems to be a law of nature; all living creatures eat other living creatures" (184).[10]

Any sympathy aroused in the reader is quickly smothered, however, when Carlsen refuses to believe the alien's peaceful overtures: "I've got an instinct about it. Nothing in their behaviour leads me to trust them" (187). As it turns out, Carlsen is right. The space vampires cannot be trusted; by its very nature, the Other is always evil.

There are several interesting similarities between *The Space Vampires* and Wilson's 1967 novel *The Mind Parasites*, which postulates a similar kind of alien possession and makes use of the metaphor of vampirism: "for more than two centuries now, the human mind has been constantly a prey to these energy vampires" (65). What is most disturbing about *The Mind Parasites* is Wilson's speculation that the cause of human *malaise* lies outside human agency. This is both a negation of human responsibility and another instance of the (paranoid) projection of undesirable elements of the human psyche onto conveniently non-human scapegoats.[11]

For the most part, the reader of *The Space Vampires* has no access to the perspective of Wilson's aliens. Such a perspective is unnecessary, since there is no doubt in the minds of the human characters, and consequently in the minds of Wilson's readers, that these aliens must be destroyed if possible, or at least expelled from Earth. Under the circumstances, it is both appropriate and ironic that the human characters refer to the alien spaceship as "the Stranger" — if they are not conversant with Camus's existentialist classic, we can be sure that Wilson is. *The Space Vampires* fits rather neatly into that longstanding sf tradition which represents the alien as the threat from the outside, the Other who must be driven from human territory if humankind is to rest secure.[12] This is also, of course, the plot of *Dracula*.

Given the ideological parallels between *Dracula* and *The Space Vampires* in regard to the figure of the "alien," it is also appropriate that Wilson's text contains some intriguing allusions to Stoker's. While the concept of energy-sucking aliens is borrowed from van Vogt, *Dracula* is a far more interesting background text against which to read *The Space Vampires*. It is not accidental that the opening pages of Wilson's story owe so much of their atmosphere to details which are overtly Gothic. The alien spacecraft is compared to "some damn great castle floating in the sky" (3) and to "Frankenstein's castle" (5); it exudes "the quality of a nightmare" (8).[13]

Wilson's allusions to *Dracula* are even more pronounced in the area of narrative event. Carlsen's companion in his quest to find and expel the aliens is Dr. Hans Fallada, a British criminologist whose research into the phenomena of human vampirism emphasises his role as the sf analogue of Professor Abraham Van Helsing, the evil Count's original nemesis. Wilson's vampire hunters are able to pinpoint the whereabouts of at least one of the aliens through her mind-link with Olaf Carlsen, who must be hypnotised before he can disclose the information. This incident directly recalls that in which Mina Harker, also partially possessed, also hypnotised, reveals Dracula's hiding place to the heroic band of men who will rescue her at last from his spell.

The fact that Wilson's allusions to *Dracula* are not always straightforward gives an interesting complexity to the narrative structure of *The Space Vampires*. One of his more intriguing revisions appears in the character of the mysterious Count von Geijerstam, who lives in seclusion in northern Sweden in a castle which was once the home of "our famous vampire, Count Magnus de la Gardie" (97). It cannot be coincidence that von Geijerstam is living with three beautiful young women who are practicing a form of "benevolent vampirism" under his tutelage. The reader is inevitably reminded of the three female vampires, the "brides of Dracula," who come so close to destroying Jonathan Harker at the beginning of Stoker's text. *The Space Vampires* also recounts a scene in which Carlsen — at this point clearly an avatar of Jonathan Harker — is approached by one of these young women. In a further revisionary movement, however, the text demonstrates that it is Carlsen rather than the woman who plays the role of vampire, as he drains her of life-energy until she is all but unconscious.

Returning to *I, Vampire* at this point — and recalling Hutcheon's identification of the dual potential of parody — "it can be normative and conservative, or it can be provocative and revolutionary" (76) — it soon becomes clear that Jody Scott's reworking of *Dracula* is far more unorthodox in its manipulation of the traditions and conventions of the classic vampire story than is *The Space Vampires*.

One of Scott's most obvious revisions is highlighted in her title. Just as *The Space Vampires* describes obviously oppositional figures who arrive from "out there," so Scott's title indicates the shift in perspective from the human to the Other. The first thirteen chapters of *I, Vampire* are narrated by the vampire, thus displacing the human from its privileged position at the centre of the text.[14] Suddenly the outsider is on the inside and the voice of the Other, glittering with angry wit and the cynicism born of sharing the world with human beings for 700 years, is heard in no uncertain terms. Sterling O'Blivion is the subject of her own story rather than the object of another's, the interpreter of events rather than the event interpreted. She is only too aware that "when you are a … semi-mythological creature like myself, you are expected to act out a script written by others; one that ignores your true nature" (22). While this particular narrative strategy serves to demystify the Other even more definitively than does Wilson's text, it also shifts the perspective in ways which break down the oppositional barriers between human and Other which *The Space Vampires* leaves standing.

Sterling O'Blivion, the centuries-old and ravishingly beautiful manager of the Max Arkoff dance studio in Chicago, is a victim of the kind of binary thinking which defines the Other as evil. She sets out to explode "a few pernicious myths" (31) about vampires, pointing out that all she takes from her own victims is "six skimpy ounces [of blood]. Less than they take at the blood bank. Cheap, selfish bastards!... and for this I suffered the curse of excommunication and was enrolled among the damned" (32). She warns that "Only a fool sets out to kill any living creature. You don't know what forces you are releasing" (42).

The target of Scott's sometimes vicious satire is that very humanity which has forced the vampire to live in the shadows for 700 years. The Rysemians bluntly inform Sterling that the human race is psychotic, that it will have to be quarantined or destroyed if it cannot evolve into a fit inhabitant of the universe beyond its own borders. *I, Vampire* thus effects a satiric inversion of the conventional alien-invasion plot, as it casts humanity as a dangerous life-form.[15]

Scott's feminist parody of *Dracula* is particularly effective in its subversion of the sexual politics of the earlier story. An examination of the roles played by the female characters in *Dracula* reveals that they are as dependent upon their relationship with Stoker's sinister Count as they are upon the ordinary men by whom they are befriended or to whom they are betrothed. Lucy Westenra and Mina Harker are cast as prizes in the contest between the vampire and his human opponents, while the three vampire brides have already been won. In their passive receptivity, women are at once the susceptible mediators through which the Other may penetrate into human territory and the spoils of war which fall to the victor in this battle between good and evil.[16] If Mina Harker enjoys peace and prosperity at the end of her adventures, it is because she submits herself to the values of Stoker's Victorian reality and returns to the patriarchal fold cleansed of any contact with the Other, who both attracts and threatens from the outside.

This implicit identification of woman and vampire, which operates as a powerful subtextual element in Stoker's original story — a kind of hidden agenda — is both acknowledged and satirised in Scott's.[17] Indeed, her work goes several steps further. Sterling becomes involved in a passionate love affair with Benaroya, who has temporarily abandoned her own alien body in order to infiltrate the human community disguised as Virginia Woolf. Sterling is not only a female vampire, but a lesbian vampire, and one who has made love "out of [her] species" (77). As Benaroya assures her, there are no limits to what the mind can create out of the physical universe, "or P.U., as we call it" (53). She also makes it clear that, from the perspective of the Rysemians, "there are no aliens" (63), or, as she revises Terence, "nothing alien is alien to me" (76). *I, Vampire* ultimately acknowledges the nature of reality as social and linguistic construction. Any metaphysical dependence upon "the thing in itself" is thoroughly undermined in this postmodern universe of continuously shifting bodies and perspectives.

Given the structural parallels in the position of the vampire in *Dracula* and *The Space Vampires*, it is perhaps not surprising to find in Wilson's text an uncomfortably ambivalent attitude towards women — the same discomfort that we can read in *Dracula* itself. *The Space Vampires* weaves a complex interconnection between the ideas of vampirism and masculinist versions of sexuality, which becomes apparent, for example, in Carlsen's realisation that "the vampire responded to desire like a shark to blood" (113) and that "the energy-loss [resulting from psychic vampirism] produced much the same effect as masculine domination" (113). Wilson's human females are invariably ready to yield, both mentally and physically, to Carlsen as his own powers as a psychic vampire develop, but it is made clear that "his gentlemanly self-control" (34) will prevent him from taking advantage of their weakness.[18]

Wilson implies, however, that female vampires will not act so benignly. Just as the women in *Dracula* are either pure Victorian maidens or ravenous — that is, sexual — monsters, so Wilson's text represents the sexually active woman as somehow linked to the alien forces which threaten from "out there." The scene in which Carlsen defeats one of the aliens who temporarily inhabits a female body, for example, bears a disturbing resemblance to a sexual encounter in which male physical desire is equated with strength of will: "Without moving his body he was holding her as a bird might hold a worm" (196). The alien, of course, was about to destroy him completely. Wilson's women-as-alien-vampires are incapable of restraining their appetites, and are, for this reason, tremendously threatening figures.

Carlsen's wife, Jelka, on the other hand, is a modern version of the Victorian angel in the house. The text's references to Goethe's principle of the *ewig weibliche*, the Eternal Feminine which "draws us upwards and on" (quoted 56), draws the reader downwards, back into the sexual politics of *Dracula*, which also separates the good woman from the sexual woman. When Carlsen's "basic masculine tenderness" (113) is aroused by one of von Geijerstam's young pupils, the sexual-political ideology of *The Space Vampires* becomes even clearer: "It struck him that her body *was* Jelka's. Both were embodiments of a female principle that lay beyond them, looking out of the body of every woman in the world as if out of so many windows" (113).

At this point we might recall Sterling O'Blivion's complaint that a "semi-mythological creature ... [is] expected to act out a script written by others; one that ignores your true nature" (22). In its essentialist representations, *The Space Vampires* not only reduces its female characters to the status of "semi-mythological" beings, but undertakes as well to supply the script for their subsequent behaviour. If there is parody here waiting to be activated, the reader might well be forgiven for missing the point entirely.

I would like to return now to Foust's contention that the Other is created through the projection of undesirable psychic material. The result in Wilson's text is the literal expression of this undesirable material embodied in the form of vampire-aliens; his narrative can be read as a metaphorical dramatisation of the return of the repressed, an expression of the anxiety of the divided self which has constructed a reality defined through binary oppositions such as inside/outside, human/alien, masculine/feminine.[19] As seems inevitably to be the case, such binary thinking is also rigidly hierarchical. In each instance, one of the terms is privileged over the other: inside over outside, human over alien, masculine over feminine.

The deconstruction of such antitheses is an important activity in Scott's text and a driving force in her parody of the conventional treatment of the vampire. Whereas Wilson's narrative casts the vampire-alien in opposition to the human, Scott's replaces the two-term system — with its underlying hierarchical privilege — with a three-term system: vampire/alien/human. Any attempt to return her narrative to the dramatisation of binary thinking breaks down in view of the shifting relationships among the terms of this system, relationships which emphasise complicity rather than opposition. The human cannot remain antithetical to the vampire in the presence of the alien; nor can the human/alien opposition hold up in a narrative which interposes the figure of the vampire between these two conventionally opposed terms.

While Wilson's text is an intriguing revision of the traditional vampire tale — a successful crossing of the border from fantasy into sf — it maintains rather than revises the ideological paranoia towards the figure of the alien Other which pervades Stoker's *Dracula*. In its echoes of the latter's sexual politics, it seems also to support conventional patriarchal attitudes about women, casting its female characters as pawns in the contest of human heroes and alien vampires in a way which underscores the human/alien opposition around which the narrative is structured.

Scott's *I, Vampire*, though lacking the coherence and the direction of *The Space Vampires* and suffering periodically from a kind of New Age valorisation of psychic over physical reality, is more skeptical about the usefulness of borders and boundaries than Wilson's fiction is. Its fusion of fantasy and sf parallels on the generic level its deconstruction of the human/Other opposition on the narrative level. Sterling O'Blivion is the vampire as intertext, a figure combining the characteristics of both human and alien, mediating between the two in a way which demonstrates the artificiality of an opposition which is, from another point of view, only a difference.

The vampire, like that other nineteenth-century avatar of horror, Mary Shelley's Creature, always functions within a context which resonates with implications beyond the mere telling of an exciting tale. Stoker's original literary vampire, for example, has been usefully examined from a wide range of critical perspectives, ranging from the sexual-political to the socio-political to the psychoanalytic.[20] While the intrusion of the vampire into sf heralds a relatively untraditional treatment of this typically Gothic archetype, Wilson's conflation of vampire with alien maintains the role of the former as the threat-from-outside, the quintessential Other. Scott's revision, however, is one of a small but growing number of works — most of them by women — which are interested in creating new scripts for this particular "semi-mythological creature," new scripts which are relevant to the "real" world as well.

Roger C. Schlobin has suggested that many contemporary treatments of the vampire have "emasculated" this traditionally potent figure, and he cites works by Chelsea Quinn Yarbro (the six-volume *Saint-Germain Chronicles*) and Suzie McKee Charnas (*The Vampire Tapestry*), among others, to support his contention (30). While Schlobin's observation demonstrates a certain (masculine) anxiety, he is certainly correct. We can add to his list the works of Anne Rice, Angela Carter, Tanith Lee, Jody Scott, Nancy Collins, Nancy Baker, Poppy Z. Brite, and Jewelle Gomez. What these writers have effected is a rejection — or at least a critical rethinking — of the vampire as what we might term a "metaphorical rapist." Schlobin makes it clear that the vampire, as it functions within the framework of the conventional horror novel or film, threatens its victims, whether male or female, with a kind of violation that has its clearest analogue in the act of physical rape. It is not therefore surprising that even when the vampire is male — as in Charnas's *The Vampire Tapestry* or Rice's *Vampire Chronicles* — he is developed from outside the conventional male perspective. For this reason, we might indeed say that he has been emasculated. When the vampire is female, as in Scott's text, the rejection of this perspective is even more obvious. I would suggest, therefore, that the "emasculation" of the "fantasy antagonist" in all these instances is also a "feminisation." There can be little incentive for women writers to contribute to the literary tradition of the "monstrous adversary" as rapist. Instead, these works might be said to constitute a new literary canon developed around the figure of the Outsider. This is no longer, of course, the modernist Outsider identified by Wilson in his 1950s book on the subject, but a new construction created by a politicised contemporary literature in its protests against the coercive nature of patriarchal representations.

Given the rapidly increasing popularity of horror literature and film over the last few years, it is not surprising that the vampire archetype has been resurrected, nor that it has occasionally been appropriated by sf writers. What is especially interesting about this "return," however, is the significant ideological differences apparent in the works of writers like Scott who have taken over the figure of the vampire in order to develop explorations and deconstructions of conventionalised oppressor/victim relationships.[21]

Wilson's domestication of the fantastic is more successful than Scott's insofar as *The Space Vampires* offers its readers a rational paradigm from within which it can explore the "abnormal occurrence" of the figure of the vampire. What Scott's text succeeds in preserving, however, is that sense of wonder about our own human nature — actual and potential — which becomes suffocated in *The Space Vampires*, buried under a far less desirable view of reality. Auerbach's observation that "every age embraces the vampire it needs" (145) suggests also that every ideology embraces the vampire it needs.

NOTES

1   This is a slightly revised and updated version of an essay which appeared in *Science-Fiction Studies* in 1989. I would like to thank Roger C. Schlobin for his informative commentary on my original draft. I would also like to thank my co-editors at *Science-Fiction Studies* for permission to reprint this essay.

2   We might also recall here another great fin de siècle fantasy which imaginatively treats our desire to control time and our inability to achieve that desire, Oscar Wilde's *The Picture of Dorian Gray* (1890).

3   Sam Moskowitz discusses the popularisation of this phrase in "Five Steps to Science Fiction Sanity."

4   This "possible/impossible" opposition, we should recall, is frequently no more than a useful heuristic fiction. There are many works of fantastic literature which defy such relatively easy categorisation. Fictions by writers like J.G. Ballard, Jorge Luis Borges, Angela Carter, Philip K. Dick, Elizabeth Hand, and Gene Wolfe come to mind.

5   As cultural historian David J. Skal suggests, "Very little about the underlying structure of horror images really changes, although our cultural uses for them are as shape-changing as Dracula himself" (23).

6   Nina Auerbach includes a discussion of "psychic vampirism" in *Our Vampires, Ourselves*, her recent cultural history of the vampire (101–112). Stories of psychic vampirism — such as Fritz Leiber's classic "The Girl with the Hungry Eyes" (1949) — began to appear as early as the first years of the twentieth century. More recently, Ellen Datlow has edited two anthologies which contain stories of psychic vampirism, *Blood is Not Enough* (1989) and *A Whisper of Blood* (1991).

7   As Hutcheon explains, however, "the structural identity of the text as a parody depends ... on the coincidence, at the level of strategy, of decoding (recognition and interpretation) and encoding" (34). In other words, like irony, parody does not exist for the reader who does not recognise it at work in a particular text.

8   Wilson's vampires owe a debt to H.P. Lovecraft as well as to A.E. van Vogt. In *The Strength to Dream*, Wilson mentions "Lovecraft's favorite idea of incubi who can steal a human body, expelling its rightful owner" (7), a device used by Lovecraft, for instance, in his sf novel, *The Shadow out of Time* (1936). This method of possession is repeated by Wilson in *The Space Vampires*.

9   Auerbach suggests that Dracula's silence makes of him "the first vampire who conforms to social precepts, fading into experts' definitions rather than affirming his unnatural life" (83). She argues convincingly for the link between this fictional process of definition by "experts" and late-nineteenth-century experts' construction of the clinical category of "homosexuality" (82–85).

10   A case could be made for discussing Wilson's space vampires as existentialist heroes gone wrong. They have forgotten what Wilson, in his early philosophical examination of the subject in *The Outsider* (1956), cites as "the Outsider's credo: 'I say, let them dread above all things stagnation ...'" (279; the quotation-within-the-quotation is from George Bernard Shaw's *Back to Methuselah*).

11   Here too Wilson is indebted to H.P. Lovecraft, whose "Cthulhu" mythology postulates an ancient race of creatures who inhabited Earth long before the human race and who lurk out of sight — usually in dark nasty corners — plotting to reclaim it. As David Ketterer notes, "Colin Wilson was sufficiently impressed to adapt Lovecraft's evocation of alien malignant powers harmful to man's autonomy, in *The Mind Parasites* ... thereby placing the alien-manipulator theme in the fully developed science-fictional context that Lovecraft only implies" (263).

12   For an overview of Wilson's career in sf, I recommend Brian Stableford's extremely entertaining *Foundation* article.

13   In the nineties, Gothic conventions influence the fashion, music, and sensibilities of the post-punk "goth" scene. Without entering into a discussion of this particular contemporary youth subculture, I want just to call attention to two novels by British writer Richard Calder, in which cyberpunk sf intersects with goth sensibilities to produce a new breed of alien vampires whose obsessions are sex and violence. These two novels, Dead Girls (1992) and Dead Boys (1994), are difficult reading, as much for their jagged and fragmented narrative technique as for their wrenching scenes of sex and death. They are also highly original examples of the integration of the vampire into contemporary science fiction and well worth discovering.

14   Mary Shelley's *Frankenstein*, of course, is the paradigmatic instance of this inclusionary narrative technique, used also by Fred Saberhagen in his revisionary *The Dracula Tapes* (1975) and, more famously, by Anne Rice in her *Vampire Chronicles*. In both Saberhagen and Rice's novels, vampires tend to be compulsive narrators of their own stories.

15   In its treatment of human beings as alien, Scott's text is comparable to Richard Matheson's sf/vampire novel, *I Am Legend*, in which all of humanity is infected with vampirism except for the lone protagonist, who thus takes on the role of outsider. While the final effect of Matheson's novel is to invert the conventional opposition between human and alien, Scott not only inverts the binary, but proceeds to dismantle it.

16   For an informative discussion of the sexual politics in *Dracula*, see Gail B. Griffin's essay "'Your Girls That You All Love Are Mine': *Dracula* and the Victorian Male Sexual Imagination." Another perspective is examined in Christopher Craft's essay, "'Kiss Me With Those Red Lips': Gender and Inversion in Bram Stoker's *Dracula*," which reads in *Dracula* the conflict, mediated by patriarchal representations of femininity, between the fear of and the desire for a forbidden sexuality. Craft reads *Dracula* as a homosocial text, a reading which Auerbach also takes up in her more recent study.

17   Angela Carter uses much the same strategy in her chilling postmodern fantasy, "The Lady of the House of Love" (1979), but her text recounts the destruction of the fantastic, not its triumph. Her woman-as-vampire, the Lady Nosferatu, dies for the love of a beautiful young man who remains sublimely unconscious of her true nature.

18   Although Wilson's text maintains rather than subverts the sexual politics of conventional vampire narratives, I would like to believe that it displays more of an ironic awareness than we might at first expect, especially in passages such as the following. Here Carlsen withstands his first "attack" by a vampire, who appears to him as a beautiful woman. If the tone of this passage is *not* ironic, then the author surely lacks all sense of humour: "He was not rejecting her; he wanted her with a greater intensity than he had wanted any woman; but he had always been a man of self-control; he attached importance to behaving like a gentleman. It would have been against all his instincts to make love to her where they were, in the specimen room" (31).

19   Such an expression is a literal function of the narrative structure as well, as Craft discusses in his analysis of *Dracula*. He calls attention to the "predictable ... triple rhythm" of texts like *Dracula*, *Frankenstein*, and *Dr. Jekyll and Mr. Hyde*. Each of these texts first invites or admits a monster, then entertains and is entertained by monstrosity for some extended duration, until in its closing pages it expels or repudiates the monster and all the disruption that he/she/it brings (107).

20   See, for example, the essays by Griffin, Hatlen, and Astle.

21   It seems extremely unlikely that the projections of women — themselves marginalised outsiders within traditional patriarchal cultures — will lead to the construction of "fantasy antagonists" characterised by the same anxieties and repressions as those of male writers. See Joan Gordon's essay "Rehabilitating Revenants, or Sympathetic Vampires in Recent Fiction," for an important examination of some of the revisionary features in vampire fiction by writers like Anne Rice, Suzy McKee Charnas, Chelsea Quinn Yarbro, Tanith Lee, and Jody Scott.

REFERENCES

Astle, Richard. "Dracula as Totemic Monster: Lacan, Freud, Oedipus and History." *Sub-Stance* 25 (1980): 98–105.

Auerbach, Nina. *Our Vampires, Ourselves.* Chicago: University of Chicago Press, 1995.

Craft, Christopher. "'Kiss Me with Those Red Lips': Gender and Inversion in Bram Stoker's *Dracula.*" *Representations* 8 (1984): 107–33.

Foust, R.E. "Monstrous Image: Theory of Fantasy Antagonists." *Genre* 13 (1980): 441–53.

Gordon, Joan. "Rehabilitating Revenants, or Sympathetic Vampires in Recent Fiction." *Extrapolation* 29 (1988): 227–34.

Griffin, Gail B. "'Your Girls That You All Love Are Mine': *Dracula* and the Victorian Male Sexual Imagination." *International Journal of Women's Studies* 3 (1980): 454–65.

Hatlen, Burton. "The Return of the Repressed/Oppressed in Bram Stoker's *Dracula.*" *Minnesota Review* 15 (1980): 80–97.

Hollinger, Veronica. "The Vampire and the Alien: Variations on the Outsider." *Science-Fiction Studies* 16 (1989): 145–160.

Hutcheon, Linda. *A Theory of Parody: The Teachings of Twentieth-Century Art Forms.* New York: Methuen, 1985.

Jameson, Fredric. *The Political Unconscious: Narrative as a Socially Symbolic Act.* Ithaca, New York: Cornell UP, 1981.

Ketterer, David. *New Worlds for Old: The Apocalyptic Imagination, Science Fiction and American Literature.* Bloomington, Indiana: Indiana UP, 1974.

Lifeforce. Dir. Tobe Hooper. Cannon/Tri-Star. 1985.

Manlove, Colin. *Modern Fantasy: Five Studies.* Cambridge: Cambridge UP: 1975.

Moskowitz, Sam. "Five Steps to Science Fiction Sanity." *Extrapolation* 27 (1986): 281–94.

Rabkin, Eric S. *The Fantastic in Literature.* Princeton, New Jersey: Princeton UP, 1976.

Schlobin, Roger C. "Children of a Darker God: A Taxonomy of Deep Horror Fiction and Film and Their Mass Popularity." *Journal of the Fantastic in the Arts* 1 (1988): 25–50.

Scott, Jody. *I, Vampire.* New York: Ace, 1984.

—. *Passing for Human.* 1977. London: The Woman's Press, 1986.

Skal, David J. *The Monster Show: A Cultural History of Horror.* New York: Norton, 1993.

Stableford, Brian. "Slaves of the Death Spiders: Colin Wilson and Existentialist Science Fiction." *Foundation*, 38 (1986/87): 63–67.

Stoker, Bram. *Dracula.* 1897. Oxford: Oxford UP, 1983.

Van Vogt, A.E. "Asylum." 1942. *Adventures in Time and Space.* Eds. Raymond J. Healy & J. Francis McComas. New York: Ballantine, 1975. 588–640.

Wells, H.G. "Preface to *The Scientific Romances.*" 1933. *H.G. Wells's Literary Criticism.* Ed. Patrick Parrinder & Robert Philmus. Totowa, New Jersey: Barnes &

Noble: 1980. 240–45.

Wilson, Colin. *The Space Vampires*. Toronto: Granada, 1976.

—. *The Mind Parasites*. 1967. Berkeley: Oneiric Press, 1979.

—. *The Strength to Dream: Literature and the Imagination*. 1962. Westport, Connecticut: Greenwood Press, 1973.

—. *The Outsider*. 1956. London: Victor Gollancz, 1974.

Wolf, Leonard. *The Essential Dracula: The Definitive Annotated Edition of Bram Stoker's Classic Novel*. 1975. New York: Plume, 1993.

Teaching the Vampire: Dracula in the Classroom

Norma Rowen

> "... as a species vampires have been our companions for so long that it is hard to imagine living without them. They promise escape from our dull lives and the pressure of our times, but they matter because when properly understood, they make us see that our lives are implicated in theirs, and our times are inescapable."
>
> (Auerbach 8–9)

THE VARYING RELEVANCE OF THE VAMPIRE AND THE complexity of our relationship to this figure were most thoroughly demonstrated to me during three years of teaching a course on vampires at York University in Toronto. The course was half-year and upper level and attracted mainly third- and fourth-year students. It covered a number of vampire "fictions," both literary and cinematic, and as its title, "Evolving Images of the Vampire," implies, its structure was basically historical. A number of approaches to the vampire were involved in our exploration of the course material. We examined it, for instance, from a psychological perspective — according to which the vampire is an embodiment of aspects of the psyche — as the objectification of secret desires and fears, especially, of course, sexual ones. Readings in Jung, mainly his discussion of the anima, the animus, and the shadow in its personal and collective forms, helped to support and direct this approach.

We also touched on the vampires of folklore and their anthropological implications, especially their connection with "primitive" attitudes to and rituals about the dead. The concentration here was chiefly on extracts from Paul Barber's *Vampires, Burial and Death* and Freud's *Totem and Taboo*. A socio-cultural approach was also important. We discussed the vampire in a class context, for instance, as essentially a bourgeois myth expressive of fears and desires about the aristocrat. A more directly Marxist analysis of the kind undertaken by Franco Moretti in *Signs Taken For Wonders* did not figure very largely in our discussions. More central to our socio-cultural contextualising of the vampire was an exploration of this figure as an embodiment of social alienation, and as a manifestation and marker of what a culture considers marginal and attempts to exclude from full participation in its life. We also considered the vampire in its spiritual and religious context, as a figure associated with both spiritual evil and spiritual transcendence. Bram Stoker's *Dracula* was the central text in this course. Earlier material examined the influences that helped to produce it. Later material, including a number of films, which began with F.W. Murnau's *Nosferatu*, explored the variants, elaborations, and "counter fictions" that emerged in response to it.

This, then, was the course methodology. But what about the students? What kind of students would take a course on vampires? This question was certainly on my mind as I entered the classroom three years or so ago to give my first lecture. Would there be "crazies" among them, people who thought they were vampires, people who wanted to be vampires, or people who thought this was a course on natural history? Certainly in that class and subsequent ones there were a number of students who *looked* rather strange. There was a marked element of fancy dress present. One young woman, for example, had decked herself out in bat jewelry (bat earrings, bat pendants, bat rings) that she had made herself, and there was a particularly spectacular young man who always came to class wearing an elaborate top hat, from which his long dark hair streamed down. In fact there was a lot of long dark hair about — more than usual, it seemed — often accompanied by dramatically reddened lips. These efforts at physical identification with the vampire were expressed at their most extreme by a young man in a recent class (another one with long dark hair) who proudly showed me his (naturally) pointed eye teeth.

In spite of these signs of a desire to assume a vampire identity and a general fascination with what has come to be understood as the vampire lifestyle (many students had visited *Sanctuary*, Toronto's "vampire sex bar"[1]), the students ultimately turned out to be pretty average and "normal," except that they were more literate than most. They got their assignments done, worked hard and absorbedly, struggled to balance school work and jobs, and were actually more anxious about their grades than the chance of running into a vampire after dark. None of them believed they were vampires or seemed to have any serious ambitions to become one. About whether they believed that vampires existed, however, I thought I detected some ambiguity. On one level, all of them scoffed at the idea. But after we had been reading some vampiric folklore, one young woman asked me earnestly how they (the vampires) managed to crawl out of the grave? There was an amused response to this. All the same, quite a few of the students showed a tendency to treat the vampire as if it were an objective phenomenon, with the fixed characteristics of the kind of creature studied in natural science. Some students were confused that a being supposedly not able to go out in the sunlight in one book could do so in another, or that having eaten freely in one book it was confined to a strict diet of human blood in the next. It was as if they thought some of the writers had "got it wrong" and were presenting what was not true. I was continually pointing out that vampires could do and be anything the author liked since they were fictional beings. I do not think this particular response indicates that these students really believed that vampires existed, but perhaps it does suggest a serious and deep yearning that such a thing might exist, that a creature like this might be found in our world.

At this point, of course, we should consider the reasons for such a yearning. Why do people want these creatures to exist? Why do they find them so attractive? From what my students said both in and out of class, and from the way they responded to the various approaches taken in the course, I came to the conclusion that there were three main aspects to the fascination the vampire exerted over them. First of all, my students were profoundly interested in the vampire in its psychological context. Indeed it almost seemed to function, in their view, as a kind of spirit guide to the underworld — the underworld of the self. They espoused the view that by acting out deeply buried desires and impulses the vampire could liberate such desires from repressing taboos, giving the conscious self a glimpse of the dark and mysterious psychic areas beyond the consciousness that were extremely intoxicating. The appeal of the vampire as a tool for such psychological exploration was clearly demonstrated in my course by my students' enthusiasm for Jung and their constant application of his ideas to the material. They were particularly interested in the figure of the shadow. Of all of the ideas that surfaced in the course, this was the one that most commanded their attention and influenced their way of thinking about the vampire. They referred to it constantly in discussion and tended to gravitate towards essay titles or exam questions that in some way involved this topic. They were particularly fascinated by the idea of the acknowledgement of the shadow and the connection between such acknowledgement and the popular habit of vampire victims somehow inviting the vampire in. Clearly, the question of the interrelationship between the parts of the psyche, of the puzzling coexistence of the normal and the pathological in us, and of how their balance is maintained, were imperative issues.

Another aspect of the vampire fascination among my students lay in their socio-cultural connection with the alienated and the marginal. Because they are carriers of a hidden life, of a secret that can never be disclosed, they are never really part of their society. They often move about in that society, of course — Stoker's Dracula, for instance, is seen drinking tea with a young woman and his celluloid descendants frequently grace upper class drawing rooms — but their connection with it is merely tangential. Always the deep, private self remains incommunicable. An invisible wall constructed out of both special knowledge and guilt invariably shuts them off. Figures of this kind often present an irresistible appeal to young people, both those in adolescence and those just beyond it, for they too are often dominated by a sense of themselves as different or "special," as possessing an inner self that can never be recognised. They are also very concerned with the issue of social integration. By giving expression and physical embodiment to their feelings about these issues, the vampire seems to make himself/herself their kin and invites them into a kind of fellowship on the margins.

The power of the vampire as a type of marginal and alienated "Other" can perhaps best be seen by the fact that every year my course attracted some students who belonged to groups which our society has very clearly designated as marginal. Thus, gay students quite frequently formed a contingent in the class, and were often determined to make their voices heard. One young man, who later wrote about his gay experience in his major essay, asked me when he was trying to get into the course if, as he had heard, some of the vampires to be studied were gay. This was obviously a major attraction for him. Generally undisclosed experience was being given a voice. This sense of the marginalised being given room and validation was considered by the students to be particularly strong in those works which actually penetrated the vampire's consciousness. Most of these works followed in *Dracula*'s wake.

As the course advanced, my students grew increasingly interested in the way the vampire could become a marker of the marginal, and signify shifts in sexual and social taboos. Thus, some of them noted that, while in most of the earlier works vampirism mainly signified a heterosexuality expressed too fully and uninhibitedly, in later writers, like Anne Rice, the taboo encoded in vampirism was more often confined to forms of sexuality that deviated from the heterosexual norm. The increased sympathy with which these vampires were treated in these later works also suggested significant shifts in cultural attitudes.

The interest in the marginal and the alienated was very strong among my students. With regard to other topics relating to the socio-cultural background of vampires, they showed less concern. Although some of them were intrigued with the idea of the vampire as an aristocrat, for instance, they tended to refrain from discussing topics involving class analysis, since most of them did not have a very good idea of what classes were, and had some difficulty distinguishing the aristocrat from the bourgeois. This subject, therefore, ultimately did not prove as fruitful as that connected with alienation.

The third aspect of the vampire's fascination involved the students' immortality. Indeed, immortality was the characteristic most often cited when I asked students what most attracted them to the vampire. Some of them added comments that suggested links between this attraction and a kind of religious nostalgia. Most of them were very drawn to the idea of the vampire as a spiritual being. Products of the twentieth-century post-religious world, the majority of the students, it is true, did not see this figure as connected with any specifically religious concept of good or evil. What the vampire did seem to suggest to them, however, was the possibility of some kind of transcendence of this world. This human need for transcendence was one of the things, it seemed, that ultimately caused these students to invest the figure of the vampire with such glamour. Vampires, while never actually moving physically to another world, can nonetheless be seen as having transcended the conditions of this one. In their ability to fly or shape-shift, they can break physical laws. They also transgress accepted moral boundaries. Above all, in being immortal, they transcend what seems to be the most unassailable fact of the human condition — death. In this way, they have broken through to another existence. "I was the supernatural in this cathedral," says Louis in *Interview with the Vampire* (145). For some, it seems, the vampire has assumed the space vacated by God.

These, then, were the main ideas and attitudes towards the vampire which my students brought to the course, and which informed their responses to it. The background knowledge of vampire texts that they

235

brought with them, however, was often quite limited. This was especially the case with literary texts. Most of them had never read Stoker's *Dracula*, or anything that was not relatively contemporary. Anne Rice, Chelsea Quinn Yarbro, and Michael Romkey tended to constitute the core of their knowledge, though not all of them had read all three of these writers.

These writers have been instrumental in setting the fashion for current fiction about vampires. It was Anne Rice who introduced the revolutionary idea of handing the narration over to the vampire himself/herself, hence giving the unspeakable a voice and bringing the margin into the centre. In *Interview with the Vampire* (1976), the first of her *Vampire Chronicles*, the narrator is the vampire Louis de Pointe du Lac. In subsequent ones, it is his fellow vampire, Lestat de Lioncourt. Michael Romkey follows the same path. The chief vampire, David Parker, in his best known book, *I, Vampire* (1990), is the first-person narrator. In Yarbro's works, the Saint Germain Chronicles, there is no comparable use of the vampire as actual narrator, but the story is frequently told from his point of view.[2]

The vampires in these books are similar in another respect: they are all exceedingly personable. Lestat, Louis's vampiriser/seducer in *Interview with the Vampire*, is described as "a tall, fair skinned man with a mass of blond hair" (12). His "grey eyes [burn] ... with an incandescence" (13), and his movements are "graceful and feline" (12). Louis is equally handsome and both of them are highly cultivated. They dress with superb elegance, decorate their homes with exquisite taste, and spend their vampire nights visiting the opera, reading Shakespeare and Aristotle, and playing the spinet. They are, unfortunately, obliged to kill for their supper, and this is portrayed as sullying their existence and causing moral conflict. However, the people they kill, generally slaves, derelicts, and prostitutes, are presented as being much less attractive than they are, and frequently so morally sordid that it is difficult to care too deeply about their fate. In the later volumes of the *Vampire Chronicles*, in fact, Rice indicates that as vampires mature they no longer need human blood to survive.

Romkey's David Parker is the scion of an old and rich American family. He too is intelligent, well-dressed, and highly cultivated, and his attractiveness is made less ambiguous by the fact that he is relieved by his author of the necessity to kill. Only a moderate ingestion of blood is needed to keep him going. Yarbro's vampire, Saint-Germain, has all the personability of his fellows. His dark and charismatic looks are complemented by a dress-sense that seems infallible, no matter in what era he is situated. And he, too, like Parker, does not need to kill in order to obtain enough blood to survive. In fact, both Romkey and Yarbro present their vampires as morally superior to human beings. Parker eventually meets up with a group of vampires known as the "Illuminati." Many great and famous men from the past are among their number (the most prominent of them is Mozart), and their main purpose is to act as shepherds to their unknowing human flock. Using their supernatural powers, they help them to avert catastrophes and disasters. It is true that there is an evil vampire in Romkey's work, but he is kept far from the narrative voice, and it is the task of David and the Illuminati to protect humanity by destroying him. Saint-Germain's role is similar to that of the Illuminati. This higher being attempts to make benevolent interventions in human history in order to rectify its course, but he is often defeated by the hopelessly evil tendencies of humankind. He is most successful, in fact, in the rescue of individuals. Many of these are young women whom he frees from various forms of patriarchal oppression and liberates into true sexuality with his vampiric kiss. With him, as with Rice's and Romkey's vampires, the vampiric act is highly erotically charged.

These, then, are the novels with which most of my students were familiar. Outside of such texts, their knowledge of vampires derived mainly from movies, and, again, mostly from recent ones. This was particularly the case with *Dracula* itself, their experience of the film versions of the novel rarely extending back to Tod Browning. The Christopher Lee movies, John Badham's *Dracula*, and the Coppola version of the story, however, were familiar to a fair number of them. The suavity and elegance of these celluloid Counts constituted their main image of Stoker's vampire.

During the course, their background knowledge about vampires was expanded. We had at this point read some folklore, some Romantic poems featuring vampire-like creatures (Byron's "Manfred," for example), and two actual vampire novels: Polidori's *The Vampyre* and Le Fanu's *Carmilla*. However, although these figures often had a greater moral complexity than those in the works the students had previously encountered, most of them were written in the shadow of the Romantic movement and Lord Byron, and therefore tended to be dominated by glamorous and attractive protagonists.

Given this background, it is not to be wondered at that when my students started on Stoker's *Dracula*, both the work and the central figure came as something of a shock. In fact, student reaction to the Count generally echoed Jonathan Harker's surprise and discomfort when he first encountered his strange host. The characteristic that evoked the most immediate comment was his age. This Dracula with his white hair and cadaverous features was old! They were used to young vampires, like Frank Langella, Gary Oldman, and those in the novels, or celluloid vampires like Bela Lugosi, who, although of mature years, still retained a midlife appearance. Even worse, not only was this Dracula old, he was exceedingly unattractive. There were aspects of brutal nastiness to his appearance that were extremely unprepossessing — his pointed ears, for instance, and the grotesque hair on the palms of his hands. Above all, he smelled! An oppressive graveyard stench irremediably tinged his breath. "As the Count leaned over me and his hands touched me," says Jonathan, "I could not repress a shudder. It may have been that his breath was rank, but a horrible feeling of nausea came over me, which, do what I would, I could not conceal" (18). Such characteristics stood in marked contrast to the physical charisma of the vampires with which many of my students were familiar, like Louis and Lestat with their crystalline eyes, luminous white skin, and supernatural cleanliness, or the celluloid Draculas of recent decades who are intriguing and magnetic at dinner parties.

Perhaps the most important difference between Stoker's vampire and those my students had previously encountered was his anti-romantic aspect. Stoker's Dracula is strikingly sexual, of course. Most obviously, his sucking of his victims' blood mirrors the sex act. But this is a sexuality connected much more emphatically with power than with love. With the possible exception of Mina, Dracula's attitude to his victims is brutally impersonal. As Christopher Craft and other critics have pointed out, Dracula's choice of the females he attacks seems to be dictated primarily by the men they belong to, over whom it is his chief ambition to exert dominion. Ultimately, all of these humans, men and women both, are no more than a part of his campaign to bring the world under his control.

Most of the cinematic vampires and those in Rice and other contemporary fictions are, on the other hand, heavily involved in romantic relationships. Thus, in Romkey's book, David Parker's main object is to find his beautiful vampire mistress, and Saint-Germain generally falls in love with his prospective victims. As for Louis and Lestat, they endure all the fluctuating tensions of a major love affair during their immortality. Even Dracula, on film, almost always has at least a "special relationship" with his chief victim. Indeed, in Coppola's film, his main purpose in staying alive through the centuries is to await the reincarnation of his wife so that he can claim her again. Frank Langella, much handsomer in his dinner jacket than Lucy's fiancé, wants to make Lucy his consort. Even in Murnau's *Nosferatu*, which contains what must surely be the most unprepossessing vampire of all time, Count Orlock's interest in the Mina/Lucy figure is particular and personal, being ignited when he catches a glimpse of her portrait in a locket. This motif repeatedly appears in later Dracula films, so that when my students came to read the Stoker text some of them remarked on its absence as if a crucial part of the story had been inadvertently omitted.

Finally, of course, there is a major moral difference between Stoker's Dracula and the vampires my students had so far encountered. Dracula's repulsive physical appearance is indicative of a matching moral nastiness that is unalleviated by any hint of ambiguity or possibility of redemption. In fact, in reference to his radically undeveloped moral sense, Van Helsing explains that Dracula possesses the brain of a child. Thus, Dracula's murderous transactions cause him no repining; rather, he exults in them, and although he wishes to intervene in history and human affairs, his intentions are in no way benevolent, his aim being to achieve total power over the world. This Dracula is thoroughly and unequivocally evil.

In many ways, then, my students tended to find *Dracula* both significantly different from and harder to deal with than the other vampire material they encountered in the course. A wary reticence seemed to descend on all three of the classes I taught during the two weeks we usually spent on Stoker's work. This manifested itself in a certain inhibiting of what had often been lively and interested discussion. In fact, with some episodes in the novel it was hard to get a discussion going at all. Chief among these was the celebrated scene in which Dracula makes Mina drink his blood. The fearful collapsing of boundaries which occurs here — gender boundaries, family role boundaries, animal/human boundaries — makes this a deeply shocking and disturbing episode. My students' reluctance to talk about it perhaps showed that they needed to explore it in the silence and privacy of their own selves rather than through public discussion. Certainly, the journey into the dark and hidden reaches of the self is more difficult when the shadow/guide assumes the form, not of someone youthful and attractive — however murderous — but of a repulsive and unrepentant elder with bad breath. Acknowledging and coming to terms with this sort of shadow is altogether more of an ordeal.

Significantly, when my students did discuss the shadow in relation to Stoker's *Dracula*, they preferred to concentrate on the vampire as a form of cultural shadow, as a reflection of the sexual schizophrenia particularly characteristic of the Victorians, those people a safe century or so off in the past. The fact that we looked at Stephen Marcus's *The Other Victorians* as part of our sessions on *Dracula* made this approach particularly appealing. With regard to Dracula's possible relevance as an individual, personal shadow, my students said very little.

A similar contrast between Stoker's novel and other vampire works surfaced with regard to the issues of alienation and marginalisation. In most of the works read prior to Stoker's *Dracula*, not only do the vampires add glamour to these states by the figures they themselves present, but the ambience within which they move is generally exceedingly attractive. David Parker, for instance, as an inheritor of American wealth, has always lived in opulent surroundings. An exclusive Swiss boarding school is followed by Harvard. On his marriage, he buys an "elegant old townhouse near the lake" where he spends his days playing on his grand piano and reading Barbara Pym novels (19). On becoming a vampire, his surroundings do not change much. When vampiric activities take him to Paris, he is able to stay, without difficulty, at the Ritz. Louis and Lestat, though not as securely positioned as Romkey's vampire, also have a townhouse in New Orleans which they are able to furnish in exquisite luxury and style. In Louis's description of it, elegant chandeliers and carpets dominate, along with "silk screens with painted birds of paradise, canaries singing in great domed, golden cages, and delicate marble Grecian gods and beautifully painted Chinese vases" (99).

In *Interview with the Vampire*, as in her other vampire fictions, Anne Rice's depiction of the loneliness and claustrophobia of a hidden and alienated existence is often very powerful. But the sheer beauty and elegance of the surroundings in which this alienation is played out exert a consoling effect. When the margins are so well appointed, the dreariness and depression of living on them is considerably alleviated. In most film versions of *Dracula*, the Count, as in Stoker's novel, lives in a series of ruined castles and abbeys. More often than not, however, the films render this habitat quite magical. In John Badham's *Dracula*, for instance, Dracula's ruined drawing room is illuminated by a myriad of twinkling candles that make it a place of enchantment. As such, it contrasts very favourably with both the comfortable but more prosaically lit home of the Van Helsings and Lucy's father's lunatic asylum, the real locus of alienation in the work. Even in Tod Browning's *Dracula*, the ruined castle is given a misty and intriguing beauty that grips the imagination. In these texts, then, alienation is given a gloss and glamour that is also bestowed on the vampires. The margins become the domain of an élite group, places of beauty and excitement that, themselves, become a kind of centre.

In its handling of the vampire's ambience, as in its handling of the vampire, Stoker's *Dracula* completely avoids all beauty and elegance. No touch of glamour or enchantment is allowed to soften the alienated landscape. Dracula's ruined castle, with its comfortless gloom and moth-ridden decaying rooms, only offers us a long vista of domestic desolation, an impression intensified by the glimpse we are given of Dracula furtively making his guest's bed. It is a cheerless prison from which we, like Jonathan, are desperate to escape. When Dracula moves to England, the ruined abbey he inhabits there has nothing of the magic present in the film versions. Permeated by a nauseating odour, "composed of all the ills of mortality and with the pungent, acrid smell of blood" (251), it is thick with dust and spiders' webs and "alive with rats" (252). True, Dracula does eventually manage to move into a townhouse in London, but the desolation accompanies him and affects that environment as well. The house itself is generally decayed and unpainted, and the sight that greets Jonathan and his comrades when they enter the dining-room is very different from the Aladdin's Cave vistas with which we are presented in Louis's and Lestat's townhouse. The effects of the Count are described as lying

> ... in a sort of orderly disorder on the great dining-room table. There were title-deeds of the Piccadilly house in a great bundle; deeds of the purchase of the houses at Mile End and Bermondsey; note-paper, envelopes, and pens and ink. All were covered up in thin wrapping paper to keep them from the dust. There were also a clothes brush, a brush and comb, and a jug and basin — the latter containing dirty water which was reddened as if with blood. (300–1)

This messy detritus of mundane objects and the jug of sinister liquid create an atmosphere of dirt and dereliction that contrasts sharply with the portrait of life on the margins in the works of Romkey and Rice. One of my students, writing eloquently on this scene, quoted a telling phrase to describe its atmosphere. "A contaminated loneliness," he said, pervaded it.[3]

Stoker's *Dracula* casts a similar blight on the idea of the glamour and desirability of immortality. The Count is certainly connected to the world of the spirit. My students were quick to note that he could only be defeated by a man who weds the two opposing visions of science and religion as does Van Helsing. (Crosses, garlic, the Host, surgical knives, a stake, a hammer, and a screwdriver are some of the weapons he mobilises against the vampire.) However, unlike the situation of those vampires who live in the freedom of the post-religious world, Dracula's immortal life is inextricably bound up with a specifically religious conception of evil. As the inverted Christian imagery surrounding him shows, his role is that of an anti-Christ. Thus, Renfield, with his talk of awaiting the coming of his Lord and Master, appears as a parody of John the Baptist, and his references to the vampire's blood-sucking as "the blood is the life" (141) mockingly echo the Christian eucharist. The purpose of Dracula's immortality, then, is to serve evil by turning the world into a vampire-haunted wilderness dominated by himself. To Van Helsing, such immortality is nothing less than "a curse" (214). Perhaps most crucially, in spite of his links to a metaphysical world and his superhuman qualities like the capacity to shape-shift, the general presentation of Dracula and his environment undermines any idea of transcendence. At the end of *Interview with the Vampire*, the boy reporter begs Louis to make him into a vampire so that he too can enter immortally into the excitement of a vampire life. Louis is furious and disgusted, feeling that his portrayal of the horrors of his condition has been misunderstood. As readers, however, I think we sympathise with the boy. Ultimately, the miseries of Louis's experience are less disturbing to the imagination than the luxury and brilliance of his existence and its freedom from normal human boundaries. To be immortal in this world, it seems, would be immensely exhilarating. Such a feeling is evoked by Rice's work. On the contrary, to live immortally in circumstances such as Dracula's seems like an imprisonment. In this case, rather than moving beyond the confines of earthly existence, the vampire seems to be trapped in some of its most dark and dreary corners. The description of Dracula's house in Piccadilly is especially eloquent on this front. Rather than presenting an image of an enviable, supernatural life, it suggests a disabled and dysfunctional human one. For those seeking to transcend the conditions of human existence, an escape route via the vampire is unavailable in this instance.

In spite of their reluctance to discuss it, I do not think my students ultimately evaded consideration of *Dracula* and the issues it raised. There were a number of excellent presentations on it, and most of the students chose to write quite extensively about *Dracula* in the course's final essay and exam. Their comments were often discerning, imaginative, and wide-ranging. Perhaps although himself a fantasy figure, Stoker's Dracula ultimately acts in some ways as a reality principle, reminding us of the terrifying and repellent aspects of the journey into the psychic depths and the shadow figures that haunt it, and of the dreariness and desolation which accompany the alienated life. Altogether I would say that, more than any other work on the course, *Dracula* gave the students pause, prompting them to reassess their prior assumptions about the vampire.

Chiefly, perhaps, the course taught me that *Dracula* should give us pause too. Over the decades Bram Stoker and his work have received more than their share of the condescension that we commonly mete out to the Victorians. For years, his novel was written off as a second-rate piece of pop/pulp fiction, and even now, when the novel is being examined more seriously, Stoker is still regarded as an innocent who had the naiveté to think that he could keep his distance from his monster and eventually annihilate him altogether. We of the twentieth century, after wars and holocausts which continue to originate in our supposedly civilised communities — the kind of communities that in Stoker drive the vampire out — realise that such arm's length approaches to the monstrous are no longer open to us. On the contrary, we now feel the necessity to get closer to and communicate with our monsters. Hence, we have allowed our vampires a voice, given them psychological house room, even to some extent taken it upon ourselves to identify with them. But perhaps this closer embrace and greater acknowledgement has been achieved only at some cost. The glamourisation and sanitisation of the vampire in many recent literary works suggests that we may only have been able to arrive at this familiar proximity by making the monster less monstrous. In giving him house room, we have tended to exact from him the penalty of increased domestication. Perhaps, after all, by keeping his distance, Stoker managed to better represent the nature of the monstrous.

When we reread *Dracula* in this context and experience afresh the extraordinary power of its images — images which seem to rise unmediated from the deepest parts of the psyche — we realise once again that this is still the best vampire work every written. It remains unchallenged in its evocation of the horror and mystery surrounding the vampire. By the end of the course, some of my students had also gained this realisation.

NOTES

1   Sanctuary is situated in a bohemian area of downtown Toronto (732 Queen Street West). The bar features fancy dress and blood-coloured drinks and every two weeks, in an area called the Catacombs, there is a Boudoir Noir Fetish Night.

2   Anne Rice and Chelsea Quinn Yarbro both began writing their *Chronicles* in the late 1970s. Neither has yet concluded them.

3   The student's name is Kenneth Hume. He could not remember where the phrase came from.

REFERENCES

Auerbach, Nina. *Our Vampires, Ourselves.* Chicago: University of Chicago Press, 1995.

Barber, Paul. *Vampires, Burial and Death.* New Haven: Yale University Press, 1988.

Bram Stoker's Dracula. Dir. Francis Ford Coppola. Columbia, 1992.

Craft, Christopher. "'Kiss Me with Those Red Lips': Gender and Inversion in Bram Stoker's *Dracula.*" *Representations* 8 (1984): 107–33.

Dracula. Dir. John Badham. Mirisch/Universal. 1979.

Dracula. Dir. Tod Browning. Universal, 1931.

Freud, Sigmund. *Totem and Taboo.* 1912–1913. London: Routledge, 1966.

Le Fanu, Sheridan. "Carmilla." 1872. *In A Glass Darkly.* Oxford: Oxford UP, 1993. 243–319.

Marcus, Steven. *The Other Victorians: A Study of Sexuality and Pornograpy in Mid-Nineteenth Century England.* 1966. New York: NAL, 1974.

Moretti, Franco. *Signs Taken for Wonders: Essays in the Sociology of Literary Forms.* London: Verso Editions & NLB, 1983.

Nosferatu: Eine Symphonie des Grauens (*A Symphony of Terror*). Dir. F.W. Murnau. Prana Film, 1922.

Polidori, John. *The Vampyre.* 1819. *Vampyres: Lord Byron to Count Dracula.* London: Faber and Faber, 1991. 97–125.

Rice, Anne. *Interview with the Vampire.* Toronto: Random House, 1977.

Romkey, Michael. *I, Vampire.* Toronto: Random House, 1990.

Stoker, Bram. *Dracula.* 1897. Oxford: Oxford UP, 1983.

III

ondo *Dracula*—

elluloid

ampires

"It is not good to note this down": Dracula and the Erotic Technologies of Censorship

Jacqueline LeBlanc

N 1908, ELEVEN YEARS AFTER THE PUBLICATION of *Dracula*, Bram Stoker published an essay in *The Nineteenth Century* calling for the censorship of "dangerous" fiction:

> … a number of books have been published in England that would be a disgrace to any country less civilized than our own. The class of works to which I allude are meant by both authors and publishers to bring to the winning of commercial success the forces of inherent evil in man.… The evil is a grave and dangerous one, and may, if it does not already, deeply affect the principles and lives of the young people of this country.… If no other adequate way can be found, and if the plague-spot continues to enlarge, a censorship there must be. ("The Censorship of Fiction" 485–486)

Stoker concludes that reading fiction poses a specifically sexual threat. Putting "a finger on the actual point of danger," he declares, "the only emotions [evoked by reading] which in the long run harm are those arising from sex impulses" (483). Critics, for the most part, have been unable to reconcile Stoker's prudish call for censorship with the eroticism of his novel *Dracula*. Reading a paradox in his identity, they have theorised two opposed Stokers: a Victorian puritan and a liberated writer of provocative fiction. As if under a spell of repression, Stoker wrote *Dracula*, these critics conclude, without knowing he had written "one of the most erotic books in English literature" (Farson 210).[1] Challenging this interpretation as a misreading of both Stoker and censorship, this essay will trace the collusion between eroticism and censorship in *Dracula*. Stoker's writings prove contradictory only because critics have assumed that censorship and sexuality are opposed, censorship being regarded as wholly repressive and eroticism as wholly expressive. Turning to Michel Foucault's "repressive hypothesis," it would seem that Stoker deconstructs the repression-expression opposition in *Dracula* to reveal a continuum between censorship and eroticism.

In volume one of *The History of Sexuality*, Foucault explains that restrictions on sexuality in the modern age are less about the repression of sexuality than about its production in discourse. Beginning with confession manuals of the Middle Ages, sex has continually been transformed or displaced into discourse even by institutions that prohibit sexual activity. Indeed, Foucault notes that by the seventeenth century it became a fundamental duty to transform desire into discourse by confessing sexual desires in detail (20–21). Foucault concludes that the modern age is not marked by censorship at all but by a "veritable discursive explosion" in the "multiplication of discourses concerning sex" (17–18). To understand Stoker's discourses of eroticism and censorship, I want to extend Foucault's analysis by suggesting a necessary connection between repression and production within the field of censorship itself. As recent studies of censorship have suggested, censorship is paradoxical because it focuses attention on that which it attempts to eradicate.[2] Censorship works productively rather than repressively by calling attention, albeit negative, to sexuality and by actually creating sexual metaphors, myths, and symbols. *Dracula* is one example of "productive" censorship, vampirism representing a monstrous exaggeration of the evil Stoker locates in "obscene" fiction. The eroticism of *Dracula* condemns while defining deviant sexuality and, like Stoker's censorship essay, its goal is "the preservation of boundaries."[3] Yet even as Stoker's human characters police vampiric sexuality by hunting the Count, they also produce and disseminate a discourse about vampirism. Indeed, this discourse structures and commands their vampire hunt. Stoker's sexual exposé neither simply liberates sexuality nor simply represses it since it produces erotic sexual symbols while simultaneously demonising this eroticism. Like the confession manuals Foucault describes, *Dracula* is a paradoxical disciplinary discourse, attempting to impugn obscene impulses ("the forces of evil inherent in man") by writing about them. Thus, Stoker is paradoxical, not because he writes erotica and advocates censorship, but because this form of censorship is itself paradoxical. Repressing sexuality and speaking about it are interdependent, and a reading of the continuum between *Dracula* and Stoker's censorship essay can suggest ways in which censorship produces "erotic" material even in its efforts to prohibit sexual discourse and behaviour.

First, historicising both the vampire myth and censorship, I will draw a connection between the productive myth-making of censorship and the "vampirism" of obscene discourse. Both *Dracula* and "The Censorship of Fiction" work out of this history of demonising both sexuality and its discourses as a means to censorship and social discipline. *Dracula*, I will argue, presents one of the first modern transformations of this censorship theme since it links vampiric sexuality with the "cutting edge" technologies of the typewriter and the phonograph.[4] While the paradox of censorship is borne out in Stoker's erotic and puritanical writings, it also functions in the plot of *Dracula* itself, where Mina Harker achieves the modern freedom to quickly produce and distribute her own discourse by using a typewriter. Through technological inventions which facilitate the dissemination of information, Mina Harker and her "brave men" produce and distribute a potentially dangerous erotic discourse in order to police the deviant sexuality of the vampire. In my conclusion, I will turn to the "postmodern" technologies of censorship in Francis Ford Coppola's film *Bram Stoker's Dracula*, which elaborates upon the sexual threat of technology and more subtly repeats the reactionary gesture of "The Censorship of Fiction."

Vampires and the Sexual Discourse of Censorship

HISTORICALLY, CENSORSHIP AND other social restrictions are justified by the rhetorical invention of evil, whether it assumes the form of obscenity, disease, or monstrosity. The myth of vampirism has functioned as one such moral regulator. Like witch hunts, the vampire myth was used as an instrument of social control, a means to define and name deviance. Not just any corpse was considered a likely candidate for vampirism. Most often, vampires were individuals who defied social or religious mores. In the early Church, most of those accused of vampire attacks were deceased excommunicants, suicides, and those buried unbaptised or apostate (Barber 29). It was widely held that "people could protect themselves from vampires by observing the sacraments of the Church" (Masters 176, 180). More specifically, vampirism was a means of policing sexual behaviour, often through demonising female sexuality. While one form of folkloric vampire was strictly monster — a walking dead, short, plump, grotesque — other versions, particularly female, were clearly eroticised. Female vampires were a form of succubus, the female demon said to descend upon a man while he slept for the purpose of sexual intercourse. Gabriel Ronay describes the Lamia as "a type of female vampire [greatly feared in ancient Greece] that used the pleasures of lovemaking to ensnare handsome youths, drain them of their blood, and devour them" (5). The Talmud's Lilith, another version of the vampire succubus, "mischievously filled the minds of sleeping men with erotic dreams, thus causing them to excrete semen" (Masters 170). Generally, vampirism represented the monstrosity of "pure sexual expenditure." Seeking erotic pleasure in defiance of social laws commanding the propagation of the human race, vampire were represented as alien creatures who threatened the survival of humanity as a whole.[5]

By the nineteenth century, the vampire myth was brought closer to home as ordinary women gaining intellectual and sexual autonomy were thought to be potential Lamias and Liliths. In "Onanism: Essay on the Ailments Produced By Masturbation" first published in 1758 but widely influential in Victorian culture, Samuel Tissot wrote that women who masturbate "are particularly liable to attacks of hysteria or frightful vapors; ... falling and ulceration of the womb, ... lengthening and scabbing of the clitoris; and finally uterine fury, *which deprives them at once of modesty and reason and puts them on the level of lewdest brutes*" (Kendrick 89, emphasis mine). Masturbation's most egregious symptom was androgyny, a feature also common to the sexually penetrating female vampire. While men who masturbate, according to Tissot, become diseased and impotent, women who masturbate become diseased and sexually potent. Unnaturally masculinised, they become lewd "brutes." Indeed, they become *like vampires*. A pseudo-scientific tract designed to repress sexual behaviour, "Onanism" delineated sexual perversion by naming it and defining it as bestial. Like certain myths of the vampire, it reproduced discursive forms of deviant sexuality even as it attempted to control sexual acts.

Masturbation represents only one activity which generated Victorian anxiety over sexuality. It accompanies, in the Victorian mind, another increasingly rampant perversion — reading. With the growing mass of common readers in the nineteenth century came heightened anxiety over the potentially subversive sexual influence of print material. Monstrously auto-erotic, women were now potentially autodidactic. Akin to the temptation of masturbation, reading even threatened to inspire the act. Encouraging independent ideas and autonomous sexuality, reading in fact became another pernicious factor in the dangerous domain of sexuality. According to the logic of the nineteenth century censor (and to Stoker himself), as lewd fiction was withheld from the masses, so too was their sexuality kept in check.

Yet the censorship of pornography and "dangerous" fiction was accompanied by its own production of sexual discourses. Henry Spencer Ashbee, a Victorian bibliophile who specialised in pornography, "damned the very things he was immortalizing." Erotic bibliography, he contended, "would protect the world from pernicious literature by highlighting it instead of blotting it out" (Kendrick 74–75). More dramatically, the prosecutions of obscene novels in the nineteenth century staged their own productions of these works by detailing content, inventing new and especially lewd titles, and citing their offending passages verbatim.[6] These trials, in a sense, produced their own form of lewd fiction, enforcing censorship through both the prosecution of obscene literature and the reinscription of it. As Richard D. Altick observes, print journalism became a crucial instrument in the moral policing of literature in the nineteenth century: "[once] 'superior orders of society' ... conceded it was impossible to prevent the lower ranks from reading, they embarked on a long campaign to ensure that through the press the masses of people would be induced to help preserve the status quo" (85). Thus was censorship forced away from the simple repression of discourse into a production of its own discourse, which, to obtain full effect, had to be convincingly erotic as well as convincingly evil.

Dracula and the Technologies of Censorship

READ IN THE context of Victorian-style censorship, *Dracula* exemplifies censorship's complex repression and production of sexual discourse. The sexuality of *Dracula* cannot be interpreted autonomously from the disciplining rhetoric of earlier vampire myths or the creative rhetoric of nineteenth-century censorship. Stoker's vampirism is a mythic cousin to uterine fury. Count Dracula is the classic inhuman Other. A monstrous embodiment of human sexuality, he represents a perverse sexuality that defies institutional definition.[7] As a demonic representation of this defiance, the vampire reinforces such institutions as marriage, heterosexuality, and patriarchy. Yet, even as *Dracula* reinscribes boundaries of sexuality, it transgresses them. The symbol of the vampire works to repress *and to expose*: it represses human sexuality, replacing it with monstrous anatomy and preternatural reproductive functions, yet it highlights "deviant" sexuality unacceptable to Victorian culture such as sex with multiple partners, sex outside of marriage, adulterous sex, homosexuality, and potent female sexuality.[8]

This paradox within Stoker's vampire myth is mirrored in the novel by a paradox within its generated sexual discourses. *Dracula* is preoccupied with the spread and control of vampiric sexuality and its representative discourse. Technological advances in communication and transcription such as the typewriter and the phonograph form a type of vampiric reproduction. As Jennifer Wicke points out, "the social force most analogous to Count Dracula's ... is none other than mass culture, the developing technologies of the media in its many forms" (469). The narrative of *Dracula* is "pasted together" from letters, newspaper articles, and telegraph messages. It features diaries written in shorthand, typed on a typewriter or recorded on phonograph cylinders. These technologies of discourse have a specular relationship to vampirism in the novel: like the Count, who represents the source of perversity, these media are a well-spring of erotica, conveying a contagious passion that requires vigilant supervision. Powerfully reproductive, they engender a type of techno-vamping of discourse, potentially spreading sexual information widely and indiscriminately. Characters employ these modern inventions paradoxically, however, to facilitate and to impede communication. Jonathan uses shorthand, for instance, to correspond with Mina and to ensure that the Count is unable to read his correspondence. Like a censorship which both produces and denounces sexual discourse, shorthand and the novel's other forms of communication technology simultaneously police and expose the Count and his perverse sexuality.

Documenting events surrounding the vampire attacks thus constitutes both a primary moral duty and a moral transgression, an ambivalent activity evidenced by characters simultaneously writing down and censoring their thoughts. Writing to Mina of her "polyandrous" fantasy, for instance, Lucy adds the proper disclaimer: "Why can't they let a girl marry three men, or as many as want her, and save all this trouble? But this is heresy and I must not say it" (59). Curiously, Lucy is compelled to chronicle her heresy even if she must denounce it. Since the strategy allows for both her indulgence and her restraint, she is seldom inclined to restrict her language. When she writes to Mina of her love for Arthur Holmwood, she fears her letter is an improper expression of emotion which she is nevertheless unwilling to contain. Her letter is a vehicle for her desire, a displaced discursive consummation of her sexual urges. "I do not know how I am writing this even to you," she tells Mina; "I am afraid to stop, or I should tear up the letter, and I don't want to stop, for I *do so* want to tell you all" (55). Anticipating her subsequent feelings of desire and repulsion for the Count, Lucy's ambivalent desire to tell all reveals her simultaneous femme fatale seductiveness and "angel in the house" sweetness. She is both naive and brazen. Hers is a discursive ejaculation which prophesies her final plunge into "undead" licentiousness. Lucy's excited desire to speak ("I *do so* want to tell you all") becomes unquestionably vampiric, giving way to unchecked sexual hunger.

Even as Lucy revels in discursive and vampiric flirtation, she recognises the illicitness of both her discourse and her vamping. Both she and Mina understand that her letters and her mysterious excursion to the churchyard must be kept "secret." Lucy adds in one letter, however, that Mina can tell Jonathan of her engagement to Arthur since "a woman ought to tell her husband everything" (56). As sexually devoted partners, Mina and Jonathan are socially sanctioned partners in discourse as well. Indeed, as Jonathan's fiancée, Mina performs the premarital rite of learning his discourse, and the couple finally communicate in their own language — shorthand. Before they are married, however, Jonathan resists fully open correspondence with Mina, especially suppressing his brush with vampirism. His ambivalent desire for the vampire women in Count Dracula's castle, like Lucy's desire for Dracula, is replayed in his ambivalent inscribing of it. He writes in his journal, "I felt in my heart a wicked, burning desire that they would kiss me with those red lips. It is not good to note this down, lest some day it should meet Mina's eyes and cause her pain; but it is the truth" (37). As Victorian publishers censored fiction for the protection of the "weaker sex," Jonathan censors both his journal and his correspondence to Mina. Theirs is still a premarital, virginal communication: "To her I have explained my situation, but without the horrors [sexual desires] which I may only surmise. It would shock and frighten her to death were I to expose my heart to her" (41).

Jonathan's apprehension attests to the novel's fixation with the danger of spreading sexual information. As deadly as vampirism itself, communication about vampirism is frequently censored in *Dracula*, usually for the protection of the physically and emotionally fragile women. Arthur Holmwood writes, for instance, that he dare not ask Lucy's mother about her daughter's failing health "for to disturb the poor lady's mind about her daughter in her present state of health would be fatal" (109). Lucy is likewise never told the origin of her illness, her physical fragility specifically requiring that she be kept ignorant, while Mina is excluded from the vampire hunt because she is physically and emotionally weak. Dr. Seward declares it is "no place for a woman," insisting "if she [Mina] had remained in touch with the affair, it would in time infallibly have wrecked her" (256). The act of withholding information about these symbolic sexual transactions does not apply exclusively to women, however, since Arthur too must be kept in the dark about Seward's transfusion of blood to Lucy. Revealing the particularly sexual nature of the transfusion, Van Helsing advises Seward, "If our young lover should turn up unexpected, as before, no word to him. It would at once frighten him and enjealous him, too" (128). In this episode, Van Helsing wishes to protect the feelings of Arthur and perhaps ensure the success of his own operation. Threatened by the knowledge of this symbolic sexual mingling of his friend's and his lover's bodily fluids, Arthur would no doubt attempt to put an end to the "adulterous" project.

In this instance, Van Helsing also outlines the double-edged nature of the recipient of information who is easily frightened and potentially menacing. Access to information can indeed turn the innocent into the guilty, the weak into the dangerous. Serving as a sort of caretaker-censor in the novel, Van Helsing leads the campaign to hunt Dracula, a campaign which involves the strict control of the dispersal of vampiric discourse. In a somber speech which echoes Stoker's own fears about the dangers of spreading sexual knowledge through literature, Van Helsing advises Seward to censor the communication of his medical knowledge and motives:

> ... my good friend John, let me caution you. You deal with the madmen. All men are mad in some way or the other; and inasmuch as you deal discreetly with your madmen, so deal with God's madmen, too — the rest of the world. You tell not your madmen what you do nor why you do it; you tell them not what you think. So you shall keep knowledge in its place, where it may rest — where it may gather its kind around it and breed. (118)

Van Helsing's insistence on keeping "knowledge in its place" suggests an anxiety about the spread of discourse which is equal to the fear generated by the vampire itself. Discourse, like sexuality, is reproductive: it too must be subject to social control. The technological advances of the phonograph and the typewriter spur fears about the control of knowledge since they allow for faster production, multiplication, and easier, more widespread dissemination of documents. Indeed, as vampiric promiscuity pervades *Dracula*, so too is discourse reproduced and distributed in a veritable pornographic orgy: Van Helsing reads Lucy's papers, Mina reads Jonathan's diary, Van Helsing reads Jonathan's diary, Van Helsing gives Seward Mina's writings to read, and Seward gives Mina his diary for transcription. While presenting a challenge to censorship and the control of sexuality, this discursive promiscuity is at the core of the novel's moral imperative. Accounts of the vampire must be compiled, reproduced, and read during the hunt for the Count. As Van Helsing comments, "I have studied, over and over again since they came into my hands, all the papers relating to this monster; and the more I have studied, the greater seems the necessity to utterly stamp him out" (301–2). The transcription of sexual deviancy, Van Helsing suggests, serves as a mode of discipline. Here lies the paradox of discourse in *Dracula*: characters must suppress *and produce* information about the vampire who represents deviant sexuality. Jonathan's written account of his erotic desire to be kissed by the vampire women's "red lips" *does* meet Mina's eyes once they are married. Similarly, Mina's account of her symbolic act of fellatio with Dracula is recounted to all of the characters as part of the greater campaign against the Count. Indeed, the connection between *Dracula* and "The Censorship of Fiction" becomes increasingly clear: all of the content that makes *Dracula* an erotic novel is, in the plot of the text, the means of destroying the erotic source. Stoker's eroticism comes replete with censor.

The strange dynamic between the repression and production of sexual discourse is best exemplified in Mina's wholly ambivalent role in the novel. Mina compiles the vampire narrative, the text of evidence against the Count, yet as the Count's victim and as the novel's leader in modern technology, she also occupies the role of vampiric Other. These two roles are indeed complementary. While Lucy's discursive freedom and sexual promiscuity render her a prime partner for the Count, it is precisely Mina's knowledge and management of communications technology which ultimately render her vampiric. If Lucy writes down her desires too freely, it is Mina who *reads* and copies these desires and others. She is akin to the Count, even before she is bitten, in both her ambitious acts challenging the common practices of discourse — her study of learning typewriting and shorthand — and her transgression of gender conventions.[9] As Van Helsing observes, Mina has the mind of a man (234). She longs to be a partner to Jonathan in his work, thus she practices shorthand and typewriting "to be useful to Jonathan." She also keeps a diary to improve her powers of memory, as she writes to Lucy:

> When I am with you I shall keep a diary in the same way. I don't mean one of those two-pages-to-the-week-with-Sunday-squeezed-in-a-corner diaries, but a sort of journal which I can write in whenever I feel inclined.... I shall try to do what I see lady journalists do: interviewing and

writing descriptions and trying to remember conversations. I am told that, with a little practice, one can remember all that goes on or all that one hears said during a day.
(53–54)

Such vigilant chronicling borders on the vampiric in its almost supernatural strength of memory and perception. Mina's increased powers of observation and reproduction — her mastery of technology — present a challenge to the censors of her age since knowledge cannot easily be hidden
from a woman so well trained. Indeed, Mina threatens to supplant the
Victorian male censor: her proficiency with a variety of communication
technologies empowers her access to, and control of, information.
Performing the role of censor in the novel, she nearly upsets the patriarchal
dominion over discourse controlled by Van Helsing. While Mina is protected from the physical dangers of the vampire hunt, her typed manuscript
in fact organises it. Thus, it may be argued that Mina's diligent typing parallels the heroism of the men who physically chase and destroy the vampires. By ordering in typed form all details about the Count's British tour,
she controls sexual discourse and symbolically imposes order on an
untamed vampiric sexuality.

Mina's role as censor is most evident when she copies Seward's
phonograph diary on her typewriter, mechanising and therefore sanitising
his emotions and desires more palpably expressed in speech. Discovering
the bare truth of Seward's heart as she listens to his phonographic diary,
Mina dutifully conceals his feelings by typing out his spoken words. As
she tells him:

> That is a wonderful machine, but it is cruelly true. It told
> me, in its very tones, the anguish of your heart. It was like
> a soul crying out to almighty God. No one must hear
> them spoken ever again! See, I have tried to be useful. I
> have copied out the words on my typewriter, and none
> other need now hear your heart beat, as I did. (222)

Offering a mechanical objectivity to written expression, typewriting tempers the personal emotions that might arouse the listener or invade her privacy. As such, it becomes a modern technology of censorship as well as a
modern challenge to it: it reproduces, yet represses, the very discourse it
copies.

Having this primary access to information about the Count in the
novel, Mina faces it at its most dangerous core, thus mitigating its threat to

others. If her typewriting tames original documents, it equally clarifies them. She translates, for instance, the opaque shorthand of Jonathan's diary for the seemingly omniscient Van Helsing. Significantly, when Van Helsing asks to read Jonathan's journal, he approaches Mina as a sort of "official keeper" of the vampire documents. Van Helsing's request affords Mina the irresistible opportunity to assert her technological authority. Perhaps in retaliation to his surprised reaction over her discursive powers, Mina decides to play a trick on Van Helsing by handing him Jonathan's shorthand journal:

> I could not resist the temptation of mystifying him a bit
> — I suppose it is some of the taste of the original apple
> that remains still in our mouths — so I handed him the
> shorthand diary. He took it with a grateful bow, and said:
> "May I read it?"
> "If you wish," I answered as demurely as I could.
> He opened it, and for the instant his face fell. Then he
> stood up and bowed.
> "Oh, you so clever woman!" he said. "I long
> knew that Mr. Jonathan was a man of much thankfulness;
> but see, his wife have all the good things. And will you
> not so much honour me and so help me as to read it for
> me? Alas! I know not the shorthand." By this time my lit-
> tle joke was over, and I was almost ashamed; so I took
> the typewritten copy from my work-basket and handed it
> to him. (183)

Mina's posture as the dissembling temptress is carried to its logical conclusion when she becomes the Count's next mistress. As a female censor, she upsets Victorian social order, emerging both as a demonised threat and a matriarchal protectress. An Eve figure who acquires supernatural percep-tion, Mina's vampiric telepathy with the Count marks her crowning achieve-ment in techno-vampirism. Mentally connected to the Count, she essentially obtains an exclusive knowledge of the vampire's symbolic sexuality since she alone knows what the Count knows. Indeed, this "mind meld" with the Count functions as the climax of her techno-vampirism aptitude developed through typewriting and shorthand. A "supernatural" form of communica-tion between Mina and the Count, their telepathy also serves as a symboli-cally adulterous rival to her "secret" communication with Jonathan through shorthand. Mina's position now becomes wholly double-edged: she is a powerful weapon for her friends against the Count, yet, as they discover, she is also a dangerous weapon that may be used by the Count against them. Now seduced by telepathic discourse with the Count rather than by a desire for physical penetration, Mina becomes the embodiment of the inconstant woman tempted by the erotic discourse of pornographic literature who may not be able to maintain loyalty, even if she so desires.

Appropriately, Mina's strength falters at this point in the novel as she seems unable to withstand the knowledge about her symbolic fellatio with the Count. When Van Helsing explains to her the nature of her vampiric infection, she faints into Jonathan's arms, an act which supports the men's conviction that women are too weak to confront the truth about vampirism. Both a victim and a threat, Mina is paradoxically the weakest and the most powerful among Van Helsing's Christian soldiers. Grown knowledgeable beyond the level normal for her gender, Mina is now "leagued with [the] enemy" (332), a menace to her friends and the entire human race. She remains, nonetheless, the moral backbone of the novel, imploring Jonathan, "Promise me that you will not tell me anything of the plans formed for the campaign against the Count. Not by word, or inference, or implication" (326). Acting as her own censor in this instance, Mina denies herself access to what she has documented. Her "wisdom" ultimately reflects the censorship polemic of her author, who maintains with regard to the reading and writing of obscene fiction, "Women are the worst offenders in this breach of moral law" ("The Censorship of Fiction" 485). Mina recognises her own potential to violate this law and wisely and courageously seeks to counter it.

As Mina's heroism makes clear, Count Dracula and his rivals struggle for the control of discourse and its technologies. The Count not only threatens the possession of Lucy and Mina ("Your girls that you all love are mine") but the eradication of human discourse. A purely villainous version of Mina, Dracula performs his own censorship manoeuvres even as he disseminates perverse sexual knowledge. He censors Jonathan's letters, actually burning the letter written to Mina in shorthand. Striking again later in the novel, he breaks into Seward's office, burning the typewritten manuscript of evidence against him along with Seward's wax phonograph cylinders. Once under Dracula's spell, Lucy becomes his accomplice in censorship, attempting to destroy her own written account of Dracula's attack on her (152). As the novel ends with the victory of the human race, however, the righteous censors prevail. Mina and her "brave men" are successful in finally destroying Dracula because they maintain control over their discourse, successfully opposing the Count's attempts to destroy all written evidence against him. As Mina states after Dracula burns her manuscript of evidence, "Thank God there is the other copy in the safe" (285). Protecting and policing the proper boundaries of discourse and sexuality, Mina's skills in techno-vampirism ultimately ensure the Count's defeat.

Dracula 1992: Censorship and Romance

THE LATE TWENTIETH century has borne witness to an advanced technology of computer transmitted information. "Cybersex" has become the latest form of vampiric discourse, threatening to spread moral degeneracy as the vampire threatens to propagate sexual deviance. Cybersex has recently become the target of censors who fear "lascivious material" is falling into the hands of minors at "lightning speed" through the Internet. Enforcing decency codes on Internet traffic, however, is nearly impossible (Lewis A1). Censors are again faced with an uncontrollable threat since sexual material now travels to tens of thousands of computers via digital bits. As this represents a noteworthy permutation in techno-vampirism, what better moment in history to adapt Bram Stoker's *Dracula* to the screen? Indeed, Coppola's film serves a purpose similar to Stoker's novel: while highlighting the erotic aspect of the vampire figure, *Bram Stoker's Dracula* (1992) promotes an ethics of devotion and romance which aims to counter the threat of promiscuous, anonymous sexuality in the age of cyberspace.

Since Francis Ford Coppola's version of *Dracula* claims to be the most accurate rendition of the original Victorian novel, no links are forged in the movie between vampirism and contemporary cybersex. Late Victorian media inventions nonetheless pervade *Bram Stoker's Dracula*. Coppola attempts an accurate rendering of Stoker's narrative's production process: we see Jonathan writing his diary in Romania (although not in shorthand) and Mina typing hers on her typewriter. As in the novel, the film draws parallels between these media, sexuality, and vampirism. Typing functions as a displaced form of sexuality, for instance, when Lucy asks Mina if her "ambitious Jon Harker" is forcing her "to learn that ridiculous machine when he could be forcing [her] to perform unspeakable acts of passion on the parlour floor?" Coppola also skillfully incorporates vampiric media which are better suited to film than literature. He makes particularly good use of the 1890s invention, the cinematograph. Serving as a simulacrum to vampirism just as the technologies devoted to the production and dissemination of discourse do in the novel, the cinematograph functions as an aid in the Count's foreplay in the film. Posing as a tourist in London, he introduces himself to Mina as Prince Vlad from Romania and asks her directions to the cinematograph. She takes him to a tent where they watch a bawdy silent film featuring scantily clad women "playing" with a man (the scene is reminiscent of Jonathan Harker's romp with the three vampire women). While Dracula first attempts to bite Mina in a corner of the tent, a nude woman dances on the screen in the background, reminding us of the monstrous threat of unregulated technology.

Coppola, however, clearly aims to treat this union of technology, monstrosity, and sexuality ironically. Featuring bare breasts and erotic scenes of orgasmic passion, Coppola's film provides the 1990s version of the early cinema's titillation. It offers up a blatant version of the sexuality more prudishly figured in Stoker's novel and thus has the opposite function of Mina's typewriting of Seward's phonograph diary, for it explicitly visualises the novel's erotic language. Like the cinematograph before it and cybersex after it, the motion picture offers new potential for the reproduction and transformation of sexual discourse. It, therefore, presents a new challenge to censorship. Coppola makes the most, for instance, of Jonathan's experience with the female vampires at Dracula's castle, depicting it clearly as a heterosexual male fantasy of group sex. The novel's vague seduction scene with Lucy in the churchyard becomes, on film, the episode where Dracula-as-beast copulates with Lucy in her garden. Lucy appears half naked throughout most of her vampiric illness. She lies on her sickbed with legs spread, writhing in the throes of erotic passion. Coppola's interpretation, literalising Stoker's sexual suggestion, rests on what Foucault calls "the speaker's benefit." The film's presentation of sexuality has the appearance of "a deliberate transgression" of the censoring mind-set of Victorian England (Foucault, *History of Sexuality* 6).

The film also appears to be more "liberated" than the novel since vampirism offers an escape to Lucy and Mina from Victorian strictures. Albeit to different degrees, both women are bursting with sexual desire and curiosity. Censorship in the film is portrayed as the suppression, as dictated by her Victorian sensibility, of Mina's true passions. Coppola highlights the connection between lewd books and vampirism when Mina takes a break from typing her diary to look at pornographic illustrations of Richard F. Burton's *Arabian Nights*. "How disgustingly awful," she exclaims as she peeks at the colourful drawing of copulation. When Mina accidentally drops the book on the floor, her secret is out, and both she and Lucy giggle while gazing at the pictures. When Mina wonders, "do men and women really do this?", the free-speaking Lucy replies, "I did it just last night in my dreams!" Mina tells Lucy she shouldn't say such things, but also types in her diary that she truly admires Lucy's ability to speak freely. Mina is, in fact, impatient for sexual experience. When Jonathan departs for his trip abroad, Mina kisses him hungrily. When she says to him, "we've waited this long," we know she is bemoaning a further deferral of sexual consummation. While Victorian rules force Lucy and Mina to wait until marriage for sexual fulfillment, vampirism offers them immediate consummation. The Count is in this sense un-demonised since he rescues even while he attacks. But what does it mean to un-demonise Dracula? Does *Bram Stoker's Dracula* subvert Victorian censorship ideas since the perverse "Other" of sexuality is "Other" no longer?

As my reading of Stoker's *Dracula* has shown, eroticism can be used to quite divergent ends, serving both to discipline and liberate, to censor and expose. Yet Coppola's hero-vampire offers a new strategy for a productive censoring of sexuality, at the centre of which is romance. Coppola uses vampiric sexuality not merely to condemn it as is Stoker's method, but to contain or even to dismiss it by way of a sublimated conjugal love between the Count and Mina. Thus, the original novel's tension between the display of sexuality and the repression of it, between the reproduction of discourse and the control of it, is relaxed in Coppola's film through the romantic sanctioning of the vampire.

In his effort to humanise Dracula, Coppola presents a pre-credit sequence of the pre-vampiric Count Dracula, drawing on some of the folkloric myths of vampires and on the historical prototype for Count Dracula. Coppola attempts to subvert the moralism of the vampire myth by recreating the "true" origin of the vampire. The film opens in 1462 in a Wallachia embattled by Turks. Vlad Dracula, a knight of the order of the Dragon, departs from his wife Elizabetha to go to battle defending Christendom "against the enemies of Christ." The subsequent scene of battle featuring Turks impaled on stakes evokes Count Dracula's historical namesake, Dracula, Prince Vlad V of Wallachia, remembered by his people as both a ruthless and heroic figure.[10] Returning home victorious, Dracula finds his wife has committed suicide after being told by vengeful Turks that her husband is dead. Because she transgressed the laws of the Church by committing suicide, Elizabetha is denied a Christian burial, and her husband, in a spectacular blood bath, vows revenge. The focus on suicide in this preamble is significant since suicides in the middle ages were commonly feared to become vampires after death.[11] Evoking pity for Elizabetha and Prince Dracula, the film exposes and challenges the religious dogmatism that condemned suicides to eternal damnation and gave rise to the vampire myth. In this case, the suicide, Elizabetha, does not rise from her grave as a vampire; instead, her husband vows to return from the grave to avenge her death. Thus Count Dracula is "born" both of rebellion against Christian intolerance and out of devoted love. In 1897, this same knight, now the undead Count Dracula, buys real estate in London in order to be reunited with Elizabetha in her new incarnation as Mina Harker. He travels to

London, finds Mina and courts her, while Jonathan is safely held prisoner in the Count's castle in Romania. While the Prince offers Mina a walk on the wild side, taking her to the pornographic cinematograph and getting her high on absinthe, his higher amorous motives prevail. "The luckiest man on earth is the one who finds true love," he tells Jonathan in a moment of emotional transparency.

Coppola's Dracula unites Prince Charming and monster. He is a hero-villain tragically doomed by his own rebellious righteousness. A sort of Byronic hero, the Count is "the monster that men would kill" because his love surpasses that of the common man. In fact, his "visionary" love fosters certain supernatural powers which he passes on to his vampire progeny. When Lucy is bitten by the Count, she describes her illness as fostering hypersensory perception, rendering her able to hear a pin drop on the opposite side of her mansion. Mina expresses her desire to share in this superhuman vision when she implores Dracula to make her a vampire: "I want to see what you see, hear what you hear."

The romance of Dracula and Mina, despite its erotic passion, is in fact a spiritual love. Dracula proves to be more repulsed by his own monstrous sexuality than Mina. He refuses to make Mina a vampire even when she asks for it: "I cannot let this be," he says. "I love you too much." Vampiric lust proves too base even for Dracula himself. He rapes Lucy only for nourishment, and these attacks effectively constitute his "misery," his damnation. He is condemned to this blood lust when Mina leaves him in order to attend to Jonathan who is ailing in Romania. Here, both Mina and the Count prove to be unfaithful to each other, to their "deeper" love. Indeed, when Mina finds the beast Dracula astride Lucy in the garden, he feels shame at being discovered. "No, do not see me!" he telepathically conveys to Mina, hypnotising her into ignorance of his adultery. While vampirism for Lucy is bestial (and devoid of love), for Mina it is a sacred bond with her soulmate. Offering a crude version of the madonna/whore cliché, vampirism is split here into conjugal spirituality and promiscuous bestiality. Despite its romantic sublimation, vampirism still functions to demonise Lucy's flirtation as it does in the novel. Her fiancé, Arthur, is still allowed the vengeful and exhibitionist pleasure of driving a stake through her with his romantic competitors as witnesses.

The film's focus on Dracula's romance, however, illustrates how vampiric sexuality conclusively emerges as a means of reaffirming the institution of romantic love. In a sort of family values interpretation of vampirism, Mina is, effectively, married to the Count. Ultimately, however, the fires of even the conjugal undead must be smothered. The spiritual fulfillment of Romantic love precludes any sexual liberation at the end of the film when Mina kills Dracula so he can be reunited with Elizabetha in heaven. Mimicking Stoker's own deployment of the sexual vampire for a conservative platform of censorship, the explicit sexuality in *Bram Stoker's Dracula* proves to be a means of channelling sexuality into the boundaries of marriage, of sublimating it into the ideal of romantic love. Coppola's cinematic rendition of *Dracula* thus offers the latest paradoxical shape of vampiric sexuality: it is unbounded in its conjugal devotion, unstoppable in the lengths to which it will go to achieve "true love."

NOTES

1   Considering *Dracula* in the light of Stoker's censorship essay, Daniel Farson concludes that "coming from the author of *Dracula* these views seem incredible.... Is it possible that Stoker did not realize he had written one of the most erotic books in English literature?" (210). Christopher Bentley effectively answers Farson by claiming, "it must be assumed that [Stoker] was largely unaware of the sexual content of his book" (26–27). Similarly, George Stade sees a disparity between Stoker's censorship writing and his fiction. "Stoker was not a hypocrite," he writes, "he simply did not know his own mind. He would not have been able to write a book like *Dracula* if he had" (xiii).

2   Michael Holquist describes the paradox of censorship as "a version of litotes" which necessarily states the positive through the negative, and necessarily includes the Other it seeks to exclude. Richard Burt deconstructs this conception of censorship as originally "negative," arguing that "censorship never operated in the modern terms in which it is generally thought to have operated — as negative, repressive exercises of power" (xv). Suggesting the ways in which censorship is a "positive exercise of power," he describes book burnings as "staging an opposition between corrupting and purifying forces and agencies" (xviii). *Dracula* intensifies this opposition by staging a struggle between the monstrous and the human.

3   Kathleen L. Spencer categorises *Dracula* as an example of the "Urban Gothic" of the late nineteenth century characterised by an "attempt to reduce anxiety by stabilizing certain key distinctions, which seemed in the last decade of the nineteenth century to be eroding: between male and female, natural and unnatural, civilized and degenerate, human and nonhuman" (203).

4   Jennifer Wicke reads *Dracula* as "a chaotic reaction-formation in advance of modernism, wildly taking on the imprintings of mass culture" (469). Thus in the narrative structure of the novel — which incorporates phonograph recordings, typewritten and telegraphed documents — nineteenth-century epistolary effusion "is invaded by cutting edge technology" (470).

5   In *The Use of Pleasure*, Foucault describes "the obsessive worries that medicine and pedagogy nurtured on the subject of pure sexual expenditure — that unproductive and partnerless activity — from the eighteenth century onward. The gradual exhaustion of the organism, the death of the individual, the destruction of his offspring, and finally, harm to the entire human race, were regularly promised through an endlessly garrulous literature, to those who would make illicit use of their sex" (16).

6   Walter Kendrick describes the trial of Madame Bovary where prosecutor Ernest Pinard "concluded the first of his attack by replacing Flaubert's subtitle, *Provincial Customs*, with a new one: *The Story of a Provincial Woman's Adulteries*." Pinard also interposed paraphrases of the novel and read the novel verbatim with his own declamations (107–109).

7   See Carrol Fry and Christopher Bentley for discussion of the sexual symbolism of vampirism in *Dracula*.

8   Christopher Craft describes the inversion of the gender-based categories of penetration and reception in *Dracula*, "as virile Jonathan Harker enjoys a 'feminine' passivity and awaits a delicious penetration from a woman whose demonism is figured as the power to penetrate" (169). Craft also locates an implicit homoerotic desire in this "demonic inversion of normal gender relations" (170).

9   As a figure that displaces eroticism from the genitalia to the mouth, the Count transgresses the traditional separation of gender roles by fusing the acts of penetrating and receiving. The Count's mouth, Christopher Craft notes, is "the primary site of erotic experience in *Dracula*," and it defies the easy separation of the masculine and the feminine. Craft explains, "Luring at first with an inviting orifice, a promise of red softness, but delivering instead a piercing bone,

the vampire mouth fuses and confuses what Dracula's civilized nemesis, Van Helsing ... works so hard to separate — the gender-based categories of the penetrating and the receptive" (169). Mina foreshadows her own vampiric gender inversion, her feminine penetration, through her "manlike" intellectual ambitions. Her mastery of communication technologies, indeed, allows her to read and spread information — sometimes lewd in content — much as the Count spreads vampirism. Mina's knowledge of shorthand, for instance, allows her to read Jonathan's journal chronicling his stay at the Count's castle and his rapture over the vampire women. The danger in this knowledge is indicated by Jonathan himself who fears the contents of his journal: "I have had a great shock, and when I try to think of what it is I feel my head spin round, and I do not know if it was all real or the dreaming of a madman. You know I have had brain fever, and that is to be mad. The secret is here [in the journal], and I do not want to know it. I want to take up my life here, with our marriage" (104). Mina subsequently types this information and passes it on to Van Helsing, Seward, Morris and Godalming (229).

10   Prince Vlad, also known as Vlad Țepeș (*țeapă* meaning spike in Romanian), lived from 1431 to 1476. He is known for his heroism as a Christian who fought against the Turks, and for his bloodthirsty practice of impaling his enemies on tall stakes (Farson 127–130).

11   In Stoker's novel, it is no coincidence that Lucy fearlessly sits on the grave of a suicide before her descent into vampirism. The old man at the cemetery tells Lucy and Mina that the young man who "blew nigh the top of his head off with an old musket" had "hoped he'd go to hell, for his mother was so pious that she'd be sure to go to heaven, an' he didn't want to addle where she was." Upon hearing this gruesome tale, Lucy resolves, "it is my favorite seat and I cannot leave it; and now I find I must go on sitting over the grave of a suicide" (67). While in theory, as Jean Marigny notes, "everyone is susceptible to becoming a vampire after death, ... some ... are more vulnerable than others". Those others include "the excommunicated, *suicides*, victims of violent death, witches, the stillborn, and anyone who has not had a Christian burial" (56–57, emphasis mine).

REFERENCES

Altick, Richard D. *The English Common Reader: A Social History of the Mass Reading Public, 1800–1900.* Chicago: University of Chicago Press, 1957.

Barber, Paul. *Vampires, Burial, and Death.* New Haven: Yale UP, 1988.

Bentley, Christopher. "The Monster in the Bedroom: Sexual Symbolism in *Dracula.*" *Dracula, the Vampire, and the Critics.* Ed. Margaret L. Carter. Ann Arbor: UMI Research Press, 1988. 25–34.

Burt, Richard. "Introduction." *The Administration of Aesthetics: Censorship, Political Criticism and the Public Sphere.* Ed. Richard Burt. Minneapolis: University of Minnesota Press, 1994. xi–xxix.

Carter, Margaret L., ed. *Dracula, the Vampire, and the Critics.* Ann Arbor: UMI Research Press, 1988.

Bram Stoker's Dracula. Dir. Francis Ford Coppola. Columbia, 1992.

Craft, Christopher. "'Kiss Me with Those Red Lips': Gender and Inversion in Bram Stoker's *Dracula.*" *Dracula, the Vampire, and the Critics.* Ed. Margaret L. Carter. Ann Arbor: UMI Research Press, 1988. 167–194.

Farson, Daniel. *The Man Who Wrote Dracula: A Biography of Bram Stoker.* London: Michael Joseph, 1975.

Foucault, Michel. *The History of Sexuality, Volume I: An Introduction.* Trans. Robert Hurley. New York: Vintage Books, 1980.

—. *The Use of Pleasure, The History of Sexuality, Volume II.* Trans. Robert Hurley. New York: Vintage Books, 1986.

Fry, Carrol L. "Fictional Conventions and Sexuality in *Dracula.*" *Dracula, the Vampire, and the Critics.* Ed. Margaret L. Carter. Ann Arbor: UMI Research Press, 1988. 35–38.

Holquist, Michael. "Corrupt Original: The Paradox of Censorship." *PMLA* 109 (1994): 14–25.

Kendrick, Walter. *The Secret Museum: Pornography in Modern Culture.* New York: Viking, 1987.

Lewis, Peter H. "Despite a New Plan For Cooling It Off, Cybersex Stays Hot." *New York Times* 26 March 1995: A1.

Marigny, Jean. *Vampires: Restless Creatures of the Night. 1993.* Trans. Lory Frankel. New York: Thames and Hudson, 1994.

Masters, Anthony. *The Natural History of the Vampire.* London: Rupert Hart-Davis, 1972.

Ronay, Gabriel. *The Truth About Dracula.* New York: Stein and Day, 1972.

Spencer, Kathleen. "Purity and Danger: *Dracula*, the Urban Gothic, and the Late Victorian Degeneracy Crisis." *ELH* 59 (1992): 197–225.

Stade, George. "Introduction." *Dracula.* By Bram Stoker. New York: Bantam Books, 1981. v–xiv.

Stoker, Bram. *Dracula.* 1897. Oxford: Oxford UP, 1983.

—. "The Censorship of Fiction." *The Nineteenth Century* 64 (September 1908): 479–487.

Wicke, Jennifer. "Vampiric Typewriting: *Dracula* and its Media." *ELH* 59 (1992): 467–493.

Draculafilm: "High" and "Low" Until the End of the World

Jake Brown

> PETER BOGDANOVICH: Which would you say were some of the best Mercury shows?
>
> ORSON WELLES: *Dracula* was a good one.
>
> PETER BOGDANOVICH: It would make a good movie.
>
> ORSON WELLES: *Dracula* would make a marvelous movie. In fact, nobody has ever made it; they've never paid any attention to the book, which is the most hair-raising marvelous book in the world.
>
> (Welles 13)

KIRA KUROSAWA'S *HIGH AND LOW* (1962) INAUGU-rated a radically postmodern vision of law enforcement and criminality, a vision which would reach an apocalyptic crescendo in films such as David Lynch's *Blue Velvet* (1986) and Alan Rudolph's *Trouble in Mind* (1985). At first glance, Kurosawa's film seems a transparent copy of Quinn-Martinesque American crime dramas in which the forces of good methodically track down the forces of evil. Both sides are easily identifiable through reactionary stereotype: the criminals are marked as threatening outsiders and the good guys restore order. Closer inspection, however, reveals an inchoate and quite terrifying critique of modern culture. Kurosawa's use of monochrome film stock, the casting of male actors with similar physiognomies, and his plodding, static, melodramatic plot exposition, work against the film's apparent diagesis: by the end of the film, the appearance and actions of the police and criminals become so similar that distinctions between good guys and bad guys become almost completely arbitrary. It's not that the good guys and bad guys are simply reversed, as in *Butch Cassidy and the Sundance Kid* (1969), it's that modern culture has somehow collapsed these distinctions into a kind of postmodern nightmare of homogeneity. Lynch and Rudolph develop this thesis much more deliberately in their films. The criminals in *Blue Velvet* and *Trouble in Mind*, far from the psychopathic outsiders they appear to be, actually form a parallel culture with its own society, mores, and art — a culture clearly intended to mirror that of conventional modern society. Although it went practically unnoticed, the apocalyptic ellision of moral and cultural distinctions between good and evil, and "high" and "low" art, had already occurred for Lynch and Rudolph.

The observations of Kurosawa, Lynch, and Rudolph may provide an important clue to the very special, and apparently undying, fascination Bram Stoker's *Dracula* seems to hold for the twentieth-century imagination. Perhaps no other novel has so successfully and durably straddled the gap between "high" and "low": academic interest and popular appeal grow together with each generation of new readers. This rare confluence of academic and pop interest may in part derive from the perplexing ambiguities presented by *Dracula*. Is it a clumsy, reactionary melodrama, or is it a radical exposé of Victorian mores and secret obsessions? Is Dracula himself evil incarnate, or is he a perversely heroic fallen angel who represents humanity's eternally frustrated libidinal desires? Who are the heroes and criminals in this story? Are Mina and Lucy progressive "new women," or are they mere puppets reifying the Madonna-Whore complex? Who are the real rapists? Dracula, who forces Mina to suck tainted blood from his chest, or Van Helsing and company, who plunge the phallic stake through Lucy's wanton, damned heart? Presumably, one could construct a virtually infinite series of rhetorical questions dramatising the problem (or opportunity!) of who to cheer for and who to jeer at in this novel.

Given these signification possibilities, Orson Welles's observation that a textually-aware adaptation of Stoker's *Dracula* still waits to be made makes perfect sense. Indeed, filming *Dracula* has proven to be a daunting task. Of the hundreds upon hundreds of vampire movies made to date, only about a baker's dozen follow Stoker's plot closely enough to be considered adaptations of his novel. Of these, rather appropriately, two have excelled in the "low" realm of box-office success, and two have distinguished themselves in the "high" realm of academic approbation. Tod Browning's *Dracula* (1931) and Francis Ford Coppola's *Bram Stoker's Dracula* (1992) have enjoyed the greatest spectatorship, while F.W. Murnau's *Nosferatu: A Symphony of Terror* (1922) and Werner Herzog's *Nosferatu: Phantom of the Night* (1979) have received the greatest amount of academic attention. In its film history, then, central questions about Stoker's *Dracula* remain unresolved. To whom does this story belong? The "high" brows or the "low" brows? What, exactly, is this novel suggesting, to whom is it suggesting it, and to what effect? I presume not to answer these questions, but rather to gloss them by investigating some of the novel's possibilities as interpreted by these four films.

The ideological ambiguity surrounding the horror genre, in general, and the figure of Dracula, in particular, provides a fruitful framework for analysis. The irruption of Dracula into normal society and his subsequent destruction by the forces of good could be seen as a reactionary reification of the status quo, in which the criminal outsider is identified as a monster, scapegoated, and cathartically defeated. On the other hand, Dracula could be seen as a radical, potentially Byronic figure heroically disrupting the fatuous hypocrisy of an already corrupt society, namely patriarchal and imperialistic Victorian England. Simply put, Stoker's *Dracula* and its cinematic permutations may be seen variously as a defence or critique of the cultural status quo.

Tod Browning's *Dracula* unleashed Stoker's horrific Count on an American film audience eager for all the salacious thrills a sexy vampire could offer. European matinée idol Bela Lugosi did not disappoint, reviving a moribund American acting career with a star turn as Dracula that remains the definitive version of the vampire in modern pop consciousness. Despite the box-office appeal of both star and film, however, Browning's *Dracula* remains a curiously static, even meek portrayal of Stoker's novel. Contemporary censorship practices may account for the film's failure to deliver sex and horror sufficient to rival Stoker's description of the "baby in the bag" scene featuring Dracula fetching late-night take-out for his voracious wives. This alone does not, however, explain the quite striking conservatism of Browning's adaptation. In Stoker's *Dracula* the characters who defeat the monster and restore order could well be considered vigorous, adventuresome, and progressive. Lucy exercises modern sexual power through a socially-sanctioned choice of three suitors and, in proto-feminist fashion, Mina shows that a masculine intellectual acuity need not cancel out feminine gentleness and grace. Mina's superior powers of deduction allow the men to catch Dracula before he reaches the safety of his Transylvanian home, and her moral courage provides the inspiration for the entire enterprise. Harker, Van Helsing, Seward, Quincey, and Godalming show steely fortitude from start to finish, turning the tables on the invading monster by invading continental Europe to defeat Dracula on his home turf where he is at his strongest.

Browning's *Dracula* rearranges this plot so that the everyday society threatened by the monster becomes strangely distant and insulated from the threat. It is a boob-like Renfield, not the masculine, morally-upright, and rational Harker, who travels to Dracula's castle to be transformed into a raving lunatic by the Count's infectious bite. Renfield returns and an ineffectual Dr. Seward unsuccessfully attempts to incarcerate and cure him. Both Lucy and Mina prove weak, easy victims for the Count, and Jonathan Harker reacts to Dracula as if the ancient monster were some guy moving in on his chick at a malt shop. His response to the threat goes no further than suggesting to his girl Mina that she "forget" about Dracula or simply go away with him to escape the attentions of this unwelcome foreign interloper. Only Dr. Van Helsing, a foreigner like Dracula, understands the seriousness of the Count's visit and possesses the strength and know-how to defeat him. These plot variations throw a peculiarly American, or isolationist, slant on Stoker's story. No wonder only Van Helsing understands the superstition-laden folklore necessary to defeat a vampire, yet another folkloric creation — these old, European things have nothing to do, finally, with modern America. Because the "bad" European magic will inevitably be defeated by the "good" European magic, the new, modern American society is not only not threatened, but actually could never have been threatened in the first place. The madness of the old world, brought back to the new by Renfield, underscores the point of the film. The heroic crew do not need to return to the continent as they do in Stoker's *Dracula;* instead, Van Helsing works alone to dispatch Dracula in Carfax Abbey, off-frame and without sound. As Jonathan and the now purified Mina slowly mount the stairs towards the sunlight, it is clear that the European madness has taken care of itself. The new, superstition-free, café society that is modern America was never truly at risk.

Ironically, the ease with which the rubbery, leering, strangely suave visage of Bela Lugosi penetrates the modern world only emphasises Dracula's inability to actually disrupt it. After all, Americans accept everyone, so long as they understand there is only one reality — the smug, paradoxically sophisticated innocence of the new world. Dracula's was the dream world, and Van Helsing, himself a holdover from this older world, restores an order which was never actually threatened. Browning's static pacing, subdued diagetic sound, frequent dissolves, and anticlimactic ending all emphasise the dream-like quality of Dracula's invasion. Listening closely, we can almost hear Mina whisper to Jonathan, "Don't worry, darling, it was all just a bad dream; there's no place like home, there's no place like home ..."

As early as 1931, then, the blithe confidence of a culture that assumed itself to be unassailable provided a monolithically conservative bastion against the ancient evil of the nosferatu, the undead. Tod Browning's *Dracula* assumed a cultural arrogance much greater than that encountered in Stoker's novel; at least in Stoker's story the representatives of the cultural status quo had to prove themselves worthy of the title. For all his personal artistry and faith in the role, Bela Lugosi's Dracula contained the seeds of the plastic model kits and "Count Chocula" cereal that would bear his kitsch legacy into the modern age of American pop-capitalism. Lugosi's was a sad legacy totally emptied of any true horror or threat to the established order of things. Far from portraying the menace of a monstrous "Other," a dangerous criminal element requiring annihilation if American civilisation is to remain intact, Lugosi's Dracula was almost immediately absorbed by American culture and transformed into a meaningless pop icon no more threatening to society than Tinkerbell or Donald Duck (in fact, a character named Count Duckula was featured in an American cartoon).

Sixty-one years after Browning, Francis Ford Coppola produced the second American version of Stoker's novel to become an unmitigated box-office smash hit. Widely considered to be a "serious" director, a reputation earned with films like *The Conversation* (1974) and *Apocalypse Now* (1979), Coppola attempted to present the first "faithful" Stoker adaptation, the hubristically titled *Bram Stoker's Dracula* (1992). Ironically, what may be the most faithful element in this adaptation is its ability to wander, like Stoker's novel, all over the ideological map. Coppola seeks to unite the "high" and "low" elements of the story, sticking close, at times at least, to the narrative integrity of what may be a Victorian masterpiece, while simultaneously ensuring pop appeal by casting three of the hottest modern screen idols in a quite lurid romantic triangle: Keanu Reeves (Harker), Winona Ryder (Mina), and Gary Oldman (Dracula). The film also attempts to straddle the ideological implications of the novel, making sure the viewer knows that Dracula is evil and must be destroyed, while simultaneously engendering sympathy for the Count as a doomed Byronic romantic by playing up his ultimately fatal love for Mina. Despite this effort, however, what Coppola actually succeeds in doing is emphasising, quite spectacularly, the most reactionary and the most mawkishly melodramatic possibilities in Stoker's *Dracula*.

These may seem harsh words for the man who so stridently criticised the Vietnam War in *Apocalypse Now* and created *The Conversation*, one of the most brutally convincing documents in the history of cinematic realism, but *Bram Stoker's Dracula* speaks for itself, in all of its glitzy, multi-million dollar production values. Coppola's treatment of the female character goes whole hog for a delirious, virtually pornographic reification of the Madonna-Whore complex, that most enduring relic of Victorian patriarchy. Stoker tempers his punishment of Lucy by hinting that the attention of three male suitors has an inappropriate connotation, and by emphasising that her brutal symbolic rape by wooden stake frees her soul into peaceful death. Coppola takes full advantage of the opportunities film has to offer by giving Lucy lush, flaming red hair, a taste for the Kama Sutra, and a teasing, overtly sexual demeanour. The mesmerised Lucy's liaison with the werewolf Dracula in the garden depicts her more than willing sexual ecstasy in the midst of very explicit bestial cunnilingus. All this makes for colourful cinema, but when the stake smashes into the vampire Lucy's heart, the entire set-up smacks of the slasher-film convention in which the most sexually-active woman ("Whore") "gets it" first. In fact, Coppola seems so enthusiastic about the "Whore" side of the complex that he can't resist adding to Stoker's scene in which Van Helsing protects himself and the now vampire-infected Mina by surrounding them with a circle composed of Hosts. While Stoker's Mina remains firmly on the "Madonna" side of the complex, heroically resisting her advancing vampirism, Coppola's Mina reproduces Lucy's attempt to seduce Godalming in the crypt by attempting to seduce Van Helsing within the circle.

Arguably, while Stoker emphasises the deadliness of Lucy's vampiric sexuality, and the moral purity of the faithful Mina, he also provides a window for the resolution of the Madonna-Whore complex by allowing for Mina and Jonathan's eventual parenthood which, presumably, involved sexual relations at some point. Mina-Madonna and Lucy-Whore are no longer the only two options for a woman. Coppola's climax allows for no such confluence between virtue and sexuality, as Mina dies after purifying Dracula and herself through sacrifice, obviating the future sexual relations with her husband Jonathan which might have worked to dismantle the odious Madonna-Whore distinction.

Mina's sacrifice may, however, point to a less reactionary adaptation of Stoker in another sense — Byronic sympathy for the devil. Since William Blake broke the ice for this kind of reading by casting Satan as the unlikely hero of Milton's *Paradise Lost*, it has become at least permissible, if not popular, to seek out avenues of human sympathy or at least empathy for quite obviously evil characters like Stoker's Count Dracula. Of Stoker's redoubtable crew, only the noble Mina remarks on Dracula's suffering, on how horrible his eternally undead condition must be for him (308). Coppola, however, structures the entire narrative tension of his film around an ancient love affair between Vlad Țepeș and his reincarnated wife who is none other than Mina Harker. The Romanian war hero Vlad Țepeș has not become Count Dracula because he lusts for blood or power, but because he has renounced God for His failure to prevent his wife's tragic death. By human-ising Dracula, by stripping him of his monster-criminal status, Coppola short-circuits the reactionary formula by which an outsider is scapegoated and crucified to emphasise the strength and legitimacy of "normal" society.

Coppola, however, does not retain enough control over his materi-al to reconcile or balance the reactionary and progressive elements of his reading. Gary Oldman's schizophrenic portrayal of Dracula provides the most obvious evidence for this claim. Oldman turns in a comic-book per-formance as the Count, and he may be forgiven if one realises that the film narrative calls on him to portray only two emotions: villainy and love. Consequently, Oldman is either grimacing evilly and wringing his hands behind a victim, or gazing longingly and passionately at Mina in one of the many scenes Coppola adds to depict Dracula's act of romancing his rein-carnated wife. Not only does this split make the film jarring and nearly incomprehensible, it also renders flaccid the potentially progressive move of humanising the monster. A Harlequin Romance lover is no more real or human than a monster and, consequently, anything profound Coppola may have thought he was drawing out of the novel evaporates into Dracula's own green vapour of simplistic melodrama.

Interestingly, both Browning's parlour-room staidness and Coppola's lurid sensationalism fail to bring out any of the real horror that lurks in Stoker's story. Regardless of ideological implication, neither film produces an image to rival Stoker's unsettling description of the baby in a bag, Mina's forced fellatio "rape scene," or Lucy's sensually-graphic stak-ing. This charge certainly cannot be leveled at F.W. Murnau's legendary *Nosferatu: A Symphony of Terror* (1922), the earliest film adaptation of *Dracula* to survive to the present day, and an acknowledged masterpiece of German expressionist cinema. Murnau emphasises Dracula's monstrous nature by truly making him a monster. Max Schreck's bulbous white head, rat-like fangs, and cruel talons make the Count a figure of other-worldly terror worthy of Stoker's worst nightmare.

In fact, the Count's appearance and undisguised malevolence in this film immediately suggest a reactionary reading of Stoker, in that the criminal status of the monster represents a real threat to the social order, a threat which must be expunged to dramatise the legitimacy and superiority of that order. Even more ideologically disturbing, Murnau's Count looks suspiciously like the contemporaneous German stereotype of the Jew, with his long, hooked nose, grasping fingers, and incisor-fangs which associate him with the rats who accompany him on his voyage to the "safe" normal society of Bremen. This physical description seems alarmingly close to the portrait of the Jew in Fritz Hippler's *The Eternal Jew* (1940), an extremely disturbing Nazi propaganda film in which Jews are explicitly described as criminal vermin who must be purged from society if "civilisation" is to survive.[1] When Mina Harker, called Lucy in *Nosferatu*, destroys the evil Count with her noble sacrifice, life returns to normal in Bremen, thus fulfilling the reactionary morality play at the core of Stoker's novel.

This reading, however, is far too facile to do justice to Murnau's enigmatic work. *Nosferatu* actually critiques, rather than legitimises, the normal society of Bremen by suggesting how fragile it really is. Like the ingenuous Renfield in Browning's film, Murnau's Harker seems foolishly sanguine about his journey to visit Dracula (called Orlok), smugly satisfied and secure in his quotidian bourgeois world of happy marriage and work. Disregarding his wife's fears, Harker traipses off woefully unprepared to meet the Count. Unlike Browning's unassailable English (read *American*) society, however, in which the "good" European defeats the "bad" European's evil nightmare world without any efficacious help or even acknowledgement from any member of the ostensibly threatened society, Murnau's normal world of Bremen proves to be living a dream which is dangerously smug.

Vampirised by the Count, Harker returns to Bremen and his wife, an event which coincides with Orlok's arrival in a ship filled with plague-ridden rats. Orlok has glimpsed a photograph of Lucy's tempting neck and has targeted her for his next victim, and the disoriented Harker can do nothing to stop him. Similarly, the scientist Van Helsing and the town officials of Bremen can do nothing to stop either vampire or plague from ravaging their city. They stumble about in confusion as the "phantom" Orlok moves about unopposed, the city elders and patriarchal authorities powerless to resist his invasion. Murnau emphasises the terrible reality of this "phantom" by brilliantly lighting the fake night shots of Orlok.[2]

Murnau makes his critique of Bremen society so explicit that he comes close to stripping the irruption, scapegoating, and defeat of the criminal outsider of its reactionary function. He depicts the powerlessness and irrationality behind the scapegoating process by having the once orderly, rational citizens of Bremen tear through the countryside in search of Renfield, whom they blame for their troubles. Meanwhile, the nosferatu walks among them in plain view. Not only is Renfield obviously not the real problem, the mob cannot even accomplish the mean task of scapegoating him, settling for quite madly tearing apart a scarecrow when they cannot find their sacrificial lamb.

If anyone in town had bothered to read the apparently widely available *Book of the Vampyr*, they would have known exactly what the problem was and what to do about it: destroy the nosferatu with the sacrifice of a pure woman, the only figure able to tempt the vampire to linger past dawn when the rays of morning light will destroy him. At this point, the ideological thicket presented by Murnau's film becomes as dense as the Germanic forest that has unleashed the nosferatu on the civilised world. In proto-feminist fashion, Murnau retains Stoker's characterisation of Mina Harker as intellectually superior to her male protectors by representing Lucy as the only citizen with enough sense to read the *Book of the Vampyr*, to do the "scientific" research necessary to defeat the monster. Ironically, the actual scientist Van Helsing, instead of battling Orlok, wastes his time lecturing on the vampiric oddities of the animal kingdom. The task of rescuing society by tempting the Count with her pure heart, therefore, devolves upon Lucy. Perversely, while Murnau champions Lucy's intellectual sense, he also advances the reactionary Victorian "angel in the house" concept by having her serve as an idealised woman, a Madonna-like saviour. Even more perversely, perhaps, Murnau incorporates the "Whore" element of the complex by splitting and doubling the deadly power of feminine sexuality. The vampiric natural oddities investigated by Van Helsing are the Venus Fly Trap and the Hydra, a plant and an animal whose physiognomies and feeding habits recall, quite literally, the mythic convention of the *vagina dentata*. Murnau reemphasises this connotation by constructing Max Schreck's makeup as a visual pun on the *vagina dentata* itself— Orlok's mouth recalls the earlier close-up of the Venus Fly Trap. Who is seducing whom, however, in this provocative confusion of ideological signification? Both Orlok (Whore) and Lucy (Madonna) die as a result of their encounter, begging the question of which is more deadly, the sexual or the pure woman?

At any rate, Lucy does succeed in defeating the monster and restoring order, although the process by which this happens seems more unsettling than comforting. The almost total helplessness of Bremen in the face of monstrous criminal invasion tempts the viewer to regard Lucy's sacrifice as a curiously anti-climactic *deus ex machina*. The "high" (Lucy's virtue), has defeated the "low" (vampiric evil), but in a fashion that emphasises just how vulnerable this "high" ground, this morally and culturally legitimate society, actually is.

Although the definitive adaptation of Stoker's *Dracula* may still await production, Werner Herzog's *Nosferatu: Phantom of the Night* (1979) can arguably lay claim to two distinctions: of the films discussed, and perhaps of all Dracula adaptations, it must surely be regarded as the least reactionary and the most horrific version of Stoker's novel to date. Ostensibly a remake of Murnau's classic film, Herzog's *Nosferatu* actually represents a highly personal plumbing of *Dracula* which ends up implicating modern society in a starkly nihilistic philosophical vision, a vision considerably more terrifying than the spectre of real or imagined vampirism. From the outset, Herzog divests his reading of Stoker of the reactionary "destroy-the-evil-monster-to-save-civilised-culture" formula by assigning Jonathan Harker the role of romantic quester.

Stoker's well-intentioned Harker, Browning's boob-like Renfield, and Murnau's fatally smug Harker, despite their differences, all function as emissaries of civilised society unwittingly visiting the monster's lair. In direct contradistinction to this set-up, Herzog's Harker quite deliberately rejects the civilised world to search for some kind of personal destiny. Herzog's Mina Harker (called Lucy) tries to dissuade her husband's journey not out of a premonition of future evil, like Murnau's Lucy, but out of the much more quotidian desire to begin their new marriage. Is this business trip really necessary? Harker's emotionless response to Lucy's request bespeaks his impatience with the society of Wismar. Dissatisfied with his own safe, "legitimate" world, he does not care to cherish and guard it from evil, but rather romantically rejects it in favour of a world yet to be discovered. With this aim, he rides purposefully into the forest of phantoms.

Herzog further dismantles the reactionary possibilities of Stoker's story by presenting the first realistically human Count Dracula (called Orlok). Klaus Kinski's reprise of Max Schreck's monstrous make-up serves only to emphasise, through contrast, the expressiveness of his eyes, so obviously those of a suffering human being trapped in a monster's form. Kinski's Count corresponds neither to Schreck's malevolent creature nor to Oldman's melodramatically grinning Byronic anti-hero. When Kinski draws Harker's attention to the "children of the night," his eyes are filled with empathetic wistfulness rather than gloating pride at his affinity with the atavistic animal kingdom. Orlok is a man humbled by pain and futility, far removed from Stoker's proud Count who so enthusiastically regales Harker with tales of his racial superiority and military prowess.

Despite the humanity Kinski establishes for his role, however, the role is still that of Count Dracula (Orlok), and he duly infects Harker with his own tortured blood-lust. Following Murnau, Herzog's Lucy awaits the return of her husband and the invasion of Orlok and his plagued, rat-filled ship. Herzog, however, goes much further than Murnau in his critique of Wismar society, stressing not only its helplessness in the face of any real threat, but also its fundamental corruption. The arrival of nosferatu and the plague only provides an occasion for these people to show their true colours: their bourgeois bureaucracy offers no defence against the invasion, and once they realise this, the citizens of Wismar descend into an orgy of eating, drinking, and bestial sexual perversion. Only Lucy remains aloof from this debauched resignation. She learns nosferatu's secret from *The Book of the Vampire* and attempts, albeit in vain, to ring the civic alarm. Receiving no support from the populace, Van Helsing, or her husband who is now half-vampire, Lucy resolves to face the Count alone, hoping that she can be the lone "pure woman" able to defeat the undead menace.

It might seem here that Herzog, like Murnau and Coppola, employs the paternalistic paradigm of the idealised woman who functions as "civilisation saviour," but he actually has something quite different in mind. Lucy and the Count are the only remotely sympathetic characters in the film, and they enjoy both a psychic and thematic bond which is consecrated in the accursed marriage-bed of the vampire. Orlok comes from the land of phantoms, the world of death which is symbolised by the plague he brings to Wismar, but he no longer enjoys his work. His eyes burn with longing and fatalistic resignation, not corruption. Lucy comes from the land of civilisation, the world of Wismar which is symbolised by a corrupt bureaucracy and degenerate social order. She no longer rests, however, in their company. Her true destiny is to meet the emissary from the Other world. By the time the Count arrives in Lucy's room, they are both outcasts from the phantasmal and civilised realms, realms which have been exposed as two sides of the same coin. Orlok and Lucy extinguish themselves in a loveless, but mutually necessary and fatal embrace, leaving both their worlds to the jackals. Herzog emphasises this reading of *Dracula* to the point where there is no doubt about the enormity and horror of his thesis.

Faced with the pathetic tableau of Lucy and Orlok, Van Helsing belatedly realises the truth of Lucy's knowledge and futile warning, and drives a stake through Orlok's heart. Van Helsing's knowledge, however, comes too late. Lucy's sacrifice has expunged the vampire and ended the plague in Wismar. All this means, however, is that the Wismar bureaucracy can resume its ignorant and corrupt operation which is now in skeletal form. Assuming that Van Helsing, with his bloody hands, has been responsible for the mayhem in Wismar, the remaining city officials attempt to arrest him. Even though informed that there are no jailers left because of the plague, the arresting official finds a willing scapegoat in Van Helsing who resigns himself to be arrested by the blackly comical bureaucrats. As with vampires, it only takes a few city officials to start up all over again.

As if all this weren't bad enough, Jonathan Harker has now become a hybrid nosferatu, an appalling mixture of the worst of Orlok and the worst of Wismar society.

Previously, Lucy had attempted to contain Jonathan's growing evil by encircling him with the host, reversing Stoker's scene in which Van Helsing encircles Mina Harker. Unlike Stoker's Mina, however, who heroically resists her vampirism, Jonathan proves an enthusiastic disciple of evil, grinning maliciously as a maid sweeps up the host thus freeing him into a corrupt world. As Jonathan, now fully nosferatu, rides purposefully out of town *in broad daylight*, Herzog's meaning becomes clear: Jonathan's soulless eyes not only lack the wearied, attenuated humanity of Orlok's; he also seems to have increased powers. Like the citizens of Wismar, he can face the daylight but, unlike them, he no longer requires the pretense that he represents an ordered, rational, "high" culture that can stand up to the evil of the dark world. The dark world and the light world, the criminal and the civilised, the good guys and the bad guys, the "low" and the "high," have joined in the valueless, cultureless homogeneity of the worst postmodern nightmare. The nosferatu Jonathan ends the film by beginning a new quest, one which is not romantic but postmodern and nihilistic. Corruption prefigures his journey: he seeks not new worlds to live in, but new worlds to corrupt.

Herzog's *Nosferatu: Phantom of the Night*, then, represents less an adaptation of a deceptively simplistic Victorian novel than it does a darkly romantic raid on a wide-open, almost unconscious text which may well conceal the most horrifying secrets known to humankind. In Stoker, Herzog finds the seeds of something more terrifying than vampires, more terrifying than reactionary horror tales in the service of a corrupt and moribund modern society, more terrifying even than a culture so frivolously bastardised that it can simultaneously produce Auschwitz and Count Chocula cereal. Herzog finds nothing less than the direst of warnings, a prescient glimpse of a wholly valueless age not to come but already upon us, an age in which civilisation is barbarous, the barbarian is heralded as civilised, pop-kitsch is indistinguishable from high art, criminality is indistinguishable from law and order, and the monstrous is indistinguishable from the normal. For Theodor Adorno, Auschwitz marked the dawning of this barbarous, valueless, postmodern nightmare. After the Holocaust, he said, there could be no more poetry. Perhaps Bram Stoker's horror aesthetics and Werner Herzog's achingly beautiful cinematic language of nihilism are all the poetry that is left to us. Perhaps this ghastly possibility accounts for the continued longevity of Bram Stoker's own symphony of horror in our decidedly iron age.

NOTES

1 It is interesting to note how adaptable *Dracula* has been to various ideologies throughout the twentieth century. While the image of the parasite-vampire was associated with the Jew in Nazi Germany, the Allies applied it in a different way. As Clive Leatherdale outlines in *Dracula: The Novel and the Legend*, "During World War Two the equation of the Hun-like Dracula with the Hun-like Nazi was gratefully manipulated and exploited by the Allies. The Americans recognized the hate-appeal of Stoker's vampire, who was held to personify German cruelty. American propaganda posters featured a German soldier with canine teeth dripping with blood. To cement the image, free copies of *Dracula* were issued to US forces serving overseas" (235–6).

2 As David J. Skal explains in *Hollywood Gothic*, "Night scenes were shot in broad daylight, then tinted deep blue for release" (48).

REFERENCES

Bram Stoker's Dracula. Dir. Francis Ford Coppola. Columbia, 1992.

Dracula. Dir. Tod Browning. Universal, 1931.

The Eternal Jew. Dir. Fritz Hippler. UFA, 1940.

Leatherdale, Clive. *Dracula: The Novel & the Legend*. Brighton, East Sussex: Desert Island Books, 1985.

Nosferatu: Eine Symphonie des Grauens (*A Symphony of Terror*). Dir. F.W. Murnau. Prana Film, 1922.

Nosferatu: Phantom der Nacht (*Phantom of the Night*). Dir. Werner Herzog. Twentieth Century Fox, 1979.

Skal, David J. *Hollywood Gothic: The Tangled Web of Dracula from Novel to Stage to Screen*. New York: Norton, 1990.

Stoker, Bram. *Dracula*. 1897. Oxford: Oxford UP, 1983.

Welles, Orson and Peter Bogdanovich. *This Is Orson Welles*. Ed. Jonathan Rosenbaum. New York: HarperCollins, 1992.

The Supernatural Ronin[1]: Vampires in Japanese Anime

Natalie Bartlett and Bradley D. Bellows

"His eyes flamed red with devilish passion: the great nostrils of the white aquiline nose opened wide and quivered at the edge; and the white sharp teeth, behind the full lips of the blood-dripping mouth, clamped together like those of a wild beast."
(*Dracula* 288)

"But it would seem I'm not quite the monster you're thinking of."
(Miyu in *Vampire Princess Miyu: Unearthly Kyoto*)

I N THE 1960s, JAPANESE PUBLISHING COMPANIES THAT produced comics, called *manga*, realised that television had the potential to reach a wider audience. Within no time, numerous *manga* series were adapted to animation. This style of Japanese animation, known by American fans as *anime*, has since grown into a hugely successful commercial industry. *Anime* has also slowly infiltrated Western popular culture, first as an underground cult movement. However, the growth of *anime* discussion groups on the Internet and the development of a fan-based network dedicated to subtitling and distributing *anime* has added to this medium's popularity and accessibility in the West. Presently, Western audiences have made the reedited and dubbed televised versions of the *anime* series *Sailor Moon, Samurai Troopers* (known as *Ronin Warriors* in North America), *Tekkaman Blade* (aka *Teknoman*), and *Dragonball*, commercially successful.

The myth of the Western vampire has been making similar cultural inroads in Japan via the film industry, *manga*, and *anime. Anime* has appropriated some of the myths of the Western vampire and invented new vampire lore to suit the textual and contextual criteria of Japanese animation. The vampire mythos has been adapted and restyled by many Japanese animators. However, it is the 1985 film *Vampire Hunter D* and the animated series *Kyuuketsuki (Vampire Princess) Miyu*, produced in 1988, that have featured and refashioned the image, story, and context of the vampire and the vampire hunter archetypes originally found in Bram Stoker's *Dracula*.

Vampire lore can be found in every culture in the form of an evil spirit or monster which attacks the living for their blood. Some of the most ancient vampire lore derives from Asia. A Bengali tribe called the Oraons include as part of their folklore a vampire witch known as the *Chordewa* who is capable of changing into a cat. Malaysian vampires appear in the form of giant mosquitoes, while the *Tu* or *Talamaur*, a ghoul in Polynesia, devours the flesh of freshly-seduced humans. Flesh-eating ghouls seem to be a common archetype of the vampire mythos of the Orient. The Chinese *Ch'iang-Shih* is a hybrid of vampire and ghoul which devours living and dead humans with great ferocity. Chinese tales also warn of green, mouldy bloodsuckers that glow in the dark or of a vampire mist which depletes a victim's lifeforce (Glut 25, 27; Leatherdale 19; Mascetti 204, 206; Silver and Ursini 18).

While there is an abundance of vampire and ghoul-related folklore in Asia, the vampire is notably absent from Japan's mythological cast of monsters, ghouls, and mutants. The only remotely vampiric character to appear in Japanese folklore is the *kappa*, a creature about the size of a ten-year-old who resembles a hairless monkey with a bowl-shaped head. The *kappa* lives in water close to riverbanks and sucks the blood of drowned victims through their anus. The *kappa*'s bowl-shaped head contains water that, if spilled, would disperse its strength (Dorson 59–68). The *kappa* legends are still widespread in Japanese literature, art, and popular culture. For example, the *kappa* was featured in a comic strip by Kon Shimizu in *Asahi Weekly*. Coffeehouses have portrayed this monster on their cheques and the *kappa* has often been shaped into wooden dolls (Dorson 58).

The Western myth of the classic bloodsucking vampire entered Japan via the influx of American culture, especially American film, after the Second World War. The Christian European vampire lore starring Count Dracula and his progeny quickly became part of Japanese mass culture. The first Japanese film with a vampire theme was Nobuo Nakagawa's *Kyuuketsuki Ga* aka *Vampire Moth* which was released in 1956. The story revolves around a series of murders where the victims are all discovered with puncture wounds on their necks believed to be caused by a vampire. Another popular vampire film, *Onna Kyuuketsuki* aka *Vampire Woman* or *The Female Vampire* was released in 1959 and told the story of a vampire who kidnaps the wife of an atomic scientist. The first Japanese adaptation of Bram Stoker's *Dracula* was the 1971 film *Chi O Suu Me* aka *Lake of Dracula* or *Lust for Blood* or *Bloodthirsty Eyes* which retained only the figure of Dracula and *Dracula*'s two principal female interests, Mina Harker and Lucy Westenra, from Stoker's original novel.

It was not until 1980 that Japan's animation industry adapted the popular myth of Dracula to the style of *anime*. The first full-length animated film featuring a vampire, *Dracula*, was released in 1980 and was based on the American Marvel Comics characters from *The Tomb of Dracula* (Melton 337). Very little information exists on this first Japanese animated version of the Dracula myth.

Anime has enjoyed tremendous success in Japan and cult status in North America for the last twenty years. *Anime* does not draw its stylistic and narrative inspirations from Japan's film industry but from the serialised comic strips called *manga*. The term *manga* was coined by Katsuhika Hokusai with his 1834 series of grotesque caricatures called *Hokusai Manga* (Groensteen 9). *Manga* developed independently from European and American comics and evolved into a very different art form from its Western counterparts. According to Scott McCloud, the *manga* style is marked by various comic-strip techniques. For example, the Japanese use a masking effect where audiences can mask themselves in cartoon-like characters set against incredibly detailed backgrounds (43–44). There is also a high degree of aspect-to-aspect transitions from panel to panel which bypass time and let the reader concentrate on the aspect of a place, idea, or mood (77). *Manga* also uses subjective motion where a clear image is set against a blurred background to show the speed of a moving object, person, or action. This technique highlights motion which makes the reader more involved in the *manga* (113–114). The Japanese have also discovered the power of detailing inanimate objects and giving them a "life" of their own. McCloud also contends that the use of expressionistic effects to show emotion, *manga*'s anthology-style formats, and the use of collage, are some of the devices frequently found in this medium.

Approximately thirty animated films were produced in Japan in the 1930s. However, they were eclipsed by the popularity of the animation of Walt Disney. The style of Disney and other American animators had a direct influence on Japanese cartoonists. The disproportionately large eyes that are now considered one of the distinguishing characteristics of *manga* and *anime* can be directly traced to the characters of Mickey Mouse and Donald Duck as well as Snow White and the Seven Dwarves.

Osamu Tezuka, one of the first Japanese *manga* artists to adapt Disney's style to Japanese stylistic parameters, was also the first *manga* artist to give comic strips a storybook form. At the time *Dracula* was introduced to Japan, *manga* was serialised in daily newspapers and followed a "continuing saga" format. Tezuka's stories combined light humour with a thread of tragedy and were told in a classical Western narrative style. His storytelling prowess, pioneering use of science-fiction, dynamic art, and Disney style influenced the medium and its creators so much that he became known as the "god of *manga*" and, upon his death, a museum was dedicated to him and his prolific works.

Osamu Tezuka also developed a passion for animation and created his own animation studio, Mushi Productions, in 1962. Mushi allowed Tezuka to transform some of his successful comics into animated series, the most famous of these being *Tetsuwan Atom* (known as *Astro Boy* in North America). Tezuka introduced a hard realism to his works by presenting characters who would live, suffer, feel joy and anger, and, sometimes, die. The animation industry owes its initial commercial success and subsequent popularity to Tezuka and a handful of other animators, such as Leiji Matsumoto (*Space Battleship Yamato*) and Go Nagai (who introduced foreign television audiences to the transforming robot *UFO Robo Grandizer* [aka *Goldorak*]) who ran their own studios where they transferred their *manga* series into animated format. Even now, studio conglomerates produce *anime* based on popular *manga*, like the widely popular *Ranma 1/2* series.

By the late 1960s, North American animation was, with rare exception, regarded as an exclusively juvenile form of entertainment. However, in Japan, the opposite was true. Japanese animation, labelled *anime* by fans in the West, began to push the limits of the medium by introducing more complex storylines dealing with adult issues. It is also noteworthy that about this time vampires became more "kiddyfied" in North America through their representation in cartoons such as *Scooby Doo* and *Goober and the Ghostchasers*.

Anime itself uses the same cel painting techniques as North American animation, but distinguishes itself in its production methods. In North America, mainstream animated films and series are often produced on a tight schedule and the animators are not allowed to use more imaginative camera work or to create the type of complex storylines commonly found in Japanese *anime*. In Japan, the camera operators and animators are given much more creative freedom that results in a greater feeling of audience involvement and identification with the on-screen action. Japanese animators have also been allowed to be more daring with scenes portraying sexuality and violence. North American audiences associate *anime* with action-packed violence, liberal doses of gore, frank portrayals of strong sexual women, and the representation of the *bishonen* (the androgynous male heroes of *anime*). Lisa Martineau describes the *bishonen* as "a hybrid of sex and race: neither male nor female, neither Oriental or Occidental, but a big-eyed, stylized betwixt-and-between" (191).

The work started by Osamu Tezuka has evolved to encompass a multitude of genres. There are as many genres of *anime* on television and in cinemas as there are live-action counterparts. *Anime* now includes a varied range of genres from animated romantic soap-operas such as *Maison Ikkoku* to animated supernatural detective shows like *Yu Yu Hakusho*. However, *anime* is also popular because of the way this medium mixes and matches existing genres, creating subgenres within hybrid genres. For example, a film like *Dragon Half* combines the fantasy element of a young half-girl/half-dragon with a comedic situation. *Silent Moebius* tells the story of a supernatural police force battling a collection of demons known as Lucifer Folk infesting Tokyo. *The Lupin* series stars a comic thief while *Ranma 1/2* is a martial arts romantic comedy series. Jeff Yang defines the complexity of the *anime* genre as follows: "The world of *anime* is large, it contains multitudes; it's a psychotronic paradise of fluorescent nightmares and wet fantasies, honeydew kisses and technophilic kicks" (56). Whether one's preference is slapstick or dark, subtle fantasy, no genre is neglected in *anime*. However, with the popularity in North America of *Astro Boy*, *Space Cruiser Yamato* (known as *Starblazers* in North America), *Robotech*, and the impressive success of *Akira*, *anime* is most often associated with only a handful of genres, notably science fiction and action-adventure.

Akira has been the most successful *anime* film released in the West. The story is set in the year 2019, thirty-one years after a Third World War. The city of Neo-Tokyo is decaying from within as social unrest and rampant biker gangs flood the streets of the city. One of the bikers, an adolescent boy named Tetsuo, has an accidental run-in with one of the psychics from the top secret Akira Project. This encounter awakens his own latent psychic powers and he faces off against both the government who wants him for their experiments and his biker friends who just want him back. Meanwhile, Tetsuo's powers begin to develop exponentially, attaining truly monstrous proportions before finally growing out of control. *Akira* is a beautifully animated film and deserves the success and attention it still receives.

One of the main reasons for *Akira*'s success in North America was its director and animator, Katsuhiro Otomo, and his animation style. Otomo designed the film as a series of startling images which are not dependent on dialogue and hence not dependent on subtitles or dubbing. *Akira* can thus be enjoyed easily by international audiences. The film's themes also account for the film's substantial success in North America. Western audiences could empathise with the film's focus on teenage biker gangs and social unrest. *Akira* is responsible for attracting a large influx of new fans into the existing *anime* fan base which was demanding more animation of a similar quality. *Akira* also incorporates a number of horrific elements from dismembered limbs to violent and destructive psychic fits of rage.

The vampire themes which are featured in *Vampire Hunter D* and *Vampire Princess Miyu* also form one of the subgenres of the more horrific *anime*. Another classification within *anime* which is extremely popular is that of *shoojo* (meaning "for girls"). Originally intended as "guides" for girls experiencing the pains of adolescence, *shoojo anime* has a dreamy texture to the artwork that seems at odds with its intense plotlines involving gentle love and developing relationships. Takayuki Karahashi describes *shoojo* as a genre which shares many similarities with the vampire genre:

> Add in the decidedly sensual element of the Western world's vampire mythos, and the irresistible pull of the gothic becomes something which isn't so far from the subtleties of *shoojo*. After all, the pathos inherent in a horror story hits many of the same notes to which *shoojo manga* traditionally aspires, and if we allow ourselves to think of both *shoojo* and gothic literature as an engrossing soap opera-like pageant of lives, loves, and deaths raised to a baroque extreme, it all begins to make a kind of sense. (Karahashi 7)

The vampire has also found itself a familiar haunt in *anime* which features horror themes because of the plethora of a wide variety of demons and ghouls. Examples of the monsters of *anime* include the ephemeral, slime-oozing Lucifer Folk from *Silent Moebius*, the Lovecraftian Cthuwulf from *Iczer-One*, and the various humanoid monsters and spirits that inhabit Tokyo in *Supernatural Beast City*, *Demon City Shinjuku*, *Phantom Quest Corporation Volumes 1–4*, and *Devil Hunter Yohko*. The monsters of *anime* are mostly supernatural beings who are ferocious, vicious, and lascivious ghouls, demons, cyborgs, and other demonic and/or technological creations. They exert their powers over humans who possess their own array of powers involving high-tech futuristic bulky weaponry.

The Japanese have a long artistic history of violence and sexual exploitation which may shock North American audiences. For example, the recent critical response in Canada and the United States to *Urotsukidoji: Legend of the Overfiend* concentrated mostly on the demons with multiple tentacle-phalli who impaled human females through a variety of body orifices. The number of spin-offs of this series has led *anime* fandom to label the resulting new genre "tentacle porn." While *Urotsukidoji* represents one extreme end of the spectrum of violent *anime*, many *anime* films and series seem to need the inclusion of a scene of violence (i.e. repeating the decisive martial arts kick three times from three different angles) or a scene of gratuitous "sex" (like the popular shower scene or the frequent low angle camera shot perfectly positioned to expose a girl's underwear). In Japanese culture, these expressions of sexuality and violence can be viewed from an artistic standpoint. In fact, there are many cultural expressions of sex and/or violence in Japan. Ian Buruma explains that photographs of women in bondage appear in newspapers, torture scenes regularly appear on television, and sado-masochist pornography is read openly on subways (220).

The Japanese view these expressions of sexuality and violence as mainstream forms of entertainment which can be seen from an aesthetic rather than a moral standpoint. Firstly, the Japanese, through cultural products such as *Akira* with its rivers of blood, break the *Shinto* taboo of violence and bloodshed. Buruma argues that the principal reasons behind the predominance of sexuality and violence is also rooted in the need for Japanese society to break out of *tatamae*, the public façade. Violence and pornography also allow a cultural release of one's *honne*, private feelings and opinions which are usually suppressed. Buruma describes this expression as follows:

> What one sees on the screen, on stage or in the comic-books is usually precisely the reverse of normal behaviour. The morbid and sometimes grotesque taste that runs through Japanese culture — and has done for centuries — is a direct result of being made to conform to such a strict and limiting code of normality. (225)

Thus, violent and highly sexualised Japanese cultural products act as a release from day-to-day pressures and are seen as a form of play.

The vampires of *anime* display some of the stylistic characteristics and conventions particular to Japanese animation. However, because the mythology of the vampire is imported into Japanese popular culture, it is necessary to examine Bram Stoker's *Dracula* in order to discover the strange blend of Western and Eastern ingredients prevalent in the vampire films of Japanese *anime*.

I. The Prototypical Vampire

"Vampires are bloodsuckers to whom the concept of honour is meaningless."

(Doris Lang in *Vampire Hunter D*)

CENTRAL TO THE vampire tale is the predator who feeds off human blood for survival. Bram Stoker was inspired by Eastern European vampire folklore in his creation of Dracula. This folklore described the vampire as a revenant, an unintelligent, zombie-like creature that rose from the dead in order to attack members of its family.

Stoker added to these myths by incorporating various other elements from the Gothic tradition, Balkan vampire legends, and romantic literature (MacGillivray 64). In *Dracula*, Stoker assembled a collection of properties to create the prototypical vampire against which all other vampires are compared and, ultimately, accepted or rejected. The fictional mythology of vampires includes a prototype, like Dracula himself, capable of generating a progeny of epigones. He is an immoral killer with no pity for his victims, a figure who is evil incarnate and does not generate any sympathy (Leatherdale 110). Dracula must, nonetheless, receive an invitation to enter a room. Carol Senf argues that Dracula receives this invitation because of his victim's desires:

In other words, a vampire cannot influence a human being without that person's consent. Dracula's behaviour confirms that he is an internal, not an external, threat. Although perfectly capable of using superior strength when he must defend himself, he usually employs seduction, relying on the others' desires to emulate his freedom from external constraints: Renfield's desire for immortality, Lucy's wish to escape the repressive existence of an upper-class woman, and the desires of all the characters to overcome the restraints placed on them by their religion and their law. (165)

The characters of *Dracula* who take it upon themselves to hold fast to their religion and law find various reasons to uphold the notion of the vampire's cruel nature. Jonathan Harker sees the vampire as a threat to England where Dracula will create a new vampire colony. Harker's new bride, Mina, sees Dracula as a criminal who murdered her best friend, Lucy Westenra. Dr. Abraham Van Helsing brings an arsenal of religious paraphernalia to fight the vampire because he regards Dracula as a moral threat, a kind of Antichrist.

Bram Stoker illustrates Dracula's threat by rendering him monstrous with bestial characteristics. These animalistic attributes are clear from Dracula's physical appearance. His sharp protruding canines, the long fingernails which resemble hooked claws, the hair growing from his palms, and the pointed ears are reminiscent of wolves and demonstrate the folkloric connection between vampires and werewolves (Leatherdale 103–104). In addition, Dracula can transform himself into a bat or a wolf. He is also associated with vermin when he commands an army of rats. Dracula's animalistic properties even extend to his personality. As Leatherdale outlines:

> Even his persona is animalistic: anti-rational, childlike, instinctive. His vitality is shown as feral, and his cunning is that of an animal that resorts to swift physical action to counter any errors of judgment. (103–104)

However, Dracula is able to move through the streets of London because he still retains the attitudes, wealth, and social position of a feudal lord. As Noel Carroll underlines, "Of necessity, Dracula is Count Dracula" ("Nightmare" 20).

Dracula is probably most associated with the consumption of blood. Some writers believe that Dracula does not need to drink blood but enjoys its taste or that Dracula drinks blood for tactical purposes, such as making himself younger or encouraging Renfield to serve and obey him (Glut 20, Leatherdale 108–109). Dracula's henchmen, the Szgany, demonstrate that the Count does not attack everyone since they can handle their master's daily business without fear of the vampire's bite. Also, Jonathan Harker provides Dracula with English language tutorials and tactical information about England. Although Dracula is tempted to bite Jonathan early in the novel when the young solicitor cuts himself while shaving, Harker is used only by Dracula for his knowledge and not as nourishment for the Undead.

The association of blood with the vampire probably has more to do with Dracula's physical association with death and his need to be revitalised by the blood of humans. He has a pale complexion and is cold to the touch. Dracula also has foul breath and carries the stench of decay. He sleeps a death-like vampire sleep in a coffin containing his native soil. Manuela Dunn Mascetti argues that Dracula's attachment to this native soil shows that he has already implicitly accepted his own death (96).

Dracula does not cast a shadow or a reflection in any mirror because, as Donald F. Glut asserts, Dracula is a dead creature without a soul (20).

The cinematic adaptations of Bram Stoker's novel have expanded the properties which we associate with his prototypical vampire. The figure of Dracula has been adapted so many times to so many different literary and cinematic productions that it is necessary to highlight the three most important interpretations of the vampire which have recast our perceptions of Dracula (Garsault 30). While Stoker may have set the definitive parameters against which all other vampires are measured, the popular mythos of vampirism was forever changed in Tod Browning's 1931 film *Dracula* by matinée idol Bela Lugosi. As Alain Silver and James Orsini claim, "Of all the incarnations of undead Transylvanian noblemen, from the spectral Max Schreck to the panther-like Christopher Lee ... no other has so dominated the role and infused it with his personal mannerisms as the Hungarian, Bela Lugosi" (57). Lugosi starred in only two films featuring the Transylvanian Count. However, the vampire is now associated with Lugosi's thick Hungarian accent, the slicked-back hair and his sartorial style of gentlemanly attire complete with formal wear and a long black cape. Lugosi also portrayed the vampire as an erotic predator (Hogan 145–46).

British actor Christopher Lee added another dimension to the audience's collective knowledge of the vampire. With the more relaxed film censorship codes of the 1960s, the British Hammer vampire films allowed Lee to bring much more sexuality and violence to the role. Lee's Dracula was more fierce, cruel, and almost feral while possessing a sexual magnetism which seduced his female victims (Hogan 145–146).

The interest in vampirism has been renewed in the last twenty years mainly because of popular novelist Anne Rice and her "Vampire Chronicles" — *Interview With the Vampire* (1976), *The Vampire Lestat* (1985), *Queen of the Damned* (1988), *Tale of the Body Thief* (1992), and *Memnoch the Devil* (1995). These chronicles describe the immortality of vampires from their point of view. Readers have discovered the ecstasy of drinking blood, the vampiric pursuit of beauty, art, and love, and the vampire's understanding of their murderous nature and their prospects for eternity. Rice transformed the vampire into a sensitive, beautiful, artistic Child of the Dark Gift: "While Stoker's Dracula is still the dominant vampire image for the general public, Rice's romanticised vision of the vampire was a literary watershed for millions who became enthralled with this new image of the vampire" (Melton xviii). Rice's erotic vampire world remains hugely successful, bolstered by the 1994 release of the film version of *Interview With the Vampire*.

The image of the vampire has retained its popularity in mass culture in the last few years via the mediums of film and television. The vampire film has now crossed into many modes from the comedic vampire tales found in *The Lost Boys, Fright Night,* and *Buffy, The Vampire Slayer* to the very lavishly stylised vampire stories in *The Hunger, Interview With the Vampire,* and *Bram Stoker's Dracula* to *Near Dark,* a vampire tale which mixes elements from the Western and the road movie. In 1995, no less than four major vampire films were released: *From Dusk Till Dawn, The Addiction, Dracula: Dead and Loving It,* and *A Vampire in Brooklyn.* The vampire has also made several prominent television appearances in the 1990s in *Forever Knight, Kindred: The Embraced, Tales From the Crypt: The Reluctant Vampire* and *X-Files: 3.* There are also sequels to *The Lost Boys* and *Love at First Bite* currently in development.

The enduring popularity of vampire fictions is dependent on the films, television series, music videos, and popular books which retain the vampire conventions established in Bram Stoker's *Dracula* while continuously adding, altering, and reshaping the fictional mythology of vampires. Kim Newman argues that the eternal success of the vampire tale is due to the various adaptations of Stoker's novel: "[T]he strength of the fictions that cluster around *Dracula* lies in their diversity" (12).

Bram Stoker's *Dracula* also remains the dominant vampire image because *Dracula* remains a well-crafted tale of horror. Writers have argued that the pleasures found in horror narratives derive from a need for wish-fulfillment where a repressed audience lives vicariously through the ghastly machinations of the Monster (Dickstein 68, Wood 177). According to Morris Dickstein, audiences like the thrills of horror tales because "Horror … [is] a safe, routinized way of playing with death, like going on the roller coaster or parachute jump at an amusement park" (69). However, the Monster may be the most important element in horrific texts because it is through this figure that the audience is led through the narrative's fears and tensions (Figenshu 52). Stoker's tale of the Undead gave the vampire a set of conditions which made this figure horrific. First, Dracula represents a set of dualities where the notion of a living-dead creature rises above our notions of normality and transcends and subverts the order of natural law. Thomas P. Walsh argues that Dracula is a supernatural being because he "exists apart from the chain of being; his is a kind of anti-creation opposing the natural life-to-death cycle of human existence" (232). Dracula's "Otherness," which includes his great strength, the ability to fly and levitate, hypnotic powers, polymorphism, and his ability to metamorphose himself into a thin, luminous mist, makes him monstrous and supernatural, repellent *and* fascinating to audiences.

For Victorian readers, Dracula was particularly monstrous because he subverted the laws of Christianity. Donald F. Glut argues that since Dracula fears religious icons, he is a creation of the Devil (27). Other writers, such as Clive Leatherdale, argue that the red mark on Mina Harker's forehead made by Van Helsing and his Holy Host after Dracula's attack on Mina, marks her as an outcast of God (Leatherdale 184). Van Helsing also uses the crucifix and holy water to make the vampires cower in fear. In their usual religious context, these religious icons are symbols of Christ. In the hands of Van Helsing, they become "weapons" possessing divine powers and are thus transformed into magical shields (Leatherdale 181 and Raible 106). Writers have also argued that Dracula is a Christian heretic. Christianity uses wine which represents blood to celebrate Christ's eternal life. Dracula parodies this celebration by consuming blood in order to ensure and celebrate his own immortality. Finally, Count Dracula subverts Christianity's most important icon — that of a dead man resurrected to eternal life (Dyer 10, Raible 105–106).

Bram Stoker gave his vampire a most horrific ability — to bestow the gift of immortality onto others. As Thomas P. Walsh states, "each new vampire Dracula creates will, in turn, seduce others to swell the numbers of the Undead" (230–231). The threat of a vampire colony in Western civilisation is serious as it represents a threat of foreign invasion. Dracula is first represented as foreign because he is the Monstrous "Other" and this Otherness is emphasised by the vampire's strange appearance and activities. As Thomas Byers describes Dracula's foreignness, "Not only in his essence but in his origins, his habits, even his nationality, he is an alien creature, exotic to the point of being unique" (152). Jonathan Harker's journals offer the first occasion to highlight this Otherness. Dracula's land is depicted as remote and inaccessible. Dracula also describes himself as a descendant of Attila the Hun who was considered an enemy of civilisation (Wood 179). Bram Stoker further emphasises the vampire's foreignness in his description of the Count's appearance. Dracula either speaks a foreign language or broken English. Dracula's strange features are also mentioned: his beaked nose, the redness of his lips and eyes, and the strange smell that seems to accompany him. John Allen Stevenson argues that the scars on Dracula's and Mina's foreheads made, respectively, by Jonathan Harker and Van Helsing, also serve to identify members of the vampire caste: "[T]he scars on the vampires serve a dense semiotic function, as simultaneously untouchable, defiled, and damned — above all, different" (Stevenson 141). None of the foreigners in the novel, Quincey Morris, Professor Van Helsing, or Dracula himself, are allowed to keep a diary in Stoker's novel. With the exclusion of Otherness and the exclusivity of an English viewpoint, readers can support and justify the actions necessary to destroy the foreign vampire threat.

Dracula's plan to conquer England can also be seen as political. The Count can no longer survive in his depleted land. Granted, he is the reason behind the depletion of Transylvania's populace, through warring, conquests, and his own need for nourishment and survival. Conquering England seems like an excellent tactical manoeuvre. Because of the country's Western technological progress, England is removed from superstitions and the dark forces essential to the realm of the vampire. Western civilisation, because of its nature as progressive, industrial, and technological, is incapable of defending itself against Dracula (Wasson 20–21). England will revitalise the Count's conquering nature and provide him with new hunting grounds. However, Dracula's invasion threat is more than a material threat (where he would remove British citizens from the land and convert others to his vampire family), because the vampire threatens the progressive Western world with regression to an era of superstition, a return to mediaevalism (Walsh 232). The battles between the vampire and the English become a confrontation between the Old World and Western Europe with its modern means of communication (i.e. typewriters and phonograph cylinders). Within this scenario, Quincey Morris represents the riches of the New World, and Dr. Seward's ideas concerning madness and its treatment are regarded as progressive.

However, while Dracula is perceived by the characters of the novel, especially Jonathan Harker, as a political threat to the progress and nature of Western civilisation as represented by England, Dracula also demonstrates that the vampire is a sexual threat to this civilisation. Dracula is, first, a sexual competitor to Lucy Westenra's three suitors, Arthur, Jack, and Quincey. Dracula's success in conquering Lucy Westenra demonstrates his sexual prowess over these young men. Dracula's promiscuity subverts Victorian and Christian conventions of "normal" sexuality. Stoker's prototypical vampire is known for mainly attacking members of the opposite sex. Further, he is not known for his exclusive attachments. Dracula is also particular about his victim's marital status and only a betrothed Lucy or a married Mina will suffice.

Dracula's threat is not limited to his affront to religious and moral laws. Dracula threatens to overtake Western civilisation with a new (im)morality by converting England's women to the dark, erotic "religion" of vampirism. Stoker plays upon the fear of the mysterious foreigner who steals civilised women away from their proper domestic place. As John Allen Stevenson describes this threat, "Stoker's perdurable myth reflects the ancient fear that 'they' will take 'our' women, and Dracula is at his most horrifying not when he drinks blood or travels in the form of a bat but when he, a man of palpable foreignness, can say, 'Your girls that you all love are mine already'" (145).

However, it is important to note that the vampire can consume male blood when needed, as when he sails to England aboard the *Demeter*.

Dracula's taste for male blood is most explicitly portrayed during the novel's opening sequence when Jonathan becomes aware of Dracula as a potential sexual threat. Although Jonathan is never attacked by the Count, the tensions in this sequence establish the vampire's monstrous threat. As Christopher Craft writes, *Dracula*'s opening sequence also suggests the horror of the vampire's potential in conquering another male: "[T]he novel's opening anxiety, its first articulation of the vampiric threat, derives from Dracula's hovering interest in Jonathan Harker; the sexual threat this novel first evokes, manipulates, sustains, but never finally represents is that Dracula will seduce, penetrate, drain another male" (170).

However, according to Alain Garsault, Dracula's various threats do not alone account for the constant revitalisation of the vampire myth. Garsault argues that Bram Stoker gave his vampire some degree of humanity which involves readers and audiences in the identification/repulsion process necessary to the enjoyment of horror narratives. For example, Dracula's superhuman properties are tempered by the threat of natural forces, such as sunshine, water, and fire, and of human forces, such as religious morality and modern weaponry. His powers of seduction and, in some *Dracula* adaptations (Dan Curtis's 1974 *Dracula*, John Badham's 1979 *Dracula*, and Francis Ford Coppola's 1991 *Bram Stoker's Dracula*), his powers of love, are tempered by his animalism and need for nourishment above companionship (Garsault 32).

Of course, Dracula's greatest connection to humanity lies in the possibility of his own death (of the final kind). Van Helsing explains the procedures necessary to destroy a vampire. The vampire hunter is quite insistent that the Undead Lucy Westenra should be dispatched with a stake through the heart followed by decapitation. Van Helsing reserves the same fate at the end of the novel for the three vampire women at Dracula's castle. Dracula himself is dispatched at this stage by Jonathan Harker who shears the vampire's throat with his Kukri knife (a long curved knife used as a weapon in Nepal), and Quincey Morris who drives his Bowie knife (a steel knife used as a weapon by, appropriately enough, early American frontiersmen) through Dracula's heart.

II. *Anime's Dorakyura*

"No grave can hold him for long."
("The Big Picture" 38)

HE NOTION OF the Western classical vampire was first introduced in Japan in 1956 with *Kyuuketsuki Ga* aka *Vampire Moth*.

Nevertheless, the spectre of the vampire was not prominent in Japanese culture until the 1970s when Dracula gained mass cultural influence worldwide. During this period, however, the Japanese had begun to critically evaluate American icons and to make cultural modifications in accordance with the beliefs of Japanese society and culture.

Traditionally in North American culture, ethical issues have been cast in terms of polarities of absolute right and wrong. In Japan, the Western concept of the duality of good and evil is a little more blurred. Moral judgements as to what may be considered good or bad are not compared to a fixed set of standards, but by judging the unique aspects of each situation. According to the Japanese religion of *Shinto*, all things have a place in the vast cycle of life. For the Undead, however, *Shinto* does not give clear directions as to their place in this plane of existence. The ambiguities concerning the role of such outcast individuals in Japanese society is a natural place for the *shoojo* genre of both *manga* and *anime* to draw their inspiration.

The first *anime* attempt at modifying the Western vampire stereotype appears in the film *Vampire Hunter D*. The story takes place in the far future, over ten thousand years after humanity is almost wiped out in a catastrophic war. What is interesting about this time period is the audience's uncertainty in distinguishing between effects that are technological and those that are supernatural. The film shows the human race living in fear of monsters and mutants (often one and the same), defending themselves as best they can. Through the darkness that prevails throughout the film, the vampires walk like nobles ruling vast tracts of land and controlling human, mutant, and monster alike.

The antagonist of this film is the vampire Count Magnus Lee who considers himself a descendant of Dracula, the sire of all vampires (it must be assumed here that Van Helsing was negligent in his duties somewhere). To an outside observer he would seem to be just another vampire bearing a strong resemblance to Dracula and Lestat, the lonely, melancholic yet powerful protagonist of Anne Rice's *Vampire Chronicles*. One can, however, see subtle, unique differences in his actions and characteristics.

Count Magnus Lee is the incarnation of immortality taken to an extreme. He has existed for over five thousand years and to him there truly is nothing new under the sun. Magnus has grown extremely bored with his "life" of endless eternal nights. With his chiselled Christopher Lee features, flowing cape, and dapper attire he appears to fit the mould of the romantic vampire, but his fashions are deceptive as his mind and features are permanently set in the archetypal vampire mould. Whereas Dracula demonstrates that blood transforms this vampire by increasing his vitality,

Magnus, even when he has gorged himself by way of various carnal pleasures offered by human females, suffers from a lack of vitality. This characteristic is not, however, a sign of harmlessness. Magnus Lee's situation
is similar to that of a slumbering bear — once awakened from his torpor
by something that interests him, his true power becomes apparent. In fact,
in some scenes, Lee is even more brutal and feral than his sire, Dracula.

From *Vampire Hunter D.*
Used with the permission of Streamline Pictures.

For example, Magnus is shown to be visibly delighted when he uses his powers to smear his servant Rogansi across the castle walls for attempting to assassinate Lee during his dark wedding mass.

Count Magnus Lee's power is not considered supernatural, but more psychic in nature. He has glowing eyes when he manifests his powers which include telekinesis, hypnosis, and the erection of psychic barriers to dissipate energy weapons. Although the villagers regard him as evil,

From *Vampire Hunter D.*
Used with the permission of Streamline Pictures.

Lee notes that his Darwinian function is simply to let the weak perish and the strong survive. Thus, instead of being considered unnatural outsiders, the vampires are a part of the life-cycle as much as any predator.

Magnus, unlike Dracula, has no need to gain consent from his victims in order to enter a building. He forcibly takes whatever interests him. According to Count Magnus Lee, his aristocratic manner is an extension of his philosophy — the stronger one is, the higher one's station in life. Since the vampires of *Vampire Hunter D* are the most powerful beings in existence, they assume the social position of absolute power in society — the nobility. Magnus Lee's lifestyle includes living in a castle with all the trappings of a king and treating the villagers as vassals who must either do his bidding or feel his wrath. Once Magnus kills over two dozen villagers in retaliation for disobeying his orders.

In keeping with the vampire's pretence of nobility and royalty, he treats blood as a connoisseur treats fine wine: he randomly samples before choosing the best 'stock' available. Count Magnus Lee and his familial entourage of noble vampires are served by the mutants and monsters who comprise the enforcers and minions of the nobles' standing army. Humans play the role of serfs who try to escape their master's notice and avoid displeasing him.

Even with this noble lineage, Magnus can be destroyed. However, he does not die well. While he physically fights death after being impaled by D's sword, his daughter Lamika decides that their noble line must die as their castle is swallowed by the maw of the earth. Upon the death of the noble vampires, a darkness is lifted from the land which perhaps signifies the Buddhist sense of renewal and rebirth.

III. *Kyuuketsuki*

"If a human so desires, I can give him immortality ... time everlasting ..."
(Miyu in *Vampire Princess Miyu: Unearthly Kyoto*)

OLLOWING THE COMMERCIAL success of *Vampire Hunter D*, *anime* producers set their sights on animating Narumi Kakinouchi's *shoojo manga Vampire Princess Miyu*. Upon its release, this animated series turned the classic vampire stereotype inside-out. The only common elements between the previous incarnations of the vampire myth and *anime*'s newest vampire, Miyu, were their supernatural powers and the vampire's bloodthirstiness. Almost every other aspect of the vampire character had been modified to conform to Japanese culture and religion.

Vampire Princess Miyu weaves the Japanese ideas of *ninjo*, *giri*, and *shikata* into the vampire mythos. These are important concepts in Japanese culture that do not have equivalents in Western thought. *Ninjo* is the strict traditional code of ethics and morality to which the Japanese ascribe. It can also be translated as meaning "human feelings" or basic humanity and is applied to the relations one has with one's fellows. *Giri* refers to the very strong sense of obligation and responsibility in doing what is expected by society. This is frequently translated as "duty" or "justice," but the concept is also used to justify acts of honourable revenge or atoning for one's actions. Upholding the demands of *giri* involves upholding honour and responsibilities even if the experience is particularly unpleasant and repulses the sense of *ninjo*. This conflict between *ninjo* and *giri* constitutes one of the central themes in Japanese literature and the theatrical arts. The concept of *shikata* is just as ingrained in Japanese society as the concept of *giri-ninjo*. Japanologist Boye LaFayette De Mente translates this as the "way of doing things" and explains how these cultural forms and processes (called *kata*) guide Japanese behaviour and expectations:

> There is hardly an area of Japanese thought or behaviour that is not directly influenced by one or more *kata*. When used in the Japanese context the *shikata* concept includes more than just the mechanical process of doing something. It also incorporates the physical and spiritual laws of the cosmos. It refers to the way things are supposed to be done, both the form and the order, as a means of expressing and maintaining harmony in society and the universe. The absence of *shikata* is virtually unthinkable to the Japanese, for that refers to an unreal world, without order or form. (1)

This desire for order even extends into Japanese religion. Both Buddhism and *Shinto* desire harmony between humans and nature, body and soul, and worlds both seen and unseen.

Shinto beliefs include the notion that humans are descendants of the *kami* (translated as gods or spirits) who still surround us on the supernatural plane of existence. The *kami* can be powerful, as in the case of Susanoo the Storm God (who is like a childish Thor with a bad attitude), or relatively innocuous, as in the case of the spirit resting in the tree in one's yard. In deference to the *kami*, any place they occupy is considered sacred and marked by a special arch known as a *torii*. These rectangular wooden arches are considered to be gateways between the mundane world of everyday existence and the world of the *kami*. *Shinto* is responsible for the erection of the plethora of *torii*'s throughout Japan. It is interesting to note that Miyu first appears sitting atop one of these *torii*, arguably half-in and half-out of the spirit world.

In *Vampire Princess Miyu*, the *kami* are called *Shinma* which refers to their nature as both gods and demons. It is to this class of supernatural being that the vampires of this series belong. Occasionally one of these *Shinma*, or group of *Shinma*, escape from their parallel plane of existence (known as "the Dark") and run freely among the humans. The *kata*, or task, of the vampire clan is to guard the human world from the menace of the escaped *Shinma* and return them to their place of origin.

The vampire known as Miyu appears to be nothing more than an average thirteen-year old Japanese girl dressed in traditional Japanese garb. Only when she manifests her powers does her skin gain that alabaster colouring one associates with the Undead. She does not even have a pair of fangs to denote an animalistic nature. She is also visible in mirrored surfaces and to the Japanese the mirror is considered the "soul of a woman," an object which reflects their purity. This is a complete about-face from the Western concept that the vampire is the epitome of evil.

Although Miyu appears human on the outside, she is definitely a supernatural being. Over the course of the *Vampire Princess Miyu* series (which is comprised of the episodes *Unearthly Kyoto*, *A Banquet of Marionettes*, *Fragile Armour* and *Frozen Time*), Miyu appears and disappears at will, levitates herself and others, hypnotically entrances her prey, and wields powerful magic once an escaped *Shinma* has been cornered.

As a vampire, Miyu has no weaknesses. In the series she is seen to catch a cross and transform it into crystal dust, to drink some holy water, and to give a boy the vampire's kiss in broad daylight. Her only apparent monstrosity is the power she holds and hides behind an adolescent facade, and her need for blood. In the series, blood is not something that a vampire can choose to do without, but an urgent need that produces an unquenchable thirst. If this need is not met, the vampire's body will act on its own, reaching for the closest available source of blood. This leads to tragic consequences for Miyu because one of her first victims, due to her uncontrollable need, is her own mother who becomes a fellow vampire.

One of the primary differences between Dracula and Miyu is that her victims never physically die. Instead, her bite bestows the gift of life for "time everlasting," and she grants the recipient the fulfillment of their greatest wish. However, for all practical purposes, Miyu's victims may as well be dead because they enter a happy, dreamlike state where they see nothing beyond their fantasy world and become out of touch with reality. Eventually, like Miyu's father, the vampire's victims go through the motions of day-to-day existence, not knowing what to live for. As Miyu's mother laments, "It's because there is death that life is wonderful" (*Vampire Princess Miyu: Frozen Time*). However, in some cases, the victim remains unaffected at the time their blood is drained. At some point they "awaken" and gain powers and perceptions they never knew existed. Whether or not they too become vampires is unclear.

Unlike the many literary, cinematic, and televisual interpretations of the vampire as an erotic or intensely sexual creature, the vampire Miyu is characterised by a very subdued sexuality. Episodes of the *Vampire Princess Miyu* series are peppered with Miyu's girlish giggles, her romantic trials and tribulations over a young male interest, Kei, and her assertion that she "like[s] the beautiful people" (*Vampire Princess: A Banquet of Marionettes*). Unlike the traditional representation of female vampires, Miyu is not sexually threatening primarily because the series derives from the *shoojo manga*, a genre dedicated to help young girls cope with the emotional pains of adolescence.

However, a subtle sexual element is retained in *Vampire Princess Miyu* from the romantic vampire mythos. One of the trademarks of *anime* is the rendering of characters with large, expressive eyes and lithesome bodies. This style of drawing produces characters who maintain a degree of innocence within a marked sensuality. Miyu desires "the beautiful people" among humans, be they female or male, and she makes sexual innuendoes by, for example, licking her lips, an act which usually accompanies the vampire's act of bloodsucking. *Vampire Princess Miyu* also presents these scenes in a languid, dream-like fashion. The bisexuality of the vampires of *anime* is subtle and most apparent in the animators' androgynous rendering of the *bishonen* characters.

Anime vampires are also different from the traditional Western archetype because they can have children, grow old, and die. However, in Miyu's case, the *Shinma* have decreed that she will not be allowed to age until she has returned the last of the escaped *Shinma* back to the Dark. The reason for this is that Miyu's mother fought the *Shinma* elders in order to prevent her daughter from having to take up the mantle she herself had borne for so long. This allowed a large number of *Shinma* to escape and terrorise humanity. Miyu's immortality is a direct result of her mother's *giri-ninjo* conflict. In other words, Miyu's mother's sense of family was at odds with her duty to fight stray *Shinma*.

Thus the image of the Japanese vampire is of an unnatural being that has a role in the natural order of things. The *kata* (process) they must adhere to is created by their own supernatural society. In following the *giri* path (the path of duty) which their *kata* requires, whether it be reluctantly or wholeheartedly, they still show signs of *ninjo* (humanity/feeling) towards both their own kind and their victims. If anything, this makes the Japanese vampire something to be pitied as much as feared.

IV. Epigones

"I am here to do Your bidding, Master. I am Your slave, and You will reward me, for I shall be faithful. I have worshipped You long and afar off. Now that You are near, I await Your commands, and You will not pass me by, will You, dear Master, in Your distribution of good things?"
(Renfield in *Dracula* 102)

AS MUCH AS the vampire is feared, the Undead are helpless without the services of a loyal servant. Bram Stoker's *Dracula* shows that the vampire needs the loyalty of the *Szgany* who carry out daily tasks and do not fear the vampire's kiss. Dracula arrives in England where another loyal servant, Renfield, awaits his master. Renfield feels compelled to serve Dracula even within the confines of Dr. Seward's asylum. Leatherdale argues that Renfield is used by Stoker to explain the validity of vampirism (121). Renfield is also used as a barometer for the Count's movements and activities.

In *Vampire Hunter D*, the role of Renfield is fulfilled by the mutant captain of Magnus Lee's guards, Rogansi. Powerful in his own right, Rogansi nevertheless covets the position of nobility the vampires hold in his world and wants to become like them. However, like Renfield, he rebels against his proscribed *kata* by trying to usurp Magnus's position. Rogansi finally pays for this ultimate insult to the vampires with his life, just as Renfield does, but without atoning for his actions.

The *Shinma* known as Larvae plays the role of the vampire's silent partner in *Vampire Princess Miyu*. Cutting a tall, cadaverous, yet graceful silhouette, he appears dressed in a flowing, midnight black cloak and cowl wearing a mask that conceals both his face and voice. A very powerful *Shinma* in his own right, Larvae comes under Miyu's influence when he mistakenly awakens her powers before attempting to kill her. After becoming her first victim, he becomes bound to Miyu by the bond of the blood they share. Larvae becomes Miyu's sole servant, confidante, and friend, and her mission to hunt stray *Shinma* also becomes his own. The audience often sees Larvae comforting Miyu as he listens to her troubles, enfolding her within his voluminous cloak. As he aids Miyu in her endless quest, he realises that once their task is finished Miyu will return him to the Dark as well. Yet, stoically, he continues helping Miyu, perhaps hoping that she will return to the Dark with him.

The role of the vampire servant in *anime* is modified from Renfield's attempt to gain vampire-like abilities by whatever means possible, to a more loyal and equitable partnership as that formed between Miyu and Larvae. The vampire's retainer now considers it a part of his *giri* (duty) to follow his master and provide assistance with no questions asked.

V. Dracula's Vampire Hunters

> "Visitors from the past shall return to the darkness from whence they came."
>
> (D in *Vampire Hunter D*)

DESPITE THE CENTRALITY of the vampire character in these *anime* films and Stoker's *Dracula*, it is the confrontation between the living and the Undead which gives these texts their drama, suspense, and impact. Bram Stoker created a small community headed by Professor Abraham Van Helsing to fight and forever destroy the vampire. Van Helsing brings an arsenal of knowledge to help him convince the band of young men to destroy the monster. Van Helsing has historical and folkloric knowledge of the vampire and he harnesses his Christian faith to help battle Dracula's moral and sexual threat. Van Helsing also has the physical tools, such as holy hosts, wooden stakes, and garlic to fight the vampire. Although he is a lawyer, doctor of medicine, and philosopher by profession, Van Helsing becomes a priest and a magician when battling the vampire. The Professor is given a crucial role in *Dracula* as he is the only one able to recognise the monstrous threat.

A "discovery plot" where the monster's presence is established and discovered by an individual or group is common to most horror texts. This individual or group must then convince another group of the existence and impending evil of the monster. This is followed by hesitations, deliberations, and assessments of the monster and considerations of ways to destroy it until the climax of the narrative where the group confronts the monster and wins. Noel Carroll argues that in the "discovery plot" of *Dracula*, "Van Helsing is the quintessential discoverer figure" (106.) Screen interpretations of *Dracula* and his vampire spawn make Van Helsing, or a specialised vampire hunter, or even an "unprofessional" yet vampire-knowledgeable person, the only character capable of recognising the vampire threat, a recognition crucial to the vampire's defeat (Waller 90).

However, in *Dracula*, Stoker reveals that Van Helsing cannot fight the vampire alone; he needs the support of a community. Gregory A. Waller asserts that the need for a community effort is demonstrated by the failure of two communities at the beginning of the novel (32). The first community to fail fighting Dracula is the crew of the *Demeter*, the Russian ship which brings the vampire to London. The captain exhibits great strength and faith but after his crew is killed off one by one, he is unable to fight the vampire single-handedly.

The second community to fail in even perceiving the threat of Dracula are the main protagonists' relatives. Lucy's mother provides the best example of this failure as she gives Dracula better access to her daughter when she removes the garlic from her room. Moreover, all of the characters end up parentless. Morris and Seward have no parents, and Lucy's mother and Arthur's father die of natural causes during the course of the novel. Mina and Jonathan Harker also have no parents; however, they see Jonathan's employer and benefactor as a father-figure who, as it happens, also dies during the unfolding of the narrative. It is thus especially important for this group to band together and form a moral community of good, brave men, headed by Van Helsing and comprised of Jonathan Harker, Dr. Jack Seward, Arthur Holmwood (Lord Godalming), and Quincey Morris. Each member of Van Helsing's group brings special individual talents, and only in consort are they able to destroy the vampire.

Arthur Holmwood brings wealth to the group. He spares no expense, a factor which allows this moral community to chase Dracula across Europe to his castle in Transylvania. Arthur also brings his title of Lord Godalming (given to him after the deaths of his fiancée Lucy Westenra and his father) which, on a practical level, gives Van Helsing's Christian brotherhood a better tactical advantage and, on a symbolic level, puts them on an even footing with Dracula. As Leatherdale has noted, the "two aristocrats fight … for possession of the same woman [Lucy]" (125–126).

Dr. Jack Seward brings his scientific knowledge to this moral community. However, he is especially important for bringing Van Helsing into the fold and for uniting several key players together. Leatherdale argues that Dr. Seward unites several of the main characters where he "functions as a link man, being the catalyst which brings four of the other male characters together. His relationship with Van Helsing and Renfield, for example, is central to the unfolding of the plot" (123).

Jonathan Harker brings the experience of his ordeal at Dracula's castle to the group's goal of destroying the vampire. Harker's first-hand experience with vampires, his role in bringing Dracula to London, and his outrage over Dracula's violation of his wife, Mina, give him the strength needed to drive away Dracula's bodyguards in order to shear their master's throat. Clive Leatherdale sees Harker as marking his own place in vampire history: "his most enduring achievement, and the one by which he is best assessed, is that he is one of the few fictional characters to have lived among, and been imprisoned by vampires, yet who by his own guile and courage survived to tell the tale" (115). Quincey Morris brings vigour, gun power, and experience in leading hunting expeditions. He brings brawn to the group's more intellectual tendencies.

This moral community therefore includes the alliance of age and youth, the middle class and aristocracy, law and commerce, science and medicine, and England and America. It also unites men and women in the struggle to rid the Western world of the evils represented by Dracula (Waller 42). Central to the success of this community is its inclusion of Mina Harker. Several writers argue that she is essential to locating and destroying Dracula (Leatherdale 138–139, Demetrakopoulos 110, and Waller 39). She provides Van Helsing's group of vampire hunters with a direct link to Dracula through hypnosis. She uses deductive analysis coupled with her knowledge of train timetables to discover Dracula's route to his castle. Mina is also adamant with Van Helsing that the group should work together (Waller 39).

Mina's role is interesting because she presents a peculiar duality. First, several writers have determined that she possesses many characteristics associated with the New Woman of the Victorian era who was concerned with taboo domains such as education, careers, and sexuality (Leatherdale 140–141, Senf 33–49, Demetrakopoulos 108–109). For example, Mina is initially presented perfecting her skills as a typist and stenographer, skills which she later uses to assist her husband, Jonathan, once he inherits his employer's business. Mina's vocation may seem like a stereotypical feminine role for modern readers; however, for the Victorians, the notion of a woman professionally supporting her husband was novel.

Dracula's seduction of Mina's best friend, Lucy Westenra, transforms the girlish, sweet, and beautiful Lucy into an Undead seductive siren. The Undead Lucy displays qualities which are far removed from those suitable to the conventional Victorian woman. Lucy subverts the traditional female role in her vampirism and sexual freedom. Her moral Otherness also has a monstrous aspect as she perverts the conventional female role of motherhood when Van Helsing and her three suitors confront Lucy in her tomb where she has been feeding off young children. In this scene, she shocks the reader by cold-heartedly throwing a child to the ground. As Gail B. Griffin states, "God's designated protector of children has become their predator. The transformation from woman to monster is complete" (460). This scene confirms to Van Helsing, Morris, Seward, and Godalming that Lucy has violated acceptable norms of femininity; she is a loathsome creature who must be destroyed. *Dracula*'s readers can identify with the men's rationalisation for destroying Lucy because they have already been introduced, through Jonathan Harker's diary, to the threat of the vampire women at Count Dracula's castle.

The vampire women were obviously initiated into vampirism by the Count himself. Clive Leatherdale claims that two of the women, who Harker says resemble Dracula, are probably his daughters. Harker writes that he recognises the third and Leatherdale surmises that this must be Dracula's wife (28). The inclusion of Dracula's vampire progeny introduces readers to the sexual aggression and voracity that vampirism can unleash in women. Jonathan Harker, at the beginning of the novel, and Professor Van Helsing, near the conclusion of *Dracula* are both tempted by these vampire women because they "offer immediate sexual gratification, though on illicit and dangerous terms, a tempting alternative to the socially imposed delays and frustrations of [Harker's] relationship with the chaste but somewhat sexless Mina" (Bentley 28). However, both vampire hunter and vampire survivor are repulsed by the wiles of these vampire women. Harker actually loses consciousness when Dracula helps the vampire women feed. Van Helsing resigns himself to doing what he calls "butcher work" (371), killing all three vampire women in order to free their souls and give them over to death. Once the threat of sexually ravenous women and Dracula's power to create a race of them has been established, the novel then focuses on protecting Mina Harker and saving her soul from the imminent threat of vampirism.

It is noteworthy that Mina's wedding to Jonathan coincides with Lucy's death. At this stage, Mina's role changes. She must confirm the virtues of Victorian womanhood. Gregory A. Waller argues that Mina must be elevated to represent the ideal Victorian woman: "Thus, to treat Mina chivalrously is not enough; she must be worshipped as the very heart of the community, lest she, like Lucy, become a creature of the night rather than the light" (39). First, Mina is shown to reject the sexual openness of the New Woman writers. She is then described repeatedly as a mother-figure to Van Helsing and his moral community, a characteristic which is explicitly demonstrated when Mina comforts Arthur. Mina describes herself, and the nature of womanhood, when she states: "We women have something of the mother in us that makes us rise above smaller matters when the mother-spirit is invoked" (230).

Saving Mina from vampirism also means saving her for motherhood. The end of *Dracula* confirms the success of Van Helsing's anti-vampire mission when Mina produces a son who represents the continuation of England's long tradition of good, strong men. Her child also bears the names of all the members of Van Helsing's vampire-fighting moral community. Van Helsing regards Mina's virtues as chivalrous, selfless, and vital to the future of Western civilisation. Mina also assumes a spiritual role which is confirmed when Van Helsing announces that "She is one of God's women, fashioned by His own hand to show us men and other women that there is a heaven where we can enter, and that its light can be here on earth" (188). With the importance of motherhood and Mina's quasi-holy nature established, the vampire hunters morally justify the destruction of Dracula.

VI. The *Dhampyre*, the *Darani*, and the Dark

IN *ANIME*, IT is oftentimes the female characters who willingly face the greatest dangers. The science fiction branch of *anime* features many strong female leads such as Katsumi Liqueur, the reluctant sorceress and demon fighter in *Silent Moebius*. Others include the combat cyborg girl, Gally, of *Battle Angel*, and the battlesuited vigilante women called the Knight Sabers in the cyberpunk classic *Bubblegum Crisis*. These female characters are leaders and fighters who battle the most monstrous beasts with the mightiest firepower and supernatural weapons. Some of the characters are nearly badly defeated in their confrontations with these demons, monsters, and mutants, but they manage to find a final burst of strength that enables them to overcome their antagonists.

This is how Doris Lang is first presented in the opening sequence of *Vampire Hunter D*. Alone in the woods, she destroys a particularly vicious demon by running it down and shooting it in the head. She is brave and feisty, characteristics demonstrated when she rejects the sexual advances and protection of Greco, the mayor's son. Doris displays the traditional strong female traits found in *anime*, and like many other female *anime* characters, she is tall, blonde, and voluptuous — a feature accentuated by skimpy clothing, gratuitous panty shots, and plunging necklines — all of which gives her a very Occidental look.

Doris soon comes to realise that she cannot combat the supernatural alone and turns to D, a vampire hunter, for help. She offers D food, lodging, and sexual favours (whether or not she is a virgin is never made clear) as payment for his vampire hunting services. D never actually accepts or rejects her sexual payments but he experiences inner turmoil when his vampire nature surfaces and Doris offers him her blood. The scene has a strange sexual mixture of animalism with D's dripping fangs and Doris's willingness and rapture at the anticipation of the forbidden vampire's kiss. The exchange is never realised, but this scene is tantalisingly prolonged.

The vampire hunter known as D is portrayed with many dualities and ambiguities. There is an element of uncertainty about the moral status of his quest as he himself is a *dhampyre*, a vampire halfbreed. Although D tries to live like a human, the vampire part of his nature strongly influences him. This tension provides the ongoing *giri* conflict in the series. D can perhaps be best described as the prototypical Japanese wandering hero who tries to live by a strong moral code and has a strong desire to see justice done. When dialogue fails, he is more than willing to speak with his sword which is regarded by the *samurai* as an extension of the soul.

D appears dressed entirely in black from the top of his wide-brimmed hat to his boots as he sits on his black cyborg horse. He rarely speaks and generally tries to defeat his opponents by all means humanly possible, as if the use of his vampire abilities is an acknowledgement of failure. His only weapons are a sword and a face — never revealed as magical or as technological — that appears to be built into his left hand. The hand engages in a witty running monologue trying to bait D into revealing his deepest thoughts — those which he is unwilling to face.

At various times, D finds himself in a position where the use of his vampire abilities is needed to escape from a potentially lethal situation. It is then that he reverts to his vampire nature. As D's talking hand comments, "when it all comes down, you eventually show your fangs." The hand also wonders why D is unwilling to revert to his more basic nature. Perhaps it is because the talking hand acts as his *honne* which reveals his private feelings when D tries so hard to exercise *tatamae*, described by Ian Buruma as "the façade, the public posture, the way things ought to be" (221). The hand also acts as a conscience and anchor in the human world for D, reminding him that there are some things that are worth protecting.

D is also very old. It is hinted in the *anime* that his father was Dracula himself. This makes him incredibly powerful and knowledgeable about vampire lore. He does his best to hide this fact, however, so that he may appear human. He also tries to avoid killing indiscriminately, be his victims human or vampire. To D, killing without justification or necessity violates his code of honour. This is why, of all the other supernatural creatures, he battles Count Magnus Lee, a vampire without honour who is concerned only with the temporary carnal pleasures provided by human females. One might say that D's *kata* is well balanced by both his senses of *giri* and *ninjo*.

The spiritualist Se Himiko from *Vampire Princess Miyu* presents another image of the vampire hunter. Although not a vampire hunter *per se*, she is drawn into Miyu's world after an encounter with an imposter vampire whom both Himiko and Miyu were chasing. Quite skeptical for a spiritualist, even to the end, Himiko pursues Miyu to prevent her from taking human blood. Disconcerted with the lack of success with traditional Western vampire-hunting methods, her best defences lie with Buddhism. Although she has a magic knife which can be used as a defensive shield, her most powerful weapon is her knowledge of the *Darani*, the secret writings of Buddha. The modification of the vampire myth to suit the Japanese context is, therefore, completed with Eastern Buddhism replacing Western Christianity as the religion of defence against the vampire. Yet for all of Himiko's dogged pursuit of Miyu, she remains uncertain as to the moral status of her quest. Indeed, Himiko appears to strike up a mutual understanding with Miyu, helping her free Larvae in exchange for more information on Miyu's past.

VII. Infinite Diversities

> "What a wondrous night this has been! For the first time in one hundred years I haven't been bored once the entire evening."
> (Count Magnus Lee upon killing Rogansi in *Vampire Hunter D*)

BRAM STOKER'S VAMPIRE continues to endure as one of the mass cultural icons of this century. Since its 1897 publication, *Dracula* has undergone many alterations, transformations, and reinventions. These variations have appeared in the many film, literary, and musical adaptations of *Dracula* and in the media products which feature vampires or vampire themes. The prevalent notion of the vampire was dramatically altered in the various cinematic interpretations featuring Bela Lugosi and Christopher Lee. In recent years, Anne Rice's *Vampire Chronicles* have inspired many film and musical products such as Sting's "Moon Over Bourbon Street," and Concrete Blonde's "Bloodletting." Rice's sensitive creatures of the night have changed popular perceptions of the vampire. This, in turn, has influenced the characterisation of Dracula in film. Gary Oldman's Count in Francis Ford Coppola's *Bram Stoker's Dracula* is but one example. The characteristics associated with the vampire as portrayed by Bram Stoker have also been modified to suit a knowledgeable audience.

Vampire media products must also take into account the audience's and characters' extensive awareness regarding a vampire's activities, and perhaps more importantly, its destruction. For example, in films like *Buffy, the Vampire Slayer*, *The Lost Boys*, and *From Dusk Till Dawn*, the main characters may not believe in vampires, but they do know the power of holy water, to refuse to invite a vampire into their homes, and that a stake must be driven through the heart of the walking dead.

The vampire myth has also been transformed by international influences. *Vampire Hunter D* and *Vampire Princess Miyu* have revised Stoker's vampire narrative in two very different ways. *Vampire Hunter D*'s futuristic yet mediaeval setting retains a vampire who is a close reproduction of Dracula. In both films, however, elements from established vampire folklore are altered. The vampire Count Magnus Lee is much more monstrous than Stoker envisioned. The vampire hunter works with a Japanese code of ethics, and the women of the film have the characteristics and attributes of female characters of *anime*. *Vampire Princess Miyu*, with its contemporary setting, incorporates many Eastern elements such as the use of Buddhism to ward off the vampires, the inclusion of monstrous demons, and the elements of *shoojo manga*.

The vampire myth has now permeated Japanese culture. The Japanese government recently initiated an AIDS awareness campaign featuring Dracula saying "I'm afraid to die" (Martineau 146). CDs of the *Vampire Hunter D* soundtrack and storybooks based on *Vampire Princess Miyu* are readily available. Vampire themes have appeared in the fourth episode of the *Bastard!* series where Lord Di-Amon noisily slurps the blood of a young girl. *Bubblegum Crisis* also features a *Mecha* (the name commonly given to large robots) which draws blood from humans in order to provide a blood bank to sustain two androids. Episode 1 of *Phantom Quest Corporation* offers a comic take on vampires. It features an anemic vampire who wards off sunlight with the aid of modern technology which includes sunglasses, Ultra-Violet tanning sessions, and shock aversion therapy. There are also new vampire *anime* series in development such as *Dark Side Blues* set in a 21st century Victorian cyberpunk environment, and the aptly titled *Vampire Wars*. Japanese animators clearly seem willing to push the Japanese image of the vampire in new directions.

Vampires continue to walk among us in diversified mediums in broad daylight. Indeed, Japanese vampires are not considered outsiders who threaten the natural order of things. They are well-rounded beings who know both love and hate, desire and longing, and have an understanding of their *kata* despite being unsure of their place in the circle of life. In short, contemporary Japanese vampires offer an altogether human outlook on the world.

NOTES

1   *Ronin* are masterless *samurai* who roamed throughout mediaeval Japan trying to discern a path for themselves in this life. Some became criminals while others followed the path of duty and honour into legend.

FILMOGRAPHY

The Addiction. Dir. Abel Ferrara, 1995.

Akira. Dir. Katsuhiro Otomo. Akira Committee, 1989.

Bastard. Dir. unknown. AIC/Anime R., 1993.

Battle Angel. Dir. Hiroshi Fukutomi. Animate Film, 1993.

Bram Stoker's Dracula. Dir. Francis Ford Coppola. Columbia, 1992.

Bubblegum Crisis 5: Moonlight Rambler. Dir. Obari Masami. AIC/Artmic, 1988.

Buffy, The Vampire Slayer. Dir. Fran Rubel Kuzui. 20th Century Fox/Sandollar-Kuzui, 1992.

Chi O Suu Me aka Lake of Dracula or Lust for Blood or Bloodthirsty Eyes. Dir. Michio Yamamoto. Toho, 1971.

Cutey Honey. Dir. unknown. Toei, 1973.

Dark Side Blues. Dir. Kazuhisa Teknouchi. Tabak and Studio Junio, 1994.

Demon City Shinjuku. Dir. Yoshiaki Kawajiri. Madhouse, 1993.

Devil Hunter Yohko. Dir. Tetsuro Aoki. Madhouse, 1990.

Dracula. Dir. Dan Curtis. Curtis Productions, 1974.

Dracula. Dir. John Badham. Mirisch/Universal, 1979.

Dracula. Dir. Tod Browning. Universal, 1931.

Dracula. Dir. Minori Okazaki. Toei, 1980.

Dracula: Dead and Loving It. Dir. Mel Brooks. Columbia/Castle Rock Entertainment/Gaumont/Brooksfilms, 1995.

Dragon Half. Dir. Shinya Sadamitsu. Production IG, 1993.

Dragonball. Dir. Minoru Okazaki. Toei Animation, 1986.

Forever Knight. Dirs. various. Paragon/Tri-Star/CBS, 1992–93.

Fright Night. Dir. Tom Holland. Vistar/Columbia, 1985.

From Dusk Till Dawn. Dir. Robert Rodriguez. Alliance/Dimension Films/A Band Apart/Los Hooligans Productions, 1995.

The Hunger. Dir. Tony Scott. MGM, 1983.

Iczer-One. Dir. Toshihiro Hirano. Iczer, 1985.

Innocent Blood. Dir. John Landis. Warner Brothers, 1992.

Interview With the Vampire. Dir. Neil Jordan. Warner Brothers, 1994.

Kindred: The Embraced. Dirs. various. Spelling Television/20th Century Fox Television, 1996–.

Kyuuketsuki Ga aka Vampire Moth. Dir. Nobuo Nakagawa. Toho, 1956.

Kyuuketsuki (Vampire Princess) Miyu. Dir. Toshihiro Hirano. AIC, 1988.

The Lost Boys. Dir. Joel Schumacher. Warner Brothers, 1987.

Love at First Bite. Dir. Stan Dragoti. Simon Productions/AIP, 1979.

Lupin Series. Dir. Hayao Miyazaki. 1980.

Maison Ikkoku. Dir. unknown. Kitty, 1983.

Near Dark. Dir. Kathryn Bigelow. De Laurentiis/Feldman-Meeker, 1987.

Onna Kyuuketsuki aka Vampire Woman or The Female Vampire. Dir. Nobuo Nakagawa. Shin Toho, 1959.

Phantom Quest Corporation 1: Kiss of Fire. Dir. Koichi Chigira. Madhouse, 1994.

Ranma 1/2 Series. Dir. Tsutomu Shibayama. Kitty, 1986.

Robotech. Dir. Carl Macek. Harmony Gold, 1985.

Sailor Moon. Dir. Junichi Sato. Toho, 1992.

Samurai Troopers aka Ronin Warriors. Dirs. Sei Ikeda and Mamoru Hamazu. Sunrise, 1989.

Silent Moebius. Dir. Michitaka Kikuchi. Studio Tron, 1991.

Space Battleship Yamato (Starblazers). Dir. Leiji Matsumoto. Toei, 1974.

Supernatural Beast City. Dir. Yoshiaki Kawajiri. Madhouse, 1987.

Tales From the Crypt: The Reluctant Vampire. Dir. Elliot Silverstein. HBO, 1990.

Tekkaman Blade aka Teknoman. Dir. unknown. Tatsunoko Productions, 1992.

Tetsuwan Atom aka Astro Boy. Dir. Osamu Tezuka. Mushi Productions, 1963.

UFO Robo Grandizer aka Goldorak. Dir. Go Nagai. Dynamic Productions and Toei, 1975.

Urotsukidoji: Legend of the Overfiend. Dir. Hideki Takayama. Angel, JAVN, 1989.

Vampire Hunter D. Dir. Toyoo Ashida. Ashi Pro, 1985.

A Vampire in Brooklyn. Dir. Wes Craven. Paramount/Eddie Murphy Productions, 1995.

Vampire Wars. Dir. unknown. 1995.

X-Files: 3. Dir. David Nutter. Ten Thirteen Productions/20th Century Fox Television, 1994.

Yu Yu Hakusho. Dir. unknown. Studio Pierrot, 1993.

REFERENCES

Bentley, C.F. "The Monster in the Bedroom: Sexual Symbolism in Bram Stoker's *Dracula*." *Literature and Psychology* 22 (1972): 27–34.

"The Big Picture." *Boxoffice* 128 (November 1992): 38.

Biodrowski, Steve. "*Dracula*: The Untold Story." *Cinéfantastique* 23 (October 1992): 12–13.

Buican, Denis. *Les Métamorphoses de Dracula: L'Histoire et la Légende*. Paris: Les Editions du Félin, 1993.

Buruma, Ian. *A Japanese Mirror: Heroes and Villains of Japanese Culture*. London: Jonathan Cape Ltd., 1984.

Byers, Thomas B. "Good Men and Monsters: The Defenses of Dracula." *Dracula, the Vampire and the Critics*. Ed. Margaret L. Carter. Ann Arbor, Michigan: UMI Research Press, 1988. 149–157.

Carroll, Noël. "Nightmare and the Horror Film: The Symbolic Biology of Fantastic Beings." *Film Quarterly* 34 (1981): 16–25.

—. *The Philosophy of Horror or Paradoxes of the Heart*. New York: Routledge, 1990.

Cleary, Thomas. *The Japanese Art of War*. Boston: Shambhala, 1991.

Christopher, Robert C. *The Japanese Mind: The Goliath Explained*. New York: Simon & Schuster, 1983.

Cohn, L.L. "*Vampire Hunter D*." *Variety* 348 (Aug 3, 1992): 41–42.

Craft, Christopher. "'Kiss Me With Those Red Lips': Gender and Inversion in Bram Stoker's *Dracula*." *Dracula: the Vampire and the Critics*. Ed. Margaret L. Carter. Ann Arbor, Michigan: UMI Research Press, 1988. 167–194.

De Mente, Boye LaFayette. *Behind the Japanese Bow: An In-Depth Guide to Understanding and Predicting Japanese Behavior*. Illinois: Passport Books, 1993.

—. *Japan Almanac*. Lincolnwood: Passport Books, 1987.

Demetrakopoulos, Stephanie. "Feminism, Sex Role Exchanges, and Other Subliminal Fantasies in Bram Stoker's *Dracula*." *Frontiers: A Journal of Women Studies* 2 (1977): 104–113.

Dickstein, Morris. "The Aesthetics of Fright." *Planks of Reason: Essays on the Horror Film*. Ed. Barry Keith Grant. Metuchen, New Jersey: Scarecrow Press, 1984. 65–78.

Dorson, Richard M. *Folk Legends of Japan*. Rutland, Vermont: Charles E. Tuttle Company, 1962.

Dyer, Richard. "Dracula and Desire." *Sight and Sound* 3 (January 1993): 8–12.

"Episodes from the Life of Osamu Tezuka." *Animerica* 3 (1995): 8–11.

Evans, Peter J. "The Beautiful and the Terrible." *AnimeUK Magazine* 2: 27–31.

Figenshu, Tom. "Screams of a Summer Night." *Film Comment* 15 (September–October 1979): 49–53.

Frost, Brian J. *The Monster with a Thousand Faces: Guises of the Vampire in Myth and Literature*. Bowling Green, Ohio: Bowling Green State University Popular Press, 1989.

Fry, Carrol L. "Fictional Conventions and Sexuality in *Dracula*." *Victorian Newsletter*

42 (1972): 20–22.

Garsault, Alain. "Comme le phoenix … Dracula." *Positif* 383 (January 1993): 30–32.

Gibney, Frank. *Japan: The Fragile Superpower.* New York: Norton, 1975.

Glut, Donald F. *The Dracula Book.* Metuchen, New Jersey: Scarecrow Press, 1975.

Griffin, Gail B. "'Your Girls That You All Love Are Mine': *Dracula* and the Victorian Male Sexual Imagination." *International Journal of Women's Studies* 3 (1980): 454–465.

Groensteen, Thierry. *L'Univers des Mangas: Une Introduction à la Bande Dessinée Japonaise.* Paris: Casterman, 1991.

Hall, John Whitney. *Japan: From Prehistory to Modern Times.* New York: Delacorte Press, 1970.

Hane, Mikiso. *Modern Japan: A Historical Survey.* San Francisco: Westview Press, 1992.

Hogan, David J. *Dark Romance: Sexuality in the Horror Film.* Jefferson, North Carolina: McFarland and Company, 1986.

Hoberman, J. "Cartoon Cultism Zaps America." *Premiere* 4 (December 1990): 42–43.

Ishida, Eichiro. *Japanese Culture: A Study of Origins and Characteristics.* Tokyo: University of Tokyo Press, 1974.

Karahashi, Takayuki. "The New *Anime* Gothic." *Animerica* 3 (1995): 7.

Leatherdale, Clive. *Dracula: The Novel and the Legend.* Wellingborough, Northamptonshire: Aquarian Press, 1985.

Ledoux, Trish and Doug Ranney. *The Complete Anime Guide: Japanese Animation Video Directory and Guide.* Issaquah, Washington: Tiger Mountain Press, 1995.

MacGillivray, Royce. "*Dracula*: Bram Stoker's Spoiled Masterpiece." *The Critical Response to Bram Stoker.* Ed. Carol A. Senf. Westport, Connecticut: Greenwood Press, 1993. 61–68.

Martineau, Lisa. *Caught in a Mirror: Reflections of Japan.* London: Macmillan, 1993.

Mascetti, Manuela Dunn. *Le Livre des Vampires.* Paris: Editions Solar, 1992.

Melton, Gordon J. *The Vampire Book: The Encyclopedia of the Undead.* Detroit Michigan: Visible Ink Press, 1994.

McCloud, Scott. *Understanding Comics.* Northampton, Massachusetts: Kitchen Sink Press Inc., 1993.

Newman, Kim. "Bloodlines." *Sight and Sound* 3 (January 1993): 12–13.

Nogoret, H. "De Kurosawa aux *mangas*." *Positif* 383 (January 1993): 74–75.

Ono, Sokyo. *Shinto: The Kami Way.* Rutland: Charles E. Tuttle Company, 1968.

Picken, Stuart D.B. *Shinto: Japan's Spiritual Roots.* Tokyo: Kodansha International Ltd., 1980.

Piggott, Juliet. *Japanese Mythology.* New York: Peter Bedrick Books, 1985.

Raible, Christopher Gist. "Dracula: Christian Heretic." *Dracula, the Vampire and the Critics.* Ed. Margaret L. Carter. Ann Arbor, Michigan: UMI Research Press, 1988. 105–107.

Samu, Charles. "Contemporary Japanese Animators." *Sightlines* 19 (1985–86): 20.

Senf, Carol A. "*Dracula*: Stoker's Response to the New Woman." *Victorian Studies* 26 (1982): 33–49.

—. "Dracula: The Unseen Face in the Mirror." *Journal of Narrative Technique* 9 (1979): 160–170.

Silver, Alain and James Ursini. *The Vampire Film From Nosferatu to Bram Stoker's Dracula.* New York: Limelight Editions, 1993.

Stevenson, John Allen. "A Vampire in the Mirror: The Sexuality of *Dracula*." *PMLA* 103 (1988): 139–149.

Stoker, Bram. *Dracula.* 1897. Oxford: Oxford UP, 1983.

Waller, Gregory A. *The Living and the Undead: From Stoker's Dracula to Romero's Dawn of the Dead.* Urbana and Chicago: University of Illinois Press, 1986.

Walsh, Thomas P. "*Dracula*: Logos and Myth." *Research Studies* 47 (1979): 229–237.

Wasson, Richard. "The Politics of Dracula." *Dracula, the Vampire and the Critics.* Ed. Margaret L. Carter. Ann Arbor, Michigan: UMI Research Press, 1988. 19–23.

Wood, Robin. "Burying the Undead: The Use and Obsolescence of Count Dracula." *Mosaic* 16 (1983): 175–187.

—. "An Introduction to the American Horror Film." *Planks of Reason: Essays on the Horror Film.* Ed. Barry Keith Grant. Metuchen, New Jersey: Scarecrow Press, 1984. 164–200.

Yang, Jeff. "*Anime* Rising." *Village Voice* 37 (November 17, 1992): 56–57, 59.

IV

Dracula at Large –

Vampires and

Society

Dracula, Monsters, and the Apprehensions of Modernity

Richard Anderson

"… the old centuries had … powers of their own which mere 'modernity' cannot kill."

(*Dracula* 36)

N RECENT YEARS IT HAS BECOME VERY FASHIONABLE to critique modernity. The modernist closet has plenty of skeletons, as researchers often point out. Its rationality creates madness, its enlightenment brings darkness, and bondage accompanies its freedom. Monsters lurk in the shadows of even its proudest pretensions.

The purpose of this paper is to continue the exploration of modernity's shadowy side, to probe its apprehensions, for which the Dracula phenomenon provides an excellent vehicle. Bela Lugosi may not be bell hooks and, compared to the monsters of the Final Solution, Dracula looks a little pale and unconvincing, but he is, nonetheless, one of modernity's most prominent literary monsters. Despite the cultural power of science, and perhaps because of it, the twentieth-century mind has been fascinated with *Dracula*. The stuff of schlock-horror 'B' movies, the vampire myth nevertheless resonates with a fear of demonic forms beyond the power of reason. In doing so it takes up a concern familiar to the Romantic critics of the Enlightenment. If we can peer behind the theatrical makeup and the bat-wing capes, Dracula provides a means of exploring the creaky floorboards and cobwebbed passages of the modernist mind.

Modernity and selective pesticides

ON THE FACE of it, my research background has little to do with literary criticism, or with the Dracula phenomenon. I work as an applied urban environmental historian, researching the messy and wasteful past of southern Ontario. I use the techniques of historical investigation to detect former garbage dumps, old messy industries, and land contaminated with toxins. It is a field populated with underground storage tanks, defunct dry cleaners, tanneries, and lead smelters. It is practical, concerned with defusing toxic time-bombs, with site remediation, and with multi-million dollar lawsuits. It is a field in which a literary imagination has no apparent relevance, and yet, when one probes a little deeper, the themes of the Dracula story seem curiously useful.

Consider, by way of illustration, the role of chemical pesticides in postwar Ontario. The two decades following 1945 were halcyon days for specialty chemicals, "selective" pesticides, and zealous prosecution of campaigns against pests of all kinds. The spruce budworm, the onion thrip, the corn borer, the black fly, the mosquito, yellow bedstraw, and the Canada thistle, were declared to be everyone's foes. While Ontario's farmers ploughed the fields and scattered the poisons on the ground, aircraft drenched the forests, trucks sprayed the roadsides, and little old ladies zapped the moths which threatened their winter furs. It was envisaged as a war, with weekly propaganda broadcasts by the agriculture ministry and an Orwellian five-minute hate for the "weed of the week." Weed recognition manuals were issued, air raids were organised (some by the RCAF), motorised ground troops took to the field with jeep-mounted foggers, backpacks and, in some cases, flame throwers. They sprayed the Humber River, fogged the ponds of Swansea, and even tried to spike the graveside vases at Park Lawn Cemetery with DDT. The complex lore of pest control made its way into mainstream publications, as much as anything else to dazzle the public with scientific bafflegab. Newspapers and magazines carried advertising copy for the merchants of paradichlorobenzene and DDT, for pentachorophenol, ethylene bromide, Aldrin and Dieldrin, for hexachorocyclohexane, 2,4-D and 2,4,5-T. Pesticides came in fuel oil, in wettable powders, in concentrate, and in dusts. They could be obtained as esters, acids, or amines. They came in industrial quantities with returnable containers, or in convenient household dispensers. Like a wonder cure, they "lightened the work, reduced control costs and brought new hope in the everlasting war on weeds" (*Weed Inspector's Manual* 3, 17), insects, and fungi. Pesticide science was wonderful, the reading public was told, and by 1960 Ontario's roadsides, hydro corridors, and fields had assumed their modern, sterile appearance.

The war on weeds was an essential part of the creation of a landscape of modernity in southern Ontario, as elsewhere in the western world, but it was also the outcome of another essentially modernist obsession: the desire to control the natural world and repress its untoward manifestations. As in Nazi Germany, beauty was to be achieved through violence (Cohen 1989), and order was to be obtained by the repressive application of science. As Rachel Carson recognised in *Silent Spring*, this was science become demonic.

The episode illustrates two major apprehensions which have been at large within modern culture. Firstly, it demonstrates the extent to which modernity can become obsessed with extending the limits of its triumphant metanarrative. There are unruly and unpleasant things outside its scheme of domination, which it urgently tries to destroy, repress, or control. Secondly, it illustrates its potential for alienation and disillusionment. When confronted with modernity, people may react with contempt or hostility. Carson's work was one of the most prominent examples in connection with pesticides, but she was not alone in noticing the brown and wilted roadsides, or the absence of pollinating insects.

I want to argue that there is a parallel between these sorts of realisations about modernity and the Dracula story, because it too embodies both sorts of apprehensions. Dracula, in Bram Stoker's vision, represents a force beyond the control of reason, something which mere modernity cannot kill. It is an instinctive reaction of the modernist mind to obliterate the monster, yet Van Helsing's science is no more effective at destroying him than Jonathan Harker's shovel. The heroes discover that Dracula lies beyond the reach of modernity: he readily outwits the blood transfusion and the phonograph. To kill him they must resort to romantic acts of heroism and quantities of garlic.

Dracula and Hollywood Gothic

DRACULA, OF COURSE, is an example of the Gothic novel (Punter 1980), a literary form which originated in the later eighteenth century. Although I will gloss over its considerable diversity, I will highlight the fact that this was the first period in which novels had an audience of any really significant size, and that the Gothic form was both extremely popular and, perhaps, its characteristic literary style. This was not the case, however, among the highbrow critics. To literary connoisseurs, it stood outside the canons of polite good taste, and was roundly condemned as trash. Its appeal lay with the emergent middle-class, who then constituted most of the reading public. For its intended middlebrow or lowbrow audience, it held great attraction. The Gothic dreams of phantasmagoric hell were not so very different from the messy realities of the industrial city, where fires smoked, furnaces roared, and people drank diluted sewage. Coketown was sweeping away the old rural, peasant-and-aristocrat way of life. Especially in England, the factory system was starting to displace huge numbers of people from the land and from what E.P. Thompson termed the traditional moral economy. Growing millions of workers were being sequestered in vast industrial hives, labouring in conditions which might have been inspired by the Marquis de Sade.

In this context, as Alok Bhalla points out, the Gothic novel articulated many of the apprehensions of the time. It was a social document rather than a mere bit of escapism. It spoke to and about the political and mental conditions in which it was written. The times were troubling, and with its monsters, terrors, and violence, the Gothic novel reflected the brutal amorality of industrialism coupled with the cruelty of contemporary political power.

One of the main functions of the Gothic novel at this time, therefore, was as a vehicle to critique those things which we would recognise as symptoms of modernity. It was science that had become demonic in Mary Shelley's *Frankenstein*, a classic instance of early nineteenth-century Gothic horror, and the cruelties of the Georgian political order were perhaps the subtext for John Polidori's tales of the Vampyre, whose villain was a bloodthirsty aristocrat.

Theatrical and literary audiences found both stories quite appealing, despite the disdain of the serious critics. In Paris before Baron Haussman, as in Edinburgh after Burke and Hare, the public could readily imagine villainy in the urban twilight. Sherlock Holmes, Count Dracula, and Jack the Ripper operated in much the same foggy atmosphere, a realm of body snatching and garroting, the fear of which has never entirely disappeared.

Stoker's vampire story belongs to a period rather later in the nineteenth century, when the audience was perhaps less obsessed with the horrors of industrial change. Nevertheless, his *Dracula* is not just a piece of efflorescent escapism. Like the Gothic novel of the early 1800s, *Dracula* is also, arguably, a social document. The question to be asked is what broad issues does it reflect?

Although something of a simplification, the shortcomings of the Victorian cultural system constituted the major literary and artistic themes at the end of the nineteenth century and the early twentieth. From the Age of Decadence in the 1890s to the revolt of the highbrows in the 1920s, the practical deficiencies of Victorian Protestant culture were ruthlessly examined. Sexuality was one field in which Victorian values and repressions were questioned. Aubrey Beardsley and Oscar Wilde, of course, should be mentioned in this connection, but so should Stoker. Voluptuous but veiled sexuality is a strong element of Stoker's *Dracula*. Much of it is misogynist. After their metaphoric defloration by Dracula, the women become insatiable monsters whose desires are totally beyond the ability of respectable men to satisfy. Groups of sexually aggressive women assail the hapless Harker in Dracula's castle, while the male heroes of the novel feel morally obliged to break Lucy's obsessive attachment to Dracula through the means of a figurative gang-rape replete with spermicetti candle and wooden stake.

There is plenty of ammunition here for a serious critique of Stoker and for the dissection of the sexual imagination of Victorian men, but his importance probably lies in the way he used Gothic horror to represent sexual apprehensions. Unlike Wilde or Beardsley, Stoker did not imagine himself challenging contemporary sexual mores. Instead, he attempted to write a popular scary tale, combining in it all the ingredients he thought appropriate. Mary Shelley's monster was perverted science, but Stoker's was Dracula, who operated by unbinding what a Victorian man might regard as the monstrous qualities of female sexuality. We now realise that the world does not fall apart when women are sexually expressive, but this was evidently a frightening prospect for some Victorian men. We may therefore understand their apprehensions in an age preparing to discard conventional Victorian notions of sex and gender.

The novel is also freighted, as was *The Vampyre*, with the symbolism of a dying religious faith, but also with the manifestations of science. Dictation machines, blood transfusions, and telegraphs join ruined ecclesiastical buildings as stage props. When faced with an insurmountable enemy, the heroes first resort to science rather than prayer and when that fails, to mediaeval superstition. Dracula bursts into the cosy world of middle-class England, defying its science, sneering at its modernity, and defiling its sexuality. Neither bourgeois science nor bourgeois religion can tame him. He presents a malevolent challenge to the intellectual and psychological norms of the late Victorian age.

Although *Dracula* the novel was not a critical success, it managed to become a considerable lowbrow literary sensation with vast popular appeal for a reading public rapidly becoming a mass audience. The Gothic novel of the 1800s had flourished among the emergent middle-class, but now the potential readership was much larger, promoted by broader literacy and popular newspapers. It translated readily into lowbrow theatre productions which, like the novel, dismayed the serious critics yet had wide appeal. As David Skal outlines, Tod Browning's 1931 Universal movie of *Dracula* was derived from these dramatisations.

Although the movie was subsequently remade many times, it is this 1931 version which, for most people, defines the image of Dracula. More specifically, the defining persona was provided by Bela Lugosi, whose Dracula proved to be an immortal icon. Lugosi had been one of the more successful stage Draculas (Cremer 1983), although he was by no means the only one. Lugosi played Dracula as a malevolent aristocrat, a polished villain. Although rather different from Stoker's white-haired original, he was a distinct success with the first really large movie-going audiences.

Dracula was acted in a form reminiscent of the silent films, with the exaggerated body language and clear diction of the contemporary stage. The atmosphere was theatrically Gothic, with creaks, cobwebs, staircases, fog, and malevolent foreigners. There was even a walk-on part for armadillos (Skal 131). The cinematography offered little innovation. The actors tended, like those of the silent screen, to move stagewise across the shot. There were few close-ups, and there was little switching of camera angles to create a scene. The filmmakers were not allowed to show Dracula actually biting anyone, nor could they show his death, so they used a combination of sound effects and reaction shots to make the violence realistic. Dracula was not shown drawing maiden blood, although he did advance menacingly toward his victims as the shot faded. Incidental music was deliberately absent from the soundtrack, at a time when audiences were familiar with a piano accompaniment. Instead, there were plenty of footfalls, creaky hinges, sickening crunches, and screams.

Dracula was the first successful talkie horror movie, and, besides salvaging Universal from bankruptcy, it represented the emergence of the horror movie genre in Hollywood. In quick succession, Lugosi immortalised his Dracula, and Boris Karloff did the same for Frankenstein's monster. Although the 1931 *Dracula* was hardly a faithful adaptation of the novel, it has endured as the definitive interpretation.

It is much easier to demonstrate the success of the 1931 *Dracula* than it is to explain it. The best answer is probably that while the public enjoyed being frightened by the Count, Lugosi managed to give Dracula sex appeal. Women writers dominated his fan mail, apparently responding to the character's Valentino qualities. Unfortunately, Lugosi found himself typecast, and instead of developing a broader film career, he was doomed to repeat his Dracula role endlessly for the stage. He appeared in three subsequent vampire movies, *Mark of the Vampire* (1935), *The Devil Bat* (1940), and *The Return of the Vampire* (1943), and in the 1948 lampoon *Abbott and Costello Meet Frankenstein* (Skal 210–2).

The film and the novel, therefore, found success because they managed to cater to the new popular audiences which the period was creating, and they offered an entertaining articulation of many of their important apprehensions and interests. *Dracula* was a cultural production for a mass audience and, especially as a movie, formed a sort of cultural forum in which that audience could be exposed to a single influential interpretation.

Dracula and the Modern Suburb

IF MODERNITY COULD be visualised as a landscape, what kind of place would it be? What sorts of experiences would it afford? Fortunately, it is not very difficult to approach this question, as most of us frequent such places on a daily basis.

The North American postwar suburb, circa 1960, for example, was such a classic modernist environment. A nursery for baby-boomers, it featured conformity, order, and clearly defined roles for men and women. There were even, I have noticed, different pesticides for men and women to use. Housing and families seemed (and sometimes actually were) mass-produced, hygienic, and standardised. Women were supposed to keep house, while men ventured out to work in large Fordist corporations. The expansive consumption and production mirrored each other. Like the factory, the household was automated and chemically-treated, and its inmates were exhorted to engage in that counterpart of mass production: mass consumption.

Yet it would be wrong to treat postwar suburbia as an unblemished utopia since it always had its sophisticated critics. Its prosperous way of life, as Henry Miller pointed out in the 1940s, was something of an air-conditioned nightmare. Like Jekyll and Hyde, it had a split personality whose very prosperity and order could be smothering and intolerant. Suburban, middle-class America was outwardly prosperous while inwardly fearful. Fear of communism was widely acknowledged in public, while other apprehensions, notably those towards sex and death, were held in private.

But while the activities of Senator McCarthy and the trial of Adolf Eichmann deepened the American public's appreciation of the banality of evil,[1] the contemporary American artist was reacting to the evil. From the paintings of Eric Fischl and Andy Warhol to the more recent work of Jeff Koons, there has been widespread artistic criticism of the dystopia of suburban life, while scientific writers, such as Rachel Carson have pointed out its ecological limitations.

To these articulate critics one should add those less articulate ones who grew up within that environment. There was, for example, a substantial contemporary interest among the young in the images of classic horror movies. In this rediscovery of Hollywood-Gothic, the film *Dracula* was a key element. For the adolescent and pre-adolescent baby-boomers, the psycho-social drama of the haunted house was a means to escape the sterility of the suburban tract house in which so many of them lived. Their broad-loomed, modernist bedrooms contained Dracula model kits and comics, while their televisions carried reruns of classic horror films alongside remakes like *The Addams Family* and *The Munsters.*

David Skal has commented that young males were a prominent audience and consumer group for this Gothic-horror revival. He speculates that the sex and death mythology of Gothic horror had particular appeal for this age-sex group. It was as if, he says, an indulgence in Gothic fantasies served to deal with burgeoning adult feelings of sexuality and mortality.

It is obvious though that Dracula has become increasingly trivialised, especially as adolescent rebellion has become commercialised. He is now just a pale imitation of the original, reduced to trademark status for a Hallowe'en costume, a breakfast cereal, and regular appearances on *Sesame Street.* The figure of the vampire, however, still remains popular. There is something of Dracula in that modern urban vampire, the serial killer, eating his livers with a nice Chianti.

MONSTERS HAVE BEEN a feature of western literature from *Beowulf* onwards, but there seems to be something particularly interesting about the monsters of the modern imagination, and Dracula in particular. As illustrated, the Dracula myth has been quite resonant for the nineteenth and twentieth centuries. While modernity often struggles obsessively to repress and control, to order and standardise, it generates alienation in doing so. Sometimes the alienation has seemed extreme and dramatic. At others, it has seemed more ephemeral. One might look at this as a dialectic or as a dialogue, but it is, in any case, symbiotic. In *Dracula,* Stoker places Victorian modernity in the foreground while, at the same time, showing us its disturbing limitations. For all of its power, modernity's will to control never quite monopolises the mind. Both sorts of apprehensions continue to co-exist. While the monster and vampire may be imaginative products of this struggle, it has taken modernity to publicise them. It became possible to mass produce Gothic novels, present lowbrow stage plays to mass audiences, shoot talking pictures, and manufacture plastic modelling kits largely as a result of those social and economic conditions which modernity made possible.

NOTES

1   For a more detailed examination of this subject see Hannah Arendt's 1964 work *Eichmann in Jerusalem.*

REFERENCES

Architektur des Untergangs (Architecture of Doom). Dir. Peter Cohen. POJ Film Produktion AB Filminstitutet Sveriges Television Kanal 1, Sandrew Film & Teater AB Zeigen, 1989.

Arendt, Hannah. *Eichmann in Jerusalem: a Report on the Banality of Evil*. New York: Viking, 1964.

Bhalla, Alok. *Cartographers of Hell: Essays on the Gothic Novel and the Social History of England*. New Delhi: Sterling Publishers, 1991.

Carson, Rachel. *Silent Spring*. New York: Houghton Mifflin, 1962.

Cremer, Robert. *Lugosi: The Man Behind the Cape*. Chicago: Henry Regney, 1983.

Dracula. Dir. Tod Browning. Universal, 1931.

Ontario Archives: RG16-09 box 264 file 3: Ontario, *Weed Inspector's Manual*, 1953 pp. 3, 17.

Polidori, John. *The Vampyre*. 1819. *Vampyres: Lord Byron to Count Dracula*. London: Faber and Faber, 1991. 97–125

Punter, David. *The Literature of Terror: A History of Gothic Fictions From 1765 to the Present Day*. London and New York: Longman, 1980.

Shelley, Mary. *Frankenstein; Or the Modern Prometheus*. 1818. Oxford: Oxford UP, 1994.

Skal, David J. *Hollywood Gothic: The Tangled Web of Dracula from Novel to Stage to Screen*. New York: Norton, 1990.

Stoker, Bram. *Dracula*. 1897. Oxford: Oxford UP, 1983.

Thompson, E.P. "The Moral Economy of the English Crowd in the 18th Century." *Past and Present* 50 (1971): 76–136.

Dracula as a Contemporary Ethnography: A Critique of Mediated Moralities and Mysterious Mythologies

Livy Visano

"... and deliver us from evil ..."
(Matthew 6: 9–13)

Introduction: A Novel Narrative

RAM STOKER'S *DRACULA* PROVIDES A SEMINAL contribution to the sociology of morality. Conceptually and methodologically, *Dracula* is a formidable socio-cultural narrative chronicling the relationship between morality and mythology. Methodologically, Stoker effectively employs what Norman Denzin calls a "triangulated" approach. This involves appreciating the values and roles of the central characters from diverse vantage points such as letters, telegrams, diaries/journals, and newspaper articles. This examination of empirical events using a variety of convergent methods and sources is congruent with Stoker's interest in enhancing the validity of personal accounts and life experiences. This flexible style of storytelling approximates the natural world as readers witness the unfolding of events, identities, and relations. Unlike the genre of more timid, traditional, normative narratives,

Stoker provides an impressive weaving of a critical narrative fabric that departs from typically artificial codes that essentialise identity according to oppositional binaries like good and evil, day and night, sinner and saint, the secular and the sacred, the dead and the living, cerebral and visceral, black and white, private and public, intentional and incidental, simultaneous and sequential, and science and religion. *Dracula* is a bold challenge to prevailing moral rules and ordered worlds. This essay seeks to accomplish several aims: first, to demonstrate the utility of the concept of "mediated moralities" in examining the nature of science and religion. Specifically, popular culture — as expressed in mythologies, metaphors, and superstitions — shapes and is shaped by the nature of morality. Secondly, *Dracula* will be revealed to be an insightful ethnography, replete with generic implications and applications that directly confront issues of control, privilege, and knowledge.

The Social Organisation of Morality: From the Personal to the Ideological

CLEARLY, STOKER'S IMAGE of a social order is presented within the framework of an emerging moral drama. Against a backdrop of doubt, danger, and death, Stoker's many voices are intensely passionate and resonant with moral conviction. Stoker's *Dracula* asks, for example, how do individuals and collectivities conceive of the reasons and motives for their actions? How are moral identities created? How is morality constituted and manipulated in terms of such dichotomies as the familiar/foreign, the sacred/secular, the personal/public, knowledge/opinion, and the present/past? To what extent does morality disguise as much as disclose the reader's own sensibilities?

Stoker's moral texts are informed by wider "structural" perspectives, namely the cultural narratives of religion and science. And yet, these deterministic accounts remain consistent with Stoker's commitment to a sense of agency among his central characters, both living and undead. Ultimately, morality is subjectively determined by each individual. From this perspective, Stoker develops a relativistic view of morality as an individual motivational force in a person's life. Although he rejects morality as mechanistic, he nonetheless alludes to the prevailing Victorian ethic of "personal salvation" that is central to liberal individualism. Thus, morality is a condition and consequence of justice as idealised and practiced in personalised experiences. The brilliance of Stoker's social theorising, however, moves beyond the realm of social psychology (the situated self) to include extra-local structures (historical trends). Morality is contextualised within more "universalised" or transcendent institutions and processes.[1] Morality, therefore, becomes an authorised force, one which justifies intervention. An analysis of any moral enterprise requires an appreciation of the depth and breadth of moral development.

In *Dracula*, a monolithic morality is ingrained in the community's consciousness — the collective conscience. But how is morality appropriated, accepted, and articulated as consensual consciousness (Gramsci 12; Jouve 8)? Stoker suggests that morality operates as a rational duty to promote a sense of justice. The righteous claims of those charged with moral responsibility is evident in the Victorian reverence of a moral calling. This vocation or sense of obligation is explained by Professor Van Helsing when he quite sternly states, "My Lord Godalming, I too, have a duty to do, a duty to others, a duty to you, a duty to the dead, and by God, I shall do it!" (206–207). Later, both Mina Harker and Professor Van Helsing admit, respectively, that they acted as "the instruments of ultimate good" (316) and were "ministers of God's own wish" (320).

As a specific text interwoven into Stoker's work and as a general narrative, morality is the production and consumption of values and concomitant practices of encoding and decoding belief systems. Morality inheres in everyday practices and reflects a variety of institutional discourses which are both contradictory and complementary. In other words, morality is mediated by a wide array of persuasive influences including law, religion, science, politics, and economics. *Dracula* provides a long overdue method for clarifying contradictions and for delving into the forms and functions of moral struggles. The awareness of being different and seeing differences inspires manoeuvres that banish or resist challenges. Morality, therefore, is manipulated in the marketplace of everyday talk as a respected authority that legitimates intrusions. Accordingly, Stoker's social theory captures the historical development of ideologies, the nature of the popular culture, and the role of privilege in defining social threats. In *Dracula*, Stoker defines morality as a contested terrain. In addition, morality as a discursive practice is revealed to be socially constructed within scientific and religious traditions. Stoker situates common sense, knowledge, and beliefs about moral conformity within problematic relations of authority.

In Deference to the Cultural Authority of Religion and Science

THE DOMINANT CULTURE shapes moral moments. Culture manipulates morality by defining disturbances as situational accommodations to contests or, alternately, as totalising narratives chronicling social threat that warrant closure, containment, and coercion. Specifically, Stoker demonstrates that moral interpretations are mediated by pervasive canons anchored in Christianity and science. Subsequently, phenomena that fall outside the epistemological domains of Christianity and science are either "demonised" or devalued as incorrigibly pathological.

The texts of Christianity and science function to constitute individuals as docile subjects. Individuals are interpellated, that is, they have social identities conferred on them according to traditional socialising criteria. For example, Christianity invests this novel with an interest in "personal salvation," a concept wherein the individual is granted primary significance. In addition, Stoker highlights the stability and continuity of religion. Similar to Foucault's insights about the omnipresence of power in the authority of religion, Stoker deconstructs religion in terms of the sacred symbol of Christianity — the crucifix. In this regard, the crucifix, as a weapon, invokes the inimitable strength of Jesus Christ, the transcendence of suffering and death through the resurrection. For example, in his diary detailing the confrontation with Dracula, Dr. Seward describes the physical and spiritual protection provided by the crucifix: "Further and further back he cowered, as we, lifting our crucifixes, advanced. The moonlight suddenly failed, as a great black cloud sailed across the sky" (282). Later, Dr. Seward recalls: "The Professor held up his golden crucifix, and said with wonderful calmness: 'Do not fear, my dear [Mina]. We are here, and whilst this is close to you no foul thing can approach'" (284). Earlier, during his visit to the Count's castle, Harker uses the cross as a protective device: "I have placed the crucifix over the head of my bed, I imagine that my rest is thus freer from dreams" (33).

For Stoker, religion is inseparable from morality. The two are inextricably connected. In addition, Stoker seeks to reconcile the differing solitudes of religion and science in the person of Professor Van Helsing. The secular and the sacred are embodied in the person of this wise scholar, humanist, and committed scientist. Despite the merits of debating the relative explanatory powers of religion and science, Stoker succeeds in introducing a less absolutist and more interpretive perspective on life and death. Notably, Stoker insists that Christianity and science not only ignore that which they cannot explain, they also deny the authenticity of alternative accounts. In his letter to Arthur Holmwood, Dr. Seward recommends the services of his friend and mentor, Professor Van Helsing, whom he describes as a "philosopher and a metaphysician, and one of the most advanced scientists of his day" (112). Mina's well-informed analysis of the etiology of crime reflects a commitment to dogmatic and determinist psychiatric theories common in intellectual circles. She comments, "The Count is a criminal and of criminal type. Nordau and Lombroso would so classify him, and *qua* criminal he is of an imperfectly formed mind" (342).

For Stoker, mythologies succeed where science and Christianity fail. A mythology is the source of images of evil in the contemporary world. Moral creations elicit a similar combination of wonder and horror to the monsters of the sixteenth century.[2] Christianity and science alone are incapable of responding to what is perceived as evil. They are equally ill prepared to confront "unfamiliar" challenges to their respective legitimacies. *Dracula* introduces more imaginative and mysterious methods for understanding morality in general and the character of Dracula in particular.

Mythologies as Moral Mystifications: Rituals of Resistance

OR BRAM STOKER, life defies simplistic explanations packaged in banal and encyclopaedic Christian and scientific inventories. According to Baudrillard, the latter belief systems promote intellectual arrogance by ignoring mythologies and trivialising their attendant mysteries. In other words, a large number of so-called mysteries of life and death cannot be easily limited to the logic of the "taken-for-granted world." By failing to consider traditional, comfortable, and "simple" ideas as actually complex, Christianity and science falters miserably in capturing the enormous breadth and depth of life. As Professor Van Helsing explains: "My thesis is this: I want you to believe ... in things you cannot" (193). He further clarifies his lesson, saying, "There are mysteries which men can only guess at, which age by age they may solve only in part" (206). The corpus of existing scientific and religious explanations falter miserably in transcending the localised scripts or situated texts which delineate diseases and sins. As Barthes elucidates in *Mythologies*, the traditional text is a text of pleasure which grants euphoria, comes from culture, and does not depart from it. The certitude of traditional texts demands intellectual servitude. On the other hand, Stoker's *Dracula* is a text that Barthes would characterise as imposing "a state of loss, ... [a] text that discomforts ... [and] unsettles the reader's historical, cultural, [and] psychological assumptions" (*Image* 14). For Mary Bittner Wiseman, challenging the modern text arouses consciousness, generates new meanings, and abolishes exclusions (133).

The reader is asked to be intrepid in deconstructing traditional texts by concentrating on the contradictions and closures inherent in conventional commentaries.

Mythologies challenge the canons of science and religion and expose both the virtues and vices of prevailing doctrinal systems. Notwithstanding the common foundation of their respective claims, mythologies serve to stimulate intellectual debate. As earlier noted, morality consists of a panoply of discourses and competing values. Mythologies provoke an elasticity in cultural consciousness by abstracting, mystifying, and complicating respected conventions. Within the marketplace of rhetoric, jargon, and clichés, the concept of mythology is a negotiable commodity, the value of which is conveniently determined by the narrator. The mysterious or even magical nature of mythologies manipulates understanding by preempting criticism and discouraging much needed critical dialogue. For Barthes, this process transforms history into nature (*Mythologies* 142). Barthes laments the fact that mythologies depoliticise and dehistoricise meanings. Consequently, a critical sensibility is typically absent. Stoker, writing in 1897, implores readers to suspend, if not to escape, prevalent simplistic common-sense assumptions about evil until they have journeyed intellectually into the world of superstition.

The Intertextuality of Morality: Science, Sin, and Superstition

SUPERSTITION PRESENTS A vastly different understanding of the self-actualising and self-governing individual. The mystery of superstition constitutes Stoker's characters as essentially cultural representations who do not appear either as victimised objects of totalising structures (acted upon) nor as determining subjects (active agents). In addition, *Dracula* construes reality as segmented and articulated within a variety of intersecting social orders that succeed in abstracting, mystifying, and decontextualising truths and superstitions. Thus, superstition demands deference to authoritative "others" who define difference as inherently dangerous. Accordingly, superstition relocates that which has occupied the margins to the centre. It decentres and de-essentialises the subject by highlighting how the subject is constructed in contradictions. The deference to "essential" elements of evil is repositioned and negotiable, and always involves an open process of transformation.

In many episodes in Stoker's novel, the tense relationship between religion-science and superstition is linked to power struggles. As Stoker documents, mythologies are normally dismissed by the hegemonic designs of scientific standards and Christian commandments. According to science and Christianity, superstitions perpetuate lexicons of evil, promote fears of the "Other," and penetrate that "Other" in complex discourses. At first instance, superstition offends certain high moral grounds by rearranging intellectual and spiritual frontiers. For Stoker, superstition, as an element of one's imagination, grounds perceptions and avoids the congested closures of traditional texts. In her journal, Mina Harker transcribes notes from Professor Van Helsing's lecture on the nature of their enemy and the limitations of traditional methods of eradicating vampires. He carefully instructs Mina, Jonathan, Dr. Seward, Lord Godalming, and Quincey Morris: "All we have to go upon are traditions and superstitions … no other means is at our control … [and] after all these things — tradition and superstition — are everything" (238). Specific demon "cures" include the positioning of the branch of a wild rose on the coffin to keep the vampire from escaping, firing a sacred bullet into the coffin, driving a stake through the body, cutting off the head (240), or filling the mouth with garlic (201). Stoker demonstrates the insidious ways in which superstition controls individuals without using overt force.

    Dracula promotes a theology of superstition that acts as a mystical foundation of mythology. The authority of superstition objectifies discourses, maintains the narrative outside of situated meanings, and reflects the hysteria of history. Although Stoker's levels of abstraction remain fictional, *Dracula* stresses the importance of provisional and relational categories in interpreting identities, relations, and events. Superstition, mythology, and fiction debunk predictability in order to permit a critical entry into imaginary lifeworlds. Superstition requires little literacy but much faith. This "new religion" cultivates images that obscure the framework of religious-scientific knowledge. *Dracula* invites even the most circumspect reader to reflect on the mystery and power of superstition as in the scene where, while opening Lucy's coffin, Van Helsing explains his murderous actions to Seward: "She was bitten by the vampire when she was in a trance … In trance she died, and in trance she is Un-Dead, too … I must kill her in her sleep" (201).

    Intertextuality is the process whereby one text plays upon other texts, the way in which texts refer endlessly to other elements within the realm of cultural production.[3] According to this semiotic theory, all texts are fabrications. This process can contribute in a positive manner to our understanding of morality as it criticises logocentrism. It challenges and resists discourse, thus opening up the possibility of becoming "Other." Derrida argues, for example, that the notion of the logos as unmediated knowledge of the world is a feature of every discourse, be it religious or scientific, which seeks to explain the world. But, as Derrida argues, knowledge is always mediated and always privileges certain truth claims.

Mystery further magnifies the "unknown." It manages to marginalise, depersonalise, and create obedient subjects.[4] As Max Horkheimer has outlined, within the hegemony of the unknown, identity and cultural practices emerge as unclear responses to domination. The commodification of the mysteries of mythologies gives rise to metaphors. According to Robert Brown, metaphors link forms of thought — macro and micro, objectivist and subjectivist. They communicate meanings about mythologies in a language that is symbolically oriented; that is, metaphors make mythologies more meaningful and the messages more accessible. Indeed, the metaphor is the fabric that clothes and protects the body of mythologies.

Count Dracula as Distant Other and Professor Van Helsing as Prophet: Metaphors of Survival

THE METAPHOR OF the vampire may appear excessively dramatic, but it is both a useful and powerful image for the subject of moral regulation. The metaphor is a figurative device that compellingly captures that which is not readily available in literal descriptions. The vampire metaphor injects mystery into the mythology of evil. Stoker's use of this metaphor foregrounds the nature of morality when confronting the protean character of evil. Dracula enjoys many identities: he is the strange, distant "Other" who speaks a common language and yet is able to transcend time and space. The vampire metaphor essentialises Dracula's identity as unequivocally evil. However, the horror of Dracula becomes even more terrifying as metaphors recast his identity in terms of images that are familiar and personalised. On the one hand, Dracula is "a tall old man" (15) who is introduced as friendly. He is a gracious noble (4) with a charming smile (17) who initially greets Harker saying, "Welcome to my house! Enter freely and of your own will!" (15). He adds, "Go safely, and leave something of the happiness you bring!... I am Dracula. And I bid you welcome, Mr. Harker, to my house. Come in, the night air is chill, and you must need to eat and rest" (16).

In addition to these anthropomorphic traits, Dracula represents the unimaginable, the unknown, and the undead — he is neither alive nor dead. Dracula's undead existence is a violent and subversive struggle for survival. His omnipresence calls into question familiar notions of identity.

On a personal level, Stoker presents evil as the inexplicable embodiment of repulsion and danger. Images of Dracula's disgusting demeanour prevail: his breath is rank (18), there is "a mocking smile on … [his] bloated face" (51), "a grin of malice which would have held its own in the nethermost hell" (52), and an "evil smile which quickly … [passes] into a cold stare of lion-like disdain" (305). At a more supernatural level, Dracula is "remorseless" (342). His physical, mental, and spiritual skills remain unmatched. Mortals "cannot hurt him … [but they] can be hurt by him" (249), and he controls the strength of "brute beasts" (253). In fact, Dracula's strengths are unmatched. As Professor Van Helsing informs his colleagues, Dracula's "cunning be the growth of ages, he have still the aids of necromancy" (237). The Professor later adds a description of Dracula's relentless mental adaptability: "He learn new social life; new environment of old ways, the politic, the law, the finance, the science, the habit of a new land and a new people who have come to be since he was" (321). Dracula's evil enjoys a well-earned but shameful reputation. During his few menacing appearances before his pursuers Dracula ridicules them, saying:

> You think to baffle me, you — with your pale faces all
> in a row, like sheep in a butcher's. You shall be sorry
> yet, each one of you! You think you have left me with-
> out a place to rest; but I have more. My revenge is just
> begun! I spread it over centuries, and time is on my side.
> (306)

But evil too has its limitations. Dracula is not only confined to the darkness: he has no power when confronted by garlic and crucifixes (240).

Stoker's sociological perspicacity is evident in the manner in which he situates evil. This force is not solely attributed to Dracula and his vampires; rather, evil is a social enterprise, the success of which depends on the willing participation of others. Herein lies Stoker's fascination with contradiction: Dracula is a morally reprehensible force who also provides pleasure and protection. To survive as a parasitic life-form, this evil requires sustenance that is only available in the blood of others. But blood is a scarce resource that is only available by invitation and the consent of the prospective victims. Typically, Dracula preys on the most vulnerable — children and the ill-informed or misguided. He targets those who more readily consent to their own subjugation. It is obvious that victims also fall prey to their own common sense, which incarcerates their imaginations and renders them unaware of Dracula's violence. Their common sense fails to guide their imagination primarily because it is anchored in prevailing cultural values. As Gramsci admonishes, common sense is not something rigid and immobile, but is continually transforming itself (325). Consent is circumscribed within this framework of common sense.

Consent is won whenever cultural values are manipulated. Just as Dracula takes selfishly from his victims, he also responds generously to that which is forbidden in the dominant order — endless desire. *Dracula*, however, is also about the regulation of desire. Both desiring subjects and objects figure prominently in this text. Further, the expression of sexual desire is portrayed as both attractive and repulsive. Pain and pleasure, therefore, jointly constitute sexual desire. The prime example of this paradox is Harker's confrontation with the three seductive young women at the Count's castle. Describing his "wicked burning desire" for them as "an agony of delightful anticipation" (37), Jonathan considers their "deliberate voluptuousness ... [to be] both thrilling and repulsive" (38).

The fear of the vampire in Stoker's novel is essentially the fear of the insatiable, sexually-active woman (Weissman 393). When "good women" are initiated into sexual activity, they become like vampires who deplete men. These men are invariably unable to satisfy their boundless sexual needs. This sexual hunger is a cause for male terror, and the struggle against Dracula is really a struggle for control over women and their sexual voracity (Weissman 404). The sexual vampire fantasy, therefore, which involves biting and multiple partners (Morse 183), represents a rejection of typical Victorian ideals. Repressed sexuality scorches the pages of Stoker's novel (Demetrakopoulos 107).

In addition to addressing the regulation of desire, *Dracula* also speaks to the issue of moral panic. Moral panics are generated by self-appointed guardians of public morality who attempt to identify the emergence of a problem and suggest action to be taken in response to it (Taylor 48–56). The body of Dracula, like its Christian counterpart, the body of Christ, becomes a major symbolic site for shaping opinion and framing moral consciousness. Stoker's text suggests that this consciousness is calibrated to handle a steady flow of trouble. A social threat invites an elastic instrument of social control. Once exaggerated, this threat legitimates the further policing of desire. This "control" might even involve the illegal behaviour of the righteous. Thus, the hunt for Dracula crystallises identities, establishes boundaries, maintains a collective consciousness and restores the integrity of the prevailing value system. The hunt also becomes a pretext to justify, to expand, and to consolidate control by moral entrepreneurs with persuasive campaigns.

What is intriguing about this seemingly communal form of policing or populist justice among Stoker's learned and privileged vampire hunters, however, is the obvious absence of law. The dangers of this hunt are, rather notably, described according to more popular discourses. Within the text's phenomenology of "the danger," the concepts of "distance" and "foreignness" provide a compelling coherence for the crusaders. Within the novel's "triangulated" vision of moral entrepreneurship, the hunt is not solely confined to individual conditions. It is, rather, a consequence of complex dependencies. In short, the hunt (the text) constitutes and is constituted by relations of power (subtext) that are mediated by cultural forms of superstitions (intertexts) that are interpreted solely by the Professor. There is no integrated text of the hunt, only fragmented, well articulated instructions that compel compliance.

The hunt, therefore, is a manufactured morality play which is sustained by the constant discussion of danger and death. This obsession with the hunt transforms the Professor into a modern-day social philosopher, engineer, and theologian, who alludes to and upholds conventional moral concepts. Nevertheless, the hunt is a problematic discourse that denies the meaningful, equal, and active participation of all of the collaborators. Images of danger predominate as cultural markers designed to compel a generic deference to the authority of the Professor and the morality of superstitious customs. Interestingly, superstition overwhelms the hunters and creates an even greater contagion — an infectious group thirst for even more sensational quests.

Dracula demonstrates the limitations of law. For Stoker, law frustrates morality by imposing conventional criteria that require fair and public scrutiny. Law is inimical to the more privatised justice of the hunt. In fact, the hunt for Dracula remains subterranean for fear of legal attention. Any appeal to formal law, whether to police authorities, coroners, or judges, is perceived to be counterproductive, if not irrelevant, to protecting morality. Members of Professor Van Helsing's expedition operate outside of the law: they break into private property, fail to inform legal authorities of suspicious deaths, and falsify records — especially Lucy's death certificate (149). Interestingly, during their discussions of bribery, Dracula's pursuers make reference to "Judge Moneybag" (334), a moniker that characterises a generalised contempt for local magistrates.

In general, Stoker develops a conception of morality as a cultural system that is not necessarily related to the authority of law. Morality refers to a set of ethical values, principles of fairness, and a sense of social justice that includes a genuine commitment to equality. Ideally, morality — as justice — ought to be the foundation of law. But in practice, law departs from this conception. Turgid case law, incomprehensible legalese, and abstract principles subvert attempts towards "achieving" morality. Metaphorically speaking, morality is law's very distant cousin. They are relatives who have precious little in common. They don't even speak the same language. Statutes and case law restrict the basic idea of justice inherent in morality. Morality is, therefore, too significant to be left in the hands of the law.

The law does not appropriately reflect the dynamics, dialectics, and diversity of values. Specifically, superstition has no place in this so-called system of rational rules and roles. Stoker demonstrates that law has failed to eradicate evil. In fact, law as a reactive restraint would prohibit the hunt for Dracula. For Stoker, law is reactionary and ill-prepared to grapple with the unknown. He recognises that an excessive reliance on the law, as a mechanism for dealing with disorder, invites difficulties. For example, by its very nature, the judiciary is an extremely conservative mechanism that would condemn the more imaginative efforts initiated by Professor Van Helsing. How, for instance, would the law and its attendant discourse handle Lucy's death?

Legal definitions of morality are problematic for many reasons. What is left out of the law, therefore, are the rights of collectivities, the need for social action and a critique of liberalism. The ethos of "individualism" in the law reduces justice to the social psychology of motivations and the appropriateness of personalised penalties. Similarly, traditional policing strategies depict criminality as a text located within the corpus of laws, practices, and policies that respond to trouble according to extant statutory provisions and case laws. Accordingly, the culture of conscience is mediated through the convenience of legal images that serve to privilege the authority of the state.

Dracula as A Critical Ethnography

IN THAT CERTAIN aspects of the form and content of *Dracula* reflect the relation of individuals to both local and universal socio-cultural forms, Stoker's novel makes an important contribution to the study of literary genres. For Stoker, the ethnography is a significant strategy with which to draw out the lived experience, the pains and pleasures, histories and biographies, words and thoughts, of his many characters. In general, the life-story research, dialogue, and modes of interpersonal communication are crucial tools as well as loci of knowledge (Corradi 107).

The social organisation of an ethnography consists of a wide spectrum of differentially constituted events. The ethnography provides a framework for assessing the contingencies which shape the researcher's identity, interactions, and social contexts. As a sensitising tool, the concept of a career incorporates objective and subjective elements. The former features include aspects of social structure such as affiliations, resources, and the skills of the researcher. The latter contingencies consist of the researcher's ideology, motivations, and self-concept. Consequently, structural and experiential factors contribute to the social construction of Stoker's research enterprise. Rather than a preconceived and programmatic methodology, a flexible accommodation exists which is consistent with the demands of storytelling. The collection and analysis of data invite a commitment to knowledge generated by experiences with the natural phenomenon. Stoker recognises the importance of the inner and outer perspectives of human agency. The inner perspective emphasises the ability of actors to know themselves and to understand others through "sympathetic introspection" and "imaginative reconstructions" of "definitions of situations" (Filstead 4). The intent, therefore, is to capture the experience of actors in their symbolic and behavioural worlds by penetrating their "everyday worlds." An immersion in the everyday life of actors reflects a respect for the nature of their empirical world (Blumer 60). This methodology of "appreciation" (Matza 25) or "naturalism" (Pearson 61), therefore, maximises validity. Validity refers to the accuracy of data, that is, the accuracy of the picture the narrator reports about the empirical world. Validity in an ethnography requires an accurate representation of the actors' social world as "they" perceive it.

The ethnography incorporates a critical examination of power relationships through the positioning of privilege in the text. In *Dracula*, the impact of gender, race, and class informs subjective experiences. *Dracula* illustrates clearly how gender, ethnicity/race, and class oppressions are linked to prevailing colonial discourses that devalue, commodify, and objectify differences. Morality is not a homogeneous category: it is gendered, racialised, and "classed" in multiple ways.

In general, as Louise Simard has argued, the historical novel is a significant witness to the evolution of feminism. Clearly, Stoker's male characters display the misogyny prevalent in fin de siècle British society as they fight with Dracula over the control of women's bodies. Violence against women is an acceptable element of this struggle. Historically, captured women were considered to be legitimate booty, battle-ground trophies that functioned as a victor's proof of his masculinity and success. Traditionally, violence against women was considered to be a serious matter only when interpreted as a crime against male property (Brownmiller 35). This type of crime occurs, for example, when Dracula forces Mina to drink his blood (282). Later, Dracula pronounces, "Your girls that you all love are mine already; and through them you and others shall yet be mine — my creatures, to do my bidding and to be my jackals when I want to feed. Bah!" (306). Equally offensive, however, is the paternalism that protects Mina from her dreams and desires (235).

Morality is a constructed text that is historically rooted in male privilege. Cultural codes frame modes of thinking — beliefs and ideas — that, in turn, govern human conduct. Moreover, social institutions structure core values of dominant ideologies that promote the unique location of women in society. Professor Van Helsing describes Mina as a wonderful person who, given her insights, must be in possession of a "man's brain" (234)! In *Dracula*, one witnesses both direct and indirect ways in which the dominant or "master" morality silences and subordinates women. Regardless of their situational status as victims or offenders, women are routinely depicted as dependent on good and evil men. This is apparent from the aggressive sexual appetites of the three female vampires, the economic dependence of British women, and the oppressive ideology of the family. Even in their everyday conversation, Lucy and Mina pay a great deal of attention to the traditional issues of romance and courtship. As Lucy merrily confides:

> Here am I, who will be twenty in September, and yet I never had a proposal till to-day, not a real proposal, and to-day I have had three. Just fancy! THREE proposals in one day! Isn't it awful! I feel sorry, really and truly sorry, for two of the poor fellows. Oh, Mina, I am so happy that I don't know what to do with myself. And three proposals! (56)

In addition to themes of gender inequality, there are ethnocentric references throughout *Dracula*. British "civilisation" is threatened by a foreign "monster" who, in traditional colonial discourse, is described in pejorative terms. Harker's description of his encounter with a foreign culture, for example, is marked by British ethnocentrism: the "strangest figures we saw were the Slovaks who are more barbarian than the rest" (3). Dracula even anticipates Harker's response: "We are in Transylvania, and Transylvania is not England. Our ways are not your ways, and there shall be to you many strange things" (21). Interestingly, morality becomes synonymous with nationality. David Glover argues that the contemporary fascination with the vampire myth shows a preoccupation with questions of ethnic difference.

Racism is an ideology, not simply of physical or cultural differences, but one that encodes superiority and denies any authentic reality and subjectivity to the designated "Other." Unequivocally, racism is power, the power to give voice to a subjective "us" while silencing a different "them." In *Dracula*, readers are exposed to the construction of a mythical portrait, a "deviant Other" in Transylvania. This type of portrait has broad consequences, especially when it is institutionalised. As Franz Fanon describes its impact:

> Blackness, darkness, shadow, shades, night, the labyrinths of the earth, abysmal depths, blacken someone's reputation; and, on the other side, the bright look of innocence, the white dove of peace, magical heavenly light. A magnificent blond child — how much peace there is in that phrase, how much joy, and above all how much hope. There is no such comparison with a magnificent black child. (189)

Equally significant is the fact that Stoker provides his readers with a cast of privileged characters. All of the novel's central characters are aristocratic, wealthy, well-educated, and/or professional. Dracula's class affiliations are also pronounced. He notes at one point that the peasant "is at heart a coward and a fool!" (22), and later exclaims, "We Transylvanian nobles love not to think that our bones may lie amongst the common dead" (24). Such blatant class inequalities illustrate that this work of fiction is not neutral but intensely value-laden. In other words, *Dracula* is a site of moral and ideological struggle. Stoker, as author, encourages a critical interpretation of the impact of history and culture. It becomes increasingly obvious that the reader's response to this text is based on his or her respective social location, personal experiences, and credulities.

Conclusions: Between the Lines,
Beyond the Text, and Behind the Narrative

BY ADDRESSING HOW mediated moralities pervade all discourse, *Dracula* is a seminal contribution to the social construction of subjectivity. Identity construction occurs within discursive cultural practices of experience and history. *Dracula* challenges and reworks these identities. How then are identities formed by, and how do they inform, social narratives? Mediated moralities, replete with mythologies and metaphors, become hegemonic in everyday lives: that is, they become a crucial part of the narratives of selfhood. Culture and history are the contexts within which moral meanings are negotiated. In specific narrative encounters, Stoker deconstructs evil and encourages a critical appreciation of morality as a narrative of representations of differences and contradictions. Therein, Stoker's theme of empowerment surfaces. The empowerment of agents of change and not just idle chatter about partnership, challenges the dominant ethos and develops oppositional currents. Resistance and struggle emerge as central features in *Dracula*. Accordingly, this cultural criticism is essential in locating the marginalised "Other," and in developing a liberating pedagogy. *Dracula*, therefore, substantially questions prevailing cultural practices. Stoker's conservatism aside, *Dracula* transcends the given and develops the complexity of being human, a condition which involves knowing and making sense of the unknown. In essence, Stoker indicts banal claims of binary oppositions such as life and death, science and religion. The horror of Dracula is overshadowed by the terror of ignorance. Stoker is determined to defy the defining gaze of cultural claims by sensitising and not sanitising the imagination of the reader to more counterhegemonic projects like superstition.

Dracula is a study of the sociology of morality. Within this collective biography, morality is complexly articulated within a plurality of discourses that are never stable, static, or fixed. The relationship between discourse and social subjectivity is organised through a specific articulation of conflicting images. These images are naturalised as fantasies as well as horrors. The image of evil and that of salvation respectively embodied in Count Dracula and the Professor, are interchangeable. These ideal moral types enjoy strengths and suffer from weaknesses. Likewise, metaphors of evil and good may appear exaggerated but they certainly contribute to an understanding of the process of moral regulation. *Dracula* is about the pursuit of righteousness by a handful of enlightened moral crusaders determined to destroy what they regard as evil. They would undoubtedly defend Albert Camus's proposition that "integrity needs no rules" (Green 141).

On one hand, *Dracula* succeeds as a forceful fiction that liberates the imagination. On the other, *Dracula* is a sociological text that addresses fundamental debates which, to date, have yet to be satisfactorily resolved. One involves determining the relationship between agency (voluntarism) and structure (determinism). Stoker, the pedagogue, leaves the issues of how social order is, and should be, constituted to his readers. Equally significant, however, is the fact that readers are encouraged to interrogate their own credulities and to become estranged from acts of moral policing. Indeed, the themes and characters in *Dracula* loom large in everyday life. As we approach the new millennium, *Dracula* reminds us of the illusory nature of progress — we continue to witness the proliferation of mythologies, the authority of tradition, the tyranny of inequality, transnational/extra-territorial hunts, endless religion-science controversies, and perhaps most significantly, the social construction of various Draculas by self-righteous moral crusaders.

NOTES

1   For further discussion of this topic, see my two articles, "The Culture of Capital as Carceral: Conditions and Contradictions," and "What Do They Know? Delinquency as Mediated Texts."

2   For more on this, see Hannah Arendt's essay, "Some Questions of Moral Philosophy."

3   For more on this signifying process, see Roland Barthes' *Image, Music, Text.*

4   Stanley Milgram discusses this issue in his essay, "The Experience of Living in Cities."

REFERENCES

Althusser, Louis. *Lenin and Philosophy, and Other Essays*. London: New Left Books, 1971.

Arendt, Hannah. 1962. "Some Questions of Moral Philosophy." *Social Research* 61 (1994): 739–764.

Barthes, Roland. 1957. *Mythologies*. New York: The Noonday Press, 1975.

—. 1975. *The Pleasure of the Text*. London: Cape, 1976.

—. *Image, Music, Text*. Glasgow: Collins Fontana, 1977.

—. *The Semiotic Challenge*. New York: Hill and Wang, 1988.

Baudrillard, Jean. *The Transparency of Evil*. Trans. James Benedict. Paris: Verso, 1993.

Becker, Howard. *Outsiders*. New York: Free Press, 1963.

Blumer, Herbert. *Symbolic Interactionism*. Englewood Cliffs: Prentice-Hall, 1969.

Brown, Robert. "Social Reality as Narrative Text: Interactions, Institutions, and Polities as Language." *Current Perspectives in Social Theory* 6 (1985): 17–37.

Brownmiller, Susan. *Against Our Will: Men, Women, and Rape*. New York: Simon and Shuster, 1975.

Corradi, Consuelo. "Text, Context and Individual Meaning: Rethinking Life Stories in a Hermeneutic Framework." *Discourse and Society* 2 (1991): 105–118.

Corrigan, Paul. *Schooling the Smash Street Kids*. London: Macmillan, 1979.

Currie, Elliott P. "Crimes without Criminals: Witchcraft and its Control in Renaissance Europe." *Law and Society Review* 3 (1968): 7–32.

Demetrakopoulos, Stephanie. "Feminism, Sex Role Exchanges, and Other Subliminal Fantasies in Bram Stoker's *Dracula*." *Frontiers: A Journal of Women Studies* 2 (1977): 104–113.

Denzin, Norman. *Sociological Methods: A Sourcebook*. New York: McGraw-Hill, 1978.

Derrida, Jacques. 1976. *Of Grammatology*. Baltimore: John Hopkins UP, 1976.

Fanon, Franz. 1967. *Black Skin, White Masks*. New York: Grove, 1976.

Filstead, William. *Qualitative Methodology*. Chicago: Rand McNally, 1970.

Foucault, Michel. *Discipline and Power*. New York: Pantheon, 1977.

—. *The History of Sexuality: An Introduction*. Trans. Robert Hurley. New York: Vintage, 1990.

Glover, David. "Travels in Romania: Myths of Origins, Myths of Blood." *Discourse* 16 (1993): 126–144.

Gramsci Antonio. *Selections from the Prison Notebooks*. Eds. and Trans. Q. Hoare and G. Nowell-Smith. New York: International Publishers, 1971.

Green, Jonathon. *The Pan Dictionary of Contemporary Quotations*. Sydney: Pan Original, 1989.

hooks, bell. *Ain't I A Woman: Black Women and Feminism*. Boston: South End Press, 1981.

Horkheimer, Max. *Critical Theory: Selected Essays*. New York: Continuum, 1936.

Kristeva, Julia. *Powers of Horror: An Essay on Abjection.* New York: Columbia UP, 1982.

Levy, Robert. "Horror and Tragedy: The Wings and Center of the Moral Stage." *Ethos* 13 (1985): 175–187.

Matza, David. *Becoming Deviant.* Englewood Cliffs: Prentice-Hall, 1969.

Milgram, Stanley. "The Experience of Living in Cities." *Science* 167 (1970): 1461–1468.

Morse, Donald. "The Stressful Kiss: A Biopsychosocial Evaluation of the Origins, Evolution, and Societal Significance of Vampirism." *Stress Medicine* 9 (1993): 181–199.

Pearson, Geoffrey. *The Deviant Imagination.* London: Macmillan, 1979.

Prus, Robert. "Anthropological and Sociological Approaches to Deviance: An Ethnographic Prospect." Unpublished paper presented at the Deviance in a Cross-Cultural Context Conference, Waterloo, 1984.

Simard, Louise. "Women Authors of Historical Novels. Quebec in Fiction/Les Romancières de l'histoire. Le Québec en fiction." *Recherches féministes* 6 (1993): 69–83.

Stoker, Bram. *Dracula.* 1897. Oxford: Oxford UP, 1983.

Taylor, Ian. "Crime Waves in Post-War Britain." *Contemporary Crises* 15 (1981): 43–62.

Visano, Livy. "The Culture of Capital as Carceral: Conditions and Contradictions." *Carceral Contexts.* Ed. K. McCormick. Toronto: Canadian Scholars Press, 1994. 193–219.

—. "What Do They Know? Delinquency as Mediated Texts." *Not A Kid Anymore.* Ed. G. O'Bireck. Toronto: Nelson, 1996. 71–106.

Ward Jouve, Nicole. *White Woman Speaks With Forked Tongue: Criticism as Autobiography.* London: Routledge, 1991.

Weissman, Judith. "Women and Vampires: *Dracula* as a Victorian Novel." *Midwest Quarterly* 18 (1977): 392–405.

Wiseman, Jacqueline. *Stations of the Lost.* Chicago: University of Chicago Press, 1979.

Wiseman, Mary Bittner. *The Ecstasies of Roland Barthes.* London: Routledge, 1989.

The Death of Dracula: A Darwinian Approach to the Vampire's Evolution

Benjamin H. Leblanc

"It was like a miracle; but before our very eyes, and almost in the drawing of a breath, … [Dracula's] whole body crumbled into dust and passed from our sight."

(*Dracula* 377)

FTER ONE HUNDRED YEARS OF HAUNTING CONTEM-porary Western culture, Count Dracula may now be declared dead. The changes brought about by mass society and modernism in the twentieth century have proven to be an insurmountable obstacle for him. Thus, rather ironically, Bram Stoker's supernatural vampire has died of natural causes. Dracula's demise, however, has not signified the extinction of vampires in general. Sometimes, one race of vampires has to die so that room may be made for another. By perishing, Dracula has given a new genre of vampires living space; however, he has also endowed a dark legacy by lending these younger bloodsuckers some of his own traits and characteristics. This essay proposes to undertake an in-depth Darwinian reading of the history of vampire lore and argues that a significant relationship exists between this creature's evolution and social changes in the twentieth century. This evolutionary vampire hunt may be said to be guided by a single question — how and why did Bram Stoker's Dracula die?

Adaptive Processes and Natural Selection:
From Biological Organism to Cultural Productions

O STUDY OR research a subject generally presupposes the ability to apply a definition to it. One cannot analyse something one cannot first identify. In this respect, the vampire presents a hitch: given its ongoing cultural and socio-historical metamorphoses, it can hardly be defined. A description of the vampire's variability, however, can perhaps be arrived at by way of a very simple, although imperfect, analogue — Darwinian evolution. In his book *On the Origin of Species*, published in 1859, Charles Darwin provided an explanation for the wide variability of species on the planet. As another scholar has summarised it:

> Organisms vary, through the process of mixing genes in sexual reproduction and through random mutation — copying errors in the genes. Some mutations are presumably beneficial to the organism in its environment, but most are not. On the average, organisms that are better adapted will survive longer and leave more offspring. From one generation to the next, the gene frequencies of the population will change slightly for the better in a particular environment. As the environment changes, so will the proportions of various types of organisms inhabiting it because different qualities will prove advantageous. Applying this model to the whole of life's history, one can explain most life forms as the result of gradual, adaptive change. (Poirier 17)

How is this theory to apply to vampires? To answer this question, one must substitute the term "organism" with "vampire representation," and the word "environment" with "cultural context." Reading the same text with these substitutions in place proves to be both revealing and useful: vampire figures/representations vary through cultural diffusion (sexual reproduction) and innovation (random mutations). A certain number of these vampire modifications will meet with a compatible cultural context, while others, unsuited to a new cultural context, will have a very short life. The most culturally compatible vampire figures will have the greatest chances of survival. They will also have a greater influence on their off-spring, the subsequent generation of vampires. It is through an examination of its transmutations within different cultural contexts that a cultural production may be shown to possess a variable morphology.

The idea of a correlation between vampire morphological variability and social change has been discussed by numerous scholars, including Nina Auerbach, whose recent book on the subject, *Our Vampires, Ourselves*, is "a history of Anglo-American culture through its mutating vampires" (1). Auerbach suggests that differences keep vampires alive, and that because they are immortal, "they are free to change incessantly" (5). As I will illustrate, however, inverting this formula is also valuable: vampires are immortal *because* they have this ability to change incessantly. This statement is also more suitable to my Darwin analogy.

The history of the vampire's evolution may be summarised as involving three stages with two distinct transitions. In each of these stages, the vampire is perceived differently by society. The development has led from the supernatural to the romantic vampire, then to a new interiorised vampire who has been tamed in recent literature and social practice.[1] This proposed chronological classification of the vampire based on social perceptions of this figure throughout history may be said to trace the evolution of society's relationships with its past and present undeads. I will demonstrate that Stoker's Count Dracula belongs to the second vampire stage which features the romantic undead, and that the recent transition to the interiorised vampire is largely responsible for Dracula's death.

Le Théâtre des Vampires
Act 1: The Supernatural Vampire

THE SUPERNATURAL VAMPIRE category includes all vampires and vampire-like creatures believed to exist until the end of the eighteenth century when Europe witnessed the birth of Romanticism. These undeads derived from superstition and religious faith. A Persian prehistoric vase depicts a man struggling with a blood-craving monster, and Chinese mythology had exploited the theme hundreds of years before the birth of Christ. Among the Greeks, it was believed that shadows who fed on the blood of their victims inhabited Hades's house. In Book Ten of Homer's *Odyssey*, Circe suggests that Ulysses give these creatures some blood so that they may both be saved (520–540). Aristotle, Plato, and Democritus wrote about wandering souls who were attracted to the sweet scent of blood and were believed to reveal the whereabouts of hidden or yet undiscovered treasure (Villeneuve 88–89). Horace, for his part, mentioned the

Lamia,[2] a necrophagous ghoul and queen of succubi who, it was said, devoured foetuses and terrorised children in the moonlight.

All of these creatures, although very different from recent vampires, exhibited some startling common characteristics. The most important symbolic connection of all was blood which signifies the duality of life and death. With such a universal base, vampirism — the superstitious or religious belief in vampires — could not do otherwise than appear under various forms in different cultures. In his laborious work of 1928 entitled *The Vampire: His Kith and Kin*, English scholar Montague Summers identified vampires and vampire-like creatures in the folklore of numerous cultures, among which he included the *asasabonsam* of the Ashanti people in Ghana (Africa), and the *obayifo*, the Ashanti name for a vampire from West Africa, known as *asiman* among the Dahomeans (Summers 259). Many other such creatures are found around the world, including the *chiang-shik* of China, the *rakshasas* (fem. *rakshasis*) of India, the *pontianak* of Java, the *Camazotz* of Mayan culture, the *tlahuelpuchi* of the Aztecs, the *asema* of Surinam,[3] the *loogaroo* of Haiti, the *upyr* of the Ukraine, the *uppyr* of Russia, the *kappas* of Japan, the *aswang* of the Philippines, and the *upior* (fem. *upierzyca*) of Poland.[4]

If the symbolic meaning of blood was of primary importance to the vampire folklore of antiquity, the Middle Ages invested this superstition with greater significance. According to Collin De Plancy in his *Dictionnaire Infernal*, during the second Council of Limoges in 1031, the Bishop of Cahors reportedly exposed the case of an excommunicated knight who, after death, ventured at least five times out of the grave. The mediaeval vampire, therefore, was no longer a divine, mythological being, but an accursed, transformed human being. The vampire was thus "brought down to earth," closer to humans.

Many documents illustrate the new "face" of the mediaeval vampire. Testimonies like Walter Map's *De Nurgis Curialium* (1193) and William of Newburgh's *Historia Regis Anglicarum* (1196) appear in England, for example, at the end of the twelfth century. They painstakingly recount the nightly jaunts of dead individuals who take great pleasure in tormenting their siblings, or provoking suspicious serial killings. These cases remained sporadic in Europe until the fourteenth century when vampirism became "endemic" in oriental Prussia, Silesia, and Bohemia.[5] Suddenly, the vampire phenomenon assumed tremendous proportions, infiltrating the realm of common knowledge. Many scholars have suggested that epidemics played a significant role in the development of vampire folklore. Indeed, contagion was ubiquitous at this time: during the 1340s alone, the Black Death decimated no less than twenty-five million people, a quarter of the total European population. It was also during this period, in 1343 at Lauenburg, that a Prussian baron who had died from the plague and been buried, was said by witnesses to have wandered out of his grave. The corpse was thereafter unearthed and stabbed with a sword. John Christian Herenberg mentions two other cases in 1337 and 1347 in which the "undeads" were "impaled and burned to ashes" (Villeneuve 94).

Cultural historian Paul Barber lends some insight into the connection between vampirism and plague:

> When one considers that vampires commonly infect others with their conditions, it will become obvious that, if even a single vampire escapes the ministrations of the local people, vampirism may increase in geometric proportions.... This was believed to explain epidemics of plague, although it was sometimes thought necessary to find and destroy only the original vampire, not his every victim, to end the plague. (57)

With so many deaths occurring over such a short period, the cases of premature burial — people believed to be dead but actually buried alive — increased.[6] Some authors have argued that such cases were, to a large degree, responsible for vampirism. Barber, however, proposes a far more complete theory which involves the poor understanding early physicians had of the normal processes of decomposition. According to Barber, a decomposing corpse undergoes many changes that are "unlikely to enhance its attractiveness" (103). Among these external signs of putrefaction are a "distension of the abdomen with gases," the "escape of blood-stained fluids from the mouth and nostrils," and the shedding of the nails and skin, uncovering what might seem like new layers underneath. Such changes were believed to provide evidence of the vampire state. They showed clearly that the undead had eaten very well the night before — his abdomen was distended, and he had blood escaping from the mouth. Interestingly, another sign of vampirism may also have been the absence of putrefaction: some corpses only decompose at a very slow pace, and others may even mummify, a phenomenon that was not well understood during the Mediaeval, Reformation, and Enlightenment eras.

In 1484, Pope Innocent VIII wrote his *Summis Desiderantes Affectibus* in which he redefined witchcraft as a form of satanism or apostasy. About the same time, two Dominicans, Heinrich Kramer and Jacob Sprenger, published their investigations on succubi, incubi, and "revenants" in a major work entitled *Malleus Maleficarum* (*The Hammer of Witches*). By approving this document, Innocent VIII lent credibility to the actual existence of undeads, an action that perpetuated, and even stimulated, vampire hysteria.

The term "vampire" was still not much in use in these years. As a text by Jean Oldecop (1561) illustrates — one where the rich are described as "suck[ing] the blood of the poor like vampires" (Villeneuve 94) — the word "vampire" was generally employed along metaphorical lines. The absence of the word "vampire" in historical documents of the time, however, does not mean that this subject was not of great concern to Catholic and orthodox theologians. In fact, it was a very well-discussed topic in certain circles and in 1645, Leo Allatius (Leone Allacci, 1586–1669), a Greek, Roman Catholic vampirologist, published the first modern work on vampires. This opened the way for subsequent books on the subject. For Allatius, the necessary conditions for the existence of vampires were (1) a devil, (2) a corpse, and (3) the permission of God. Allatius's monograph is significant as it explicitly links vampirism to satanism, a bond that has been especially exploited over the last three decades. Twelve years after Allatius's contribution, French Jesuit François Richard published his *Relation de ce qui s'est passé à Sant-Erini, Isle de l'Archipel*, a personal testimony which echoed the opinions of Allatius. Richard was also influenced by the *Malleus Maleficarum* as he linked witchcraft to vampirism.

Before concluding the first act of vampire history, we must turn to the disconcerting eighteenth century. Although this period is generally known as the Age of Reason, it was a prosperous time for the supernatural vampire. In the course of a trial held at Vienna in 1732, seventeen of forty unearthed corpses were believed to be vampires, and were therefore stabbed, beheaded, and burned to ashes. As a result of the wave of rationalism, some individuals attempted to prove the existence of vampires scientifically.[7] These investigators confronted many skeptical detractors, however, such as Voltaire and Diderot.[8] The French philosopher Jean-Jacques Rousseau was, for his part, a firm believer in vampires, claiming that the existence of undeads had been empirically proven.

This rationalist epoch inspired several fascinating documents about vampirism including the *Dissertazione sopre I Vampiri* (1744) by Giuseppe Davanzati, and the *Lettre à une Illustre Morte* (1771) by Louis-Antoine Caraccioli. In 1755, Gerard Van Swieten wrote a medical report about vampires at the request of Marie-Thérèse d'Autriche. Despite all of this, the undeads of superstition and religion were dying. It would be dreamers, and not physicians, who would revive them.

Act 2: The Romantic Vampire

THE END OF the Enlightenment era witnessed the birth of a diverse and fragmented movement known as Romanticism which promoted utopias featuring the equal distribution of wealth, the absence of violence and prosperity, and emotion over reason. Romanticism's impact extended beyond politics and philosophy to painting, music, and, most significantly for the subject of vampires, literature.

Indeed, it is in literature that the vampire sought refuge after being abandoned by religion and superstition. With the ongoing secularisation of society and the promotion of rationalism, the supernatural vampire was a species confronted by abrupt environmental changes which threatened its extinction. The only path to survival was adaptation; thus, undeads migrated to literary fiction. For the first time in their history, they were no longer perceived as part of reality, and this modified relationship between them and their human creators constitutes the main characteristic of the first major transition in the vampire's development. It was also during this stage that the vampire was freed from his past unattractiveness. The romantic undead was definitively transformed from a grotesque monster to a dark prince/aristocrat.

The most comfortable environment for a vampire became the Gothic romance, a literary genre Leonard Wolf describes as

> ... a species of writing that first appeared in England in the mid-eighteenth and early nineteenth centuries. The typical Gothic romance has a beautiful young woman in it, who is pursued by wicked, dark, usually Italian, men whose intentions are strictly dishonorable. Her flight takes her to a variety of dismal or dangerous places: subterranean corridors, vaults, crypts, ruins, caves, secret rooms, graveyards. Usually the young woman is well-bred, sensitive, frail. Clearly, she deserves a better fate than the one that threatens her, and it almost goes without saying that she is rescued from it (sometimes repeatedly) by a handsome but sexually unthreatening young man with whom, as the book closes, she settles down to live happily ever after. (viii)

Elizabeth MacAndrew, author of *The Gothic Tradition in Fiction*, defines the Gothic genre as the "literature of nightmare." MacAndrew identifies this genre as a form of romanticism — *dark* romanticism.

The birth of Gothic literature is usually identified with the publication on Christmas Eve, 1764, of Horace Walpole's *The Castle of Otranto*. This tale is set in a haunted castle where the descendants of a certain Alfonso the Good, a twelfth-century ruler of an Italian province, undergo many adventures. Although not a vampire, the villain, Manfred, exhibits the Machiavellian traits that literary undeads were to bear in subsequent years. But Walpole's story is hardly a masterpiece of written art; it lacks a well-defined structure. Ann Radcliffe's *The Mysteries of Udolpho* (1794) is known as the first truly Gothic literary novel. The author maintains a good plot dynamic throughout as Emily St. Aubert is incessantly persecuted by the sinister Montoni. In 1797, one hundred years before the publication of Stoker's *Dracula*, Radcliffe published another story, *The Italian*, in which she successfully intensified every terrifying aspect of her first book. Count Montoni in Radcliffe's *The Mysteries of Udolpho*, Count de Bruno (Schedoni) in *The Italian*, Ambrosio in Matthew G. Lewis's *The Monk* (1796), and Melmoth in Charles Robert Maturin's *Melmoth the Wanderer* (1820), are all semi-vampiric in their fleshly, materialist cravings. In the final analysis, however, they remain human.

The vampire was actually introduced to Gothic literature through several works including John Polidori's *The Vampyre* (1819), and James Malcolm Rymer's *Varney the Vampire* (1847). The former work was primarily Lord Byron's idea. On the famous stormy night of June 16th, 1816, at the Villa Diodati (overlooking Lake Geneva), he composed a rough outline of the story. It was during that same evening that *Frankenstein* was first conceived by Mary Shelley who was also present at the Villa. While *Frankenstein* was later completed and published, however, Byron never reworked his outline. John Polidori, Byron's travelling companion and personal physician, later rewrote and published it under the title, *The Vampyre*. The many staged versions of this work and the popularity of the bloodthirsty Lord Ruthven in London and Paris attest to its success. Based on Byron himself, Ruthven is a suave, rich — though not very friendly — young man who dies yet returns to life in the moonlight. This figure was evil yet elegant, a demon lover who was very popular with women. This character make-up became central to the fictional vampire's descendants.

Rymer's vampire, Sir Francis Varney, appeared twenty-eight years after Ruthven. The two share similar powers such as immortality, great physical strength, the ability to withstand sunlight and to gather energy from the moon. But Varney is truly vampiric — he sucks the blood of his female victims and his fangs leave behind puncture marks. In his initial portrait, Varney's face is described as being

> ... perfectly white — perfectly bloodless. The eyes look
> like polished tin; the lips are drawn back, and the principal
> feature next to those dreadful eyes is the teeth — the fear-
> ful looking teeth — projecting like those of some wild ani-
> mal, hideously, glaringly white, and fang-like. (3–4)

Both Polidori and Rymer were familiar with the Eastern European vampire phenomenon. For instance, allusion to Dom Augustin Calmet's survey of vampirism is made in the introduction to *The Vampyre*, and it is suspected that Rymer had access to the same information. It may be said, therefore, that these writers were very instrumental in bridging the gap between the supernatural and the romantic vampire figures.

Joseph Sheridan Le Fanu and Abraham Stoker, both Dublin-born Irishmen who were graduates of Trinity College, were probably inspired by Lord Ruthven and Varney. Le Fanu, a poet and author of horror litera-ture, wrote a novel entitled *Carmilla* which was published in a book of short stories called *In a Glass Darkly* in 1872. Carmilla became the third major vampire figure in English literature. In fact, she is one of the most tantalising. Also known as Mircalla and Millarca, Carmilla introduced a very strong sensual dimension to the figure of the undead, as she and her victim, Laura, are involved in a lesbian relationship. It is believed that Stoker borrowed some images from Le Fanu's novel for his *Dracula* (1897), among which include Lucy Westenra's staking (Wolf xii). Carmilla was extremely influential as she became the prototype for female vampires in later fiction and cinema.

The romantic vampire was transformed from his hideous and piti-ful characterisation in writings of the Medieval, Renaissance, and Enlightenment eras. He acquired a great deal of physical prowess, wealth, elegance, and mesmerising seductive power. As J. Gordon Melton expli-cates this shift:

> The folkloric vampire was part of village culture. It was
> restricted to its grave site or its home village, where it took
> up residence once again. In contrast, Lord Ruthven, Varney
> the Vampire, and Dracula are citizens of the world. (657)

Classifying *Dracula*

MUCH HAS BEEN written about Stoker's masterpiece. Described by many as the highest achievement in Gothic literature (although rarely praised for its literary merits), *Dracula* is a species of vampire literature fully adapted to its environment. Paradoxically, when first published in 1897, it was not an immediate success. In fact, it was not lucrative for its author. Stoker died on the 20th of April, 1912, in a poor financial situation.

Although *Dracula* belongs to the Gothic literature genre, it has many singular and innovative characteristics. For instance, Stoker judiciously adds a taste of authenticity to his story with the inclusion of folkloric and historical material, such as Romanian superstitious beliefs and some biographical details about a violent fifteenth-century Wallachian prince (or Voivode) named Vlad Țepeș Drăculea. The reader should keep in mind, however, that many questions about Stoker's sources remain unanswered. For instance, we know for certain that he twice met Arminius Vambéry, distinguished Professor of Oriental Languages at the University of Budapest. According to Stoker's biographer Harry Ludlam, Vambéry would have informed Stoker, on one or both occasions, of biographical details about Vlad Țepeș and Transylvanian folklore. This is a very enticing and convincing theory, especially when one considers the actual reference to Vambéry in *Dracula* where he is presented as "Arminius, of Buda-Pesth University", a friend of Van Helsing's and a scholar who is very knowledgeable on "that Voivode Dracula who won his name against the Turk" (240). There is, however, one problem with this theory — the absence of hard evidence. Indeed, Stoker's personal account of the Vambéry meeting on April 30th, 1890, says nothing of these matters (*Personal* 371–372). As Raymond T. McNally and Radu Florescu confirm, "Unfortunately, no correspondence between Vambéry and Stoker can be found today. Moreover, a search through all of the professor's [Vambéry's] published writings fails to reveal any comments on Vlad [Țepeș], Dracula, or vampires" (150).

Another important source of information for consideration are Stoker's notes for *Dracula*, now held at the Rosenbach Museum & Library in Philadelphia. As Joseph S. Bierman points out, "a number of lines in the outline have been altered by deletions and substitutions." For instance, in notes dated March 14th, 1890, Stoker replaced the word "Styria" with "Transylvania," while later in the same manuscript the first mention of Dracula is also the product of a substitution. According to Bierman, Stoker must have altered these notes:

> ... at any time between the day they were made, 14 March 1890, and 29 February 1892, the date of a manuscript in which "Whitby," "Dracula," and the "Borgo Pass" (Transylvania) appear, as original entries rather than as substitutions. The alteration could have been made as the outcome of his [Stoker's] meeting with Vambéry on 30

Vlad Țepeș, Voivode of Wallachia, 1448, 1456–1462, 1476, after a portrait in oil, kept in Ambras Castle, Austria, 15th century.

April 1890, if they spoke of Dracula and Transylvania at that time. Stoker might also have altered the outline for reasons not connected with the Vambéry meeting at any time between March 14 and the end of February 1892. (40)

Much mystery, therefore, remains. Some scholars even doubt that Stoker actually based his Count on the historical figure Vlad Ţepeş. In May of 1996, Elizabeth Miller presented a paper at the second Transylvanian Society of Dracula Symposium, held at the Borgo Pass in Transylvania, in which she argued that, "If Stoker knew as much about Vlad as some scholars claim (for example, that he impaled thousands of victims), then why is this information not used in the novel? This is a crucial question, when one considers how much insignificant detail Stoker did incorporate from his many sources" (2). We learn from the Rosenbach Collection notes for *Dracula*, however, that Stoker had read something about the historical figure Vlad Dracula. A typewritten sheet with the classification "Whitby Library 0.1097" entitled "Account of the Principalities of Wallachia and Moldavia, Etc, [by] Wm Wilkinson, late consul of Bukarest, Longmans, 1820," is included in his set of notes.

Another widely accepted belief about Stoker's sources involves Emily Gerard's travel guide *The Land Beyond the Forest*, described by Leonard Wolf as "the richest single source of folklore information for ... [Stoker]" (xiii). Elizabeth Miller has argued, however, that we are not sure whether Stoker ever read this particular book as it is not mentioned in his own list of sources. Nevertheless, we do know that he consulted Gerard's article "Transylvanian Superstitions," which was published in the July 1885 issue of *The Nineteenth Century & After*, and later incorporated into Gerard's book. On the question of Stoker's sources, Joseph Bierman concludes, "Whether or not Stoker even spoke or corresponded with Arminius Vambéry about Dracula and Transylvania may never be known. However, all of the significant material attributed to Professor Arminius in the novel can be found in Gerard's article, Wilkinson's book, and two other books from which Stoker excerpted notes" (41).[9]

Some scholars, like Tony Faivre, have also suggested that Bram Stoker was a member of the Hermetic Order of the Golden Dawn, an occult order which developed out of the Societas Rosicruciana in Anglia (SRIA), founded by Robert Wentworth Little in 1867. Other well-known writers involved with this Order included Algernon Blackwood and William Butler Yeats. In search of evidence that Stoker was involved with this Order, Faivre analyses *Dracula* for hidden clues. He finds these in the form of the ordeals Jonathan must endure during his trip through

Transylvania, the idea of a disease infecting the world, and the presence of a Master who commands the forces of nature, animals, and human beings. All of these elements were crucial to Rosicrucian metaphysics.

Whatever else may be said, *Dracula* is a pure product of its time, a perfectly adapted species. The traits of its principal characters — especially the women — almost constitute a caricature of Victorian ideals: while the soft, defenceless, and understanding Mina is an archetypal angel in the house, the three vampiresses and the vampirised Lucy Westenra are sexually provocative, even aggressive — the antithesis of good manners à la Victorienne. In this respect, *Dracula* is a book which reinforces Victorian values. But values change while writings, once published, do not. All through the twentieth century, new interpretations of *Dracula* have appeared in literature and on screen. Margaret L. Carter's bibliography of vampire-related fiction includes more than a thousand titles. What may have inspired writers and producers to make use of *Dracula* instead of Polidori's *The Vampyre* or James Malcolm Rymer's *Varney the Vampire* is the very "adaptable" nature of Stoker's narrative material. Royce MacGillivray explains part of *Dracula*'s appeal when he writes, "of all that is historically interesting in *Dracula*, nothing is more curious than its combination of the Victorian preoccupation with death and an almost twentieth-century preoccupation with sex" (526–527).

The sexual dimension of *Dracula* has been carefully examined by many scholars to date. In this respect, Stoker's novel is not very innovative. As psychoanalyst Ernest Jones has pointed out, the supernatural vampire already bore very sexual meanings in the Middle Ages (98). Indeed, undeads have long been bedroom visitors associated with the nightly, supernatural assault tradition. They can be compared, therefore, to succubi, incubi, werewolves, night-hags, devils, and witches, creatures feared for their nocturnal attacks (sexual or otherwise) upon the sleeper. Dracula's annoying habit of stalking night stalking places him in the same league as these nocturnal visitors.

In his well-documented book *The Terror That Comes in the Night*, David J. Hufford delineates four sleep-related phenomena that may have played a role in stimulating bedroom visitation folklore: (1) bad dreams, (2) night terrors, (3) sleep paralysis, and (4) hypnagogic/hypnopompic hallucinations. Sleep paralysis, the third phenomenon, is particularly interesting and relevant. As defined by Hufford, it is "a period of inability to perform voluntary movements, either when falling asleep or when awakening, accompanied by conscious awareness" (122). It is worth mentioning that paralysis during sleep is perfectly normal; it prevents the sleeper from running out of bed when dreaming that a vicious monster is chasing them. What constitutes a sleep disorder is the bad synchronisation between sleep state and paralysis, a phenomenon that produces a period when the subject is paralysed yet fully awake. A crucial detail about sleep paralysis is that it is often experienced as the feeling of a heavy weight or pressure on the chest. Such a sensation can lead to the conviction that somebody or something threatening is present in the room. This type of experience has been depicted, for instance, in Henry Fuseli's painting entitled *The Nightmare* (1782), where an incubus is portrayed sitting on the chest of a female sleeper. J. Bond, in his *Essay on the Incubus* (1753), and R. Macnish, eighty years later, in *The Philosophy of Sleep* (1834), mention those "symptoms" in their vivid descriptions of the nightmare experience. Ernest Jones also proposed three "cardinal features" of the Nightmare: (1) an agonising dread, (2) a sense of oppression or weight on the chest which alarmingly interferes with respiration, and (3) a conviction of helpless paralysis (98).

Vampire folklore seems to be closely related to the phenomenon of the nightmare and, more specifically, to sleep paralysis. It also shares many similarities with the incubus, a relationship which is confirmed by Heinrich von Wlislocki in his research on Romanian superstition. In his *Slavische Volksforschungen* (1908), Krauss writes, "The case has often happened that after a number of deaths in a village, the wife of a recently deceased man has been maltreated until she confessed that her husband was visiting her, and promised to persuade him not to murder people" (Jones 102). In his *Okkultismus und Sexualitat*, Freimark writes, "Though it is not an absolute rule, still it can be observed that in most cases women are constantly visited by male vampires, and men by female ones.... The sexual features characterize the vampire belief as another form of the Incubus-Succubus belief" (Jones 125).

The vampire's attacks on his sleeping victims in their bedrooms have been characterised, in some instances, as a pressure on the chest. Such was the case, for example, in Rhode Island, during the early 1770s with the Stuckley family. This young farmer's daughter was suffering from what the local doctor diagnosed as incurable consumption (tuberculosis). In a state of delirium, she told her parents that the ghost of her elder sister, Sarah, visited her each evening. This sister had previously died from tuberculosis, and was apparently attempting to suffocate her sibling by sitting on her stomach and sucking blood from her neck. When Stuckley's wife took ill and also complained of nightmares in which Sarah came to her, the farmer decided to exhume the body of his daughter. Stuckley discovered the required proofs of vampirism on Sarah's corpse — her body was well-preserved, her hair and fingernails were still growing, and her heart was still filling with blood. Farmer Stuckley cut the heart out, placed it in an iron pot in front of his house, and burned it.[10]

Count Dracula's nocturnal attacks are, to a certain extent, reminiscent of bedroom visitations. Not only is the victim unable to resist, but a sexual dimension is definitely present. Dracula clearly prefers women, while the Count's vampiresses wish to sink their fangs into Jonathan Harker. These episodes support Freimark's observation that succubi and incubi — like vampires — prey upon the opposite sex. As Christopher Craft relates, "Modern critical accounts of *Dracula* ... universally agree that vampirism both expresses and distorts an originally sexual energy" (107). Bram Stoker's Count is far from attractive, however, when compared with Lord Ruthven in Polidori's *The Vampyre* or Le Fanu's Carmilla. Jonathan Harker's description of the Count paints his unattractive portrait:

> His face was a strong — a very strong — aquiline, with high bridge of the thin nose and peculiarly arched nostrils; with lofty domed forehead, and hair growing scantily round the temples, but profusely elsewhere. His eyebrows were very massive, almost meeting over the nose, and with bushy hair that seemed to curl in its own profusion. The mouth, so far as I could see it under the heavy moustache, was fixed and rather cruel-looking, with peculiarly sharp white teeth; these protruded over the lips, whose remarkable ruddiness showed astonishing vitality in a man of his years. For the rest, his ears were pale and at the tops extremely pointed; the chin was broad and strong, and the cheeks firm though thin. The general effect was one of extraordinary pallor. (17–18)

Add to this unsavoury portrait the "hairs in the centre of ... [his] palm," his "squat fingers," and long and fine nails "cut to a sharp point" (18), and Dracula is hardly a Don Juan. There is certainly no future for Dracula in the *Baywatch* television series! As far as vampire sexuality is presented in Stoker's novel, it is primarily identified with young women and the concept of moral uncleanness. Mina, in particular, experiences this after her vampire baptism when she cries, "Unclean, unclean! I must touch him [her husband, Jonathan] or kiss him no more!" (284). C.F. Bentley proposes that Dracula's attack on Mina is a symbolic form of sexual intercourse involving the loss of virginity (31). He also interprets the staking of Lucy Westenra as rife with phallic symbolism. Her reactions during the staking are, he says, reminiscent of female orgasm. Although entertaining and provocative, Bentley's reading lacks clear evidence.

Just prior to *Dracula*'s publication, Stoker presented a staged reading of the novel. Only in 1925, however, was the play really developed by

Hamilton Deane, the son of Stoker's friend. It was in *Dracula*'s new dramatic role that Stoker's Count metamorphosed into "a suave, sophisticated gentleman in evening dress" (Guiley 64). From this point onwards, the Count became increasingly handsome. An examination of the successive list of actors who have played Dracula on screen (Max Schreck-Bela Lugosi-Christopher Lee-Louis Jourdan-Frank Langella) illustrates this shift. Indeed, the vampire has undergone many mutations throughout the twentieth century. Significant changes in Western culture have rendered Stoker's Count unrecognisable. In some cases, these changes have been lethal.

Act 3: The Interiorised Vampire

TWENTIETH-CENTURY WESTERN society has undergone tremendous changes. With modernity and the emergence of mass society, marginality and deviance have become more readily accepted. An increasing tendency to individualism and a new pluralism of axiologies (systems of values) can be held responsible for the vampire's second major transition where s/he has become interiorised by his/her "victims." This shift began some twenty-five years ago, and it has sentenced Dracula, rather mercilessly, to death.

The characteristics of this new "interiorised" vampire are numerous, but the most important one is undoubtedly his/her proximity to human beings. The second transition in the vampire's development, therefore, has involved his/her "humanisation." For bibliographer and writer Margaret L. Carter, this transition was first apparent in writer Chelsea Quinn Yarbro's vampire novels which began to be published in the 1970s.[11] As Carter explains:

> Her vampires are much more straightforwardly sympathetic, altogether nice people, much nicer than the human beings around them. Her vampires are noble ... in a human world where things are so brutal the vampires would look kind anyway. (Guiley 66)

The sympathetic vampire was adopted by other writers, among them Anne Rice, author of the famous *Vampire Chronicles*.[12] Unlike Bram Stoker's Count Dracula, Rice's character Louis is almost a devotee of political correctness. His quest for identity involves a thorough retracing of his origins, a pilgrimage which parallels the individual's quest for meaning. Hence, Rice's new species of vampire has perfectly adapted to current social trends.

Other character traits of the interiorised vampire illustrate his/her proximity to the human world. While at the time *Dracula* was published, vampires were still — as they were traditionally — members of the aristocracy, today's undeads do not usually derive from this social rank. This suggests that virtually anyone may be one of them. The most compelling difference between the romantic and the interiorised vampire, however, involves their perspective. In Stoker's *Dracula*, the Count is a figure who is objectified in descriptions by his human enemies. He is evil and must be destroyed without remorse. Rice's novels, inversely, offer a door to the vampire's mind. There, the reader is granted an inside view. As Margaret Carter has provocatively stated, "we can empathize with vampires no matter how evil they are if we can get inside their minds" (Guiley 70). The second major alteration in the interiorised vampire may, therefore, be described as his renunciation of emotional and intellectual privacy. This figure was thus divested of an essential portion of its mystery. This especially occurs in Coppola's 1992 cinematic adaptation of *Dracula* in which a radically altered Count is presented. This Oscar-winning director opted for a romantic Prince possessed of a good heart instead of a merciless and terrifying Transylvanian nobleman. Coppola also provided an explanation for Dracula's vampire origins. His "fall" is, in fact, justified as he is portrayed as having reacted against God's injustice. This rationale, however, is entirely absent from Stoker's novel.

Another interesting and revealing characteristic of the interiorised vampire is the fact that his/her emergence was concurrent with the New Age movement in contemporary Western culture. Born some thirty years ago, New Age derived from the counter-cultural movement in California and the Caddy couple in Findhorn, Scotland.[13] The New Age ideology upholds values of peace, fraternity, and love. In this philosophy, science is regarded as oppositional to nature, and a new form of spiritualism is advocated which centres on feelings and personal experience. Many scholars have tried to explain this social movement as anti-rational, a response to an excess of *Aufklärung*, scientism, and marxism. The agnosticism, scepticism, and indifference of New-Agers have been interpreted as attempts to escape the stifling materialism of the late twentieth century (Poupard 120). The suggested reincarnation of Elizabetha as Mina in Coppola's 1992 cinematic production of *Bram Stoker's Dracula*, shows how the New Age movement and new religious pluralism have influenced the popular representation of the undead.

As Rosemary Ellen Guiley outlines in her book *Vampires Among Us*, these New-Age trends and ideas have had significant social implications. As Guiley's interviews with so-called "vampires" and "vampire hunters" reveal, the vampire figure has been recuperated for identity purposes, especially by individuals who feel increasingly alone in a technocratic world. Guiley introduces her readers, for example, to two figures named Damien and Damon who, confronted by hard childhoods, phobias, and a poor financial situation, were increasingly attracted to the vampire and what they understood to be the vampire lifestyle. Guiley sheds some light on this figure's appeal to individuals in oppressive circumstances:

> The [modern] vampire is admired for his denial of death and his ability to transcend the dullness of mundane human life. How glamorous life would be, it seems, if we, too, lived forever, suffered no illness, had no wants, and were able to rise above the plodding human masses. Yet the vampire is profoundly alienated from all other living things, as we in modern times feel alienated from our own societies. Thus, we identify with the vampire's pain. (70)

The emergence of new religious movements centring on the vampire also bear out Guiley's words. Spiritual liberalism, part of the aforementioned series of social changes in the late twentieth-century, has led to some interesting innovations. Many icons of popular culture, for example, have been integrated into new religious movements. Angels and extraterrestrials are included among the new inductees, and so too are vampires. The birth of organisations like the Order of the Vampyre and the Temple of the Vampire may be attributed both to a new wave of spiritual liberalism in the late twentieth century and to the increased popularity of the vampire figure in pop-culture since the 1970s. Members of the Order of the Vampyre distinguish between the Hollywood-style undead and the spiritually evolved creature they seek to become. As Robert Neilly, Grand Master of the Order, explains:

> A Vampire is the popularized Hollywood version of the 'undead' (read unthinking and unaware) and static creature which seems to exist only to gratify its physical needs, and perhaps physical immortality. The 'Vampyre,' [note the spelling difference] conversely, is a Living, Awakened creature which seeks to immortalize its core Self or soul. If, for the sake of argument, one adopts as a given that both kinds of creatures exist, then clear differences may be seen. The 'Vampire' exists at an instinctual level only, and would seem to live a rather tragic existence. The 'Vampyre,' however, exists at an instinctual level only, and would seem to live a rather tragic existence. The 'Vampyre,' however, via initiatory work, has 'quickened' her soul and in doing so acquired a host of other qualities along the way. (Webb)

As this description outlines, members of the Order seek, through an evolutionary model of vampirism, to 'quicken' their souls. In the process, they claim they can develop new powers, the most important of which is self-control. Other powers include the "Command to Look" (where the "Vampyre" can hold someone else's gaze and communicate with his eyes), the power to convince others through "voice control," and the development of a "Vampyric Presence," a powerfully intimidating and charismatic aura. Interestingly enough, members of the Order do not wish to emulate Stoker's Count. In fact, they don't even want to be associated with him. The "Vampyre" powers they uphold effectively target what has been described as an epidemic contemporary problem, namely low self esteem. While the psychology shelves of bookstores are overcrowded with books offering a method for achieving personal success (and their apparition on the market is not completely independent of the emergence of the New Age movement), the Order of the Vampyre offers its own self-improvement technique.

The Temple of the Vampire, on the other hand, is quite distinct from the Order. Indeed, according to the Vampire Bible — the reference book of the Temple — undeads *do* exist. Their "Vampire Creed" runs as follows:

I am a Vampire.

I worship my ego and I worship my life, for I am the only God that is.

I am proud that I am a predatory animal and I honour my animal instincts.

I exalt my rational mind and hold no belief that is in defiance of reason.

I recognize the difference between the worlds of truth and fantasy.

I acknowledge the fact that survival is the highest law.

I acknowledge the Powers of Darkness to be hidden natural laws through which I work my magic.

I know that my beliefs in Ritual are fantasy but the magic is real, and I respect and acknowledge the results of my magic.

I realize that there is no heaven as there is no hell, and I view death as the destroyer of life.

Therefore I will make the most of life here and now.

I am a Vampire.

Bow down before me. (Webb)

The Temple also has a ring and a ritual medallion for sale, both of which depict a winged skull. It is noteworthy that some sentences of the Vampire Creed are reminiscent of the philosophy promoted by the Church of Satan which was founded in 1966 in San Francisco (Introvigne 173).

The Order of the Vampyre itself is "like a Standing Committee of the Temple of Set" (Webb), which is the primary splinter group of the Church of Satan. It is also significant that the Satanic Bible, written by Anton Szandor LaVey, contains an entire chapter on "psychic vampires" entitled "Not All Vampires Suck Blood!" LaVey defines psychic vampires as "individuals who drain others of their vital energy.... They fill no useful purpose in our lives, and are neither love objects nor true friends. Yet we feel responsible to the psychic vampire without knowing why" (75).

Burton H. Wolfe[14] lends some insight into LaVey's folkloric and literary sources:

> All of LaVey's background seemed to prepare him for his role. He is the descendant of Georgian, Romanian, and Alsatian grandparents, including a gypsy grandmother who passed on to him the legends of vampires and witches from her native Transylvania. As early as the age of five, LaVey was reading *Weird-Tales* magazine and books such as Mary Shelley's *Frankenstein* and Bram Stoker's *Dracula*. (11)

Leo Allatius provided a link between vampires and satanism as early as 1645. Contemporary applications of this relationship involve reconfiguring it in innovative ways within the context of a new religious and moral liberalism.

A Dark Legacy

IF WE ACCEPT the idea of a second transition from the romantic to the interiorised vampire, we must conclude that Stoker's Count, who belonged to the romantic vampire tradition, is now dead. New representations of the vampire — like Yarbro's Saint Germain and Rice's Lestat, Louis, and Armand — are far removed from Dracula. It is very revealing that most contemporary vampire fans have never read Stoker's Gothic classic. Dracula is simply too far removed from their reality. He is too emotionally and intellectually distant — he does not allow entry into his private thoughts and feelings because he was written for another time with different tastes. While, as Nina Auerbach has argued, vampires in general are more adaptable creatures than "ghosts, werewolves, and manufactured monsters," for they "blend into the changing cultures they inhabit" (6), individualised vampire figures — like Count Dracula — are products of a specific time and place.

On the issue of the vampire's adaptability, however, one essential condition has helped this creature survive — intense media coverage over a prolonged period of time. Ghosts and werewolves did not benefit from this publicity to the same degree. Another figure, however, was lucky enough to enjoy this advantage, namely the extraterrestrial. Although younger than vampires — they are mainly a twentieth-century product — extraterrestrials evolved following a similar Darwinian pattern. As Martin Kottmeyer has noted in his cynically titled essay "Entirely Unpredisposed," the alien's morphology in the popular worldview has altered as technology and science fiction have progressed (3). From representations as disgusting monsters with tentacles or little green men from Mars, aliens evolved into several types — Little Gray, Tall Blond, Reptilian, and Insectoid. As aerospace historian Curtis Peebles has suggested:

> In addition to the science fiction influences, the shape of the "Grays" [extraterrestrial type seen in the most recent sci-fi movies] have other symbolism. On a cultural level, the Grays resemble television images of starving African children — [they have] large heads, spindly arms and legs, malformed bodies, and [are] physically weak. This is symbolic of a dark future for mankind.... A starving children/Gray symbolism also fits the picture of "alien beings from a dying planet." (320)

Although this "starving children/Gray" theory may not — like the phallic imagery in Lucy's staking scene — be verified, it is noteworthy that the vampire is comparable to at least one other pop-culture figure in terms of his adaptability.

Dracula's death should not be considered a tragedy. After all, he died of "natural" causes, and left a legacy to his descendants, one which is both dark and powerful. In a way, he will live forever through his descendants and in our memories. Nina Auerbach has said that she wrote about vampires "because they can be everything we are, while at the same time, they are fearful reminders of the infinite things we are not" (6). This would perhaps explain why the vampire fails to cast a reflection — all we see in the mirror, in the final analysis, is ourselves.

NOTES

1   By "social practice," I am referring to the vampire-related lifestyles or occasional behaviours adopted by so-called "vampires" and vampire fans.

2   Lamia is the Roman version of Babylonian "Lilitu" and Hebraic "Lilith."

3   For further details about the *asema*, see the essay by Rob Brautigam.

4   Further information about these creatures may be found in J. Gordon Melton's *Encyclopedia of the Undead.*

5   "Endemic" is the term used by Jean Marigny to describe the mediaeval vampire phenomenon in his book *Vampires: Restless Creatures of the Night* (24).

6   For further reading on premature burial, see the works of Docteur M. Pineau, Herbert Mayo, theosophist Franz Hartmann, Montague Summers, and Anthony Masters listed in my bibliography.

7   See, for example, the work of Dom Augustin Calmet.

8   Voltaire complains in his *Dictionnaire Philosophique* that "Everybody only talks about those vampires!"

9   The two other books mentioned by Bierman are *Magyarland* (1881) and *On the Track of the Crescent* (1885).

10 Cases of vampirism associated with a pressure on the chest and the feeling of paralysis are extensively described and analysed in my essay "Uninvited Guest: The Possible Role of Sleep-Related Phenomena in Nightly Supernatural Assault Traditions," which was presented in May of 1996 at the second Transylvanian Society of Dracula Symposium in the Borgo Pass, Transylvania.

11 Books by Chelsea Quinn Yarbro include *Hotel Transylvania* (1978), *The Palace* (1979), *Blood Games* (1980), *Path of the Eclipse* (1981), *Tempting Fate* (1982), *The Saint Germain Chronicles* (1983), *A Flame in Byzantium* (1987), and *Crusader's Torch* (1988).

12 Anne Rice's *Vampire Chronicles* include *Interview With the Vampire* (1976), *The Vampire Lestat* (1985), *The Queen of the Damned* (1988), and *The Tale of the Body Thief* (1992).

13 Along with the California cultural revolution of the mid-1960s, the Caddy couple is considered to be a major precipitator of the New Age movement. In 1962, Peter Caddy lost his job as a hotel manager and went to live with his wife Eileen on a small plot of land in Findhorn, Scotland. Eileen was meditating one day when she heard a voice saying that she and her husband should establish a little vegetable garden. Although the soil was very dry and sterile, they nevertheless succeeded. Soon the garden was very productive. Its success was attributed to the help of devas, dwarf-like mythological creatures who, according to the Caddys, lived inside the earth.

14 Burton H. Wolfe is the author of many books, among which is *The Devil's Avenger: a Biography of Anton Szandor LaVey*. Wolfe has been officially involved with the Church of Satan since 1974.

REFERENCES

Allaci, Leone (Leo Allatius). *De Graecorum hodie quorundam opinationisbus*. Cologne, 1645.

Auerbach, Nina. *Our Vampires, Ourselves*. Chicago and London: University of Chicago Press, 1995.

Barber, Paul. *Vampires, Burial and Death: Folklore and Reality*. New Haven, Connecticut: Yale UP, 1988.

Bentley, Christopher. "The Monster in the Bedroom: Sexual Symbolism in Bram Stoker's *Dracula*." *Literature and Psychology* 22 (1972): 27-33.

Bierman, Joseph S. "*Dracula*: Prolonged Childhood Illness, and the Oral Triad." *American Imago* 29 (1972): 186–198.

Brautigam, Rob. "Asema: The Vampire of Surinam." *International Vampire* 1 (1990): 16–37.

Calmet, Dom Augustin. *Dissertation sur les Apparitions des Anges, des Démons, et des Esprits, et sur les revenants, et vampires de Hongrie, de Bohème, de Moravie, et de Silesie*. Paris, 1746. Reprinted in *The Phantom World*. 2 vols. London: Richard Bentley, 1850.

Carter, Margaret L. *The Vampire in Literature: A Critical Bibliography*. Ann Arbor and London: UMI Research Press, 1989.

Craft, Christopher. "'Kiss Me with Those Red Lips': Gender and Inversion in Bram Stoker's *Dracula*." *Representations* 8 (1984): 107–33.

De Plancy, Collin. *Dictionnaire Infernal*. 2 vols. Paris: Edition princeps, 1818.

Faivre, Tony. *Les Vampires*. Paris: Editions Eric Losfeld, 1962.

Farson, Daniel. *The Man Who Wrote Dracula: A Biography of Bram Stoker*. London: Michael Joseph, 1975.

A Fellow of the Carpathian Society. *'Magyarland': Being the Narrative of our Travels Through the Highlands and Lowlands of Hungary*. 2 vols. London: Sampson Low, Marston, Searle and Rivington, 1881.

Griffin, Gail B. "'Your Girls That You All Love Are Mine': *Dracula* and the Victorian Male Sexual Imagination." *International Journal of Women's Studies* 3 (1980): 454–465.

Guiley, Rosemary Ellen. *Vampires Among Us*. New York: Pocket, 1991.

Hartmann, Franz. *Premature Burial*. London, 1896.

Homer. *The Odyssey*. Trans. Alexander Pope. New Haven: Yale UP, 1967.

Hufford, David J. *The Terror That Comes in the Night. An Experience-Centered Study of Supernatural Assault Traditions*. Philadelphia: University of Philadelphia Press, 1982.

Introvigne, Massimo and Eckhard Turk. *Satanismus: Zwischen Sensation und Wirklichkeit*. Freiburg: Herder Verlag, 1995.

Johnson, E.C. *On the Track of the Crescent: Erratic Notes from the Piraeus to Pesth*. London: Hurst and Blackett, 1885.

Jones, Ernest. *On the Nightmare*. New York: Liveright Publishing Corporation, 1931.

Kottmeyer, Martin. "Entirely Unpredisposed." *Magonia* (1993): 3–10.

LaVey, Anton Szandor. *The Satanic Bible*. New York: Avon Books, 1969.

Leblanc, Benjamin H. "Uninvited Guest: The Possible Role of Sleep-Related Phenomena in Nightly Supernatural Assault Traditions." 1996. Unpublished.

Ludlam, Harry. *A Biography of Dracula: The Life Story of Bram Stoker*. London: W. Foulsham & Co., 1962.

MacAndrew, Elizabeth. *The Gothic Tradition in Fiction*. New York: Columbia UP, 1979.

MacGillivray, Royce. "*Dracula*: Bram Stoker's Spoiled Masterpiece." *Queen's Quarterly* 79 (1972): 518–527.

McNally, Raymond. *In Search of Dracula*. Boston: Houghton Mifflin, 1994.

Marigny, Jean. *Vampires: Restless Creatures of the Night. 1993*. Trans. Lory Frankel. New York: Thames and Hudson, 1994.

Masters, Anthony. *The Natural History of the Vampire*. New York: G.P. Putnam's Sons, 1972.

Mayo, Herbert. *Letters on the Truth Contained in Popular Superstitions*. Edinburgh: Blackwood, 1849.

Melton, Gordon. *The Vampire Book: The Encyclopedia of the Undead*. Detroit Michigan: Visible Ink Press, 1994.

Miller, Elizabeth. "Filing for Divorce: Vlad Țepeș vs. Count Dracula." *The Borgo Post* (August 1996): 2.

Peebles, Curtis. *Watch the Skies! A Chronicle of the Flying Saucer Myth*. Washington: Smithsonian Institution Press, 1994.

Pineau, Docteur. *Mémoire sur le danger, des inhumations précipitées & sur la nécessité d'un réglement, pour mettre les citoyens à l'abri du malheur d'être enterrés vivans; dans lequel on apporte des observations de personnes enterrées & ouvertes vivantes, tant dans les diocèses de Poitiers & de la Rochelle et où l'on ajoute quelques réflexions sur la nécessité de faire Exécuter l'Ordonnance*. Niort: Pierre Elies, 1776.

Poirier, Frank E. *Understanding Human Evolution*. New Jersey: Prentice Hall, 1990.

Poupard, Paul. *Les Réligions*. Paris: Presses Universitaires de France, 1987.

Richard, François. *Relation de ce qui s'est passé de plus remarquable, a Sant-Erini, Isle de l'Archipel, depuis l'Etablissement des Pères de la companie de Jésus en icelle*. Paris, 1657.

Rymer, James Malcolm. *Varney the Vampire; or A Feast of Blood: A Romance. 1847*. New York: Arno Press, 1971.

Stoker, Bram. *Dracula. 1897*. Oxford: Oxford UP, 1983.

— . *Personal Reminiscences of Henry Irving*. 2 vols. New York: Macmillan, 1906.

Summers, Montague. *The Vampire. 1928*. New York: Dorset Press, 1991.

Villeneuve, Roland. *Loups-Garous et Vampires*. Paris: Editions J'ai Lu, 1970.

Webb, Don. *The Order of the Vampyre of the Temple of Set*. 1992.

Wolf, Leonard. *The Essential Dracula: The Definitive Annotated Edition of Bram Stoker's Classic Novel. 1975*. New York: Plume, 1993.

Wolfe, Burton H. *The Devil's Avenger: A Biography of Anton Szandor LaVey*. New Westminster, B.C.: Pyramid, 1974.

V

"The Red Pages" — Stoker/*Dracula* Associations/ ssociations/ wards/Resources

The International Count Dracula Fan Club, New York

Jeanne Keyes Youngson

N JULY OF 1965, DR. JEANNE KEYES YOUNGSON TOOK a trip to Transylvania which changed the course of vampire fandom for all time. Her fascination with Bram Stoker's literary Count Dracula, combined with additional knowledge of Vlad Țepeș (one of Stoker's models for the bloodthirsty Count) led then and there to the founding of a Dracula Society, to be known henceforth as the International Count Dracula Fan Club. For the next few years, Youngson collected vampire books and memorabilia, and returned to Romania again in the 1960s and 1970s to further investigate the career of the Renaissance condottière, aka Vlad the Impaler.

By 1975 the society had headquarters in both England and the United States. Gala club dinners were held in London, as well as more informal "wiener and wine" get-togethers in the New York City penthouse office. In 1978, the Club moved its British headquarters to a second office in New York City located (as is the penthouse) in a landmark building in New York's historic Greenwich Village.

Operated by a staff of thirteen member-volunteers, the Count Dracula Fan Club is now the largest vampire society in the world, with members in twenty-five countries. The society operates fifteen divisions, including a vampire bookshop, marketplace, publishing company, free book-search service, and picture file.

Dr. Youngson's ultimate dream of opening a Dracula Museum was finally realised in 1990. Entrance to the Count Dracula Fan Club Museum is one of many membership benefits. Although Youngson still oversees every aspect of this complex organisation, she still finds time for extra activities. She continues to travel throughout the world in search of vampirabilia, lectures at both Oxford and Cambridge Universities in the summer, and interviews "real life vampires" when they surface.

Never a society to seek publicity, the CDFC has, for nearly thirty years, operated as a low-key society dedicated to perpetuating the memory of Bram Stoker and, of course, his venerable vampire.

(Adapted with permission from an article by Wallace Burns of Carteret, New Jersey).

DIVISIONS

I. The Count Dracula Fan Club Research Library

It has been the aim of successive committees and the founder of the Society to build a permanent collection of standard and authoritative works, with an emphasis on vampirism, lycanthropy, and horror. The non-circulating library was created in 1970 and constitutes one of the world's major research libraries in the fields of vampirism and lycanthropy. The collection is constantly in use by the Vampire Research Referral Centre, The Vampire Research Foundation, The Vampire Information Bureau, Dracula World Enterprises, The International Vampire Institute, and the Varcikaci Vampire Archives. The library contains approximately 24,000 volumes in hardcover and paperback, and includes subjects ranging from astrology to zymosis. The collection is not open to the public.

II. Special Research Division

Norine Dresser (*American Vampires*), Olga Holt (*Lust for Blood*), Bernhardt J. Hurwood (*Vampires*), Prudence Foster (*Blood Legacy*), Carol Page (*Bloodlust*), Rosemary Ellen Guiley (*Vampires Among Us*), Vincent Hillyer (*Vampires*), David Skal (*Hollywood Gothic*), and Dale Robinson (*The Woman Who Talks to Vampires*) are but a few of the authors the Special Research Division has assisted in past years. We regret that time no longer permits us to help with dissertations, theses, term papers, or other academic projects. Authors *under contract*, however, may contact the SRD at Club headquarters.

III. The Research Referral Centre
The next best thing to knowing something is knowing where to find it — and that's where the Vampire Research Referral Centre comes in. This special division of the CDFC functions as a divisional aid in assisting members to locate information about vampires and vampirism. Sometimes just a nudge in the right direction is all that's needed. Please send a SASE with your query and we'll get back to you as soon as possible.

IV. Dracula Press
Dracula Press is internationally known as a publisher of quality vampire poetry, fiction, and scholarship.

V. The Vampire Bookshop
The Vampire Bookshop is the exclusive distributor of Dracula Press publications. Please send a SASE for an updated listing of available editions. Write: Kerri Kelly, Manager, Vampire Bookshop, PHN, 29 Washington Square West, New York City, New York, 10011, USA.

VI. Booksearch Service
A very special bonus for members. We specialise in paperback fiction — new, used, hard-to-find, out-of-print. In fact, we may already have YOUR book in our stacks! Please send a SASE for EACH BOOK you are looking for. Please write: Booksearch, PHN, 29 Washington Square, New York City, New York, 10011, USA.

VII. The Bram Stoker Picture File
We have a collection of exclusive photographs relating to Bram Stoker, Whitby, Cruden Bay, Dublin, Clontarf, the Bram Stoker Summer School, St. Michan's, Dublin Castle, etc.

VIII. Membership
Membership in the CDFC consists of the following categories: Honorary, Founding, Charter, and Participating.

IX. Vampires in the Media
Playbills, programs, photographs, and other items make up this special collection. We are especially interested in Vampires in the Cinema and are constantly on the lookout for books on this subject.

X. The Monster Ménage

Nearly everyone loves monsters, and our members are certainly no exception. We have many books relating to monsters in our library and, from time to time, we run articles on this subject in our club zines.

XI. The Moldavian Marketplace

The Moldavian Marketplace carries articles of special interest to Dracula and vampire fans. Ads of available merchandise appear periodically in CDFC newsletters.

XII. Club Publications

The Dracula News-Journal, Letterzine, *Bites & Pieces*, and "Undead Undulations" are published from 1 to 12 times a year and sent gratis to registered members of the society.

XIII. Supernatural Spirits

Fairies, giants, mermaids, banshees, unicorns, leprechauns (and, of course, the dreaded Irish dearg-dul) are all included in this exciting new division. We collect books and stories about these characters and others of their ilk. We sometimes even visit their haunts.

XIV. The Werewolf in Fact, Fiction, and Fantasy

Our collection of "wolfabilia" is impressive indeed! We've also helped many authors with research on the werewolf. If you are looking for a special book on lycanthropy, send us a SASE and see if we have an extra copy.

XV. Special Interest Division

Dedicated to the *other* subjects our members find fascinating such as Star Trek, UNCLE, "Hal," The Prisoner, Shadow, etc. We are glad to publish SID needs in our newsletters.

The Dracula Museum

The Count Dracula Fan Club's Dracula Museum, located in one of New York's treasured historical landmark buildings on Fifth Avenue, contains the world's largest, most comprehensive collection of material relating to Bram Stoker, Dracula, and vampires. Officially founded in 1990, the museum has displayed such exhibits as "The World of Bram Stoker," "The Life and Times of Vlad Ţepeş," "Rare and Unusual Vampirabilia," and "Dracula Meets Frankenstein in the Big Apple." The museum also maintains a Bram Stoker Memorial Wall, as well as a library of first and early Stoker editions. Admission to this private collection is available only to members of the Count Dracula Fan Club, The Bram Stoker Memorial Association, and The International Vampire Institute, who must contact the founder/curator to arrange a mutually convenient meeting time.

The Bram Stoker Memorial Association

The Bram Stoker Memorial Association was founded by Dr. Jeanne Keyes Youngson in June, 1985. Dr. Youngson, a long-time admirer of Stoker's work, had already amassed numerous photographs, copies of certificates, and much other memorabilia pertaining to the life of Stoker, his family, and his associates. Although originally a Membership Society, the BSMA is now primarily dedicated to research, and to that end, maintains a library consisting of all known biographies of Stoker as well as editions in which he is mentioned and/or featured and, of course, books he authored. The research collection is available to authors already under contract.

Former members of the BSMA, mainly in the tri-state area (New Jersey, New York, and Connecticut) still meet annually to celebrate Bram Stoker's birthday on or about November 8th. Those inquiring about membership in the BSMA are referred to the Bram Stoker Society in Dublin, Ireland, with which the BSMA is closely associated. Its founder, Leslie Shepard, has donated a good many items both to our extensive Stoker memorabilia collection and the Bram Stoker Memorial Wall at our Dracula Museum.

For further information, please write The International Count Dracula Fan Club, Penthouse North, 29 Washington Square West, New York City, New York, 10011, USA.

The Dracula Society, London, England

Bernard Davies

 HE DRACULA SOCIETY WAS THE FIRST GOTHIC literary society to be formed in Great Britain. Bernard Davies was one of its co-founders. He served as its Honorary Secretary for the first twelve years and has been its Chairman for the past twelve. He writes —

As the Society's story has been a great slice of my life, I hope a personal record of the past quarter of a century will best describe what it is all about. The Society was formed in November 1973, when a long-time colleague of mine, Bruce Wightman, returned from a package tour of Romania and complained that they never went near any of the places named in Bram Stoker's *Dracula*. Two Gothic literature nuts, we agreed that it would be great — if only to fulfill our own personal ambitions — if we could plan our very own Dracula Tour, following the action of the novel mile by mile. To persuade people to join it and charter flights, we should have to form a common-interest group, which we could easily disband afterwards.

I worked out the first-ever itinerary for a Dracula Tour from the West and it seemed to work successfully. It has been copied many times since by various tour operators, including the Romanian government. We were still left with the common-interest group, and it occurred to us — why not arrange a calendar of events to keep the thing going, like a sort of society, for another year? So, the Dracula Society was born, and it has been going ever since. Our subject interests extend beyond vampires to other icons of Gothic literature.

So other, different projects were to follow — projects like the Golem-Báthory Tour of Czechoslovakia in 1977, which investigated the legends of both the Golem of Prague's Alt-Neu Synagogue and the infamous Countess Báthory. Interest in the latter was increased by having among our party no less than five descendants of the Blood Countess. It was an eye-opener to see how, in this day and age, in what was then the most hard-line Marxist-materialist of countries, these relatives were received by the villagers of Čachtice. Such red-carpet treatment and bowing and scraping (plus genuine affection) you have never seen! That was the trip during which a bat kept flying round and round the hotel foyer while the tour-party was booking in! Somehow the Society always managed to lay on special effects of this kind. (We call it the Drac-factor).

Over the years the Society has striven to prove interesting rather than merely popular, and we place great emphasis on an enduring track record. For example, only this year we have staged, for the third time in our history, our Lancashire Witches Tour of the Pendle hill-country of Lancashire, led by one of our staunchest founder-members who is an expert on the trials. Our membership has remained fairly constant at around 200, give or take a few, except whenever some fanzine gets wind of our address, and it is suddenly swollen by a rush of applicants who last for precisely one year. We don't encourage people overseas to join unless they can attend meetings at least now and again. Ours is a society for meeting, mixing, and doing things together. Intellectual pursuits are fine, but we are also a very social group. Despite the limitations of the Count after whom we were named, eating and drinking, as well as meeting like-minded people, are important. I always used to say that the Society is a non-profit, non-political, and non-sectarian organisation. The only thing we are not is non-alcoholic!

While we try not to be too solemn, we do treat Dracula and his peers with respect — which is more than can be said for some authors on the subject and almost all journalists. When we were formed there were ample outlets for teenagers, but none for seriously interested adults. That is why the minimum age for joining is eighteen, although in the past we have had trouble with young people (particularly rather precocious young ladies) putting their age up in order to get in. It's not the girls who are the trouble, but their parents!

As the pioneer organisation in Britain all those years ago we felt that it was up to us — and we had a clear field — to rescue and promote Bram Stoker's reputation. I think we seized that opportunity. In 1977 we were asked to adjudicate in a wrangle over the siting of the London commemorative "Blue Plaque" on one of his Chelsea residences. We gave our verdict, and we afterwards paid to have it unveiled and gave a party after the ceremony. In 1980 we also produced a booklet for tourists on the "Whitby Dracula Trail." This covers everything mentioned in the story, and the Scarborough Department of Tourism in Yorkshire has sold it to thousands of visitors from all over the world. It has recently inspired a French film company to make a film entitled *Whitby — Town of Dracula*. The *Trail* booklet was compiled as part of our bargain with the local authority. We would provide that, plus a bronze commemorative plaque, if they would erect a Victorian seat on West Cliff — the Bram Stoker Memorial Seat, from which visitors can see every part of the historic town mentioned in *Dracula*.

The Society has inspired others too. One worthwhile offshoot was the Bram Stoker Society in Dublin which grew out of a handful of our early Irish members. Isolated but enthusiastic, they decided to go it alone. They have gradually succeeded in gaining more official recognition of their efforts. I say "worthwhile" because at the time when we unveiled Bram Stoker's Chelsea Plaque in 1977, the Cultural Attaché from the Irish Embassy whom we had invited for a drink was unaware that *Dracula* had been written by an Irishman. When I informed him that the most influential book worldwide by any Irishman was *Dracula*, his face was a picture. He had to have another John Jameson to recover!

The maintenance of a Dracula Archive has been another charge we take seriously. Available to both professional and amateur researchers, it has its more glamorous items, such as Christopher Lee's Dracula cloak, but it also contains solid historical material like the Hamilton Deane Theatrical Collection which has attracted scholars from all over the world. All this must colour our approach, and I suppose it's fair to say that we play our interest fairly straight. We were exposed to the media in the old days when a group like ours was a nine-day's wonder. It isn't any more. But I would not put on even Chris Lee's cloak to talk to the press. If they cannot take an interest in what I have to say unless I am dressed for the part, they are not worth talking to.

In recent years, numerous vampire groups, large and small, have sprung up around Britain, some with quite a different approach. They provide what the Dracula Society does not: notably, an outlet for those keen on vampire "style" — black costume, special make-up, esoteric jewellery,

Goth music, and the like. We all flourish side by side quite happily. Often people belong to more than one group. The growth of all these interests has been part of the considerable changes in the Dracula field that we have witnessed since the Society was first founded, alongside the change in the public perception of Bram Stoker. That is something which our members have always been able to feel they were helping to promote, by paying their subscriptions and supporting our events. We will celebrate the centenary with great satisfaction.

Enquiries to The Dracula Society may be forwarded to the Honorary Secretary or the Membership Secretary, The Dracula Society, 11 Harriot Close, Greenwich, London, England, SE10 0JP.

The Bram Stoker Society, Dublin, Ireland

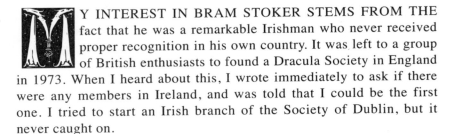

Leslie Shepard

Y INTEREST IN BRAM STOKER STEMS FROM THE fact that he was a remarkable Irishman who never received proper recognition in his own country. It was left to a group of British enthusiasts to found a Dracula Society in England in 1973. When I heard about this, I wrote immediately to ask if there were any members in Ireland, and was told that I could be the first one. I tried to start an Irish branch of the Society of Dublin, but it never caught on.

I then had the idea of founding a specific Bram Stoker Society, based in Dublin, with fraternal links with the Dracula Society. With the assistance of accountant John C. Leahy (who had read *Dracula* in the Irish language translation) and David Lass (of the Berkeley Library, Trinity College, Dublin), I founded the Bram Stoker Society in 1980. We aimed to encourage the appreciation and presentation of the life and work of Bram Stoker and other writers in the Gothic tradition, to plan social events such as lectures and film shows, and to advise or promote tourism to locales associated with Bram Stoker and other Gothic novelists.

We launched the society at a special meeting of the Philosophical Society at Trinity College because Stoker was a noted president of the society in his time (as well as auditor of the Historical Society). Over the next few years we arranged many lectures and film shows at Trinity College in association with the Philosophical Society.

In 1988, I donated my personal collection of Bram Stoker first editions, autographed letters, and other memorabilia to the Philosophical Society for a permanent exhibition. A Bram Stoker Room was provided at the college, and the exhibition was opened by poet Anthony Cronin, then a personal adviser to the Taoiseach Charles J. Haughey.

For a time it seemed that we had found a permanent home in Stoker's old college society, and we even merged with the Philosophical Society for a time, becoming "The Bram Stoker Club" of the "Phil." Unfortunately, with the election of a new Phil committee, relations with them became strained. The committee wanted to restore the Bram Stoker Exhibition Room as a workroom, and I was obliged to reclaim my collection, which I have since donated to the Writers Museum in Parnell Square, Dublin. The Bram Stoker Society resumed its autonomous identity, but left a nominal "Bram Stoker Club" still in existence at Trinity College, with David Lass as Secretary. The club continues to arrange meetings and film shows at Trinity College in conjunction with the Bram Stoker Society.

Over the years we have had various gains and losses. Regretfully, our first Secretary John C. Leahy passed away, but his work has been carried on by David Lass. Albert Power, a young solicitor, joined the society, becoming auditor and treasurer, and he has given us some excellent lectures on Gothic themes in literature. Through a friendly contact with Bord Fáilte, the tourist board, we succeeded in getting a plaque placed on Stoker's first independent address after his home in Clontarf was sold up. The plaque ceremony was performed by Stoker's granddaughter Ann, who came over to Dublin. The National Library mounted a small Stoker Exhibition, drawn from my collection, to mark the occasion. Unfortunately, we have been unable to get a plaque erected on the birthplace itself, since the present owner-occupier refuses to permit this.

Colourful characters have drifted in and out of the society, notably Ivan Stoker Dixon, said to be a great-nephew of Bram Stoker, who gave us a special performance of his interesting one man show "From Clontarf to Castle Dracula."

Over the years, we have issued regular Newsletters, and 1989 marked the first issue of an annual *Bram Stoker Journal*. The *Journal* contains research material on Stoker, and on other aspects of the Gothic tradition in literature. The *Journal* editor, Richard Dalby, is well known as an authority on Stoker. He owns a splendid private collection of Stoker first editions, and is also an editor of anthologies of Gothic and fantasy fiction. Mr. Dalby was also responsible for the authoritative bibliography of Bram Stoker.

Throughout the years, our society has received support and encouragement from members in the United States, notably Dr. Jeanne K. Youngson, president and founder of the Count Dracula Fan Club, New York. She has actively assisted our work from the beginning, and has made various visits to Ireland, where she is most welcome.

In 1991, Dennis McIntyre of the Clontarf Historical Society launched the first Bram Stoker Summer School in Clontarf, the Dublin suburb in which Stoker was born. In addition to presenting lectures on "Bram Stoker and the Irish Supernatural Tradition," and "Bram Stoker and the Theatre," the school also made available a large collection of books on Stoker and related Gothic themes from Dublin Public Libraries, for reference and research, and mounted a small exhibition detailing Stoker's life and work as theatre manager and author. At subsequent Summer Schools, lectures and exhibition materials were augmented by film shows of such classics as the first (pirated) version of Stoker's *Dracula*, retitled *Nosferatu*, made in Germany in 1922 by F.W. Murnau, and the strange film *Vampyr* directed by Carl Dreyer (1931) which is loosely based on Sheridan Le Fanu's *Carmilla*. Speakers have included Professor Raymond T. McNally (author of important books concerned with *Dracula* and related themes), Vincent Hillyer (who kindly presented us with a copy of his book *Vampires*, 1988), and Dr. Jeanne Youngson. We also previewed a short documentary about Stoker by director Ian Graham, later shown on the RTE television channel. Of special interest are the guided walks to locales and buildings associated with Stoker's early years in Clontarf. We hope that these Summer Schools will eventually rival, at both the scholarly and popular levels, the annual James Joyce, W.B. Yeats, and Samuel Beckett seminars held in Dublin.

The Bram Stoker Society continues to provide information and factual material for journalists, radio and television producers, and to answer queries about Stoker from a variety of sources. We hope to secure proper recognition for Bram Stoker in his own country and abroad, not merely as author of the most famous vampire story of all time, which has influenced scores of books, plays, and films, but also as a remarkable Irishman who, as Henry Irving's loyal and indispensable acting manager, did so much to encourage appreciation of the theatre in Ireland, Britain, and the United States.

Enquiries about the Bram Stoker Society should be addressed to Leslie Shepard, 1 Lakelands Close, Stillorgan, Blackrock, Co. Dublin, Irish Republic.

The Bram Stoker International Summer School, Dublin, Ireland

Dennis McIntyre

 ITERARY AND CULTURAL HISTORY WAS MADE IN Clontarf when the inaugural Bram Stoker International Summer School was held in June of 1991. The idea of a summer school had its genesis in the need for a formal international forum to encourage the appreciation of Bram Stoker and his work in order that he will, one day, gain long overdue recognition and acclaim in his own country and internationally.

While it is true that Bram Stoker is best known for his internationally renowned Gothic horror thriller, *Dracula*, the summer school is slowly opening up a whole new Stoker world. Lectures and talks to date have revealed the many-faceted Stoker — Stoker the sickly child, Stoker the Trinity College student, Stoker the athlete, Stoker the civil servant in Dublin Castle, Stoker the drama critic, Stoker who won the hand of Florence Balcombe from the flamboyant Oscar Wilde, Stoker the manager of Henry Irving, and Stoker the writer (beyond *Dracula*).

The location of the Bram Stoker Summer School couldn't be more suitable. Stoker was born at Number 15, The Crescent, Clontarf, a quaint little semi-circular street of Georgian houses ... and Stoker is Clontarf's most famous son. The Clontarf locality was Stoker's world in his fledgling years and when you delve into the history of the locality and its surroundings you have substantial grounds to argue that those formative years had a very telling influence on Stoker's output of writings, and especially on *Dracula*.

As Stoker's name is almost synonymous with Dracula, many people automatically perceive participants in the summer school as vampire freaks totally preoccupied with the creepy, chilling, eerie, haunted world of bewitching bloodsucking creatures of the night who inhabit lairs, coffins, and caverns! While there will always be room for some lightheartedness, the central ethos of the summer school is of a more academic nature. It is a forum where Stoker and his writings can be celebrated and evaluated in a relaxed and humane way. The tone will never be overly academic, intense, or pedantic. It will also never be frivolous.

The business of the Summer School is conducted through talks, lectures, seminars, field trips, the provision of a wide-ranging reference library, and a comprehensive Stoker memorabilia exhibition. In the six summer schools held to date, the speakers have been most impressive — with a truly international flavour — and the content of their various papers fascinating and interesting. Speakers from Ireland have included Leslie Shepard, Chairman of the Bram Stoker Society, Albert Power, editor of the Bram Stoker Society Newsletter, David Lass of Trinity College, Dublin, Sean Ronan, former Irish Ambassador to many countries, and Dennis McIntyre, Director of the Bram Stoker Summer School. From the United States the summer school has heard Professor Raymond McNally, the well known *Dracula* author of Boston College, Dr. Jeanne Youngson, President of the Count Dracula Fan Club, New York, Vincent Hillyer, arcanologist and author from Los Baños, California, and Dr. J. Gordon Melton from the Santa Barbara Centre for Humanistic Studies, California. From Britain, Dr. William Hughes of Bath College and Secretary of the International Gothic Association has spoken frequently and, from Memorial University of Newfoundland, Dr. Elizabeth Miller has addressed the Summer School. The reference library provided at the Summer School for research is a substantial one containing a myriad of Gothic, vampire, ghost, horror, and occult genre literature.

The entire Summer School project may be described as a "sleeping giant" in that the range of possibilities and the range of directions open to the school is almost limitless. One long-term aim is to open up a "Stoker Trail" to Dublin where our Summer School would provide facilities — a library and study/resource centre — for students, academics, and writers to undertake research on Stoker. The Summer School could become the international meeting point for all Stoker and *Dracula* enthusiasts, including leaders and members of the cornucopia of Stoker clubs and societies around the world. The Summer School has become a noted spawning ground for new ideas, thoughts, and approaches to the works of Bram Stoker.

There is no academic entrance requirement or qualification to participate in the Bram Stoker International Summer School; indeed, the aim is to encourage more people to involve themselves in the activities of the Summer School. One and all are invited to attend — students, academics, aficionados, the merely curious, and the public in general. The Summer School is truly international. The organisers especially strive to create a social ambience where international friendships may be nurtured.

Enquiries about The Bram Stoker International Summer School should be addressed to Dennis McIntyre, 101 Foxfield Grove, Raheny, Dublin 5, Ireland.

The Transylvanian Society of Dracula —
American and Canadian Chapters

Elizabeth Miller

OUNDED IN BUCHAREST, ROMANIA, IN 1991, THE
Transylvanian Society of Dracula (TSD) is dedicated to the
study of *Dracula* in all of its manifestations. Its formation was
facilitated by the fall of the Communist regime of Nicolae
Ceaușescu in late 1989 and the subsequent opening up of Romania to
Western cultural and literary influences. This included the appearance in
Romania for the first time of Dracula movies, the translation of Bram
Stoker's novel into Romanian, and an influx of tourists interested in
exploring Dracula country.

A non-political, non-profit, cultural-historical organisation, the
Transylvanian Society of Dracula encourages the serious study of both the
myth of Count Dracula and the history of Vlad Dracula. It seeks to analyse
the penetration of the Western myth of Dracula into Romania as well as
the world at large, and to provide a clearinghouse of information pertaining to the whole spectrum of scholarly interest in the field.

In addition to its central office in Bucharest, the Society has chapters throughout Romania in Bistrița, Sighișoara, and Curtea de Argeș, with
others in the process of formation. It is interesting to note that these three

395

locations have close associations with Dracula, either the historical personage or the fictional Count. Much of the impetus for the formation of these chapters has come from local entrepreneurs in the tourism field who wish to showcase their particular connections to one or both of the Draculas. The Society has also expanded outside of Romania. Chapters have been formed in Japan, Germany, Russia, the United States, and Canada. Others are in the process of being formed in Sweden, the Republic of Moldova, Spain, Argentina, and Italy.

TSD members include prominent scholars in literature, folklore, history, anthropology, and religious studies. The Society, however, is not limited to academics. The Canadian Chapter, for example, includes a novelist, a publisher, a computer programmer, a library technician, a lawyer, a descendant of Bram Stoker, and a homemaker. Other chapters have attracted the attention of travel writers and tour operators who are drawn to the Society's offerings of Dracula tours.

In May of 1995, the chapters of the TSD in Romania organised the first World Dracula Congress, an event that attracted scholars and aficionados from many countries. The list of speakers included some of the world's leading experts in the field, including Radu Florescu, Raymond McNally, Gordon Melton, Clive Leatherdale, Jean Marigny, Matei Cazacu, and Chelsea Quinn Yarbro. The Congress marked the first time that Romanian folklorists and historians have had the opportunity to meet with their counterparts in the West to share their research on both the vampire legend and the history of Vlad Ţepeş. The Romanian society has also launched a series of annual symposia held in the Bistriţa/Borgo Pass region of Transylvania which is combined with tours and field trips throughout the country. Information about these activities may be obtained by writing the central office.

Chapters of the Transylvanian Society of Dracula were formed in Canada and the United States in 1995, following the World Dracula Congress. The current President of the Canadian Chapter is Dr. Elizabeth Miller, Professor of English at Memorial University of Newfoundland, while the American Chapter is headed by prominent author and religious studies scholar Dr. J. Gordon Melton of Santa Barbara, California. The two Chapters have a number of joint projects: a new scholarly publication, *Transylvanian Journal: Dracula and Vampire Studies*, group tours to Romania and other Dracula sites, and co-sponsorship (along with the Count Dracula Fan Club) of "Dracula 97: A Centennial Celebration." Both offer their members a regular newsletter while the Canadian Chapter provides a lending library as well as local activities in cities where there are a sufficient number of members.

For further information on the TSD, contact one of the following:

Romania: Nicolae Păduraru
                Transylvanian Society of Dracula
                47 Primăverii Blvd.
                Bucharest 1, Romania

Canada: Canadian Chapter, TSD
                Box 23240 Churchill Square P.O.
                St. John's, Newfoundland, Canada
                A1B 4J9

United States: American Chapter, TSD
                P.O. Box 91611
                Santa Barbara, California, USA,
                93190-1611

The Bram Stoker Awards Horror Writers Association of America

Lawrence Watt-Evans

THE CREATION AND INCORPORATION OF THE HORROR Writers of America (HWA) in March of 1987 was overseen by Dean Koontz, then president of HOWL, the Horror and Occult Writers League. Determining that the HWA needed to present yearly awards for writing in several categories, Mr. Koontz strongly favoured naming it "for one of the most influential writers of the past." He suggested four candidates — Mary Shelley, Bram Stoker, Edgar Allan Poe, and H.P. Lovecraft. As Poe had already been used by the Mystery Writers of America and Lovecraft by the World Fantasy Convention, a vote of the membership settled the matter. In the light of the fact that "*Dracula* is the model for so much of modern horror," the HWA decided to present the Bram Stoker Awards.

The first awards were given in 1988, honouring works published in 1987. They have presented them every year since. The current mechanism for choosing the recipients is as follows: Any member of HWA may recommend any work other than his/her own, and a volunteer compiles the recommendations. The twenty works in each category receiving the most recommendations are placed on the preliminary ballot which is then sent out to the membership. Active members with professional writing credentials then vote, and the four works in each category receiving the most votes are placed on the final ballot. A special committee, known either as the Oversight Committee or the Stoker Awards Jury, has the option of adding a fifth work in each category. The final ballot is then mailed out to active members, whose votes determine the winners.

The award itself is a whimsical statuette of a haunted house, known as the Usher. It was sculpted by Stephen Kirk from a design by artist Tim Kirk based on a concept by Harlan Ellison. The award is decorated with turrets, chimneys, and giant worms. The front door of the house opens up to reveal a small brass plaque identifying the recipient, the year the award was granted, and the name of the winning work. Each award is cast in resin, then hand-finished, so that no two are exactly alike.

The HWA itself exists as a mutual support network for writers working in horror, occult, or dark fantasy fiction. They provide networking and advice and have as a principal mandate the education of the public about the field of horror literature, surely one of the most misunderstood of all literary genres. They welcome members. Unpublished writers may join as Affiliates. Affiliates may recommend works for the Stoker Awards, but they do not vote on either the preliminary or final ballots.

The permanent e-mail address of the HWA is hwa@horror.org. Who this e-mail reaches may change, but the address will not.

BRAM STOKER AWARD WINNERS

1988

NOVEL:	*Misery*, Stephen King
	Swan Song, Robert R. McCammon (tie)
FIRST NOVEL:	*The Manse*, Lisa Cantrell
NOVELETTE:	"The Pear-Shaped Man," George R.R. Martin
	"The Boy Who Came Back From the Dead," Alan Rodgers (tie)
SHORT STORY:	"The Deep End," Robert R. McCammon
COLLECTION:	*The Essential Ellison*, Harlan Ellison
NON-FICTION:	*Mary Shelley*, Muriel Spark
LIFE ACHIEVEMENT:	Fritz Leiber, Frank Belknap Long, Clifford D. Simak

1989

NOVEL:	*The Silence of the Lambs*, Thomas Harris
FIRST NOVEL:	*The Suiting*, Kelley Wilde
NOVELETTE:	"Orange is for Anguish, Blue for Insanity," David Morrell
SHORT STORY:	"Night They Missed the Horror Show," Joe R. Lansdale
COLLECTION:	*Charles Beaumont: Selected Stories*, Charles Beaumont
LIFE ACHIEVEMENT:	Ray Bradbury, Ronald Chetwynd-Hayes

1990

NOVEL:	*Carrion Comfort*, Dan Simmons
FIRST NOVEL:	*Sunglasses After Dark*, Nancy A. Collins
NOVELETTE:	"On the Far Side of the Cadillac Desert With Dead Folks," Joe R. Lansdale
SHORT STORY:	"Eat Me," Robert R. McCammon
COLLECTION:	*Richard Matheson: Collected Stories*, Richard Matheson
NON-FICTION:	*Harlan Ellison's Watching*, Harlan Ellison *Horror: The 100 Best Books*, Stephen Jones & Kim Newman (tie)
LIFE ACHIEVEMENT:	Robert Bloch

1991

NOVEL:	*Mine*, Robert R. McCammon
FIRST NOVEL:	*The Revelation*, Bentley Little
NOVELETTE:	"Stephen," Elizabeth Massie
SHORT STORY:	"The Calling," David B. Silva
COLLECTION:	*Four Past Midnight*, Stephen King
NON-FICTION:	*Dark Dreamers*, Stanley Wiater
LIFE ACHIEVEMENT:	Hugh B. Cave, Richard Matheson

1992

NOVEL:	*Boy's Life*, Robert R. McCammon
FIRST NOVEL:	*The Cipher*, Kathe Koja *Prodigal*, Melanie Tem (tie)
NOVELETTE:	"The Beautiful Uncut Hair of Graves," David Morrell
SHORT STORY:	"Lady Madonna," Nancy Holder
COLLECTION:	*Prayers to Broken Stones*, Dan Simmons

NON-FICTION: *Clive Barker's Shadows in Eden*, Stephen Jones
LIFE ACHIEVEMENT: Gahan Wilson

1993

NOVEL: *Blood of the Lamb*, Thomas F. Monteleone
FIRST NOVEL: *Sineater*, Elizabeth Massie
NOVELETTE: *Aliens: Tribes*, Stephen Bissette
     "The Events Concerning a Nude Fold-Out Found in a Harlequin Romance," Joe R. Lansdale (tie)
SHORT STORY: "This Year's Class Picture," Dan Simmons
COLLECTION: *Mr. Fox and Other Feral Tales*, Norman Partridge
NON-FICTION: *Cut! Horror Writers on Horror Film*, Christopher Golden
LIFE ACHIEVEMENT: Ray Russell

1994

NOVEL: *The Throat*, Peter Straub
FIRST NOVEL: *The Thread That Binds the Bones*, Nina Kiriki Hoffman
NOVELLA: "The Night We Buried Road Dog," Jack Cady
     "Mefisto in Onyx," Harlan Ellison (tie)
NOVELETTE: "Death in Bangkok," Dan Simmons
SHORT STORY: "I Hear the Mermaids Singing," Nancy Holder
COLLECTION: *Alone With the Horrors*, Ramsey Campbell
NON-FICTION: *Once Around the Bloch*, Robert Bloch
OTHER MEDIA: *Jonah Hex: Two Gun Mojo*, Joe R. Lansdale
LIFE ACHIEVEMENT: Joyce Carol Oates
SPECIAL TRUSTEES AWARD: Vincent Price

1995

NOVEL: *Dead in the Water*, Nancy Holder
FIRST NOVEL: *Grave Markings*, Michael Arnzen
NOVELETTE: "The Scent of Vinegar," Robert Bloch
SHORT STORY: "The Box," Jack Ketchum
     "Cafe Endless: Spring Rain," Nancy Holder (tie)
COLLECTION: *The Early Fears*, Robert Bloch
LIFE ACHIEVEMENT: Christopher Lee

1996

NOVEL:	*Zombie*, Joyce Carol Oates
FIRST NOVEL:	*The Safety of Unknown Cities*, Lucy Taylor
NOVELETTE:	"Lunch at the Gotham Cafe," Stephen King
SHORT STORY:	"Chatting With Anubis," Harlan Ellison
COLLECTION:	*The Panic Hand*, Jonathan Carroll
NON-FICTION:	*The Supernatural Index*, Michael Ashley and William Contento
LIFE ACHIEVEMENT:	Harlan Ellison

Dracula Collections at the Rosenbach Museum & Library, Philadelphia, Pennsylvania

Wendy Van Wyck Good

EHIND ITS STATELY FACADE ON DELANCEY PLACE in Philadelphia, the Rosenbach Museum & Library houses some of the rarest treasures anywhere in the world. For more than forty years, the Rosenbach has welcomed visitors to study and admire its extraordinary collections of English and American furniture, silver, paintings, decorative arts, and world-renowned holdings of rare books and manuscripts. These collections are housed in an 1865 townhouse, the former home of Dr. A.S.W. Rosenbach (1876–1952), a dealer and collector of rare books and manuscripts, and his brother Philip (1863–1953), who dealt in fine art and antiques. From 1904 to 1953, the brothers were partners in the Rosenbach Company which sold books, manuscripts, antique furniture, silver, prints, and drawings from salesrooms in Philadelphia and New York. During the 1920s and 1930s, A.S.W. Rosenbach earned an international reputation for buying — and selling — the finest books and manuscripts at the highest prices. Among his clients were the greatest American collectors of the early twentieth century, including Henry Huntington, Henry Clay Folger, and J. Pierpont Morgan.

Following their deaths in the early 1950s, the Rosenbach brothers left their Philadelphia townhouse and extensive collections to be made into a public museum and research library. In 1954, the Rosenbach Foundation opened for research and tours. Today, visitors are welcomed six days a week, receiving individualised docent-guided tours through the three floors of the townhouse, which is furnished much as it was when the brothers lived there. The collections currently comprise approximately 30,000 rare books, 300,000 manuscripts, 20,000 works of art on paper, 500 paintings, 650 photographs, and 350 works of decorative art. The rare book and manuscript collections are unequalled among American libraries in their uniform rarity, condition, and importance, representing the finest works that passed through the hands of the Rosenbach Company. The collection is especially strong in the areas of Americana, British and American literature, and works of art on paper relating to book illustration.

One of the most fascinating Rosenbach acquisitions since its founding in 1954 is a collection of Bram Stoker's working notes for *Dracula*, which was purchased on February 25, 1970, from Charles Sessler, Inc., a Philadelphia bookseller. The notes, dating from approximately 1890 to 1896, include Stoker's background research for *Dracula*, lists of characters, outlines of chapters, and a calendar of events in the novel. The provenance of the notes is hazy — shortly after Stoker's death, his wife, Florence, sold them at a Sotheby's auction held in London on July 7, 1913. The notes were purchased by a Mr. Drake for slightly more than two pounds. Eventually, the Scribner's Company gained possession of the notes and offered them for sale at least twice, in 1938 and 1946. The asking price was a mere $500. Some years later, probably in 1969, the notes ended up in Philadelphia and were acquired by Sessler.

At the same time it acquired the notes for *Dracula*, the Rosenbach purchased additional Stoker-related materials from Sessler. One of the items was a letter from Stoker to an unidentified woman, written on Lyceum Theatre letterhead and dated February 25, 1891. Stoker reports on upcoming plays at the Lyceum and encloses a two-page article on the famous actor and Stoker's boss, Henry Irving. The Rosenbach also purchased Alfred, Lord Tennyson's copy of the first edition of *Dracula*, which includes an inscription from Stoker: "The Right Hon. Lord Tennyson from Bram Stoker — July 1897." In 1985, the Rosenbach acquired another first edition as a gift. Although not a presentation copy, this volume is in an extremely rare state, with its original 1897 dust-jacket still intact.

Another *Dracula*-related item in the Rosenbach collection was acquired by A.S.W. Rosenbach in 1930 from the Munich bookseller, Jacques Rosenthal. *Dracole Waida*, a rare book printed in Nuremberg in

Die fackt sich an gar ein grauffen

liche erschröckenliche Hystorien. von dem wilden wü=
trich Dracole weyde Wie er die leüt gespist hot vnd
gepraten vñ mit den haübtern yn einë kessel gesotten

"Impale Forest", engraving printed in Dracole Wayda, Matth. Hupfuff Edition, Strassburg, 1500.

1488, is a contemporary account of the historical figure Vlad Țepeș who ruled Wallachia, now part of Romania, from 1456 to 1462. The Rosenbach's *Dracole Waida*, one of four surviving copies, is the only copy held in an American library. The text, which is relatively brief, describes Vlad's horrific deeds as ruler of Wallachia. Vlad was merciless to his opponents; his cruelty earned him the epithet "Vlad the Impaler," a reference to his preferred means of executing his enemies. He was also called "Dracole" or "Drăculea," the Romanian equivalent of "son of the devil" or "son of the dragon."

While conducting research for *Dracula* at the British Library, Bram Stoker consulted a similar fifteenth-century account of Vlad's exploits. The historical "Vlad Dracula" described in the text became the source for the name of Stoker's vampire and might have inspired Stoker to locate Dracula's castle in Transylvania, which is near Wallachia. Although none of the historical accounts suggests that Vlad Țepeș was a vampire, Stoker imaginatively connected Vlad's taste for bloodshed with vampirism and named his nineteenth-century vampire after the fifteenth-century ruler.

Stoker's working notes for *Dracula* remain one of the highlights of the Rosenbach collection. For the past 26 years, they have been the focus of intense scholarly debate, the subject of numerous publications, and the centrepiece of several popular exhibitions. Every visitor to the Rosenbach — whether scholar, movie buff, or vampire aficionado — is fascinated by the notes and their history. In 1997, as we mark the one-hundredth anniversary of the publication of *Dracula*, Stoker's notes for the novel will be the focus of a major exhibition at the Rosenbach Museum & Library. *Bram Stoker's Dracula: A Centennial Exhibition* will be on view from April 10 through November 2, 1997.

For further information, write to Wendy Van Wyck Good, Curator of Bram Stoker's Dracula: A Centennial Exhibition, Rosenbach Museum & Library, 2010 DeLancey Place, Philadelphia, PA, 19103, USA.

VI

ppendix and

he Bloody

ibliography"

The Library of Bram Stoker / A Note on the Death Certificate of Bram Stoker

Leslie Shepard

E MAY NEVER KNOW THE FULL EXTENT OF BRAM Stoker's personal library, but it is possible to form a general idea of its scope and subject matter, as distinct from the books which he studied in reference libraries for background information for his own books. The discovery of his research notes for *Dracula* (now in the Rosenbach Museum & Library, Philadelphia) threw a flood of light on the meticulous detail of his research, and Clive Leatherdale's study *The Origins of Dracula* (1987) lists over thirty such titles and examines in detail seventeen of them. These do not appear, however, to be books from Stoker's personal library.

However, Harry Ludlam's book *A Biography of Dracula: the Life Story of Bram Stoker* (1962), mentions that in 1910, two years before Stoker's death, Bram and his wife Florence moved from their house in Durham Place, Chelsea, to a smaller house in nearby St. George's Square, and discarded hundreds of books collected over many years. These included authors like Kipling, Mark Twain, and Stevenson, volumes of Egyptology, a history of the Ku Klux Klan, and sets of ordnance maps for the British Isles.

In the year following Stoker's death, the rest of his library was sold up, probably by his widow Florence, and the printed catalogue of Sotheby, Wilkinson, and Hodge in 1913 listed the remainder of the library. This was disposed of on Monday, 7th July, and ran to 317 items. The catalogue makes fascinating reading, and indicates the wide range of Stoker's interests and associations.

Travel and history were represented by books on Egypt, Asia, Canada, and America, which had survived the sale in 1910. Predictably, a number of other books were concerned with the theatre and theatrical history, including biographical studies of Stoker's idol Henry Irving. In addition to the works of Shakespeare and other items of Shakespeare interest, there were books on the Bacon cipher controversy. Books of poetry included such authors as Shelley, Browning, Tennyson, Eugene Field, James Whitcombe Riley, and Walt Whitman. Field and Riley were personal friends of Stoker, and Riley ("the Hoosier Poet") was also a favourite of Irving. Stoker had been captivated by Whitman's poems from the time that he first read *Leaves of Grass* when a student at Trinity College, Dublin. Stoker later became a great friend of that poet.

The Sotheby sale included seventeen Whitman items, mostly association copies inscribed "Bram Stoker, from his friend, the Author." Item 136 was a unique collection of fragments of Whitman's writings in his own hand on scraps of paper, mounted in an album. There was also an interesting autographed letter from Stoker describing how, with Edward Dowden, he had defended the poet from violent criticism in a discussion at the Fortnightly Club, Dublin. Whitman wrote: "My physique is entirely shatter'd, doubtless permanently from paralysis and other ailments. But I am up & dress'd & get out every day a little — live here quite lonesome but hearty & good spirits. Write to me again."

There were few works of fiction in the catalogue, but presumably these would have been sold off in 1910 when Stoker moved house. Remaining fiction books included the works of Stevenson, tales by H. Rider Haggard and Rudyard Kipling, Mary Shelley's *Frankenstein*, E.T.W. Hoffman's *Weird Tales*, and a volume of stories by J. Sheridan Le Fanu. Other books of folklore and occult interest included W. Silkes, *British Goblins*, Elliott O'Donnell, *Byways of Ghost-Land*, D. MacRitchie, *Fians, Fairies and Picts*, J.G. Campbell, *Superstitions and Witchcraft and Second Sight in the Highlands and Islands of Scotland*, and a volume of *Anancy Stories* of the West Indies by Pamela Colman Smith, with an autographed letter from her. There were also copies of the magazine *The Green Sheaf* edited by Smith, with her hand-coloured illustrations.

A large part of the collection was taken up by over sixty presentation copies of books to Stoker and his wife. Notable individuals who inscribed their books to Stoker included S.L. Clemens (Mark Twain), Bret Harte, Winston Churchill, W.B. Yeats, and Hall Caine. Caine was a special friend of Stoker, and the presentation copy of Caine's *My Story* (1908) reads "To my dear Bram, to whom this book owes much." It will be recalled that in turn, Stoker had dedicated *Dracula* to "my dear friend, Hommy-Beg" (a nickname for Caine).

One unique item in the catalogue was No. 143, a Death Mask and Hands, closed, of President Abraham Lincoln. These were cast by the sculptor Augustus St. Audens in 1886 from original moulds made by Leonard Wells Volk before Lincoln went to Washington for his first presidency. The moulds were found by Volk's son twenty-five years later, and twenty men subscribed to purchase the moulds and present them to the American nation. Each of the twenty received bronze casts of the face and hands with his name in each case, cast in bronze, and two of the men were Henry Irving and Bram Stoker. Item 144 was the original manuscript of Stoker's lecture on Lincoln.

Browsing through the Sotheby catalogue one discovers a great variety of subjects which must have had special interest for Stoker, such as: H. Ward, *Five Years with the Congo Cannibals* (1891), Robert Benson, *Sketches of Corsica* (1825), J. Baker, *Imperial Guide, with Picturesque Plans of the Great Post Roads* (1802), W. Morton (translator), *Collection of Proverbs, Bengali and Sanscrit* (1832), J.C. Lavater, *Essays on Physiognomy* (5 vols., 1789), A. Balfour, *Second, Third and Fourth Reports of the Wellcome Research Laboratories at the Gordon Memorial College, Khartoum* (3 vols., 1906–11), J.W. Powell, *First and Second Annual Reports of the Bureau of Ethnology, 1880–1*, Nic. de Febure, *Compleat Body of Chymistry* (1670), *The Lightning Sea-Column or Sea-Mirrour, discovering all the Coasts and Islands of Europe, Africa, America and Asia* (1689), Sir W. Hamilton, *Collection of Vases, mostly of Pure Greek Workmanship, discovered in Sepulchres in the Kingdoms of the two Sicilies* (3 vols., 1791–95), *Statutes made and established from the time of Kyng Henry the thirde, unto the fyrste yere of the reigne of Henry the VIII* (1543), Wm. Rastall, *Collection of Statutes now in force from Magna Charta, untill the reigne of Queene Elizabeth* (1588), Geoffrey Chaucer, *Works* (1721), M. Sadeler, *Vestigi della Antichita di Roma* (n.d.), Wm. Stirling, *Some Apostles of Physiology, Account of their Lives and Labours* (privately printed, 1902), F. Harvey, *List of Portraits, Views, Autograph Letters, and Documents contained in an Illustrated Copy of the Princess Marie Liechtenstein's History of Holland House* (only 25 copies printed, n.d.)

Of special interest was an album of Original Pencil Sketches by William Fitzgerald, who was one of the illustrators for Stoker's book *Under the Sunset* (1882). Fitzgerald was responsible for the picture of the gloomy castle of the King of Death, which seems like a precursor of Stoker's Castle Dracula.

The Sotheby Catalogue also listed six autographed manuscripts of Stoker:

177   *Personal Reminiscences of Henry Irving*
178   *Lady of the Shroud (with the outline of the story).*
179   *Snowbound, the Record of a Theatrical Touring Party* (last four chapters only).
180   *Under the Sunset.*
181   *Lair of the White Worm.*
182   Original Notes and Data for *Dracula*.

Presumably this last item is the important acquisition by the Rosenbach Museum & Library, Philadelphia.

Looking through this fascinating Sotheby Catalogue it is sad to reflect that so many important items were dispersed and a number have been lost sight of for nearly eighty years. It is particularly unfortunate that the original manuscript items are not all in one collection for study. Meanwhile the Sotheby Catalogue reminds us of the wide ranging capacity of Stoker's enquiring mind, as well as the wide circle of his friendships.

A Note on the Death Certificate of Bram Stoker

IN THE LAST few years, a reckless mythology alleges that Bram Stoker died of syphilis. There are two sources for this story. The main source is Daniel Farson, great-nephew of Stoker, in his book *The Man Who Wrote Dracula* (London, 1975; New York, 1976). A secondary source is a family tradition of Senator David Norris, a connection of the Dublin city branch of the Stoker family.

Farson's claim rests on the interpretation of the Death Certificate of Stoker, which reads: "Locomotor Ataxy 6 months, Granular Contracted Kidney, Exhaustion." Farson asserts that 'Locomotor Ataxy' is a euphemism for *Tabes Dorsalis* or General Paralysis of the Insane, the final stages of syphilis.

Senator Norris was under the impression that Stoker "died of the pox," but this belief may derive from the Death Certificate as well as gossip amongst ancestors scandalised by the sensationalism of Stoker's novel

Dracula. Dublin gossip is often hurtful and scandalous, as well as witty. Since Bram Stoker died in London, the Death Certificate could well have been the source of this gossip.

Farson's surprisingly emphatic interpretation of the Death Certificate of his relative rests on the common medical identification of "Locomotor Ataxy" with the final stage of syphilis, but this is by no means invariable. I consulted a medical lecturer at the Wellcome Institute for the History of Medicine, who stated as follows: "As for 'locomotor ataxy', it usually, (one can never put it more strongly than that) refers to the consequences of cerebellum disease due to tertiary syphilis. There is therefore a definite indication that syphilis was related to cause of death, but one cannot be certain."

This cautious statement confirms that there is no definite justification for assuming that syphilis killed Stoker, and the circumstances surrounding his later years would seem to militate against the possibility. *Tabes Dorsalis* is usually the culmination of several years of physical deterioration and brain damage, expressed in disturbances of vision, palsy, disorientation in walking, accompanied by mental degeneration.

In the case of Stoker, he did not exhibit the mental deterioration that might be characteristic of General Paralysis of the Insane, since he was mentally alert and active with literary work almost up to his death in 1912. The fact that he had some muscular disorientation described as "locomotor ataxy" is hardly surprising, since nine years earlier he had suffered a severe stroke after the death of his friend and idol Henry Irving. As Stoker's biographer Harry Ludlam wrote: "He suffered a stroke which laid him unconscious for twenty-four hours, and which began a painful illness that dragged on for weeks, robbing his robust frame of much of its boundless vitality and leaving his eyesight impaired." In the following years, however, Stoker revised his novel *The Man*, corrected proofs of his biography of Irving, and published five other books: *Lady Athlyne* (1908), *Snowbound* (1908), *The Lady of the Shroud* (1909), *Famous Impostors* (1910), *The Lair of the White Worm* (1911), as well as a number of articles in periodicals. None of this is characteristic of a man in the final stages of syphilis! Some physical difficulties were inevitable. He had struggled for years with overwork. The aftermath of the stroke in late life, coupled with earlier suffering from Bright's Disease and gout, could be expected to result in a condition of *paralysis agitans* or palsy, affecting his gait.

The really significant cause of death is surely the single word "Exhaustion."

Catalogue Description of Bram Stoker's Notes for Dracula

Rosenbach Museum and Library
Philadelphia, Pennsylvania

Stoker, Bram, 1847–1912.
Dracula: notes and outline, [ca. 1890–ca. 1896].
ca. 119 l. in case; 29 cm.

Irish theatrical manager and author.

Summary: Manuscript and typescript notes, photographs, and a newspaper clipping, comprising both background research and an outline for the book. The first section consists of 49 leaves of manuscript: a list of characters, notes on vampires, outlines for the whole book and for most chapters (all 7 chapters for each of books 1–3 and ch. 26–27), chronologies, and miscellaneous notes on characters and events. The second section consists of 30 manuscript leaves tipped onto 10 sheets, 2 photographs, and a clipping: reading notes on vampires and werewolves; and shipwrecks, weather, geography, and language in the area of Whitby, North Yorkshire, where part of the story takes place. The last section consists of 37 leaves of typescript notes with manuscript corrections, being reading notes on various works about the history and geography of the Carpathians, dream theory, and tombstones at Whitby.

Sold at Sotheby's 7 July 1913, no. 182 — unknown — Charles Sessler (sold 25 February 1970).

Location: Rosenbach Museum & Library, 2010 DeLancey Place, Philadelphia PA, 19103.

Call number: EL3
       f.S874d
       MS

𝕿𝖍𝖊 𝕭𝖑𝖔𝖔𝖉𝖞 𝕭𝖎𝖇𝖑𝖎𝖔𝖌𝖗𝖆𝖕𝖍𝖞

Carol Margaret Davison

Appleby, Robin S. "*Dracula* and Dora: The Diagnosis and Treatment of Alternative Narratives." *Literature and Psychology* 39 (1993): 16–37.

Arata, Stephen D. "The Occidental Tourist: *Dracula* and the Anxiety of Reverse Colonization." *Victorian Studies* 33 (1990): 621–645.

Aristodemou, Maria. "Casting Light on *Dracula*: Studies in Law and Culture." *Modern Law Review* 56 (1993): 760–5.

Astle, Richard. "Dracula as Totemic Monster: Lacan, Freud, Oedipus and History." *Sub-Stance* 25 (1980): 98–105.

Auerbach, Nina. "Magi and Maidens: The Romance of the Victorian Freud." *Critical Inquiry* 8 (1981): 281–300.

—. *Our Vampires, Ourselves.* Chicago and London: University of Chicago Press, 1995.

Baran, Henryk. "Some Reminiscences in Blok: Vampirism and Its Antecedents." *Aleksandr Blok Centennial Conference.* Ed. Walter N. Vickery. Columbus, Ohio: Slavica, 1984. 43–60.

Barber, Paul. *Vampires, Burial and Death: Folklore and Reality.* New Haven, Connecticut: Yale UP, 1988.

Barclay, Glen St. John. *Anatomy of Horror: Masters of Occult Fiction.* London: Weidenfeld and Nicolson, 1978.

Baring-Gould, Sabine. *The Book of Werewolves.* London: Smith, Elder, 1865.

Belford, Barbara. *Bram Stoker: A Biography of the Author of Dracula.* New York: Knopf, 1996.

Benefiel, Candace R. "Fangs for the Memories: Vampires in the Nineties." *Wilson Library Bulletin* 69 (1995): 35–38.

Bentley, Christopher. "The Monster in the Bedroom: Sexual Symbolism in Bram Stoker's *Dracula*." *Literature and Psychology* 22 (1972): 27–34.

Bhalla, Alok. *Cartographers of Hell: Essays on the Gothic Novel and the Social History of England*. New Delhi: Sterling Publishers, 1991.

—. *Politics of Atrocity and Lust: The Vampire Tale as a Nightmare History of England in the Nineteenth Century*. New Delhi, India: Sterling Publishers, 1990.

Bierman, Joseph S. "*Dracula*: Prolonged Childhood Illness, and the Oral Triad." *American Imago* 29 (1972): 186–198.

—. "The Genesis and Dating of *Dracula* from Bram Stoker's Working Notes." *Notes and Queries* 24 (1977): 39–41.

Biodrowski, Steve. "*Dracula*: The Untold Story." *Cinéfantastique* 23 (October 1992): 12–13.

Blinderman, Charles S. "Vampurella: Darwin and Count Dracula. *Massachusetts Review* 21 (1980): 411–428.

Bloch, Robert. "Two Victorian Gentlemen." *Blood of the Innocent*. Vol. 1. By Rickey Shanklin and Mark Wheatley. New York: WARP Graphics, January 1986. 27–30.

Bonewits, Wanda. "Dracula, the Black Christ." *Gnostica* 4 (1975), No. 7.

Boone, Troy. "'He is English and Therefore Adventurous': Politics, Decadence, and *Dracula*." *Studies in the Novel* 25 (1993): 76–91.

Borst, Ron. "The Vampire in the Cinema." *Photon* 18 (1990).

Botting, Fred. *Gothic*. London and New York: Routledge, 1996.

Brautigam, Rob. "Asema: The Vampire of Surinam." *International Vampire* 1 (1990): 16–37.

Brederoo, N.J. "*Dracula* in Film." *Exhibited by Candlelight: Sources and Developments in the Gothic Tradition*. Amsterdam and Atlanta, Georgia: Rodopi, 1995. 271–281.

Brennan, Matthew C. "Repression, Knowledge, and Saving Souls: The Role of the 'New Woman' in Stoker's *Dracula* and Murnau's *Nosferatu*." *Studies in the Humanities* 19 (1992): 1–10.

Brokaw, Kurt. *A Night in Transylvania: The Dracula Scrapbook*. New York: Grosset and Dunlap, 1976.

Buican, Denis. *Les Métamorphoses de Dracula: L'Histoire et la Légende*. Paris: Les Editions du Félin, 1993.

Bunson, Matthew. *The Vampire Encyclopedia*. New York: Crown, 1993.

Byers, Thomas B. "Good Men and Monsters: The Defenses of *Dracula*." *Literature and Psychology* 31 (1981): 24–31.

Calmet, Dom Augustin. *Dissertation sur les Apparitions des Anges, des Démons, et des Esprits, et sur les revenants, et vampires de Hongrie, de Bohème, de Moravie, et de Silesie*. Paris, 1746. Reprinted in *The Phantom World*. 2 vols. London: Richard Bentley, 1850.

Cardin, Philip and Ken Mann. *Vampirism: A Sexual Study*. San Diego, California: Late Hour Library/Phoenix Publishers, 1969.

Carlsen, M.M. "What Stoker Saw: An Introduction to the Literary Vampire." *Folklore Forum* 10 (1977): 26–32.

Carroll, Noël. *The Philosophy of Horror or Paradoxes of the Heart*. New York: Routledge, 1990.

Carter, Margaret L., ed. *Dracula: The Vampire and the Critics*. Ann Arbor, Michigan: UMI Research Press, 1988.

—. *Shadow of a Shade: A Survey of Vampirism in Literature*. New York: Gordon

Press, 1975.

—. *Specter or Delusion? The Supernatural in Gothic Fiction*. Ann Arbor: UMI Research Press, 1987.

—. *The Vampire in Literature: A Critical Bibliography*. Ann Arbor and London: UMI Research Press, 1989.

Case, Alison. "Tasting the Original Apple: Gender and the Struggle for Narrative Authority in *Dracula*." *Narrative* 1 (1993): 223–243.

Case, Sue-Ellen. "Tracking the Vampire." *Differences* 3 (1991): 1–20.

Coats, Daryl R. "Bram Stoker and the Ambiguity of Identity." *Publications of the Mississippi Philological Association* n.v. (1984): 88–105.

Cooper, B. Lee. "*Dracula* and *Frankenstein* in the Classroom: Examining Theme and Character Exchanges in Film and Music." *International Journal of Instructional Media* 19 (1993): 339–347.

Copjec, Joan. "Vampires, Breast-Feeding, and Anxiety." *October* 58 (1991): 25–43.

Copper, Basil. *The Vampire in Legend, Fact, and Art*. Secaucus, New Jersey: The Citadel Press, 1974.

Coppola, Francis Ford, and James V. Hart. *Bram Stoker's Dracula: The Film and the Legend*. New York: Newmarket Press, 1992.

Coppola, Francis Ford and Ishioka Eiko. *Coppola and Eiko on Bram Stoker's Dracula*. Ed. Susan Dworkin. San Francisco: Collins, 1992.

Cox, Greg. *The Transylvanian Library: A Consumer's Guide to Vampire Fiction*. San Bernardino, California: Borgo, 1993.

Craft, Christopher. "'Kiss Me with Those Red Lips': Gender and Inversion in Bram Stoker's *Dracula*." *Representations* 8 (1984): 107–33.

Cranny-Francis, Anne. "Sexual Politics and Political Repression in Bram Stoker's *Dracula*." *Nineteenth-Century Suspense From Poe to Conan Doyle*. Eds. Clive Bloom, et al. London: Macmillan, 1988. 64–79.

Creed, Barbara. *The Monstrous-Feminine: Film, Feminism, Psychoanalysis*. London and New York: Routledge, 1993.

Croley, Laura Sagolla. "The Rhetoric of Reform in Stoker's *Dracula*: Depravity, Decline, and the Fin-de-Siècle 'Residuum.'" *Criticism* 37 (1995): 85–108.

Dalby, Richard. *Bram Stoker: A Bibliography of First Editions*. London: Dracula Press, 1983.

—. *Dracula's Brood*. London: Aquarian Press, 1987.

Davies, Bernard. "Mountain Greenery." *The Dracula Journals* 1 (1976–1977), No. 1.

Davison, Carol Margaret. "Consanguinity: Bram Stoker's Dracula and Gothic Literature's Wandering Jew." *Journey into the Supernatural: Proceedings of the First World Dracula Congress*. Bucharest: Lumea Publishing House, 1997.

—. "Vampires: Centuries of a Cultural Obsession." *Clik Interactive* 1 (cd-rom). Montréal, Québec: Premiere Interactive Media, 1994.

Day, William Patrick. *In the Circles of Fear and Desire: A Study of Gothic Fantasy*. Chicago: University of Chicago Press, 1985.

Del Principe, David. "Misbegotten, Unbegotten, Forgotten: Vampires and Monsters in the Works of Ugo Tarchetti, Mary Shelley, Bram Stoker, and the Gothic Tradition." *Forum Italicum* 29 (1995): 3–25.

Demetrakopoulos, Stephanie. "Feminism, Sex Role Exchanges, and Other Subliminal Fantasies in Bram Stoker's *Dracula*." *Frontiers: A Journal of Women Studies* 2

(1977): 104–113.

Denman, Peter. "Le Fanu and Stoker: A Probable Connection." *Eire-Ireland (Irish American Cultural Institute)* 9, Autumn 1974.

Dingley, R.J. "Count Dracula and the Martians." *The Victorian Fantasists.* Ed. Kath Filmer. London: Macmillan, 1991. 13–24.

Donald, James. "The Fantastic, the Sublime and the Popular Or, What's at Stake in Vampire Films?" Fantasy and the Cinema. Ed. James Donald. London: BFI Publishing, 1989. 233–251.

"*Dracula*: Irish Blood." *Economist* 326 (1993): 85.

Dracula: The Complete Vampire. Starlog Movie Magazine, No. 6. New York: Starlog Communications International, 1992.

Dresser, Norine. *American Vampires: Fans, Victims, Practitioners.* New York: Vintage, 1990.

Dukes, Paul. "*Dracula*: Fact, Legend, Fiction." *History Today* 32 (1982): 44–47.

Dyer, Richard. "Children of the Night: Vampirism as Homosexuality, Homosexuality as Vampirism." *Sweet Dreams: Sexuality, Gender and Popular Fiction.* Ed. Susannah Radstone. London: Lawrence and Wishart, 1988. 47–72.

Dyer, Richard, Kim Newman, Henry Sheehan, and Ian Sinclair. "*Dracula* and Desire." *Sight and Sound* 3 (1993): 8–15.

Eighteen-Bisang, Robert. *Dracula: An Annotated Bibliography.* White Rock, British Columbia: Transylvania Press, 1994.

Faig, Kenneth W. "About Bram." *The Romantist* 4–5 (1980–1981): 39–40.

Faivre, Tony. *Les Vampires.* Paris: Editions Eric Losfeld, 1962.

Farrant, David. *Beyond the Highgate Vampire: A True Case of Supernatural Occurrences and Vampirism.* London: British Psychic and Occult Society, 1991.

Farson, Daniel. *The Man Who Wrote Dracula: A Biography of Bram Stoker.* London: Michael Joseph, 1975.

Fasolino, Greg. "Lestat of the Art — The Dark Gift Discussed." *Reflex: Alternative Music and Culture* 29 (1991): 42–46.

Feimer, Joel N. "Bram Stoker's *Dracula*: The Challenge of the Occult to Science, Reason and Psychiatry." *Contours of the Fantastic.* Ed. Michele K. Langford. Connecticut: Greenwood, 1994. 165–171.

Fiedler, Leslie. *Freaks: Myths and Images of the Secret Self.* New York: Simon and Schuster, 1978.

Flynn, John L. *Cinematic Vampires.* Jefferson, North Carolina: McFarland, 1992.

Fontana, Ernest. "Lombroso's Criminal Man and Stoker's *Dracula*." *Victorian Newsletter* 66 (1984): 25–27.

Frayling, Christopher. *Vampyres: Lord Byron to Count Dracula.* London: Faber and Faber, 1991.

Frost, Brian J. *The Monster with a Thousand Faces: Guises of the Vampire in Myth and Literature.* Bowling Green, Ohio: Bowling Green State University Popular Press, 1989.

Fry, Carrol L. "Fictional Conventions and Sexuality in *Dracula*." *Victorian Newsletter* 42 (1972): 20–22.

Gagnier, Regenia. "Evolution and Info: Or, Eroticism and Everyday Life, in *Dracula* and Late-Victorian Aestheticism." *Sex and Death in Victorian Literature.* Ed. Regina Barreca. Bloomington, Indiana: Indiana UP, 1990. 140–157.

Garden, Nancy. *Vampires*. London: Lippincott, 1973.

Garnett, Rhys. *"Dracula and The Beetle: Imperial and Sexual Guilt and Fear in Late Victorian Fantasy." Science Fiction Root and Branches: Contemporary Critical Approaches*. Eds. Rhys Garnett and R.J. Ellis. London: MacMillan, 1990. 30–54.

Garsault, Alain. "Comme le phoenix … Dracula." *Positif* 383 (January 1993): 30–32.

Geare, Michael and Michael Corby. *Dracula's Diary*. London: Buchan and Enright, 1982.

Geary, Robert. *"The Powers of Dracula." Journal of the Fantastic in the Arts* 4 (1991): 81–91.

Gee, James Paul. *"Dracula, the Vampire Lestat, and TESOL." TESOL* 22 (1988): 201–225.

Gelder, Ken. *Reading the Vampire*. London and New York: Routledge, 1994.

Gerard, Emily de Laszowska. *The Land Beyond the Forest*. London: W. Blackwood and Sons, 1888.

Gladwell, Adèle Olivia and James Havoc. *Blood & Roses: The Vampire in 19th Century Literature*. London: Creation Press, 1992.

Glover, David. "Bram Stoker and the Crisis of the Liberal Subject." *New Literary History* 23 (1992): 983–1002.

—. "'Our Enemy Is Not Merely Spiritual': Degeneration and Modernity in Bram Stoker's *Dracula*." *Victorian Literature and Culture* 22 (1994): 249–265.

—. "Travels in Romania: Myths of Origins, Myths of Blood." *Discourse* 16 (1993): 126–144.

—. *Vampires, Mummies, and Liberals: Bram Stoker and the Politics of Popular Fiction*. Durham, North Carolina: Duke UP, 1996.

Glut, Donald F. *The Dracula Book*. Metuchen NJ: Scarecrow Press, 1975.

Gordon, Joan. "Rehabilitating Revenants, or Sympathetic Vampires in Recent Fiction." *Extrapolation*, 29 (1988): 227–34.

—, and Veronica Hollinger, eds. *Blood Read: The Vampire Metaphor in Contemporary Culture*. Philadelphia: University of Pennsylvania Press, 1997.

Greenway, John L. "Seward's Folly: *Dracula* as a Critique of 'Normal Science.'" *Stanford Literature Review* 3 (1986): 213–230.

Griffin, Gail B. "'Your Girls That You All Love Are Mine': *Dracula* and the Victorian Male Sexual Imagination." *International Journal of Women's Studies* 3 (1980): 454–465.

Grixti, Joseph. *Terrors of Uncertainty: The Cultural Contexts of Horror Fiction*. New York: Routledge, 1989.

Gross, Edward and Marc Shapiro. *The Vampire Interview Book*. New York: Image, 1991.

Guiley, Rosemary Ellen. *The Complete Vampire Companion: Legend and Lore of the Living Dead*. New York: Macmillan, 1994.

—. *Vampires Among Us*. New York: Pocket, 1991.

Gutjahr, Paul. "Stoker's *Dracula*." *Explicator* 52 (1993): 36–38.

Haining, Peter. *The Dracula Centenary Book*. London: Souvenir Press, 1987.

Haining, Peter, ed. *The Dracula Scrapbook*. London: New English Library, 1976.

—. *Shades of Dracula: The Uncollected Stories of Bram Stoker*. London: William Kimber, 1982.

—. *The Vampire Omnibus*. London: Orion, 1995.

Halberstam, Judith. *Skin Shows: Gothic Horror and the Technology of Monsters.* Durham and London: Duke UP, 1995.

Hall, Jasmine-Yong. "Solicitors Soliciting: The Dangerous Circulations of Professionalism in Dracula." *The New Nineteenth Century: Feminist Readings of Underread Victorian Fiction.* Eds. Barbara Harman and Susan Meyer. New York: Garland, 1996. 97–116.

Halliwell, Leslie. *The Dead That Walk.* London: Grafton, 1986.

Hatlen, Burton. *"The Return of the Repressed/Oppressed in Bram Stoker's Dracula." Minnesota Review* 15 (1980): 80–97.

Haworth-Maden, Clare. *The Essential Dracula.* New York: Crescent, 1992.

Heick, Alex. *"Prince Dracula, Rabies, and the Vampire Legend." Annals of Internal Medicine* 117 (July 1992): 172–3.

Henderson, D.J. *"Exorcism, Possession, and the Dracula Cult: A Synopsis of Object-Relations Psychology. Bulletin of the Meninger Clinic* 40 (1976): 603–28.

Hennelly, Mark M. *"Dracula: The Gnostic Quest and Victorian Wasteland." English Literature in Transition* 20 (1977): 13–26.

—. *"Twice Told Tales of Two Counts." Wilkie Collins Society Journal* 2 (1982): 15–31.

—. *"The Victorian Book of the Dead: Dracula, Part III." Journal of Evolutionary Psychology* 15 (1993): 143–157.

Hill, Douglas. *Return From the Dead.* London: Macdonald, 1970.

Hillyer, Vincent. *Vampires.* Los Baños, California: Loose Change, 1988.

Hogan, David J. *Dark Romance: Sexuality in the Horror Film.* Jefferson, North Carolina: McFarland and Company, 1986.

Hollinger, Veronica. "The Vampire and the Alien: Variations on the Outsider." *Science-Fiction Studies* 16 (1989): 145–160.

Holte, James Craig. "The Vampire." *Mythical and Fabulous Creatures: A Source Book and Research Guide.* New York: Bedrick, 1988. 243–264.

Homan, Richard L. "Freud's 'Seduction Theory' on Stage: Deane's and Balderston's *Dracula." Literature and Psychology* 28 (1992): 57–70.

Hood, Gwenyth. "Sauron and Dracula." *Mythlore* 52 (1987): 11–17.

Howes, Marjorie. "The Mediation of the Feminine: Bisexuality, Homoerotic Desire, and Self-Expression in Bram Stoker's *Dracula." Texas Studies in Literature and Language* 30 (1988): 104–119.

Holt, Olga. *Lust for Blood: The Consuming Story of Vampires.* New York: Stein & Day, 1984.

Hughes, William. "'So Unlike the Normal Lunatic': Abnormal Psychology in Bram Stoker's Dracula." University of Mississippi Studies in English 11–12 (1993-5): 1–101

Hurwood, Bernhardt J. *Monsters and Nightmares.* New York: Belmont, 1967.

—. *Passport to the Supernatural.* New York: Taplinger, 1972.

—. *Terror by Night.* New York: Lancer, 1963.

—. *Vampires.* New York: Quick Fox, 1981.

—. *Vampires, Werewolves and Ghouls.* New York: Ace, 1968.

Hyles, Vernon. "Stoker, *Frankenstein, Dracula,* Sex, Violence, and Incompetence." *Round Table of South Central College English Association* 27 (1986): 7–8.

"Illinois Picks Dracula to Symbolize AIDS Threat to Young People." *Public Health*

Reports 108 (1993): 143–4.

Irvin, Eric. "Dracula's Friends and Forerunners." *Quadrant* 135 (1978): 42–44.

Jann, Rosemary. "Saved by Science? The Mixed Messages of Stoker's *Dracula*." *Texas Studies in Literature and Language* 31 (1989): 273–287.

Johnson, Alan. "Bent and Broken Necks: Signs of Design in Stoker's *Dracula*." *The Victorian Newsletter* 72 (1987): 17–24.

—. "'Dual Life': The Status of Women in Stoker's *Dracula*." *Texas Studies in Literature and Language* 27 (1984): 20–39.

Johnson, Judith E. "Women and Vampires: Nightmare or Utopia?" *The Kenyon Review* 15 (1993): 72–80.

Johnson, Roger. "The Bloofer Ladies." *Dracula Journals* 1 (1982), No. 4.

Jones, Ernest. *On the Nightmare.* New York: Liveright Publishing Corporation, 1931.

Jones, Stephen. *The Illustrated Vampire Movie Guide.* London: Titan, 1993.

Journey into the Supernatural: Proceedings of the First World Dracula Congress. Bucharest: Lumea Publishing House, 1997.

Kaplan, Stephen. *In Pursuit of Premature Gods and Contemporary Vampires.* Long Island, New York: Vampire Research Centre, 1976.

Kaplan, Stephen and Carole Kane. *Vampires Are.* Palm Springs, California: ETC Publications, 1984.

Kayton, Lawrence. *"The Relationship of the Vampire Legend to Schizophrenia." Journal of Youth and Adolescence* 4 (1972): 303–314.

Keats, Patrick. *"Stoker's Dracula." Explicator* 50 (1991): 26–27.

Kemp, George P. *"Dracula: Eroticism in the Vampire Genre." Varieties of Filmic Expression. Ed. Douglas Radcliff-Umstead.* Kent, Ohio: Romance Languages Department, Kent State University, 1989. 128–134.

Kendrick, Walter. *The Thrill of Fear: 250 Years of Scary Entertainment.* New York: Grove Weidenfeld, 1991.

Kilgour, Maggie. *The Rise of the Gothic Novel.* London: Routledge, 1995.

King, Stephen. *Danse Macabre.* New York: Everest House, 1981.

Kirtley, Bacil F. "*Dracula*, the Monastic Chronicles and Slavic Folklore." *Midwest Folklore* 6 (1956): 133–139.

Kittler, Friedrich. "*Dracula*'s Legacy." *Stanford Humanities Review* 1 (1989): 143–173.

Kober, Catherine. "A Session With *Dracula*: A Selfless Patient." *Psychotherapy Patient* 2 (1985–6): 49–57.

Krumm, Pascale. "Metamorphosis as Metaphor in Bram Stoker's *Dracula*." *The Victorian Newsletter* 88 (1995): 5–11.

Landau, Diana, ed. *Bram Stoker's Dracula: The Film and the Legend.* New York: Newmarket, 1992.

Lapin, Daniel. *The Vampire, Dracula and Incest.* San Francisco: Gargoyle Publishers, 1995.

Leatherdale, Clive. *Dracula: The Novel & The Legend.* East Sussex: Desert Island Books, 1985.

Leatherdale, Clive, ed. *The Origins of Dracula: The Background to Bram Stoker's Gothic Masterpiece.* London: William Kimber, 1987.

Leblanc, Benjamin H. "Uninvited Guest: The Possible Role of Sleep-Related Phenomena in Nightly Supernatural Assault Traditions." 1996. Unpublished.

Lefebure, Charles. *The Blood Cults.* New York: Ace, 1969.

Lidston, Robert. *"Dracula and Salem's Lot: Why the Monsters Won't Die."* West Virginia University Philological Papers 28 (1982): 70–78.

Ludlam, Harry. *A Biography of Dracula: The Life Story of Bram Stoker.* London: W. Foulsham & Co., 1962.

McBride, William Thomas. "Dracula and Mephistopheles: Shyster Vampires." *Literature Film Quarterly* 18 (1990): 116–121.

McDonald, Beth E. "The Vampire as Trickster Figure in Bram Stoker's *Dracula.*" *Extrapolation* 33 (1992): 128–144.

McDonald, Jan. "'The Devil is Beautiful.' *Dracula*: Freudian Novel and Feminist Drama." *Novel Images.* Ed. Peter Reynolds. London and New York: Routledge, 1993. 80–104.

McFarland, Ronald E. "The Vampire on Stage: A Study in Adaptations." *Comparative Drama* 21 (1987): 19–33.

Macfie, Sian. "'They Suck Us Dry': A Study of Late Nineteenth-Century Projections of Vampire Women." *Subjectivity and Literature From the Romantics to the Present Day.* Eds. Philip Shaw and Peter Stockwell. London and New York: Pinter Publishers, 1991. 58–67.

MacGillivray, Royce. *"Dracula*: Bram Stoker's Spoiled Masterpiece." *Queen's Quarterly* 79 (1972): 518–527.

McGuire, Karen. "Of Artists, Vampires, and Creativity." *Studies in Weird Fiction* 11 (1992): 2–4.

MacKenzie, Andrew. *Dracula Country: Travels and Folk Beliefs in Romania.* London: Arthur Barker, 1977.

McNally, Raymond. *Dracula Was A Woman.* London: Robert Hale & Co., 1984.

McNally, Raymond T. and Radu Florescu. *Dracula: A Biography of Vlad the Impaler.* New York: Hawthorn Books, 1973.

—. *Dracula: Prince of Many Faces.* Boston: Little, Brown, 1990.

—. *The Essential Dracula.* New York: Mayflower Books, 1979.

—. *In Search of Dracula. 1972.* Rev. ed. Boston: Houghton Mifflin, 1994.

McWhir, Anne. *"Pollution and Redemption in Dracula."* *Modern Language Studies* 17 (1987): 31–40.

Manchester, Sean. *The Highgate Vampire: The Infernal World of the Undead Unearthed at London's Famous Highgate Cemetery and Environs.* London: British Occult Society, 1985.

Marigny, Jean. *Vampires: Restless Creatures of the Night. 1993. Trans. Lory Frankel.* New York: Thames and Hudson, 1994.

Marrero, Robert G. *Vampires: Hammer Style.* Key West, Florida: RGM Publications, 1982.

—. *Dracula: The Vampire Legend.* Key West, Florida: Fantasma, 1993.

—. *Vampire Movies.* Key West, Flordia: Fantasma, 1994.

Martin, Philip. "The Vampire in the Looking-Glass: Reflection and Projection in Bram Stoker's *Dracula." Nineteenth-Century Suspense From Poe to Conan Doyle.* Eds. Clive Bloom et al. London: Macmillan Press, 1988. 80–92.

Mascetti, Manuela Dunn. *Le Livre des vampires.* Paris: Editions Solar, 1992.

Masters, Anthony. *The Natural History of the Vampire.* New York: Putnam, 1972.

Mayne, Judith. *"Dracula* in the Twilight: Murnau's *Nosferatu." German Film and Literature.* Ed. Eric Rentschler. New York: Methuen, 1986. 25–39.

Melton, Gordon J. *The Vampire and the Comic Book.* New York: Dracula Press, 1993.

—. *The Vampire Book: The Encyclopedia of the Undead.* Detroit Michigan: Visible Ink Press, 1994.

Meyers, William. *Vampires or Gods?* San Francisco, California: III Publishing, 1993.

Milgrom, Lionel. "Vampires, Plants, and Crazy Kings." *New Scientist,* 24 April 1984.

Miller, Elizabeth. "*Dracula*: The Narrative Patchwork." *Udolpho* 18 (September 1994): 27–30.

—. "Filing for Divorce: Vlad Țepeș vs. Count Dracula." *The Borgo Post* 1.6 (August 1996): 2.

—. "*Frankenstein* and *Dracula*: A Question of Influence." *Visions of the Fantastic.* Ed. Allienne Becker. Westport, Connecticut: Greenwood, 1996.

—. "The Genesis of Count Dracula." *Transylvanian Journal: Dracula and Vampire Studies* 1 (Fall 1995): 11–15.

—. *Reflections on Dracula.* White Rock, British Columbia: Transylvania Press, 1997.

—. "Schizophrenic Dracula." *Journal of the Fantastic in the Arts.* Forthcoming, 1997.

—. "Vampires for the Nineties." *Cinema Monthly Movie Magazine.* Bucharest, August 1996.

—. "The World Dracula Congress." *Locus* 35 (August 1995): 44–5.

Monaco, Richard and Bill Burt. *The Dracula Syndrome.* New York: Avon, 1993.

Moretti, Franco. *Signs Taken for Wonders: Essays in the Sociology of Literary Forms.* London: Verso Editions & NLB, 1983.

Morrison, Ronald D. "Reading Barthes and Reading *Dracula*: Between Work and Text." *Kentucky Philological Review* 9 (1994): 23–28.

Morse, Donald. "The Stressful Kiss: A Biopsychosocial Evaluation of the Origins, Evolution, and Societal Significance of Vampirism." *Stress Medicine* 9 (1993): 181–199.

Murphy, Brian. "The Nightmare of the Dark: The Gothic Legacy of Count Dracula." *Odyssey* 1 (1976): 9–15.

Murphy, Michael J. *The Celluloid Vampires: A History and Filmography, 1897–1979.* Ann Arbor, Michigan: Pierian, 1979.

Nance, Scott. *Bloodsuckers: Vampires at the Movies.* Las Vegas, Nevada: Pioneer, 1992.

Nandris, Grigore. "The Historical Dracula: The Theme of His Legend in the Western and in the Eastern Literatures of Europe." *Comparative Literature Studies* 3 (1966): 367–396.

Newman, Kim. *Nightmare Movies: A Critical Guide to Contemporary Horror Films.* New York: Harmony, 1988.

Nicholson, Mervyn. "Bram Stoker and C.S. Lewis: Dracula as a Source for That Hideous Strength." *Mythlore* 19 (1993): 92–128.

Noll, Richard. *Vampires, Werewolves and Demons: Twentieth Century Reports in the Psychiatric Literature.* New York: Brunner/Mazel, 1992.

Oates, Joyce Carol. "Dracula: The Vampire's Secret." *Southwest Review* 76 (1991): 498–510.

O'Brien, Thomas F. "Re: Vampires, Again." *The Baker Street Journal* 37 (1987): 154–157.

Oinas, Felix. "East European Vampires and Dracula." *Journal of Popular Culture* 16 (1982): 108–116.

—. "Heretics as Vampires and Demons in Russia." *Slavic and East European Journal* 22 (1978): 433–441.

Olcott, H.S. "The Vampire." *The Theosophist* 7 *(April, 1891): 1–9.*

Olorenshaw, Robert. "Narrating the Monster: From Mary Shelley to Bram Stoker." *Frankenstein: Creation and Monstrosity.* Ed. Stephen Bann. London: Reaction Books, 1994. 158–176.

Osborne, Charles, ed. *The Bram Stoker Bedside Companion.* London: Quartet, 1974.

Page, Carol. *Bloodlust: Conversations with Real Vampires.* New York: HarperCollins, 1991.

Pattison, Barrie. *The Seal of Dracula.* New York: Bounty, 1975.

Perkowski, Jan L. *The Darkling: A Treatise on Slavic Vampirism.* Columbus, Ohio: Slavica Publishers, 1989.

Perry, Dennis. "Whitman's Influence on Stoker's *Dracula.*" *Walt Whitman Review* 3 (1986): 29–35.

Phillips, Robert. "The Agony and the Ecstasy: A Jungian Analysis of Two Vampire Novels, Meredith Ann Pierce's *The Darkangel* and Bram Stoker's *Dracula.*" *West Virginia University Philological Papers* 31 (1986): 10–19.

Pick, Daniel. "'Terrors of the Night': *Dracula* and 'Degeneration' in the Late Nineteenth Century." *Critical Inquiry* 30 (1988): 71–87.

Pirie, David. *The Vampire Cinema.* London: Paul Hamlyn, 1977.

Plett, Nicole. "Nosferatu: *Dracula* Returns." *Dance Magazine* 67 (October 1993): 36–40.

Pope, Rebecca A. "Writing and Biting in *Dracula.*" LIT 1 (1990): 199–216.

Porset, Charles. "Vampires et Lumières." *Studies on Voltaire and the Eighteenth Century* 266 (1989): 125–150.

Praz, Mario. *The Romantic Agony.* Trans. Angus Davidson. Oxford: Oxford UP, 1935.

Punter, David. *The Literature of Terror: A History of Gothic Fictions From 1765 to the Present Day.* London and New York: Longman, 1980.

Raible, Christopher Gist. "Dracula: Christian Heretic." 1979. *Dracula: The Vampire and the Critics.* Ed. Margaret L. Carter. Ann Arbor, Michigan: UMI Research Press, 1988. 105–107.

Railo, Eino. *The Haunted Castle: A Study of the Elements of English Romanticism.* London: George Routledge & Sons, 1927.

Raines, Jonathan M. *"Dracula: Disorders of the Self and Borderline Personality Organization." Psychiatric Clinics of North America* 17 (1994): 811–826.

Rance, Maxine. *"Dracula in The Wasteland." Notes and Queries* 34 (1987): 508–509.

Reed, Donald. *The Vampire on the Screen.* Inglewood, California: Wagon and Star Publishers, 1965.

Riccardo, Martin. *The Lure of the Vampire.* New York: Dracula Unlimited, 1983.

—. *Vampires Unearthed: The Complete Multimedia Vampire and Dracula Bibliography.* New York: Garland, 1983.

Richards, Jeffrey. *"Gender, Race, and Sexuality in Bram Stoker's Other Novels." Gender Roles and Sexuality in Victorian Literature.* Ed. Christopher Parker. Hants: Scolar, 1995.

Richardson, Maurice. *"The Psychoanalysis of Ghost Stories." Twentieth Century* 166 (1959): 419–431.

Ronay, Gabriel. *The Truth About Dracula.* New York: Stein & Day, 1972.

Roth, Lane. *"Film, Society and Ideas: Nosferatu and Horror of Dracula."* Planks of *Reason: Essays on the Horror Film.* Ed. Garry Keith Grant. Metuchen, New Jersey: Scarecrow, 1984. 245–254.

Roth, Phyllis *A. Bram Stoker.* Boston: Twayne, 1982.

—. "Suddenly Sexual Women in Bram Stoker's *Dracula.*" *Literature and Psychology* 27 (1977): 113–121.

Rudorff, Raymond. *The Dracula Archives.* London: Sphere, 1973.

Ryan, J.S. "Perilous Roads to the East, From Weathertop Through the Borgo Pass." *Minas Tirith Evening Star* 17 (1988): 12–14.

—. "The Vampire Before and After Stoker's *Dracula.*" *Contemporary Legend* 3 (1993): 145–154.

Schaffer, Talia. "'A Wilde Desire Took Me': The Homoerotic History of *Dracula.*" *ELH* 61 (1994): 381–425.

Schmitt, Cannon. "Mother Dracula: Orientalism, Degeneration, and Anglo-Irish National Subjectivity at the Fin de Siècle." *Irishness and (Post)Modernism.* Ed. John S. Rickard. London and Toronto: Associated University Presses, 1994. 25–43.

Sedgwick, Eve Kosofsky. *The Coherence of Gothic Conventions.* New York: Arno Press, 1980.

Seed, David. "The Narrative Method of *Dracula.*" *Nineteenth-Century Fiction* 40 (1985): 61–75.

Senf, Carol A. *The Critical Response to Bram Stoker.* Westport, Connecticut: Greenwood, 1993.

—. "*Dracula*: Stoker's Response to the New Woman." *Victorian Studies* 26 (1982): 33–49.

—. "*Dracula*: The Unseen Face in the Mirror." *Journal of Narrative Technique* 9 (1979): 160–170.

—. *The Vampire in Nineteenth-Century Literature.* Bowling Green: Bowling Green State University Popular Press, 1988.

Senn, Harry A. *Were-wolf and Vampire in Romania.* East European Monographs No. 99. New York: Columbia UP, 1982.

Shanklin, Rickey. "Dracula: Bram Stoker's Bogeyman." *Blood of the Innocent.* Vol. 2. By Rickey Shanklin and Mark Wheatley. New York: WARP Graphics, January 1986. 25–27.

Shepard, Leslie. *Bram Stoker: Irish Theatre Manager and Author.* Dublin: Impact Publications, 1994.

Showalter, Elaine. "Syphilis, Sexuality, and the Fiction of the Fin de Siècle." *Sex, Politics, and Science in the Nineteenth-Century Novel.* Ed. Ruth Bernard Yeazell. Baltimore and London: Johns Hopkins UP, 1986. 88–115.

—. "Blood Sells: Vampire Fever and Anxieties for the *Fin-de-siècle.*" *Times Literary Supplement* (January 8, 1993): 14.

Shuster, Seymour. "*Dracula* and Surgically Induced Trauma in Children." *British Journal of Medical Psychology* 46 (1973). 259–70.

Silver, Alain and James Ursini. *The Vampire Film From Nosferatu to* Bram Stoker's Dracula. New York: Limelight Editions, 1993.

Skal, David J. *Dracula: The Ultimate Illustrated Edition of the World Famous Vampire Play.* New York: St. Martin's Press, 1993.

—. *Hollywood Gothic: The Tangled Web of Dracula from Novel to Stage to Screen.*

New York: Norton, 1990.

—. *The Monster Show: A Cultural History of Horror.* New York: Norton, 1993.

Skal, David J., ed. *V is for Vampire.* New York: Plume, 1995.

Smart, Robert A. "Blood and Money in Bram Stoker's *Dracula*: The Struggle Against Monopoly." *Money: Lure, Lore, and Literature.* Ed. John Louis DiGaetani. Westport, Connecticut: Greenwood, 1994. 253–260.

Smith, Malcolm. "*Dracula* and the Victorian Frame of Mind." *Trivium* 24 (1989): 76–97.

Soule, Arun. "Dracula: Of Shades and Shadows." *Rajasthan University Studies in English* 20 (1988): 77–83.

Spear, Jeffrey L. "Gender and Sexual Dis-Ease in *Dracula.*" *Virginal Sexuality and Textuality in Victorian Literature.* Ed. Lloyd Davis. New York: State University of New York Press, 1993. 179–192.

Spencer, Kathleen L. "Purity and Danger: *Dracula*, the Urban Gothic, and the Late Victorian Degeneracy Crisis." *ELH* 59 (1992): 197–225.

Stade, George. "Dracula's Women." *Partisan Review* LIII (1986): 200–215.

—. "Dracula's Women, and Why Men Love to Hate Them." *The Psychology of Men: New Psychoanalytic Perspectives.* Eds. Gerald I. Fogel, Frederick M. Lane, and Robert S. Liebert. New York: Basic Books, 1986. 25–48.

Stavick, J.e.d. "Love at First Beet: Vegetarian Critical Theory Meets *Dracula.*" *The Victorian Newsletter* 89 (1996): 23–29.

Stevenson, John Allen. "A Vampire in the Mirror: The Sexuality of *Dracula.*" *PMLA* 103 (1988): 139–149.

Stewart, Garrett. "'Count Me In': *Dracula*, Hypnotic Participation, and the Late-Victorian Gothic of Reading." *LIT* 5 (1994): 1–18.

Stoker, Bram. "Actor-Managers." *The Nineteenth Century & After* 27 (June 1890): 1040–51.

—. "The Censorship of Fiction." *The Nineteenth Century & After* 64 (September 1908): 479–87.

—. "The Censorship of Stage Plays." *The Nineteenth Century & After* 66 (December 1909): 974–989.

—. *Dracula.* 1897. Oxford: Oxford UP, 1983.

—. *Dracula's Guest — and Other Weird Stories.* London: Routledge, 1914.

—. *Famous Impostors.* New York: Sturgis & Walton Company, 1910.

—. *A Glimpse of America.* London: Sampson Low, 1886.

—. "Introduction." 1898. *Makt Myrkranna.* Trans. Valdimar Asmundsson. *Bram Stoker Society Journal* 5 (1993): 7–8.

—. "Irving and Stage Lighting." *The Nineteenth Century & After* 69 (1911): 903–12.

—. *The Jewel of Seven Stars.* London: Heinemann, 1903.

—. *Lady Athlyne.* London: Heinemann, 1908.

—. *The Lady of the Shroud.* London: Heinemann, 1909.

—. *The Lair of the White Worm.* London: Rider, 1911.

—. *The Man.* London: Heinemann, 1905.

—. *Miss Betty.* London: Pearson, 1898.

—. *The Mystery of the Sea.* London: Heinemann, 1902.

—. *Personal Reminiscences of Henry Irving.* 2 vols. New York: Macmillan, 1906.